IN THE LAND OF THE UNREAL

IN THE LAND OF THE UNREAL

LISA MESSERI

VIRTUAL & OTHER REALITIES IN LOS ANGELES

DUKE UNIVERSITY PRESS   DURHAM AND LONDON   2024

© 2024 DUKE UNIVERSITY PRESS
Printed in the United States of America on acid-free paper ∞
Project Editor: Melody Negron
Designed by Matthew Tauch
Typeset in Alegreya by Westchester Publishing Services
Printed and bound by CPI Group (UK) Ltd, Croydon, CR0 4YY
Library of Congress Cataloging-in-Publication Data
Names: Messeri, Lisa, [date] author.
Title: In the land of the unreal : virtual and other realities in Los
Angeles / Lisa Messeri.
Description: Durham : Duke University Press, 2024. | Includes
bibliographical references and index.
Identifiers: LCCN 2023031698 (print)
LCCN 2023031699 (ebook)
ISBN 9781478030232 (paperback)
ISBN 9781478025979 (hardcover)
ISBN 9781478059226 (ebook)
Subjects: LCSH: Virtual reality—Social aspects—California—Los
Angeles. | Women in technology—California—Los Angeles. |
Technological innovations—Social aspects—California—Los
Angeles. | Fantasy in mass media. | Mass media and technology. |
BISAC: SOCIAL SCIENCE / Anthropology / Cultural & Social |
SOCIAL SCIENCE / Gender Studies
Classification: LCC HM851 .M4655 2024 (print) | LCC HM851 (ebook) |
DDC 006.809794/94—dc23/eng/20230902
LC record available at https://lccn.loc.gov/2023031698
LC ebook record available at https://lccn.loc.gov/2023031699

For my father, the sociologist,
my mother, the storyteller,
and my brother, the filmmaker

CONTENTS

ACKNOWLEDGMENTS

One of the great pleasures of book writing is gathering together a community over the long duration of the project. Working on a text for years is only bearable because of the smart, passionate, and generous individuals who are willing to go on the journey with you. I am grateful for the many supportive people who helped me shape the ideas and stories in the pages that follow.

My biggest debt of gratitude is owed to the members of the VR community in Los Angeles, who welcomed me into their worlds. Marcie Jastrow and Carrie Shaw opened up their places of work to me, which not only allowed me to see the creation of VR experiences from the inside but also how these women built networks and careers that allowed them to flourish, even with the odds stacked against them. Scott Fisher has supported my research from the beginning, generously inviting me to sit in on his classes and brainstorming sessions about VR's history and present. Several other folks met with me frequently throughout my research, including Jacki Ford Morie, Nonny de la Peña, Joanna Popper, Theresa Elorriaga, Arielle Jennings, and Laura Hertzfeld. I am grateful for their insights about both VR and Los Angeles. Employees and affiliates at Technicolor Experience Center and Embodied Labs welcomed my presence, and I thank especially Tom Leahy, Erin Washington, Haiden McGill, Anna Wozniewicz, Abbey Tate, Kelsey Hess, Brian Frager, John Root, Drew Diamond, and Devon Baur. Organizers of the Women in VR community, including Jenn Duong and Julie Young, generously connected me with their colleagues, and I am appreciative for conversations with Erika Barraza, Emily Cooper, Irena Cronin, Janie Fitzgerald, Alex Gamble, Jess Kantor, Iona Mischie, Suzan Oslin, Tiffany Raber, Robyn Selly, Paisley Smith, Betsy Trapasso, and Georgia Van Cuylenburg. LA would have been a lonelier place without the camaraderie of Lena Belkor, Jennifer Wang, and Fay Wells. A National Science Foundation Scholars Award (#1748531) supported this fieldwork, allowing me the luxury of getting to learn from this community for twelve months.

I conceived of this project while at the University of Virginia. Denny Proffitt and Veronica Weser grounded me in the technology as a tool of psychological research. Colleagues in Engineering and Society and Anthropology were early sounding boards for this work, and my thanks go to Ira Bashkow, Bernie Carlson, Lise Dobrin, Rider Foley, Michael Gorman, Jim Igoe, Deborah Johnson, Susie McKinnon, Kay Neeley, Peter Norton, Tolu Odumosu, Geeta Patel, China Scherz, Kath Weston, and Caitlin Wyle. Charlottesville was made special in part thanks to friendships with Sarah Milov, Kyrill Kunakhovich, David Singerman, Mary Kuhn, Jack Hamilton, Nikki Hemmer, Murad Idris, Theresa Krüggeler, Emily Gadek, Kelly Jones, Nina Earnest, Andrew Parsons, Carrie Baker, and Melissa Levy.

At Yale, numerous people engaged with my thinking about VR before, during, and after fieldwork. Joanna Radin knows this project better than anyone else, except for perhaps Molly Crockett. Thinking with these two brilliant people cracked open aspects of this work that might not have otherwise come to light. Doug Rogers and Erik Harms have been generous and supportive mentors, reading early drafts and guiding the project (and my career) forward. For the many conversations that helped me digest this research, I am grateful to Rene Almeling, Debbie Coen, Robin Dembroff, Wendy Gilbert, Marcia Inhorn, Yukiko Koga, Noreen Khawaja, Paul Kockelman, Louisa Lombard, Jane Lynch, Eda Pepi, Jess Peritz, John Durham Peters, Nana Quarshie, Helen Siu, K. Sivaramakrishnan, Kalindi Vora, and many more than can be listed, especially faculty and students in Anthropology and the Program in the History of Science and Medicine for ample collegiality and comradery. Marleen Cullen, Jennifer DeChello, and the rest of the staff of the Anthropology department removed institutional frictions such that there were moments—even during the semester—when it was possible to focus on research. To the students who have chosen to work with me—Samara Brock, Spencer Kaplan, Manon Lefèvre, Nala Williams, and Michelle Venetucci—I am so thankful to have the opportunity to think collectively about the ways in which expertise produces the worlds we inhabit.

The first time I voiced my ideas about "the unreal" was on a walk along the Pacific Ocean with Valerie Olson, who gave me the earliest encouragement that there was a there there. As the ideas took sturdier shape, I had the pleasure of sharing parts of this project in various seminar rooms—both virtual and physical—at the Berggruen Institute as part of the Antikythera program, Brandeis University, California Institute of Technology, Harvard University, Humboldt University, Oxford University, Radcliffe Institute, University of Toulouse, University of Pennsylvania, and at Yale with both the Film and Media Studies Department and the Performance Studies working group. I owe an intellectual debt to Tom Boellstorff, who helped make the virtual an object of anthropological study. Patricia Alvarez Astacio, Marisa Brandt, Elaine Gan, Danya Glabau, Willi Lempert, and Sylvia Martin have been wonderful collaborators for growing the conversation around VR on the page, at conferences, and even in dreaming up potential, if never realized, schemes.

As we were all living our lives very online, I am appreciative that Janet Murray, J.D. Connor, Joanna Radin, Kalindi Vora, and Erik Harms took time to read an early draft of the manuscript and spend an afternoon on Zoom discussing future shapes it could take. Michelle Venetucci was an excellent research assistant leading up to this workshop, not only helping with the nuts and bolts of completing a first draft, but also helping to hash out a few unfinished ideas. During moments of insecurity, Michael Rossi, Emily Wanderer, and Rebecca Woods read excerpts and reassured me in the way only those who have known you from graduate school can. In a similar vein, Stefan Helmreich lent his precise and generous intellect to the manuscript as it neared its final state. Peter Messeri also provided sharp insight at this late stage, though he'll be disappointed to see that a Weberian analysis did not make its way in.

At Duke University Press, Ken Wissoker supported this project from its earliest stages. I'm so grateful for his thoughtful stewardship through the peer review process and his wise suggestions for how to keep the ideas from becoming too unruly. This project received input from four readers at various stages. It is hard to articulate how indebted I am to my anonymous peers for spending time with the manuscript, particularly those who read and responded to the proposal during the deeply disorienting moment that was the summer of 2020. Early production support was provided by Joshua Gutterman Tranen and later by Kate Mullen, whose organization kept things going. Thank you to the marketing and production teams, without whom the object you are reading would not exist.

For the friends who are family, I am appreciative of the bottomless support from Laura, Susan, Jeff, Rachael, and especially Tyler. And I am thankful, too, that my family are my friends. My Avalon cousins, New Haven cousins, and everyone who comes together at 60 Jeff to celebrate several times a year are all immeasurably important to me. In 2022, we lost three elders—Grandpa Sid, Aunt Kary, and Aunt Evey—whose memories will forever be counted as blessings. Grandma Sue, keep doing those exercises. I have dedicated this book to my parents, Ellen and Peter, and my brother, Jason. I realized early on that the topic of the book was an odd amalgamation of each of their—all of our—professions. That's kind of unreal.

PROLOGUE

In fall 2015, I became captivated by an episode of NPR's TED *Radio Hour*.[1] The program was about our engagement with screens and the hook of the episode cracked open a conversation that registered for me as both strange and familiar. Noting Facebook's 2014 acquisition of a virtual reality (VR) company, the host's conversation with a filmmaker-turned-VR innovator bookended the episode. VR, it seemed, was the future of screens, promising to explode the confines of the rectangle and immerse people fully in a story. The episode was peppered with grand claims, including ideas long attached to VR: that it could make one feel present in another place and that it might even reshape human consciousness. But there were newer promises, too. The VR innovator's premier VR experience did not transport the user into a fictional world, but rather into a Syrian refugee camp. There, the VR-headset wearing participant sat across from a young girl on the floor of her temporary home and listened to her describe her daily life. On the radio show, the filmmaker explained that even more than traditional storytelling, VR's immersive storytelling could instill a feeling of empathy and, he hoped, bring forth a better future for this girl and other refugees.

By early 2016, I was well into constructing a research project about how and why bettering humanity had become so central to the mid-2010s resurgence of VR. How had VR come to be positioned as a solution to social and political failings? This imagination of the technology's present and future seemed at odds with the VR of the 1980s and 1990s, textured as that earlier version was by cyberpunk escapism and desires for bodily transcendence. But in the 2010s, there emerged abundant media stories covering "good" VR projects aimed at drawing attention to problems ranging from refugee crises to environmental injustices to threats to reproductive rights.[2] The unquestioned acceptance of VR's benefit to humanity warranted investigation. After all, technologies like search engines and social

P.1 Obama takes in a VR experience in the outer Oval Office. This image was featured as a White House Photo of the Day on August 24, 2016. Photograph by Pete Souza, courtesy Barack Obama Presidential Library.

P.2 A screenshot from the satire VR game *Trump Simulator*. In the days before the 2016 election, developer Christine Barron released this short game modeled on the popular VR game *Job Simulator*. The virtual became (un)real not long after.

media platforms, which had similarly been introduced as motors for liberal humanism, were generating a growing list of harms and inequities. There was no reason to assume VR would carve out a different path. Unlike these other emerging technologies, the heart of the VR scene, I came to realize, was located in Los Angeles rather than Silicon Valley. My initial research questions formed around both this geographic peculiarity and the humanitarian promises of VR.

As US politics shifted from the Obama-era to Trumpism, the web of associations that animated VR also shifted, and in response my analytic attention expanded. In 2015, on the TED Radio Hour, VR's beneficence was located in its ability to transport someone into another person's reality. The host briefly wondered whether, in the wrong hands, that same affordance could be used in a Matrix-esque way to "change the truth." This speculative musing attached VR to concerns over the difficulty of distinguishing facts from lies in a highly simulated mediascape. In 2016, as Trump ascended to power leaving a trail of "alternative facts" in his wake, I followed the host's intuition and began to appreciate how VR might be resonant with a loosening of the fabric of reality that seemed to be happening throughout US politics and culture. The reality-hopping experiences VR offered and the reality-bending assertions of the Trump administration both seemed unreal; both seemed to be extraordinary ways of experiencing and comprehending reality. The significance of this connection would not become clear to me until well after my anthropological fieldwork had concluded.

That fieldwork was conducted in 2018, a year during which I traced the contours of an unreal technology in LA (itself famous for an industry accomplished in manufacturing unrealities). It was impossible not to juxtapose virtual reality's promise of cultivating a sense of shared humanity with national headlines that documented the Trump administration's manipulation of reality through its post-truth assault on governance, expertise, and whose humanity—whose lives—mattered.[3] This multipronged attack shook the faith, held by some, that there existed a common public reality. The Trump administration was not alone to blame for what felt like reality's fracturing. During my fieldwork, public awareness grew around social media's role in spreading misinformation and crystalizing distinct reality bubbles. The biggest investor in VR's resurgence, Facebook, came under intense public scrutiny in March 2018 when news broke that the company had allowed the firm Cambridge Analytica to harvest user data without consent such that they could serve up targeted political advertising for their clients, which included Trump's 2016 presidential campaign.

The public airing of this scandal inaugurated the "techlash," shattering the myth that technology necessarily serves the public interest.

Despite VR's financial indebtedness to Facebook, in LA the technology was positioned as an antidote to the techlash and a foundation upon which different, better futures were imagined. I came to focus on the *fantasies* that allowed such alternative realities to seem plausible. Being geographically outside Silicon Valley and thus outside of the techlash's focus, VR innovators and enthusiasts spun a fantasy of building a different kind of industry led by people from underrepresented backgrounds (a commitment that, coincident with my fieldwork, was affirmed by the #MeToo movement). This bolstered the enduring fantasy that VR's goodness came from its ability to foster understanding across difference. Such fantasies were envisioned against an awareness by the community I studied that reality, catalyzed by Trumpism, was somehow changing. If Trumpism had accelerated a feeling of unreality, VR's own wielding of the unreal, it was imagined, could blunt the damage. I tracked projects and conversations that wrestled with an awareness that people existed in different realities; that the reality of the philanthropist was not the same as that of the refugee. Though the desire was to mend rifts between realities, in authorizing some people (the philanthropist) as being the ones who get to know the reality of other people (the refugee), VR could not help but affirm the structures that elevated some people's humanity over other's.

In 2020 and 2021, as I was writing this book, reality further contorted. The COVID-19 pandemic made screens even more central to daily living, as many people learned to conduct professional, familial, and social activities virtually. But this period also illustrated the vastly different realities within the United States that people had come to inhabit. While some individuals shifted to working from home, others were called on as frontline workers and asked to put their bodies in danger. While some experienced profound isolation and devastating loss, others went about life as usual. The outright denial of the pandemic by some sectors of the public turned into ugly refusals to wear masks and eventually perverse pronouncements about bodily autonomy when rejecting lifesaving vaccines. A more jarring and acute demonstration of the loss of a shared public reality occurred when Trump lost reelection to Biden. Reality was not simply "impossible to pin down,"[4] as one journalist had described Trump's America; it reached a point of crisis when Trump and his constituents refused to believe the election outcome. On January 6, 2021, a stunned national and global audience watched a series of incongruous images play across their screens: an unruly riot on the steps of the US Capitol building, MAGA-capped men posing for selfies inside, a man in a fur-lined Viking hat with red, white, and blue face paint howling in victory, a noose and bloodthirsty chants, a Confederate flag waving next to one proclaiming "Trump 2020."

As I watched media commentators process the aftermath of the insurrection, it became clear to me that through my years of researching and writing about the VR community in LA, I had unexpectedly also been developing ways of thinking about reality that, at this moment of crisis, became salient. Reporters struggled to name what had happened, reaching for the same language of the unreal and fantasy that I had been using to describe VR. The events at the US Capitol were unreal in that they manifested a spectacular display of multiple (and conflicting) realities. During a live chat covering Trump's second impeachment trial, Sabrina Tavernise told her colleague at the *New York Times* that she was shocked that the rioters did not think they had done anything wrong. She continued, "It adds to the unreality of that day for me. How it was just truly an alternate reality that had crashed into the actual reality." The unwavering belief on the part of Trumpists that the 2020 election was stolen, resulting in an attempted insurrection, "pushed unreality from the fringes into the mainstream," Tavernise concluded.

With the ascendency of unreality, my research had helped me understand, fantasies emerge alongside truths and facts as strategies for shaping social action. Observing the mounting consequences of fantasies in the political landscape, journalist John Dickerson, speaking on *Slate*'s "Political Gabfest," diagnosed: "If the struggle of our day is between reality and fantasy, the fact that a person who engages in fantasy [referring to the congresswoman and QAnon conspiracy spreader Marjorie Taylor Greene] can get elected should be worrying. And it would only be mildly worrying if it were an outlier. But fantasy led to the sixth of January. We are still in the smoldering wreckage of a lie creating actual violence . . . as a result of complete detachment from reality."[5] And from another perspective, an arrested rioter looking back on January 6 described how time moved like frames in a movie on that day, as "fantasy slammed into reality like a car wreck."[6] For these commentators, the unreal and fantasy *felt* like the right language to describe the realities that clashed on January 6, similar to how they had become the right words for writing about VR's promise of transporting people between different lived realities. In the pages that follow, I will explore how the unreal and fantasy made sense of VR while hinting at how they also provide ways for grappling with the crisis of reality that, as evidenced by Joe Biden's plea for 2022 midterm voters to elect Democratic candidates in order to "sustain a republic where reality's accepted,"[7] remains ongoing.

I borrow the language of "reality crisis" from columnist Charlie Warzel, who named this phenomenon in the days after January 6 when pointing to Trump's years-long "assault on the truth."[8] Warzel, a tech columnist, refocused attention on the role technology plays in the construction of fantasies and unrealities. Specifically, he singled out Trump's army of followers that had been "cocooned in Facebook groups and fed a steady diet of lies."[9] Facebook materially ties together the reality crisis and VR. The 2015 *TED Radio Hour* episode that generated my interest in virtual reality presented Facebook's acquisition of Oculus VR with bemused interest. It seemed a wild (if harmless) bet that Mark Zuckerberg was making on what he anticipated being "the next smartphone, the next internet, the next thing that's going to transform our lives." Facebook has refused to take responsibility for any misdeeds, with Zuckerberg insisting that his company's purpose has only ever been about forging connections and building community.[10] In 2021, Zuckerberg changed his company's name to Meta and increased its investment in VR and immersive technologies to bring about what he claimed would be the successor to the internet: the metaverse. Zuckerberg positioned VR as the technology that would finally realize Facebook's original goal: "The dream was to feel present with the people we care about. Isn't that the ultimate promise of technology? To be together with anyone, to be able to teleport anywhere, and to be able to create and experience anything."[11] That Zuckerberg could so flagrantly ignore the possibility that the assault on reality wrought by his original platform would be replicated and perhaps even magnified on a platform that even more explicitly offers itself as a virtual reality is a stunning example of living in an alternate reality.

In the Land of the Unreal rewinds from this moment to when the reality crisis was brewing but had not yet manifested as a mass, grotesque spectacle. In Los Angeles, the epicenter of the widely exported unreality of Hollywood, the VR community imagined itself as independent from the Big Tech forces up north and worked toward crafting an alternative to business as usual. They wove together VR's humanitarian project of reality repair with more local concerns about workforce representation. While I witnessed small successes, the hoped-for better selves and societies remained elusive; good-intentioned projects often failed to address the structural issues that demanded more radical solutions. What is instructive about this community is the ways in which fantasy and the unreal were wielded to explore otherwise ways of building community and working with technology. VR permitted conversations on fractured realities, and while some of these conversations foreshadowed the dark divisions that fed into January 6, more often the beneficial possibilities of reality's malleability were probed. In this community, the unreal was not necessarily something to be feared, but something that could also direct intentions toward building better worlds. Precisely because the unreal elicits both peril and pleasure, I remain cautious of VR's utopian claims, warning against the seduction of technological fixes for entrenched, complex social problems. And yet, in striving to resist dominant narratives of what technology is and ought to be—what reality is and ought to be—there might be inspiration to take from fantasies of technologies otherwise created and deployed.

INTRODUCTION
FANTASY AND TECHNOLOGY

In July 2017, the Los Angeles County Museum of Art (LACMA) installed the US premiere of *Carne y Arena (Virtually Present, Physically Invisible)*, which, when shown at Cannes a few months earlier, was the first virtual reality (VR) experience to be selected for screening at the storied film festival. When I arrived in LA in January 2018—an anthropologist curious about VR and the people rallying around this forever reemerging technology—*Carne y Arena* was one of a few experiences that the VR community considered a must-see; this was an example of the potential of the medium. Even in early 2018, tickets were hard (and expensive) to come by. Only one person could be in the exhibit at a time, and as such tickets sold out almost as soon as they went on sale. I was lucky to be checking my email when the announcement came that a new block of tickets was released and bought one immediately.

A few weeks later, on a sunny and crisp Monday morning in February, I began my day at LACMA. In the afternoon, I would meet up with classmates with whom I was taking a VR development class to brainstorm what experience we might want to build for our final project. Though early in my fieldwork, I was busy crisscrossing the city to meet folks involved with VR, establishing a network that would eventually yield invitations allowing me to observe and engage in each stage of the process of creating a VR experience. I was also getting a feel for the larger LA community that had been activated by VR and the growing tech scene by attending industry and public events. Over the weekend, I had spent Saturday in Marina del Rey at a coding boot camp and on Sunday evening I attended a convening of Ye Olde Futurist Union at a brewery in Downtown LA where attendees debated whether VR could fix a broken reality. After a month and a half of learning the basics of how a VR experience gets made, meeting with VR innovators to learn what Angelenos thought of the medium, and attending events that both hyped and hedged VR's potential, I was excited to visit LACMA and see this much-praised piece.

My scheduled entrance time was one of the first in the morning, and as I waited to pick up the ticket, I chatted with the only other visitor there, who had the slot ahead of me. She worked in the special effects industry, and this would be her first time experiencing VR. *Carne y Arena* is written and directed by Alejandro González Iñárritu (director of movies including *The Revenant* and *Birdman*), which was part of what had made it such a draw for folks in LA, especially those like the guest ahead of me who worked in Hollywood. Iñárritu was awarded a Special Achievement Oscar for this piece in 2018, a rare accolade previously awarded in 1995 for Pixar's *Toy Story. Carne y Arena* is not a heartwarming animation, but is rather about crossing the Mexico/US border, drawing attention to the violent conditions in Latin and South America that prompt adults and children to risk their lives. Iñárritu hoped VR could be a force for good in the world by cutting through the fog of ideology and portraying the "real reality" of these migrants. In his Oscar acceptance speech, Iñárritu spoke of decisionmakers who would be voting on the future of Deferred Action for Childhood Arrivals (DACA), wondering if they ever looked one of these kids in the eyes. VR, the filmmaker believed, could allow for each of them to have this experience, offering "a slice of our complex reality so that we can understand each other and therefore love each other." He went on to explain that he does not see VR as a way to escape reality. Instead, "I am interested in technology as a tool to embrace reality and, like the immense ocean, submerge myself."[1] In *Carne y Arena*, the experiencer is immersed in a VR world where they are virtually present but physically invisible (as the subtitle of the piece reads). The experiencer thus takes on the social positioning of the migrant who is, for many of the intended viewers of this piece, present yet invisible.

A visitor individually makes their way through the four rooms of the exhibit (only the third of which contains a VR experience). The first room is dark, containing a backlit artist's statement. Iñárritu explains how VR allows him to tap into the very personal, horrific accounts of border crossing.

He calls his approach, based on interviews with dozens of undocumented people (many of whom live in LA), "semi-fictionalized ethnography." Every person encountered in the experience, though digitally rendered, is based on an actual person and an actual border crossing event. Iñárritu instructs the visitor, instructs me, to explore the virtual scene in whatever manner we choose—unlike in film, in VR the frame is gone. We, not Iñárritu, are the director. Rather than passive viewers, we are instructed to think of ourselves as active, embodied participants in the story's action.

The second room of the exhibit is cold, sterile, and bright; a short-term holding cell for crossers picked up by the Border Patrol. Stark red text painted on the wall instructs me to take off my shoes and socks and place them along with my bag in a locker, sit on the metal bench, and only enter the next room when a siren and light go off. I obey, hugging myself to keep warm. The room is littered with worn-out shoes covered in dust and grime; another text on the wall explains that these shoes were collected along the border. I wonder if the former owners of these shoes survived their crossing.

When the alarm goes off, I enter the third room. With bare feet, I can feel the coarse sand that covers the floor. Flesh and sand, *carne y arena*. There are two staff members in the middle of the dimly lit room, holding a backpack and a VR head-mounted display (HMD). A long, thick wire runs from the HMD up to the ceiling and down again, snaking on the ground out of sight. As one assistant keeps me from tripping on the wire, the other helps me into the backpack, HMD, and a pair of headphones. I am told that I can move anywhere in the room, and they will keep me from getting tangled in the wires or colliding with a wall. The VR experience starts, and I am in a scrubby desert. I don't have a body, but I can look and move all around. The sand under my feet could be the sand of this desert scene; I am virtually present but physically invisible. I remain in this desert for the seven minutes of the experience, though the activity around me ebbs and flows. For much of the experience, I am with a group of immigrants led by a coyote. Iñárritu used motion capture, filming the scenes and then overlaying the human movement with digitally rendered avatars. It's dusk in the desert, so you can't make out anyone's face too clearly. The way the bodies move feels authentic, allowing me to easily imagine that I am with this group of people in the desert. The coyote talks on a cell phone and encourages our group to keep walking. I move amongst the migrants, listening in on individual conversations conducted mostly in Spanish (which I do not speak). I find myself eavesdropping from a polite distance, though, when I talk about this experience with a friend a few days later, they say that when they "bumped" into an avatar, they were brought inside the digital body and could see organs pulsing and hear the heart pounding.

The quiet of the scene is interrupted by the sound of an approaching helicopter; there is a powerful gust of wind that I feel on my skin and the coyote yells at all of us to duck and get on the ground. Border Patrol agents arrive on the scene and begin shouting in English and Spanish. They are rounding us up. In the chaos, someone tries to run, and another is injured and can't get up even as the agent yanks their arm. There is screaming and flashlights and guns. I move around the chaotic scene, present yet invisible, trying to make sense of the different stories. People are being loaded into cars. One person says that he is an American lawyer and yet is still being arrested. I follow a woman being dragged by her arms. In the cacophony, I am slow to realize that a patrolman is pointing a gun directly at *me*. At first, I think I'm in the middle of a scene and look behind me to see who the gun is being pointed at. But there is no one there. I shuffle a few steps sideways and he traces the gun on me, shouting at me to kneel. As I realize I am no longer invisible, that I am there, the experience ends.

Not sure of the etiquette, I somberly thank the museum helpers as they remove the headset and backpack. I make my way to the final room of the exhibit, where there is a series of ten or so screens at eye level, each enlivened by a person staring out of the screen and, in text superimposed over their image, telling their story.[2] I feel the urgency of their personal narratives as they talk about why they left home, their crossing experience, their current status, and their hope for the future. Many are young and, as the interviews were recorded during the Obama administration, place much of their hope in DACA. A few weeks after my LACMA visit, a Republican-majority Congress failed to pass the Dream Act. A few months later, the US Department of Justice implemented a draconian "zero tolerance" policy, imprisoning border crossers (including asylum seekers) and separating parents from children without any protocol for reuniting these families. Reality at the border had indeed shifted since the debut of *Carne y Arena*, but not as Iñárritu might have hoped.

It is clear, then, that the success of this piece was measured not by its political efficacy but rather the affective response of the participant to this mode of aesthetic engagement that seemed to disrupt the boundaries between viewer and experiencer, physical body and virtual body, seeing and feeling. Though justice-oriented VR pieces have not spurred structural changes, they are nonetheless celebrated by those who believe that they can, for the individual, offer an impactful experience of being in another reality. During *Carne y Arena*'s premier at Cannes, the festival director praised Iñárritu for offering the film community a "Lumière moment," which, like the famous clip of a train pulling into a station that reportedly terrified the assembled audience,[3] similarly blurred the relationship between representation and reality. In an interview in the trade magazine for the Director's Guild of America, Iñárritu described what many in the industry herald as the distinguishing quality of VR as compared to theater, cinema, or the written word: one must engage not only their mind but also their body in a VR experience. He startlingly concluded, "The body does not lie. So once your body's telling you something, you know that it's true. And the wires in your brain are tricked, and then you lose a little bit of the sense of reality." In other words, Iñárritu understands VR as offering an embodied way of knowing that overrides the mind. You might rationally know you are in a museum, but your body allows you access to a truth of being with this group of immigrants; you let go of your immediate reality in order to engage with another. In his artist statement, Iñárritu describes this as a "realistically unreal experience." As a technology of the unreal, VR allows a participant to momentarily occupy multiple, even conflicting, realities. In the case of *Carne y Arena*, a white participant (such as myself) experiences a shift from the familiar position of the removed observer able to move safely through a space of violence into, when the guard points the gun, a less protected reality. Speaking of this scene, Iñárritu explained that he wanted everyone, even the most unwilling participant, to have an experience of bodily presence. He wanted them to stop thinking and start being: "So you surrender your intellectualization and become part of the experience."[4] When I took off the headset, the unrealities of the experience—both my positioning and the experiences of the migrants—became a memory. However, for those who are the narrative subjects of pieces like Iñárritu's, this unreality is not so easily shed.

Carne y Arena exemplifies the aspirations of a community of storytellers and innovators who, throughout the 2010s, positioned VR as a solution to social and political failings. For this community, such failures were borne from certain lived experiences not being *real* for lawmakers and some members of their constituencies. If rational arguments for addressing injustices have fallen on deaf ears, those building VR experiences like Iñárritu's wondered if the visceral, emotional, embodied, and unreal experience of being in another reality might surpass what words alone could do and soften rigidly held beliefs. Being somewhere or someone else—an experience often presumed to emanate from a desire to escape reality—became for Iñárritu and many other VR creators the very thing that they felt might repair reality. Could experiencing other realities generate compassion and empathy, building bridges between disconnected realities? Though the situation at the border had worsened, this didn't stop people from wondering under what circumstances VR could be leveraged to resolve the political and societal impasses that seemed to have become ever more entrenched in a world in which the belief in a singular reality had lost its sovereignty.

This book takes as its premise that virtual reality can help make sense of what reality has become and is becoming. With each new social, political, or global emergency—be it immigration, racial injustice, climate change, or a pandemic—it is increasingly apparent that there is no common consensus as to the nature of an emergency (indeed whether an emergency even exists), its consequences, or a solution. The weakening of expertise and the fragmentation of the media landscape has intensified an inability to agree on fundamental facts about the world, creating a reality crisis and paralyzing efforts to confront large-scale problems. While VR did not create this reality crisis, the projects and conversations discussed throughout this book are symptomatic of anxieties emergent from living in a fractured reality.

This fracturing cleaves along multiple axes, including the disparate aspects of identity that shape one's "lived reality" and how epistemic commitments shape one's perception of an "external reality." I am not suggesting that reality is newly torn asunder—that there had previously been a singular reality—but rather I am motivated to understand how those who might have assumed a unified reality, and perhaps even remain committed to this worldview, came, in the late 2010s, to see multiple realities as a situation in need of address. This includes the VR innovators discussed throughout this book, but parallels can be drawn outside of these pages with political commentators making sense of the Trump administration's post-truth politics and liberal progressives accounting for the privileges that shape their particular—and not universally shared—experience of the world. From these perspectives, reality was becoming undone, becoming multiple, becoming something else; it is not dissimilar to the moment I describe as unreal in *Carne y Arena* during which my reality shifted from being an observer to being implicated in the action. But from other perspectives—particularly those from people in marginalized communities—reality's multiplicity has always been a truth. Writer Sylvia Wynter argues that there is no singular human, and thus no singular reality of being a human.

However, she cautions, these very claims that posit a shared human condition structure (and are structured by) the currents of power and knowledge that maintain global inequalities.[5] As reality's fracturing comes to be felt by more people, radical futures that break from the hegemony Wynter has articulated feel possible. However, as the case of virtual reality will instruct, such admirable and bold attempts easily become recaptured by the very structures targeted for dismantling.

To be in the land of the unreal is to feel reality's fracturing. For some, the unreal is ordinary. For those whose perspectives are documented in this book, it is extraordinary. The unreal contains both possibility and threat, prompting people to wonder what collective action and change might look like when the "collective" can no longer be taken for granted. In this fractured reality, it has become frustratingly apparent that traditional strategies for civic action have become ineffective, premised as they are on norms and assumptions that no longer hold. Other methods and practices are needed, with scholars, artists, technologists, and activists embracing alternative, experimental, and speculative ways of understanding and practices of being. While not all—or even most—of the virtual reality industry is aligned with what might be considered progressive politics, VR nonetheless is an unexpected crucible in which techniques for navigating a fractured reality are being tested both explicitly (as in the case of a piece like *Carne y Arena*) and implicitly. VR raises questions—and its enthusiasts attempt answers—about the porosity of reality and the consequences of infusing it with fantasy in order to imagine other worlds that might be possible. Iñárritu experimented with how effectively VR could transport someone into another's world, hoping this could foster an empathetic understanding that would transcend the differences between lived realities. Might this reforge a common reality and allow for the emergence of a different, more humane and equitable future?

Engaging with speculation and fantasy, imagining alternative realities, and worldbuilding toward various futures feel exciting in that these methods seem to push past the standstill confronting more realist or rationalist approaches. However, as this book is situated in LA, one is necessarily reminded of the noir elements that shade sunny outlooks. The fractured reality that has facilitated these ways of thinking about and with VR is the same terrain upon which insurrectionists and authoritarians are also able to blend fantasy and reality to incite the action needed for bringing about the world as they think it ought to be. The same strategies that are imagined by VR innovators to do good in the world can, in other hands, do its opposite. This ambiguity is what makes the reality crisis challenging to navigate, demanding care and attention be paid to how worlds are imagined and created.

The Fantasies That Create Realities

Virtual reality, I am not the first to note, is at first glance a contradiction, juxtaposing two concepts not often imagined as coextensive. It is nonetheless a productive phrase, illustrating how unexpected pairings can generate modes of thinking and practice. In this book, pairing fantasy and technology is similarly generative, particularly for making sense of what reality has become.

Though technology is often associated with pragmatic pursuits (solving "real world" problems), social media technologies are central to the long-brewing reality crisis. These platforms provide infrastructure for communities that, through the spread of misinformation and conspiracy theories, create, maintain, and amplify alternative realities. VR is both conceptually and materially tied to this phenomenon, as Meta, the parent company of Facebook, is also one of the biggest investors and promoters of virtual reality. However, this book's concern with the role of technology in the reality crisis comes not from the alternative, proliferating realities of virtual worlds, but rather from an interest in those who believed that VR could act as a salve *against* multiplying and fracturing realities. At the time of my research, it was believed that this could be accomplished through narrative-driven VR pieces, like *Carne y Arena*. In contrast to social VR and games, these VR experiences were temporally discrete, experienced individually, and often accessed at museums or film festivals. These pieces were *cinematic*, dependent on expertise in storytelling as much as hardware and software know-how. A vibrant VR community thus formed in Los Angeles, shaped by those who had previously worked in Hollywood and some who had moved down from Silicon Valley. Because VR was not only cinematic but also understood as an emerging technology, LA's VR community took up familiar conversations about tech, but infused them with particular, local meanings shaped by the histories and industries of Los Angeles. This provided distinct frameworks—including fantasy—for thinking about technology and reality.

One conversation about technology that has long circulated in Silicon Valley but took on additional meanings in LA concerned projects that sought to implement technologies for "good" civic ends. Unlike "AI for Good" or, more generally, "Tech for Good" project banners that corporate entities deploy to promote implementations of their technologies in addressing underserved community needs,[6] "VR for Good" more often describes projects that are focused on improving the elite individual (who would then, it is imagined, make decisions that trickle down to the underserved others).[7] Such claims have been bolstered by laboratory research, as psychologists have offered evidence that the experience VR provides of "walk[ing] a mile in [another's] digital shoes" can, in certain contexts, foster prosocial behavior.[8] VR filmmaker Chris Milk popularized the idea that VR is the "ultimate empathy machine" in a 2015 TED talk (featured in the TED Radio Hour episode I describe in the prologue).[9] All these "tech for good" projects, VR included, need to be approached with caution.[10] Because "the good" is not a universally agreed upon concept but rather articulated through "regimes of knowledge," "tech for good" projects that emerge from Big Tech companies shape definitions of what it means to do "good" work in ways that align with their mission, namely capital accumulation.[11] Both Facebook and Google were promoting their "VR for Good" initiatives during my period of research and while I met some folks in LA who received funding through these programs for their particular VR projects, LA's "VR for Good" conversation was adjacent to but also outside of the vision coming from Big Tech. Even if some of the academic critiques of "Tech for Good" initiatives are not entirely applicable to "VR for Good" as I encountered it (these projects were not directly in service of humanitarian efforts, were not exclusively corporatized, and did not have the same privacy concerns as did the projects dependent on data collection), this phrasing nonetheless naturalizes a host of assumptions, including an uncritical acceptance of technosolutionism (that technology is the fix for social problems) and a narrative that conflates technological progress with social progress.[12] The complex relations that animate social and technical networks are masked behind the simplicity of "the good," necessitating a critical and skeptical stance when encountering such assertions.

To understand the social work accomplished by a belief that VR is "good," I contextualize it in a time and place when it was being valued by a particular community. In 2018, "techlash" was the runner-up for the Oxford English Dictionary's "word of the year," inaugurating a cultural moment when the myth of technological progress was shattering and the tech industry's harms were publicly discussed. VR's "goodness" was thus seen not as automatic but as something that needed to be underwritten by a community that was itself constituted around "good" values. In Iñárritu's Oscar speech, he briefly mentioned the less idealistic players in the VR industry, alluding to those developing the technology exclusively out of "vulgar, profit driven interests." Iñárritu might be referring to the gaming and pornography industries based in Southern California or the Big Tech companies headquartered up north in Silicon Valley. But the point was the same: he and others sought to create a different kind of community and thus, they imagined, a different kind of VR.

Put another way, the community in LA that strove to leverage VR for positive social and political outcomes was itself constructing an alternative reality that positioned itself as outside of Big Tech's harmful circuits of power, an unattainable position given the reach of these companies, their products, and their funding networks. As I worked to understand how the community maintained a belief in this positioning—how any alternative reality flourishes—the language of *fantasy*, seemingly endemic to Los Angeles thanks to Hollywood's looming presence, kept presenting itself as a way to make sense of everyday encounters and the cultural work that was being done by this community.[13] I observed how employing a technology to imagine and pursue other, better worlds took place within a meshwork of interwoven fantasies that rendered reality pliable and thus something that could be multiplied or reshaped. Fantasies, in this context, are not distinct from reality but texture the social practices through which realities are brought into being. In that sense, it is similar to how film theorists, drawing on a psychoanalytic tradition, invoke fantasy. As summarized by Todd McGowan, fantasy "serves as a way for the individual subject to imagine a path out of the dissatisfaction produced by the demands of social existence."[14] Fantasy distorts social reality and can facilitate "experiences otherwise unthinkable."[15] Which is not to say it is apart from reality, but rather that fantasy plays a significant role in structuring an individual's lived experience. Fantasy, as André Nusselder has more explicitly argued, operates as an interface between the virtual and the real.[16]

There are three fantasies that created the reality of the community that I studied: a fantasy of place, a fantasy of being, and a fantasy of representation. The *fantasy of place* centers on Los Angeles and the question of whether a city known for movie magic could also be a place of technological innovation. Los Angeles, where I lived for a year in 2018 to conduct this research, is textured by storytelling and spectacle. How might these local dynamics shape virtual reality as it left the laboratory and entered the consumer market? While VR has long been fodder for speculative fictions,[17] in 2018 filmmakers and innovators collaborated to figure out how to tell stories not *about* VR but *with* VR. Such work conjured many fantasies regarding the possibility of VR, but one that recurred with frequency (well-illustrated by Iñárritu's piece) was what I will call a *fantasy of being*. Could VR transport someone from their reality to a different reality, from their self to a different self? While such an experience could be in service of amusement, the fantasy of being directs attention toward the hope that this feature of VR could be leveraged to bring about a better human and thus a better world.

This fantasy of a better world was reflexively taken up by the VR community itself in claiming that the VR industry could be better than either tech or entertainment; it could be an industry led by those who had been underrepresented and disenfranchised in other industries. Such a *fantasy of representation* was not, however, about content, but production. In particular, this is a fantasy of women leading the VR industry. Starting in 2015 and 2016, young women in LA began building infrastructure to support the vision of a more diverse and inclusive virtual reality industry. Culminating in the founding of an influential Facebook group, initially called "Women in VR," these organizers put forth a compelling vision that VR could be an industry led by women and marginalized voices. Conversations about VR in LA were shaped by the unexpected and influential contributions of women, a dynamic that only heightened following reporting in October 2017 on the many victims of producer Harvey Weinstein's sexual predation. Women in Hollywood and beyond posted on social media their own experiences with sexual harassment and predation using the tag #MeToo.[18] This launched the celebrity-driven arm of the #MeToo movement which, when I arrived in LA in January 2018, was still gaining momentum and energizing calls to action.

These fantasies of place, being, and representation intersect and reinforce each other, underpinning the "VR for Good" ethos that many in the community I write about in this book championed. Doing a VR experience could make an individual better and, in pursuing these projects, VR could itself be a "good" industry. To be clear, fantasies of "the good" don't inevitably yield the intended better worlds. This point is made by Lauren Berlant in *Cruel Optimism*. They write about the fantasy of "the good life," explaining why people stay attached to such fantasies even as they become less attainable. Berlant is able to write about "the attrition of a fantasy" with cultural and historical hindsight.[19] The full story of the fantasies in this book are not yet known. Indeed, when I began my fieldwork in 2018, these fantasies—and the better world—felt far away. The watershed moment that the community was hoping for had not yet come, and so 2018 was a year when several companies folded, when those who entered the field hoping to make a quick buck exited without a payday, and when the most committed VR boosters were showing both weariness and hopefulness. In the United States more broadly, 2018 was a year that began with the Parkland school shootings and ended with California fires up and down the coast. It was the year of #MeToo and of Brett Kavanaugh's ascension to the Supreme Court, despite a sworn testimony of sexual assault by Christine Blasey Ford. It was a year of revelations over Facebook's Cambridge Analytica scandal and the growing techlash. It was a year when the chaos of the Trump presidency began to feel normal and when Democrats regained their majority in the House of Representatives. It was a year of outrage and persistence, of exhaustion and anticipation.

Iñárritu described his process for creating *Carne y Arena* as semifictionalized ethnography and, indeed, we all craft fictions in our ethnographies as we strive to capture a truth. To write this fiction, I suspend this place and community in time. I do not tell an all-encompassing story of VR, nor do I offer predictions for its future. Though I wrote much of this book during the COVID-19 pandemic, which made the crises and experiences of 2018 feel small, my ambition in these pages is nonetheless to capture how the fantasies I encountered during my fieldwork were of a piece with, perhaps even an antidote to, an affective understanding that the world, the place, the moment, and even the technology of VR all seemed . . . unreal.

The Land of the Unreal

Los Angeles is a fitting place from which to study both virtual reality and shifts in reality. Geographer Edward Soja emphasized that the region has long been at the vanguard of producing "artful suspension[s] of factual reality," challenging the ability "to distinguish what is real from what is imaginatively simulated."[20] He borrows the language of simulation from Jean Baudrillard who, along with Umberto Eco, wrote influentially of Southern California's hyperreality. In an essay originally written in 1992 that Soja edited and republished in 2014, he draws out the implications of LA's hyperreality for American politics. "It can be argued," he wrote, "that a reactionary form of postmodern politics consolidated rapidly in the United States after the election of a Hollywood actor and ex-California governor as president in 1980."[21] The Reagan and Bush Sr. years saw hyper-realities being successfully wielded for political gain. Shifting from Nixon-era political *dissimulation* (covering up something that is there), political *simulation* in contrast "means pretending to have something that really isn't there and working hard to make others believe that it is, really."[22] This all led to what must have felt like, for Soja who was revisiting his 1990s analysis during Obama's presidency, a culmination: George W. Bush's Iraq War, motivated as it was by the simulacrum of the unknown unknowns. Soja excerpts a quote from a Republican aide defending the war (and associated lies), who described accusatory journalists and academics as being members of "the reality-based community" who have not yet realized that the "way the world works" has changed. The aide continued, "When we act, we create our own reality."[23]

Trump's presidency—the immediate historical context for my research—transformed hyperreal politics into unreal politics. Pretenses of rational and accepted modes of reasoning that persisted (even as farce) in political dissimulation were done away with; to justify actions, members of the Trump administration instead fabricated historical events or used markers to redraw hurricane paths. It became more obvious to the attentive public that alternative realities were being constructed whole cloth, severing what had been imagined as a common reality into multiple, diverging realities. Fittingly, not only was Trump a Hollywood president like Reagan, but he was more specifically a reality-television president and thus versed in producing fictions that passed for reality. Trumpism's political simulacra spun out alternative facts and post-truths, culminating in the unreality of the insurrection at the US Capitol on January 6, 2021.

If previous writers found the hyperreal in LA, I found the unreal and found it to be a helpful descriptor of the city, VR, and the politics of the moment. The unreal holds in tension an extraordinary rendering of reality with what might be thought of as an everyday reality. The social world has always been comprised of multiple realities, but the unreal marks circumstances when such multiplicity demands attention; when the fractured commons demands repair, particularly by those who have previously put their faith in a singular reality. Unreal politics position alternative facts alongside scientific or historical facts; the unreality of virtual reality allows for the simultaneous experience of one's reality and another's reality; the unreality of Los Angeles captures how Hollywood fantasies exist alongside a diverse and sprawling metropolis.

This depiction of Los Angeles is itself only one of multiple ways to describe the reality of the city. Historian Robert Fogelson described Los Angeles as a "fragmented metropolis." The fragment of this city that constituted the site of my research were institutions and spaces primarily occupied by the elite intellectual and creative classes of LA. Where I lived and worked, how I socialized and moved through the city, brought me into contact with people similar to those working in VR and separated me from the majority of Los Angeles's residents to whom the LA I write about matters little to their daily lives. When I describe how "LA" helped me understand VR or when I talk about the ways in which Hollywood shapes the city, I am referring to this fragment of LA that I came to know. The "LA" of this book is its own virtual reality, a world apart from how many others experience and know the city.

Exemplary, then, of this LA is the Hollywood studio. On a Paramount Pictures studio tour during the first weeks of my LA residency, I first encountered "the unreal" as an emic self-understanding of the worlds conjured by the intermixtures of fantasy and reality that begin in the studio and spill into the surroundings.

Alongside a family of four on holiday from Australia, I learned about Hollywood's first studio and the movies and television shows shot on this lot. Kim was our guide and drove us around the lot in a golf cart, taking us in and out of sound stages and pointing out where classic scenes were filmed. Throughout the tour, Kim provided various examples of how film crews transform sets into other locations. On the "New York Backlot," a street whose exterior is recognizable as belonging to Brooklyn intersects with another made to feel more like Greenwich Village, and around another corner one can feel instead like they are standing in Chicago's South Side. Kim explained that sometimes reality looks fake. Los Angeles, for example, usually has crystal clear blue skies, and so there is a gigantic canvas painted a less vibrant blue, textured with clouds, sometimes used in exterior shots when LA's pristine sky strikes a false note.

As the tour proceeded, I began thinking about the similarities between virtual reality and Hollywood backlots. Both promise to transport you elsewhere and yet both, in the end, are façades—they promise a rich, full world similar to the one with which we are familiar but are surfaces that can't fully be entered; they are some other kind of world that remains out of reach. On the backlot, the different worlds collide with one another, creating a pleasurable implausibility of moving swiftly between these worlds.

I.1 It was cloudy on the day I took the Paramount tour, so the canvas matched the sky above. Photograph taken in January 2018 by the author.

Later on, while stopping to admire Paramount's iconic Bronson Gate, I was provided with a fitting description for the layering of worlds produced by both backlots and virtual reality. Kim explained that this gate is often used as a setting for films that are about Hollywood itself. On an iPad, she played for us a supercut of scenes from different movies featuring this location as an establishing shot. In one scene from the 1961 satire *The Errand Boy*, Jerry Lewis stands in front of the gate and a narrator intones, "This is Hollywood. Land of the real and the unreal." The supercut continued and other scenes played on Kim's iPad, but it is this description of Hollywood that stayed with me long after the tour.

The clip Kim showed was itself a bit of movie magic. The voiceover is not from the scene in front of the gate, but rather from the opening shot of the movie when the viewer is treated to an aerial view of Los Angeles. "This is a town," the narrator explains, "where dedicated people spend every waking hour applying their varied talents to the making of a product, the only purpose of which is to take you away from the harsh realities of life into the wondrous land of Make-Believe."[24] In the same year that this film was released, the LA-based writer Bill Davidson published a book detailing visits and interviews with the likes of Frank Sinatra and Elizabeth Taylor titled *The Real and the Unreal*. Davidson's book paints Hollywood as populated not by stars who are just like us, but rather people occupying a different, privileged reality: "There are two Hollywoods—the Real and the Unreal—and often it is impossible to tell which is which." Davidson describes the intermixing and play between the real and the unreal as what enlivens "this bizarre company town."[25]

The unreal does not remain confined to the studio lot but follows Hollywood workers back out into the city. As Leo Rosten wryly mused in his 1941 sociological study of the movie industry, "When a movie producer or actor, director or writer, goes to sleep he leaves the world of fantasy and enters the world of reality. . . . And this preoccupation with the fanciful must tend to blur perceptions of the real. . . . If Hollywood is a community of people who work and live in fantasy, then it is to be expected that their life should take on the attributes of the fantastic."[26] For the fragment of LA most influenced by Hollywood trades, fantasy and reality flow into one another such that the land of the unreal spreads beyond the studios. It is upon this land, enriched by the worldbuilding possibilities of the unreal, that virtual reality found fertile ground.

Throughout this book, I use fantasy and the unreal for similar purpose, shorthand for the shifting and multiplying of realities that, in turn, facilitate imagining and creating otherwise worlds. I use fantasy to index aspiration and, often, the future. The unreal, on the other hand, more generally describes the current state in which reality's fracturing cannot be ignored. In this land of the unreal, precisely because reality's instability is part of the everyday, there is always the possibility of reshaping reality and building new worlds. The unreal describes the backlot, the VR experience, the city itself; it describes any world built with the intention of providing access to another reality. Extending beyond VR and LA, the unreal captures the experience of living in and navigating between multiple realities. Unreality is a structure of feeling, intuiting that reality seems to have become something else; that it has multiplied, has fractured, has become virtual or fantastical.

Disciplining the Unreal

The unreal, as an analytic, telescopes across scales, allowing me to link the arguments I am making about VR in LA with not only US cultural and political shifts, but also changes in academic strategies and foci. At each of these scales, the unreal draws attention to the symptoms, consequences, and opportunities of a fractured reality. In academic thought, the loosening of constraints imposed by the enlightenment assumption of a singular reality have, in different ways, impacted the two fields from which I draw much of my theoretical and methodological commitments: anthropology and science and technology studies (STS).

In anthropology, operating in the speculative register of the unreal has opened up new avenues for rethinking the discipline's past and future. While anthropology has long attended to unreal and fantastical phenomena like magic and myth-making, these were of interest to the white colonial anthropologist's gaze precisely because such phenomena were imagined as outside of the researcher's reality. Anthropologists today recognize the colonial histories that created the separation between the "real reality" of the researcher and the "primitive reality" of the ethnological subject, and are pursuing a variety of methodological approaches to unsettle and critique both this history and attending assumptions. A speculative turn[27] has directed anthropologists to consider, as Matthew Wolf-Myer has outlined, "what sources might there be for rethinking the future? for dislodging the futures that we have been given and to think something anew? for rethinking the past that has gotten us to this point?"[28] This rethinking is required both for the liberal project but also for anthropology itself, and Ryan Jobson has suggested the need to "imagine a future for the discipline unmoored from its classical objects and referents"; from its commitments to the singular human and, I would add following Wynter, a singular reality.[29] Akhil Gupta's 2021 presidential address at the meetings of the American Anthropological Association engaged in a speculative project of asking what American anthropology might be today if it had been founded as a decolonial discipline. Gupta suggested that such counterfactual histories and attempts at "imagining otherwise" are "powerful tools for thinking about the present,"[30] perhaps opening toward what Anand Pandian has called "a possible anthropology." Pandian reframes the discipline's method of ethnography as a "practice of critical observation and imagination, an endeavor to trace the outlines of a possible world within the seams of this one."[31] Anthropologists, like VR innovators, are engaged in projects of worldbuilding that maintain the possibility that other futures are possible and perhaps most realizable through attuning to the multiple realities of the present.

In STS, the unreal is a category of concern as scholars wonder how to maintain a critique of technoscience against the backdrop of a post-truth politics that dangerously undermines scientific expertise. The discipline developed in an American and European context in which technology was accepted as a driver of progress and science had unimpeachable authority, associated as it was with accessing a singular and objective "real." Science and technology, however, are deeply human endeavors, and STS scholars traced out the social and political networks in which technoscience operates. In so doing, they positioned reality, like science, as a product of social work. Bruno Latour notes that reality's Latin root, *res*, means "to resist." The reality of an object becomes stable in so far as it is able to resist the critique of others.[32] Such a conception of reality has ramifications far beyond the object or fact being studied. As Annemarie Mol has written, this perspective "has robbed the elements that make up reality—reality in its ontological dimension—of its stable, given, universal character. [Instead,] reality is historically, culturally, and materially located."[33] Leaning into this instability, Karen Barad further challenges, "Reality is not composed of things-in-themselves or things-behind-phenomena but 'things'-in-phenomena."[34] Barad's agential realism posits reality as emergent from the intra-action between phenomena and materiality. "The real" does not lie in an object nor even does it become fixed through social consensus; reality is always in the process of becoming.

With the proliferation of post-truths and alternative facts, however, scholars in STS find a perverse version of our analytic work mirrored back. In the political arena it has become apparent that there are gains to be made by instilling distrust in mutually agreed upon facts or reality.[35] Moreover, technological platforms have proven themselves effective at forging and fostering alternative realities. Whereas unsettling reality had been a productive critical strategy in STS when science and technology had (mostly) unquestioned authority, the field must now also account for how other actors wield similar strategies for darker purposes. As Latour reflected in a 2018 interview, "Now we have people who no longer share the idea that there is a common world. And that of course changes everything."[36]

This does not lead, in my estimation, to a suggestion for doubling down on realist accounts in order to shore up scientific expertise or accepting technological "progress." The radical rethinking afforded by unreal approaches is demonstrated by the conversations in anthropology discussed above. Rather we must maintain an awareness that though elements of the unreal can be found in VR and LA and Trumpism and academic discourse, these all differ in kind. Projects of the unreal need to be contextualized, as they can contain the promise of creating new realities or the danger of nihilistic abstraction by which we come to exist in realities without any overlap.

Technology Otherwise

From STS's constructivist project that renders reality multiple stems an appeal to resist singular narratives about technology. An oft used phrase, "it could be otherwise," serves as a slogan of sorts for the discipline[37] and will also provide a refrain throughout this book as I wonder what a technology otherwise—a technology that resists Big Tech logics—could look like. The otherwise reminds the analyst that rarely is there a predetermined path along which a technology inevitably develops; different pasts are thinkable, and different futures are possible. In 2018, VR was still in the making and different communities envisioned different futures. I detail throughout this book the future that was being imagined in Los Angeles, premised on the fantasies that VR would be a good technology and that women would lead the industry. These fantasies assert that VR could be otherwise. But also there is a fantasy at work that the very nature of technology and who gets to be a tech worker could be otherwise. This fantasy was able to blossom in LA precisely because it was geographically outside of Silicon Valley and thus outside of the hegemonic center of the US tech scene. And while I refer to the work being done in LA as a *fantasy* of technology otherwise, there is also a significant lesson here for analysts of the US tech scene that, going forward, some version of this imagined otherwise might well come to be.

Although Southern California has long been host to military, aerospace, and industrial manufacturing (what, in the previous century, would have been classed as high technology enterprises), by the last decades of the twentieth century, Silicon Valley consolidated California's tech expertise and power, particularly in regard to computing and digitally networked ventures. The vision for the World Wide Web and subsequently social media (sometimes glossed as Web 1.0 and Web 2.0) were in large part conceived of and executed by Silicon Valley–based companies; software platforms and consumer hardware stole headlines and generated investment returns.

I.2 A sign for "crypto" blends in seamlessly with the "Venice" sign, a replica of the original from 1905 (rehung in 2007), which has long beckoned visitors to enjoy entertainment and escape. Photograph taken in March 2022 by the author.

Recently, speculations have intensified around "Web 3.0" (or "Web3"). This capacious term attempts to anticipate the next phase of the internet, and often assumes technologies like blockchain and artificial intelligence as drivers. Many imagine that Web3 will also include the seamless integration of virtual and physical worlds (what the phrase "spatial computing" often refers to), drawing augmented reality (AR) and virtual reality into the imaginary. What uses or experiences will make people want to partake in Web3 sociality? This indicates a broader question that was and continues to be asked about VR: What would make users want to spend time immersed in virtual spaces? One of the pathways for succeeding in the Web3 ecosystem depends less on platform development and more on content creation, and thus more suited to the talent and expertise of SoCal. Given this state of affairs, VR's prominence in LA throughout the 2010s starts to feel less like an anomaly and more like a harbinger, foreshadowing this next phase of the internet that investors and large companies are pushing toward.

The power center of the US tech industry might thus be in the process of shifting slightly away from Silicon Valley and toward Hollywood, where expertise in content development is seen as crucial for capitalizing on Web3. For those of us concerned about tech futures, we must similarly expand our geographies of attention. Scholarship in critical technology studies that has been instrumental to articulating the harms of digital technologies has largely done so by critiquing Silicon Valley actors and their ways of thinking and doing.[38] This necessary work must continue while being mindful of the changing contours of the US tech industry, particularly in cases like VR when an industry (entertainment) not often captured in our analyses of technology plays a significant role.

The reviving of a tech industry in LA has been slowly occurring over the past twenty years given the significance of content—generated by both professionals and users—in driving traffic to "Web2" platforms.[39] But even as recently as 2015, it was possible for a Silicon Valley transplant, arriving in LA, to observe that "Compared to Silicon Valley, the Los Angeles tech scene is the Wild West."[40] After all, until very recently tech companies have remained headquartered in Silicon Valley. In the early 2000s, when LinkedIn, Friendster, and Facebook were all founded, only Myspace based itself out of LA. In 2003, Netflix, headquartered in Silicon Valley, opened its first LA office, and other tech companies began quietly following. In 2012, the social media company Snapchat was founded in Venice and soon became LA's most visible success story, allowing other tech ventures to justify a beachfront location.[41] What was being called "Silicon Beach"—more by marketers than by tech workers[42]—began consolidating and if one were to ride a Bird scooter (the micro mobility company was founded in 2017 in Santa Monica) around LA's coastal neighborhoods in 2018, one would pass signs for Google, YouTube, Facebook, Postmates, Hulu, and Headspace.

Despite these familiar corporate presences, the tech scene in LA isn't a replication of the one in Silicon Valley; it is otherwise. This technology otherwise is influenced by local industries and their attending fantasies, which in turn catalyze the fantasies specific to VR that I encountered throughout my research. LA offers a reminder that technology, as a concept and an artifact, is not universal but particular to places and times. This book explores one technology otherwise among many that exist throughout the tech landscape.

Studying the Virtual

Focusing on place when studying a technology like VR might seem counterintuitive, given the connotation of "the virtual" as that which is dislocated from the physical world. However, as many scholars have discussed, the virtual is a very "real" phenomenon. Media theorist Homay King argues that before virtuality became so thoroughly associated with digital realms, it was "a contranym: it simultaneously invoked existence and nonexistence, reality and unreality, fact and fable."[43] The reality of the virtual traces back to metaphysical treatises by Bergson and Deleuze, both taking inspiration from Proust's description of memory as virtual, in that it is real but not actual.[44] Starting in the 1990s, scholars extended this Deleuzian understanding of the virtual (and its reality) to digital media,[45] though with concern that to overly associate the virtual with cyberspace would limit the meaning of the term.[46] One strategy was to place the virtual in opposition to the physical and the actual, rather than the real. Virtual worlds *are* real worlds, as anthropologist Tom Boellstorff demonstrated in his study of the virtual world, *Second Life*.[47] Boellstorff clarifies that this doesn't mean that everything in the digital realm is real. Indeed, there is already plenty in the physical realm that is itself make-believe.[48]

Studying the virtual can thus be approached through several different ethnographic framings, depending on one's interest in the sociality of persistent virtual worlds,[49] the inseparability of our digital worlds from our actual worlds,[50] or the local and global impacts of digital media.[51] While I tracked discourse about VR in the news and on social media, the focus of my ethnographic work was on how the VR community in LA constituted itself.

One of the first tasks of an anthropologist is to learn the language and so, upon arriving in LA in January 2018, I enrolled in an introduction to VR production class taught at a start-up in Marina del Rey. I also sat in on a class at the University of Southern California cotaught by Scott Fisher, who had built one of the first VR headsets in the 1980s. Between these two classes, I gained a better sense of how VR experiences are made; I gained basic literacy.

While learning the basics, I reached out to folks through the Women in VR Facebook group, attended meetups specifically for women in the VR and tech community, participated in a VR hackathon, and began running into the same people and building relationships. By late spring, I found two organizations willing to let me into their day-to-day operations. One, the Technicolor Experience Center (TEC), exposed me to the Hollywood side of the VR world and the other, Embodied Labs, brought me into a start-up trying to realize VR's potential to do good. Employees at both companies generously gave me their time and patience, allowing me to chronicle their experiences in the VR industry. In addition to spending most days at one or the other of these companies, I attended several networking events a month and socialized with the friends I'd met at events or in classes who would fill me in on their travels through the VR world. Toward the end of my time in LA, I sat down for formal interviews, both with those I knew well and those I had met only a time or two. By this point, I had some theories and ideas about VR in LA and used the interviews to refine these thoughts and think alongside those who, in the end, know the community best. The people I met throughout my fieldwork were, variously, established in their careers, just getting started, or struggling to find a way in. The naming conventions reflect relative career stability, as I refer to those further along in their careers (with their permission) by their real, full names and pseudonymize the less established.

I left LA in December 2018 but continued to keep tabs on the happenings in LA. Posts on the Facebook group, media coverage, and several industry podcasts kept me apprised of the large movements of the industry. Occasional texts from and visits with LA friends allowed me insight into the smaller movements of individuals as they continued to navigate the scene. This book, however, does not give the up-to-date scoop on VR. Instead, I tried to capture in these pages a specific community at a specific time in a specific place.

The Stories This Book Tells

The settings of ethnographic projects are not incidental or background, but deeply revealing of the communities, artifacts, and ideas anthropologists aspire to make sense of. This book therefore begins by tracing how the fantasies endemic to LA flow into the imaginations of technology and the creation of VR experiences. LA is imagined as a place of possibility, dominated by Hollywood and populated with experiments of creating worlds, futures, and realities otherwise. Like all places, LA has a unique character, and this in turn shapes and is shaped by the kinds of conversations about technology that percolate in the city. In the first three chapters, I explore different facets of LA's "technological terroir." Chapter 1, "Desert of the Unreal," emphasizes how Los Angeles has long been a place of utopian ideation. In addition to late nineteenth-century booster fantasies, midcentury collaborations between the military and entertainment industries strategized about civic betterment. Such partnerships set the institutional stage for contemporary VR and offer histories that can be mined for lessons about whose realities are prioritized and whose are marginalized in such visions of improvement.

The exploration of LA's fantasy of place continues in chapter 2, "Realities Otherwise," by suggesting that the experience of being in LA unlocks some of VR's more ineffable qualities. The architectural façades of the movie set and theme park extend throughout the city, offering a glimpse of other places and other times while moving through the urban landscape. Building on theorists who analyze LA as a postmodern city and ground zero for hyperreality, the unrealities that I encountered and that VR exemplify are but the latest shifts in reality that the city makes legible. That one seems to be able to feel reality becoming something else in LA hones an intuition for the kinds of worlds and realities that VR similarly invites into being.

Chapter 3, "Tinseltown and Technology," explores the impact Hollywood has on technological development. The history of the movie industry is also a history of technology, and it is fitting that this chapter builds from the several months I spent observing the day-to-day activities of the Technicolor Experience Center (TEC)—a small branch of the famed company that led the technological transition from black-and-white to color film. In 2018, TEC was trying to lead a transition in the entertainment industry to VR and other immersive technologies. The triumphs and frustrations I witnessed at TEC can be partly attributed to VR being simultaneously a cinematic technology and an emerging technology—a technology for storytelling as well as a technology about which stories are told. There is different expertise needed for success in these different domains and, because this distinction was not articulated, VR's failure to launch was a puzzle that devolved into a blame game between Silicon Valley and Hollywood.

Part II turns to the fantasy of being that animates VR. The immersive quality of VR is such that one can experience being somewhere else and perhaps even being someone else. Taking on the perspective of another is central to the fantasy of VR as a good technology, a technology that cultivates empathy. In chapter 4, "Being and the Other," I offer a history of VR that explains how it shifted from a technology that, in the 1980s and 1990s, promised freedom from one's body to today's fantasy of embodying another. Central to this reconceptualization of VR is the work of LA-based immersive journalist Nonny de la Peña, who translated research out of the laboratory and offered Hollywood filmmakers, including Iñárritu, a glimpse of VR's narrative potential. Many of the VR experiences with good intentions that were produced in the 2010s were designed for privileged viewers to take on the perspective of marginalized individuals. This chapter unpacks the racial dynamics at the heart of many of these empathy experiences, underscoring that being another can only ever be a façade and must be approached with caution.

In chapter 5, "Special Affect," I consider the mission of Embodied Labs, a company founded in 2016 that creates VR experiences for professional caregivers who work with elderly people. These VR experiences are premised on a similar logic that embodying another will yield insight. However, I explore in this chapter whether an empathy machine otherwise is possible—can the fantasy of being be implemented with care? Drawing on the time I spent with cofounder Carrie Shaw and her coworkers, this chapter suggests that deploying VR such that it does not *replace* the need to be with and care for others but rather *augments* such being and caring is one potential strategy for pursuing VR's fantasy of being a good technology.

Might a good industry bolster and be bolstered by a good technology? This is the question at the heart of the fantasy of representation that focuses part III. In chapter 6, "VR's Feminine Mystique," I describe how Women in VR found its voice and visibility in LA. I do not describe a utopia, but rather moments of triumph—including the successful disenfranchisement, catalyzed by the #MeToo movement, of a VR company when its male founders were charged with harassment—and moments of exclusion felt by some members of this community with regards to the label of "woman." To articulate that women could lead VR is to articulate a fantasy of a different kind of industry, and this chapter works through what strengthens and weakens this fantasy.

Finally, in chapter 7, "Making Innovation Women's Work," I consider the dynamic of the overlapping fantasies of place, being, and representation to suggest that claims by VR producers that they are "women in tech" indicates that "tech" means something fundamentally different in LA. Women described to me how the rapid growth of VR and the lack of gatekeepers allowed them to claim expertise in a manner they had been denied in other career paths. This was empowering, made more so because while they might have trained in television or film, VR associated them with the prestige of "tech." Unlike earlier moments in the history of both technology and entertainment, where a contraction of expertise limited the involvement of women, here definitions of expertise were allowed to expand with inclusion in mind. Facilitating this expansion of expertise was a recasting of storytelling as technological innovation. Who, then, gets to be an innovator who might otherwise be excluded? And could this project of building a better industry—an industry that promised to build a better world—avoid the pitfalls of the tech world against which it was defining its values?

The world in which I researched this book felt very different from the world in which it was written (and I imagine the one in which it is being read). While the cracks in a fractured reality were quite visible in 2018, the gap between different realities has since widened. In the epilogue, I will bring the conversations of this book into the present by considering the shifting ethical stakes surrounding VR's future. The fantasies of VR's good potentials are fading as the otherwise is being eclipsed by the expected. Meta and Apple have offered their corporate fantasies of VR futures, hoping to maintain their positions of dominance should we (at their insistence) begin spending even more time in virtual worlds. In the land of the unreal, there is much work to be done if technology's future is to be different from its past.

PART I
FANTASY OF PLACE

Technologies often project an aura of placelessness, of universality. Those that circulate globally, including VR, become detached from their places and communities of origin. Emplacing technologies, on the other hand, can risk reinforcing a narrative of the singular act of invention, marking a specific garage, for example, as the birthplace of an industry. There is thus a balance to strike between either erasing or overemphasizing place. My approach throughout this book is to draw out how aspects of Los Angeles elucidate certain ways of thinking about virtual reality that retreat from prominence in other locations or through its global travels. Most salient are the ways in which fantasy weaves through the city—architecturally, historically, literarily, institutionally—putting into relief themes that each of the next three chapters will in turn explore. The fantasies of LA draw out histories of the uneven impact of utopian ideations, theories that describe proliferating realities, and explanations for the impacts of Hollywood on understandings of what technologies are and ought to be. Amidst these dynamics of place, beliefs about VR as an empathy machine and aspirations for it to be an inclusive industry took shape. While these concerns circulated beyond Southern California, they are rooted in LA's VR community. The engagements with and critiques of the fantasies of being and representation that come in later chapters take their specific form through articulations of the politics that saturate the land of the unreal.

In part I, I am thus interested in how LA's "technological terroir" cultivates a particular way of thinking about and developing both VR in specific and technology more generally.[1] In chapter 1, I begin by associating VR's quest to "repair reality" with more than a century of utopian urges that have manifested in Los Angeles. In the midcentury, both the military and entertainment industries produced fantasies of a better world and, in their finding common cause, established the institutional groundwork for VR's subsequent flourishing in LA and worldbuilding endeavors. While these histories are often forgotten by the contemporary VR community, there are cautions to be remembered, as projects pursuing utopia have tended to fracture the city, elevating some realities over others. Chapter 2 turns from the fantasies that pattern LA's histories to the fantasies that infuse the everyday. In the slice of LA that I and the VR community inhabited, realities otherwise textured the experience of moving through and being in the city. Even if my fieldwork was conducted at a time when VR (like many LA transplants) was struggling to make it, the fantasy of place that permeated the cityscape made it seem inevitable that if VR was going to make it anywhere, it would make it here.[2] And so, in chapter 3, I look at how a Hollywood postproduction company attempted to guide VR's development. Evident in the daily conversations and activities at this studio was a set of expertise that positioned VR as a tool for the storyteller but lost sight of VR as also a consumer technology that many hoped would be ubiquitous in the future. Complementary to the conceptual readings of LA's fantasy of place that I offer in chapters 1 and 2, in chapter 3 I consider the material implications of the premier manufacturer of such fantasies, the entertainment industry, and its continued convergence with the technology industry. As Hollywood continues to partner with Silicon Valley, perhaps even taking the lead on immersive, content-driven platforms, consideration must be given to the divergent meanings of technology that, as chapter 3 illustrates, exist between these places.

Technological Terroir

Throughout part I, I deploy the phrase *technological terroir*[3] when thinking descriptively and prescriptively about the relationship between place and technology. This imagery draws attention to how both artifacts (a specific technology like VR) and ethos (the very concept of "tech") shape and are shaped by their local conditions. I am not, however, the first to draw attention to how place matters for studying technology. Scholars in science and technology studies (STS) have offered numerous case studies that show how local practices and communities shape objects and ideas.[4] Increasingly, there are studies that provincialize Western concepts of technoscience in order to offer analyses of other epistemologies and ontologies, as well as research that places multiple ways of knowing in conversation.[5] There is also a metadiscourse emerging that decenters the European and US concerns that typically lie at the heart of STS inquiry, highlighting that even when Global North scholars work in Global South settings, they often still address Global North concerns.[6] To attend to the local in the context of the United States, as I do in this book, illustrates the applicability of strategies often employed when studying "other" places to centers of power. My contention is that even in the state of California, different cities produce different varietals of technology and tech discourse. Technological terroir is thus a heuristic reminder for the analyst that place matters, especially when writing about technologies like the virtual and the digital, which are too readily imagined as being dislocated and fully captured by global flows. As Yanni Loukissas has observed, it is not enough to look at data sets; data settings also need attention.[7]

Terroir comes from French winemaking, where it accounts for how both the material features of the land and craft knowledge create a regional taste. "The taste of place,"[8] as terroir can be glossed, explains why the same variety of grape grown in different locations do not produce the same (tasting) wine. Heather Paxson's ethnography of artisanal cheese makers examines how terroir takes on new meanings in the American context. Paxson demonstrates that terroir also encompasses specific community values (local investment, sustainable practices) by which something like artisanal cheese comes to have commercial value. Therefore, terroir as a meaningful concept is itself something that the cheese makers Paxson worked with were producing.[9]

Technological terroir pushes beyond the understanding that certain places are better suited than others for technological development.[10]

Such approaches still accept a monolithic understanding of what is and isn't "tech." Technological terroir trains attention on local dynamics that inform ideas about technology and how these in turn "flavor" the specific innovations that are produced even if, through their circulation, their point of origin is obscured.

"Tech" is always local, but some locations come to matter more than others. Accordingly, most readers likely have a similar notion of "technology" not because it is a universal concept, but rather because one local flavor has come to dominate. How people understand tech today is largely shaped by Silicon Valley and aligned locations (including Cambridge, Massachusetts, where I myself was trained, first as an engineer and later as an anthropologist of science and technology). As media scholar Alice Marwick notes, Silicon Valley culture is local, but "[i]n its function as a global imaginary, Silicon Valley exports the Californian Ideology as a universal solution to localized problems."[11]

The Californian Ideology to which Marwick refers was first articulated by Barbrook and Cameron in 1995. Their essay warns that technology isn't inherently liberal; Silicon Valley was founded on an agnosticism that allowed its products to be imagined as furthering both left and right causes. The essay begins with an observation of what I would consider to be the technological terroir from which this ideology has grown: "[It] has emerged from a bizarre fusion of the cultural bohemianism of San Francisco with the hi-tech industries of Silicon Valley. . . . [It] promiscuously combines the free-wheeling spirit of the hippies and the entrepreneurial zeal of the yuppies."[12] If these aspects of the ideology are at times celebrated, the authors are clear to articulate the dark conditions that foster such optimism: "Yet, this Utopian fantasy of the West Coast depends upon its blindness toward—and dependence on—the social and racial polarization of the society from which it was born."[13]

The technological terroir of Los Angeles and Silicon Valley share many similarities, but I am interested in articulating a distinct Southern Californian ideology that attaches to ideas about technology and VR in LA. While part I sets the stage for thinking about LA's technological terroir and how it shapes and is shaped by VR, other characters and plot lines are needed before I can complete the story. In the final chapter of this book, I will return to the fantasies fermenting in this place to illustrate how "tech" meant something different in LA. This local meaning of tech is what facilitated the fantasies of VR as a good technology supported by a good, diverse workforce.

1

DESERT OF THE UNREAL
HISTORIES, FUTURES, AND INDUSTRIES OF REALITY REPAIR

In February, at a brewery in Downtown Los Angeles, a stage was set for a debate. Several dozen audience members sat attentively at picnic tables, sipping hoppy beers and quietly chatting while waiting for the event to begin. We were there for a convening of Ye Olde Futurist Union (YOFU), "a debate club for the galactic age."[1] With gavel in hand, Zenka, an LA-based artist, technologist, and futurist, took the stage to welcome those assembled and introduced the resolution to be debated that evening: "We need virtual reality to recreate reality." This was the third meeting of YOFU, and during 2018 it would meet a few more times to debate topics including cryptocurrency and social media. Over the course of this evening, a playful conversation unfolded structured as a tongue-in-cheek twist on Oxford-style debating. As speakers took the stage, Zenka or her co-moderator would yield the floor to, for example, the Gentleman from Sirius or the Gentlelady from the Future. Some attendees wore quasi-futuristic costumes and blacklights transformed the speaker podium into a glowing platform. The audience pounded their tables in approval of a point or hissed in disapproval. Off to the side, a room from the virtual world AltSpace, where avatars had gathered to watch a livestream of the event, was projected on a screen. Virtual spectators (themselves watching the stream on a screen in the virtual room) emitted hearts or angry faces to signal support or disagreement.

It was understood that, from the perspective of this liberal, artsy crowd living through the second year of the Trump administration, reality needed repair. The resolution being debated was not if and how reality was broken but whether VR could usher in a new reality better suited to human and nonhuman flourishing. The first debater spoke in favor of the resolution, offering an outlook and practice she termed "reality craft." VR is a tool of reality craft, the gentlelady claimed, facilitating the articulation and exploration of better worlds. People could apply lessons learned through inhabiting these virtual worlds back out in the physical world, with the hope of closing the gap between a virtual utopia and a broken reality. A typical VR event would stay in this realm of optimism, but because this was set up as a debate, the presumption of VR's inherent goodness was allowed to be interrogated. In response to this opening argument, the moderator questioned the speaker's belief that such reality craft would lead to better futures. Wouldn't dystopias similarly proliferate? An audience member similarly challenged the techno-optimism of the gentlelady debater, asking how VR can be seen as liberatory and empowering when it is being driven by large tech companies like Facebook that care only for profits and market share. The questioner wondered if VR users could avoid being captured by the politics of the companies producing the tech. A couple months later, in April, Facebook CEO Mark Zuckerberg would testify in his congressional debut, thus inaugurating a wider and growing conversation of how Silicon Valley companies ought to be regulated, but in February it was still bold to question the presumed goodness of tech. I joined the audience in pounding the table in support of this point.

With the pro-side argued and scrutinized, the debater speaking against the need for VR to recreate reality took the stage. He posited the folly of verisimilitude. Why should a technology like VR pursue realism (recreate reality) when it could alternatively push us into new representational and experiential realms? "The greatest use of VR," the gentleman from Capetown claimed, "is when we break reality apart . . . VR's power [is] in deconstructing reality." The debater provided a brief lesson on semiotic deconstruction and delivered a philosophically sprawling speech. Upon conclusion, the audience was a bit confused and half-hearted hisses and table pounds filled the brewery. The moderator, similarly lost, made a joke about feeling like she was in Plato's cave or maybe the Matrix. What is reality, anyway?

Later in the evening, a speaker who called himself an anthropologist from the future (I was delighted by this and let out a soft "whoop") took the stage to reconcile the two sides of the debate to suggest how rejecting reality might be what leads to a repaired reality. He revisited what it might mean to deconstruct reality, explaining that he traveled here from the future to describe the better world that awaits us all: a world where binaries no longer exist and the distinction between "the virtual" and "the real" has become meaningless. The world, he told us, was deconstructed such that it could be reconstructed as something better. "Welcome to the desert of the real," the time traveler said, playing the role of Morpheus from *The Matrix*, who himself was riffing on the French theorist of hyperreality, Jean Baudrillard.

But perhaps this future anthropologist should have welcomed us to the desert of the unreal. In Baudrillard's desert of the real, virtuality pervades but scraps of what used to be identifiable as the real remain. However, in the desert of the unreal, multiple realities structure the landscape, undermining any confidence that one could discern even the scraps of a singular, dominant reality. Zenka had advertised the debate as a "mixed reality" event, as some spectators were at the brewery and others were in a virtual world. Though in 2018 these realities were materially and experientially distinct, this seeded the imagination that the anthropologist from the future conveyed, in which such difference would be inconsequential—life would be lived as both virtual and real, always mixed such that distinguishing between the two wouldn't be possible or have any meaning. In such a future, reality had been repaired in that it had morphed into something else entirely. But in the present, the sharp distinction between virtual worlds and physical worlds (and the multiplicity of both the former and the latter) was rendered as both symptomatic of a fracturing that was causing harm (reality as something that needed repair) and a resource for practicing a reality craft that could ameliorate such harms. VR was positioned as symptom and solution; a contradiction that will be elaborated upon in part II. In this chapter and throughout part I, I suggest that the politics of the fantasy that VR could knit back together a common reality and thus a better world are shaped by the politics of the place from which it found a community of support: Los Angeles. To conceptualize LA and VR in tandem, I tease out aspects of LA—from its history, its geography, its literary tradition—that provide additional resources for making sense of VR. I am interested in both the ways in which LA has materially shaped VR and also modes of thinking about LA that offer conceptual framings for understanding blendings of the virtual and the real.

There are many Los Angeleses and thus many ways to write about the city and its history. One persistent trope that I will examine in this chapter is, as enacted in the debate, a belief that LA was a place where different realities and different futures could be imagined. This is the fantasy of LA as a place to make a fresh start and build something new, manifesting a reality that has been repaired.[2] As I will discuss, this has historically led to one reality being elevated over others, with devastating consequences for those whose realities were erased. As Hollywood and LA's technology industry matured alongside one another, they too became resources for the city's cycle of "repairing" reality only to further multiply and fragment the realities of the city. When expertise around VR began developing in LA in the early 2000s, LA's technological terroir infused this project with these politics of the unreal. Indeed, VR in LA was so thoroughly a creation of this place that the community has forgotten some of its own origins in order to maintain the technology as a tool for worldbuilding toward better realities. The histories in this chapter provide cautions, revisited throughout the book, for projects desiring to repair reality.

Utopia for Some

Those writing about LA's history often frame the region as one in which alternative realities might be forged. "Generations [of migrants to California] sought freedom, wilderness, prosperity, a rupture from the old ways, a new beginning" opens a book about how LA has been long imagined as a healthful place for retreat and rejuvenation.[3] In a similar vein, one of the first comprehensive histories of the region, *Southern California Country* by Carey McWilliams, describes "A land of magical improvisation."[4] Scholars rehearse this trope not because they are seduced by the fantasy but rather they are engaged with excavating what these fantasies conceal, activating the "dialectic of sunshine and *noir*" that Mike Davis has argued shapes the "city myth" of LA.[5] As will be gleaned from LA's history and attending writerly tropes, attempts (whether by early settlers or contemporary VR enthusiasts) to repair reality often result in further fracturings of reality, elevating one version of LA (and assumptions about whom the city is for) while disenfranchising others.

Just as I am interested in this aspect of LA's history as a way to make sense of VR's project of reality repair, speculative fiction author Ursula Le Guin found California's history to be a way into a critical appraisal of the literary genre of utopia. In her 1983 essay abstrusely titled "A Non-Euclidean View of California as a Cold Place to Be," Le Guin describes utopian writing as not quite real and not quite fantasy; instead, it is a practiced melding of the two. Utopian promises drew white settlers to California, as boosters advertised the appeal of frontier living and promises of a fresh start. The year-round perfect weather made it ideal for the new film industry but also designated Southern California as a place of restoration for body and mind. If in the north there was a rush for gold, in the south there was a pause for health. Revealing of whom these fantasies were for, a physician expressed in the early days of statehood, "California will be found more conducive to the highest physical and intellectual development of the Anglo-Saxon race than any other part of the globe."[6]

That utopias are steeped in white, Western colonialism is a point central to Le Guin's critique of the imaginative resources that often underlie utopian parables. Their Euclidean nature marks many utopias as celebrations of linear progress and conquest. Echoing the language from the YOFU debate, Le Guin thus warns, "To reconstruct the world, to rebuild or rationalize it, is to run the risk of losing or destroying what in fact is. After all, California was not empty when the Anglos came."[7] Le Guin, the daughter of anthropologist Alfred Kroeber, who studied the Indigenous populations of California, does not shy away from reminding the reader that California's white utopia required the genocide and decimation of the native population. She even gently critiques her father, who tried without luck to get his interlocutors to draw a map of their land. If he interpreted this refusal as a feigned inability, she proposes that they were more actively resisting Western imperialism. "The Euclidean utopia is mapped," but Native understandings of land could not be so statically represented.[8]

Today, Los Angeles has a relatively large population of Native Americans but, like most Angelenos, they too are transplants (not always by choice) from communities once spread throughout the country.[9] Before the intrusion of the Franciscan missions, the region supported the Gabrielino-Tongva Nation. Even though the settlers destroyed the population and cultural loss accompanied human loss, anthropologists and archeologists from Kroeber's generation onward could not resist imaging the Tongva as peacefully inhabiting a paradise. As academic trends ebbed and flowed,

1.1 Mural at the intersection of Abbot Kinney Blvd. and Navarre Ct. in Venice. The text reads, "From Diné to the Tongva. This Mural was painted by a Navajo Recognizing it sits on The Ancestral Land of the Tongva People to stand as a Reminder that we are . . . Still Here." The artist is Lehi ThunderVoice Eagle, who completed the mural in March 2021. Photograph taken in March 2022 by the author.

the kind of paradise shifted to accommodate new theories. First, the Tongva were imagined to have inhabited a "paradise by default" (a worry-free hunter-gatherer society) and then a "paradise by design" (a community of ecological stewards).[10] But always a paradise.

An imagination of a precontact Edenic existence for the Tongva shaped the histories written in the late nineteenth and early twentieth centuries that falsely suggested a peaceful coexistence between the Spanish missionaries and Native population. This fantasy, to requote Le Guin, "covered what in fact is." Not until McWilliams's *Southern California Country*, published in 1946, did a writer not only explain how this "mission myth" came to be but also replaced the fantasy with a description of the violent enslavement and genocide that accompanied these missions.

And yet, even in recent scholarship there is a persistent evocation of Los Angeles as a place where one can imagine repairing reality. Histories of the region often rehearse a multiethnic utopian narrative when recounting the colonial years. This narrative begins with a demographic description: in 1781, El Pueblo de Nuestra Señora la Reina de los Ángeles was founded by forty-four settlers comprised of Europeans, Mexicans of African origin, indigenous Mexicans, and mestizos. In the introduction to *Black and Brown in Los Angeles*, scholars Josh Kun and Laura Pulido treat this demographic trope with a mix of sunshine and noir. They caution against reading too much into this demography, which, they note, is often deployed to assert that LA has always been multiracial. At the same time, Kun and Pulido remark how this colonial admixture of population was a product of hope for greater equality symbolized by the frontier. They write, "Although Mexican society was characterized by deep racial inequality, along the frontier the racial hierarchy was more fluid, which is perhaps why so many Afro-Mexicans took a chance in coming north."[11]

While the Afro-Mexican population shrank over the course of the Pueblo's history,[12] Californian statehood (1850, following the Mexican-American war) brought an influx of both Anglo and Black American migrants. Historian Susan Anderson describes the period after statehood through the 1920s as the Golden Era for the Black community in Los Angeles. The fantasy of a racial utopia drew Black migrants out west. Los Angeles, Anderson writes, became a city "symbolizing escape from the racist excess of the Deep South" and thus "an object of black enchantment." And yet, alongside enchantment, there was despair: "all utopian searchers must discover, that the beautiful city of God is not of this place."[13]

Anderson describes how, on a trip to California in 1913, W. E. B. Du Bois captured the early twentieth century Black American impression of LA—an impression that simultaneously embraced the fantasy of a better way of life out west but at the same time acknowledged that this fantasy could not be fully realized by communities of color. Writing in *The Crisis*, the periodical of the National Association for the Advancement of Colored People, Du Bois began his travelogue with all of the utopian attributes of California in general and LA in specific. It was a "land of gold," when it joined the union it outlawed slavery, and more recently it had become a "tourist's wonderland" renowned for its bucolic atmosphere. And of the growing African American population, Du Bois wrote, "They are without doubt the most beautifully housed group of colored people in the United States."[14] "To be sure," he cautioned a few paragraphs later, "Los Angeles is not Paradise. . . . The color line is there and sharply drawn."[15]

Utopian aspirants seeking to repair reality fail to envision projects that account for the diversity of realities that exist in any given place. In LA, new realities can be figured, but the history shows that generations of nonwhite migrants (not to mention the people who were native to the land) confront the limits and harms of utopias that are conceived of for some but not all. As long as utopias are Euclidean, Le Guin diagnoses, reality will only be recreated in a fashion that benefits those already in positions of power. In the midcentury, high technology began merging with utopian fantasies, and the futures being imagined in Los Angeles became both more distinct and more exclusionary.

Problems of Today and Worlds of Tomorrow

As the city grew, though its boosters were no longer as prominent, their utopian ideations found uptake by practitioners in both the entertainment industry and LA's high technology sector. While receiving less attention than Hollywood, the region's investment in aerospace and, later, electronics manufacturing maintained Southern California's vibrancy as a technology sector for much of the twentieth century.[16] LA's entertainment and technology industries overlapped in projects and common causes throughout the midcentury, laying the institutional foundation upon which the VR community would be built. The fantasy of Hollywood and the practicality of military–industrial work merged in projects that often, like the boosters before, sought a repaired reality. Noir legacies from this phase of the city's

1.2 Entertainment and military have long depended on the other's expertise. During World War II, Douglas commissioned engineer Frank Collbohm, architect H. Roy Kelley, and landscape architect Edward Huntsman-Trout who, with the help of set builders from Warner Bros., camouflaged the Douglas plants. After the war, Collbohm would go on to found RAND and Kelley designed the campus. This is an image from the Douglas Santa Monica campus, showing an employee walking below the chicken mesh camouflage. Courtesy of the Santa Monica Public Library.

history include further segregating those with privilege and those without; a fracturing that half a century later, some in LA's VR community would target as a problem to be rectified.

That aerospace and entertainment both flourished in Southern California in the twentieth century might seem, at first, an unexpected pairing. However, as urban sociologist Harvey Molotch has observed, "Only on the surface are institutions like Disneyland and the US war machine and space programs opposites. The benign weather and open spaces of Southern California had something to do with their common point of beginnings. But so was the LA social climate of fantasy and exploration, equally applicable for searching the stars, amusing folks, or targeting a missile." A striking example of the coming together of these two industries can be found during World War II. After the attack on Pearl Harbor, aeronautics companies on the West Coast became potential military targets. Douglas Aircraft, located in Long Beach, was particularly conspicuous and military personnel hired architects and set designers from Hollywood studios to camouflage the factory buildings. The goal was to make the area look like, from the overhead view of an imagined Japanese bomber, a residential neighborhood. To do so, an elevated mesh of chicken wire was suspended over the Douglas buildings, supporting lightweight material sculpted into a six-block neighborhood, complete with facsimiles of roads, cars, houses, trees, and telephone poles. In the years after the war, the façade of suburban sprawl would become real as developers built what became the Lakewood suburb, a planned community not dissimilar from the Hollywood set and its cookie-cutter houses.[17]

After World War II, both the entertainment and technology industries turned their focus toward speculating about civic and urban futures. Charismatic figures like Walt Disney and Herman Kahn fused expertise from both industries to embellish their futurist visions.[18] Disneyland, which opened in 1955, created a geography in which the world of tomorrow was located next to the world of fantasy. Walt Disney himself evolved from storyteller to futurist, going so far as to imagine in Florida an Experimental Prototype Community of Tomorrow that, though built after his 1966 death as the EPCOT theme park, was intended by Disney to be a lived-in "reality made fantastic."[19] Also in the 1950s and '60s, Herman Kahn established himself as a futurist imagining worlds of tomorrow for the purpose of strategic military planning at RAND, headquartered in Santa Monica. Kahn grew up in Los Angeles and, as described by his biographer, Sharon Ghamari-Tabrizi, was a "consummate futurist, Californian in every particular." Ghamari-Tabrizi speculates how seeing the upheaval of the city in the postwar period—neighborhoods cleared to make room for the expressway—"must have influenced his notion of the shape and cohesion of the world."[20] If LA was plastic enough to become a new city, why not imagine new future realities? Kahn thus "had no qualms about moving between reality and unreality, fact and fiction, while developing an argument."[21] This resulted in his innovation of "the scenario," a method for projecting multiple futures to weigh different military options. Kahn, being an Angeleno "in every particular," influenced Hollywood and vice versa. Not only was Stanley Kubrick's Dr. Strangelove in part inspired by Kahn, but the word *scenario* came from storytelling practices of the silent film era. This naming was suggested by Leo Rosten, the sociologist turned screenwriter who (as quoted in the introduction) noted how the fantastic spilled over from the studio into the lives and livelihoods of those who worked in and around Hollywood.[22]

Kahn and Disney, as temporal, geographic, and intellectual contemporaries, illustrate the overlap between entertainment and technological enter-

1.3 The PeopleMover tram in Disneyland's Tomorrowland was imagined as a prototype for easing traffic in downtown areas. At the theme park, the future of urban areas was being figured. Photographed by Steve Fontanini for the *LA Times*, June 29, 1967. Courtesy of the *Los Angeles Times* Photographic Collection in the OpenUCLA Collections.

prises, and how in LA the mixing of fantasy, technology, and the future came to mark not only theme parks and military exercises, but also the new highways and housing developments that were being built to meet the needs of an expanding (majority white) middle class spurred by these industries.[23]

Though Disney's theme parks, Kahn's scenarios, and building projects throughout LA County all promised a future infused with technological expertise and efficiency, anyone passingly familiar with LA's history knows that World War II through to the end of the twentieth century is marked by expressions of long-brewing racial discrimination and unrest: the "Zoot Suit Riots" of 1943 where servicemen attacked Latino youth, the internment of Japanese Americans during the war, the Watts uprising of 1965, and the 1992 rebellion after the LAPD officers who beat Rodney King were acquitted, not to mention various tensions (and alliances) between Black, Brown, and Asian communities. The city's fragmentation mapped onto racial and economic segregation such that Beverly Hills could remain idyllic while neighborhoods in south Los Angeles ruptured and frayed. As historian Jennifer Light describes, the military strategists who were sitting idle after the war were drafted by local governments to apply their expertise to the new enemy of urban blight. Following Watts, the mayor of Los Angeles convened the Community Analysis Bureau. City planners partnered with RAND researchers (Kahn, however, was no longer there) to apply scenario planning to imaginations not of nuclear devastation but instead flourishing urban and civic futures.[24]

Futurists, however, proved no match for a city growing in population, diversity, and inequality. When the failure of utopia began to reach the white neighborhoods, none other than Joan Didion flew from New York City back to Los Angeles to diagnose the problem. Published in the *New Yorker* in 1993, her essay "Trouble in Lakewood," (the same Lakewood presaged by the Douglas aircraft plant camouflage), was motivated by national media coverage of "The Spur Posse." This was a group of mostly white male teenagers who were arrested for sexual crimes committed while playing a game they created for scoring their sexual conquests.[25] In her essay, Didion is concerned by more than just the moral panic surrounding this atrocious behavior. The adolescent trouble was indicative of what, by the end of the twentieth century, Didion recognized as the failure of the American Dream even for white suburbia. This mirrored Didion's more personal loss of the utopian image of California in which she grew up believing. This essay isn't entirely sentimental, but rather wants to make visible to the reader the invisible ties that connect military funding to the rest of the city, offering a causal history of the region that the white Angelenos Didion was writing about rejected or de-emphasized in order to instead blame changing demographics on their misfortunes. After the Cold War, the defense contracts dried up and the economic network that connected geographically distant suburbs like Lakewood to affluent neighborhoods like Bel Air weakened. The rise of the Spur Posse coincided with residents of Lakewood losing their jobs and a regional economic slump. Rather than blame the trouble on a depressed industry, Didion argues that white Angelenos were more likely to point to the 1992 riots and the decline of a white majority as the proximal reason for their economic misfortunes and thus the misbehaving of their boys. A strategy of blaming "the other" for the failure of realizing utopia—rather than blaming institutional failure—was in ascendency.

By the end of the twentieth century, LA as a metropolis of the future seemed harder to imagine than in earlier decades. And perhaps for that reason, when VR came to town, dormant narratives about the city found a renewed locus.

VR and the Military–Academic–Entertainment Complex

Virtual reality arrived in LA by way of aerospace and defense funding even though, decades later, I would encounter it mostly through the entertainment industry. Before it was called "VR," the dream of an immersive and responsive digital display was prototyped by Ivan Sutherland in the 1960s at MIT and Harvard. Sutherland was influenced by research that was happening at Bell Helicopter Company, and while he deemed his display "too early" and spent his career pushing forward the field of computer graphics (students he trained at the University of Utah went on to careers in defense, Silicon Valley, and entertainment, including the first president of Pixar). Sutherland was not the only one intrigued by the possibility of making the human an integrated and responsive component of a display. From 1966 until 1989, Tom Furness worked as a researcher for the Air Force at the Wright-Patterson Base in Ohio where he led foundational research and development in augmented and virtual displays, including a "Darth Vader helmet" that fighter pilot trainees could put on and be transported into a cockpit.[26] Resonant with the midcentury collaborations between military and entertainment, Furness commissioned designers at LucasArts to make his original design more aesthetically pleasing.[27] Furness's research was well funded but classified, prompting him to move his VR research to the University of Washington in Seattle in 1989 and expand his work to nonmilitary applications.

While Furness was refining his cockpit simulator, Scott Fisher spent the 1980s building what would be the first interactive and immersive VR display at NASA Ames in Mountain View, California.[28] Fisher had transferred his enduring interest in stereoscopic displays from MIT's Architecture Machine Group to the Bay Area, first to Atari Research Labs and then to NASA. Fisher's team commissioned Jaron Lanier (who coined the phrase *virtual reality* at about the same time) and his company to build a glove to interact with the virtual environment users could see in the headset Fisher and his team built. Scientists and celebrities alike visited NASA to experience VR and, with help from evangelists like Lanier and Timothy Leary, VR and cyberspace joined with other emerging digital and networked technologies, leading Silicon Valley hype in the late '80s and early '90s.

However, as VR's commercial potential failed to materialize, the problem of how to continue to develop this technology loomed over innovators.[29] In Southern California, a strategy began to emerge when recognizing that

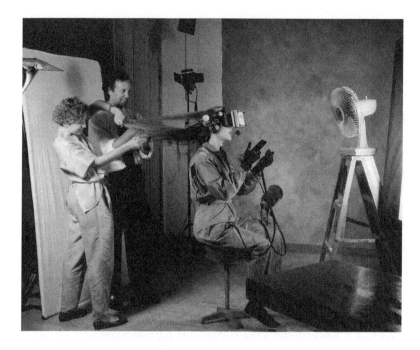

1.4 Scott Fisher, photographed in 1989, assists in holding back Sally Rosenthal's hair to create a widely circulated image of the NASA Virtual Interface Environment Workstation (VIEW). Courtesy of NASA Ames Research Center, Wade Sisler, Scott Fisher.

both defense and the entertainment industry had use for this tech. As clarified in a Department of Defense commissioned report published in 1997: "Both the entertainment industry and DOD are interested in developing immersive systems that allow participants (whether game players or soldiers) to enter and navigate simulated environments. For DOD such systems can be used to train groups of combatants . . . [and] create virtual prototypes of military systems. . . . For the entertainment industry such systems are the basis for virtual reality (VR) experiences being incorporated into location-based entertainment centers, theme parks, and video game centers."[30]

As the histories above recount, VR was far from the first application mixing military and entertainment. Indeed, this had become a regional specialty of Southern California, a key characteristic of LA's technological terroir.[31] In 1999, The US Army provided the University of Southern California with $45 million to establish the Institute for Creative Technologies, where several researchers who contributed to the 1997 report became affiliated faculty. At USC, new VR headsets were developed that could tell immersive stories for entertainment or informative purposes, train soldiers virtually, and, through the emergence of immersive therapy, virtually treat these same soldiers for PTSD.[32] Scott Fisher, along with a colleague who built the VR system with him at NASA, moved to LA and joined USC with an appointment in the School of Cinematic Arts. This set the stage for the emergence of commercial VR in the 2010s, a story that I will return to in chapter 4. For now, it is enough to recognize that VR easily occupied a slot in the LA imaginary that already existed from decades and centuries of utopian thinking that blended fact and fantasy, partnerships between military and entertainment around technology, and expectations of how the future was being imagined and created in the City of Angels.

From Virtual Reality to Civic Reality

Though I find the histories told in this chapter about LA and VR to be revealing of the community with which I conducted fieldwork, they were largely absent from conversations and perhaps even the collective memory. Such omissions are themselves reflective of a "history of forgetting," as Norman Klein has written, endemic to LA. In trying to write about Downtown Los Angeles, Klein discovered he had to blend scholarship and fiction in order to fill in the architectural absences resultant from decades of overzealous urban planning in reaction to the growth of nonwhite communities.[33] As Jocelyn Pacleb observes in her search for material traces of Japanese internment in LA, "What is remembered and what is forgotten are tied to power relations."[34] Forgetting certain histories—particularly military origins and prior iterations of LA's high tech industry—was necessary for the political work some in the VR community wanted to do. They framed VR as "new," similar to how the settlers viewed the frontier of California as "empty." This, in turn, opened up a space for the fantasies of VR as a good technology and a good industry (the foci of Parts II and III) to flourish. In returning now to the practices of the contemporary VR community, I look at one example of how forgetting various histories—even those that inform institutional structures and ways of imagining—facilitates the implementation of VR as a tool for societal betterment.

Those who gathered to debate whether VR could recreate reality assumed that imagining a better world was the first step to achieving it; that fantasy could yield reality. While this might be something most people would agree with, in Los Angeles, where Hollywood created wealth and power out of fantasy, the idea that fantasy could become real felt a bit more concrete and within reach. This is most acutely expressed in the practice of worldbuilding, by which Hollywood logics are converted into a method for achieving improved civic realities.

Worldbuilding is a term used in many contexts and with multiple lineages. Science fiction and fantasy writers use worldbuilding to describe the detailed worlds they construct to hold the narratives that themselves only explore a small piece of their creation.[35] Media and literary scholars have analyzed worldbuilding as a transmedia practice in which fans can participate.[36] However, it quickly became clear that when I encountered the term in the LA VR community, it was referring to a more specific and codified technique—one that was first developed for the movies to create cinematic futures but has since become a strategy for imagining societal futures. This strain of worldbuilding was developed by Alex McDowell, who worked as a production designer before becoming a professor at USC and creating the World Building Institute. He teaches this method to aspirational filmmakers as well as social and technological innovators, and its prevalence in the VR community both comes from McDowell's conviction that VR is best suited for worldbuilding's aesthetic holism[37] and because many of McDowell's students have, upon graduating, become VR innovators.

McDowell developed this approach to worldbuilding when he was the production designer for the 2002 blockbuster *Minority Report*. This ended up being a radically different production experience, uniquely creating the conditions for developing a novel approach to story and world development. Significantly, McDowell and the scriptwriter were hired at the same time, after Steven Spielberg had agreed to direct but tossed the original script in the garbage. Instead of the production design emerging from the narrative, as is the norm, the world "incepted the narrative. . . . The fabric of the world had triggered the story."[38] Additionally, Spielberg wanted *Minority Report* to be set in a plausible future, not an unimaginable science fiction. As a consequence, McDowell consulted a wide range of scientists, engineers, architects, and urban planners to build out the setting for the movie. Engineers from MIT's Media Lab designed the gestural system that the protagonist, played by Tom Cruise, used to manipulate the virtual interface. After production, one engineer stayed in LA, started a company, and has made real this interface that, in the movie, was still a fiction.[39]

McDowell spent the subsequent years fleshing out this worldbuilding methodology and exploring how, like the engineer's start-up, it could be leveraged beyond Hollywood toward any number of future-oriented endeavors. *Minority Report*, McDowell reflected, "provided an opportunity for entertainment and science to intersect and use fiction as a testing ground for reality,"[40] and his academic work since has further explored how worldbuilding can be a tool to "develop sustainable solutions to real-world problems."[41] Worldbuilding brings together fantasy, futurity, technoscience, and storytelling such that Hollywood expertise slips beyond the confines of the screen, just as it did when the entertainment industry was mobilized for the war effort or Disney imagined the urban fantasy of EPCOT.

Having heard about worldbuilding from many people in the VR community, I was eager to learn more from the source. After a brief email exchange, McDowell invited me to attend the final presentations of the worldbuilding class he was teaching in Spring 2018. I had been told by a student taking the class that McDowell was focusing on how worldbuilding could be used to tackle "real world" problems, particularly exploring the benefits and costs of various proposed technoscientific futures. At USC, I navigated to the Robert Zemeckis Center for Digital Arts (in which McDowell's lab is located) and entered the Ron Howard theater, a small screening room that was filled with students and guests—including both scientists and media folks who have collaborated with McDowell. At this event, students presented their final projects—a digital rendering of a street corner of the future meant to explore interactions between location, technology, ecology, and inhabitants. The class was divided into two teams, each of which built a near future world—one in Detroit, one in the Gobi Desert—and populated it with characters. Students built models of these worlds in Unity, the game engine in which many VR experiences are also built, and supposedly one could put on a headset and become a bystander on the street corner, observing the goings on. Before these presentations, McDowell and the graduate teaching assistants (TAs) provided background on worldbuilding and how students used this method. One TA explained to the audience that worldbuilding combines the actual with the fictional. The characters are made up, but based on surveys and consultations with experts. The class thus asks, as the TA put it, "Can we investigate fictional characters and get real data back?" The street corners are extrapolations of present places, based on "real" satellite imagery and demographic data with layers of imagined futures built on top. These futures do not depict the dystopian worlds that pepper McDowell's Hollywood career, but rather are hopeful of political and civic change. McDowell concluded the presentations by announcing that next semester, this same street corner approach would be used to focus on Los Angeles, applying the worldbuilding method to tackle the problem of homelessness in the city.

It was seductive to imagine that the tools of fantasy and storytelling, wielded with ease by so many in Los Angeles, could be the solution to problems that other experts have failed to solve. In June, I participated in a worldbuilding workshop meant to help flesh out the narrative of a VR experience whose development I was observing. There, I met a woman who was also an active participant in the Women in VR Facebook group. It turned out that she had been a TA for McDowell and, in addition to developing VR experiences, she ran worldbuilding workshops to help participants envision "feminist futures." Here, again, was "reality craft" and a practice of blending fantasy and reality in the hopes of building better worlds. This was stated another way at a different event I attended that featured a worldbuilding panel. As the moderator summarized, "We [must] begin to recognize that worldbuilding is the partner to advancing emerging technologies today."

In these accounts, worldbuilding was new and exciting. But from an historical perspective, it can be seen as the successor to Kahn's scenario planning and reflective of prior endeavors to merge entertainment and technical expertise in service of civic betterment. Just as scenario planning morphed from military strategy to urban planning, McDowell's approach began in entertainment but also found its way to the street corner. Nowhere in McDowell's writings about worldbuilding do I see traces of these lineages even as the same technological terroir informs this practice. "Forgetting" maintained the façade that both VR and worldbuilding were "new," which in turn concealed the civic fracturing often left in the wake of practices that, like prior utopian projects, elevated certain realities (and their need to be repaired) over others.

Conclusion

For VR to be a "good" technology, LA's VR community strove to articulate the fantasy of its potential rather than reckon with the history of its development. When examples surfaced of VR being used for purposes that conflicted with the progressive politics held by many of those in the slice of the community that I spent time with, a fortifying of the fantasy was swiftly performed. For example, the founder of Oculus, Palmer Luckey, had come to be seen by many as the antithesis of what VR ought to be. After leaving

Oculus/Facebook in 2017, he founded a company to build a virtual version of Trump's border wall, leveraging drone technology to stop immigrants from entering the US from Mexico. If Iñárritu's *Carne y Arena*, as described in the introduction, imagined VR as a way for understanding the human stories of border crossing, Luckey's company used the same technology to abstract the human as something to be surveilled and policed. On July 4, 2018, Luckey announced on the Women in VR Facebook group that he was hiring VR developers to "make America safer." Most people who posted comments responded with outrage, some demanded the moderators remove the post and ban Luckey from the group, a few tried to defend the post suggesting that his company would be better if more women worked there. I was struck by those who responded with disbelief that VR could be used as a tool of warfare.[42] Though this post provided the opportunity for VR's military origins to briefly be remembered, such association was instead rejected, and most commentators reinforced that Luckey's project was not part of the world that this community was building.

As Klein writes in *The History of Forgetting*, "We believe the romance; we need the romance. But we must realize that the myths, whether of tinsel town, of the sunny village, or of the downtown Babylon, have never represented the city accurately. They have always systematically ignored the life of [minority] communities in the city, as if . . . [they] could not exist in our imagination when we think of LA. Indeed, these imaginary cities reveal the futility of our good intentions."[43] Likewise with VR, the fantasy makes it challenging to see who is ignored and left out when pursuing "the good." As will be explored in future chapters, the fantasies that are salient to this community—the fantasy of VR as a good technology that can make better people; the fantasy of VR as an industry led by women and underrepresented voices—reject or leave unknown certain histories. In addition to LA being a place where people come in search of utopia and a land of the unreal in which entertainment and military mix freely, these acts of forgetting are also a politics of the place that inform the politics of VR.

It is clear that a lot of social work goes in to enlivening the fantasy of technology as a tool for reality repair. Returning to the essay by Ursula Le Guin, we find one attempt at unmasking that fantasy. Le Guin challenges the role that technology plays in utopian projects by including in the title of her essay the provocation that California might be a "cold place." California's cold character plays with a distinction made by the anthropologist Claude Lévi-Strauss between hot, technological societies and cold, traditional societies.[44] Le Guin disrupts the association of technology with progress: "I do not see how even the almost ethereal technologies promised by electronics and information theory can offer more than the promise of the simplest tool. . . . [T]o count upon technological advance for anything *but* technological advance is a mistake."[45] Le Guin thus imagines a future in which California has cooled its hot industries, wondering about the greater diversity of people who might flourish in such a state.

Some contemporary Angelenos share Le Guin's skepticism over technology's potential for human betterment. Back at the brewery, the VR enthusiasts who assembled that evening in February had to vote on whether VR was needed to recreate reality. Could this technology fix what was wrong with the world and help build a new reality? By a narrow margin, the resolution was voted down and we were left to wonder what, if not VR, might mend the fractured reality; what other resources—fantastical or otherwise—might serve the project of improving collective futures? The moderator offered her assessment. These debates were created in order to bring people together, understand different perspectives, and practice civil communication—a mode of engagement that seemed to be a dying art in an ideologically divided, partisan country. The debate itself was an attempt to cultivate participatory citizens, staging a hoped-for future in the present. This debate about VR enacted the better world that those gathered hoped the technology would bring about. This debate also introduced me to LA's VR community. I would encounter the hosts, debaters, and audience members throughout the year at different events and, in some cases, for longer chats about their careers and prospects. I would find further examples of this event's blending of real and virtual, fantasy and fact, humor and sincerity not only at other VR events but throughout the city itself. It thus became apparent to me that ways of understanding VR could be found not only in LA's history but also in the experience of moving through and being in the city.

2

REALITIES OTHERWISE
UNDERSTANDING VR BY
EXPERIENCING LA

Kris moved to LA in 2010. Having finished her undergrad film degree a few years earlier, she was able to take a chance and "try to make it" in LA after having won prize money from her participation in a promotional campaign for a wannabe blockbuster movie. The promotion was a marketing experiment that demonstrated an early and acute understanding of the confluence of social media and the experience economy.[1] An advertising campaign that could make potential consumers feel like part of the movie—and encourage the sharing of these experiences online—could extend movie promotion from the static and passive screen or billboard into an active and immersive experience. A few years before "FOMO" (fear of missing out) would become a cultural meme, Kris was already keen to be part of experiments in immersive and interactive storytelling. After a month of playing (and winning) a cross-country alternative reality game (in which players followed rules of the movie's world and chronicled their activities on social media), Kris used her prize money to cover rent for a few months while she navigated the unsteady career of a freelancer. Kris fittingly began her Hollywood stint as a story editor in reality television before, in 2016, switching over to the newly hot VR industry. Kris has successfully navigated the subsequent shrinking of the industry due to declining investment, securing both steady jobs at VR production companies while also working as a freelancer in leaner times.

Kris had responded to a post I made on the Women in VR Facebook group that explained my research and my interest in meeting people in LA's VR community. We met up in February for coffee near where she lives in Koreatown and chatted about her career. As our conversation ended, she kindly extended an invitation to join her for Korean BBQ that evening. Kris was meeting up with two friends who work in VR but also dream and scheme about the other kinds of immersive experiences they might create.

Over sizzling meat and, later, beer at a dive bar around the corner, Kris, Dave, and Hugo enthusiastically brought me into their world. They placed VR in the broader constellation of location-based entertainment (LBEs), which can also include escape rooms, immersive theater, theme parks, and any number of whimsical pop-ups that Angelenos document with dedication on Instagram. We swapped stories of immersive experiences we had done and dissected particularly successful ones to understand the mechanics of their storytelling and execution. Hugo is a trend spotter (having joined Oculus when they were still based in Irvine, before the Facebook acquisition) and, after leaving Oculus, began working for an augmented reality company. He sensed that both VR and AR were on newly shaky ground and saw LBEs as the next big thing. If Hugo was thinking strategically about the market, Kris and Dave were hoping to follow their passions. They had an idea for an immersive experience, they told me in a conspiratorial whisper, but they weren't yet ready to share the details with an anthropologist.

As the evening wound down, Hugo asked me why I was conducting my research in LA (and he was not the first or last to be perplexed as to why someone interested in tech was in LA). Early in my research, I was myself still a bit confused and offered an inelegant answer about being interested not in the hardware but in the content and storytelling. As someone who has worked in the VR industry in both LA and San Francisco, Hugo agreed with me that this is where the more exciting stories are being created. He paused and then apologized for sounding cheesy before observing that LA is better equipped than SF to realize the potential of VR because, "LA has always been about fantasy."

The previous chapter explored how utopian fantasies—those benefiting some, not all—have long been central to the framing of LA's history. Such dreamings cultivated a technological terroir by which the entertainment and aerospace industries—two industries essential to VR—expanded and trained overlapping practitioners. In this chapter, I offer two additional angles from which to reflect on Hugo's assessment that LA's fantasy of place nurtures VR's growth. First, I will discuss how moving through the city is often punctuated by the experience of moving between different worlds, facilitated by the fantastical architectural façades spread throughout Los Angeles. Being in this land of the unreal makes one accustomed to navigating the instability wrought by multiple realities; in this setting, VR is familiar as but another façade. I secondly consider how I am only one in a long line of scholars to have found LA's fantasies and façades intriguing. My articulation of LA (and VR) as unreal is a twenty-first-century attunement of the *realities otherwise*—the hyperreal, the real-and-imagined—that previous theorists have proposed when thinking from and about LA.

As I state in the introduction, this rendering of LA only depicts one fragment of the city. It is the fragment occupied by the creative and intellectual classes: the socioeconomically privileged. It is the fragment experienced by those for whom escapes from reality (appreciated and analyzed by Kris, Hugo, Dave, and myself) are welcome excursions, for whom noir politics can be intellectualized from a distanced arms-length, not experienced as everyday hardships and discriminations. It is the fragment of LA that was most familiar and visible to my way of being in the world, and to prior academic visitors who theorized reality from LA. Many of my VR interlocutors circulated in this fragment of LA and, significantly, this circulation fortified the boundaries of this fragment even as the VR experiences were fantasized as building connections between other (and other's) Los Angeleses. As I, along with members of the VR community, drove to meet ups in Koreatown or installations of VR pieces—to LACMA, for example, to see Iñárritu's *Carne y Arena*—we navigated highways that allowed smooth passage from one well-off or gentrified neighborhood to another. Migrant communities and homeless encampments were sped by on overpasses, existing at the periphery of this fragment. And yet, having arrived at a museum or a festival or a brewery, a VR headset promised access to these other realities: the migrant border crosser, the Angeleno beset with hunger, the racial other victimized by police. The inequities and contradictions of LA (and the world) that VR experiences and their attempts to elicit empathy were imagined as combating were instead reproduced through the act of inhabiting the fragment of LA that supported the industries needed for VR's success. To examine in this chapter the realities otherwise that saturate this fragment of Los Angeles is to foreshadow the irony that it is in such a place where a project to repair reality took hold. VR, as will be examined in part II, simultaneously embraced and sought to mitigate proliferating realities.

2.1 The sunshine and noir of façades. The Venice Canals were one of LA's first façades, envisioned by Abbot Kinney in the first years of the twentieth century to create a tourist attraction of Venice in America. Gondoliers were brought over from Italy to escort visitors through two miles of excavated waterways. Today it is a wealthy residential community but still welcomes tourists to walk along the canals. As is frequently the case in Los Angeles, extreme wealth abuts the housing insecure, illustrated by the tent city established across the street. Photograph taken in March 2022 by the author.

The exploration of LA below will thus provide a language and approach for thinking about certain politics of VR, upon which later chapters will expound. Not only, as Hugo surmises, is VR suited to LA because of its fantasies, but LA is suited to VR because the city itself offers frames for articulating VR's appeal, aesthetic, and contradictions.

Façades and Fantasies

Architectural façades are the material instantiation of LA's fantasies of realities otherwise. The proliferation of eclectic façades patterns the day-to-day experience of being in and moving through the city. My use of *façade* is drawn from its architectural meaning, the literal face of a building. But I'm thinking specifically about instances where the exterior is exaggerated and even fantastical. These façades conjure something other: an elsewhere or elsewhen. They suggest a whole world beyond the façade that, should one cross the threshold, one can enter. But often there is a mismatch between the façade and the interior. In Reyner Banham's celebrated articulation of LA's "four ecologies," he is amused by LA's fantastical architecture and intrigued (perhaps let down) when, upon entering the Brown Derby—whose exterior faithfully resembled a giant bowler hat—he discovered booths and tables like any other chain restaurant. Fantasy was relegated to the surface, a container for function.[2] There is also a negative connotation of façade that is well associated with Los Angeles. Façade conjures a phoniness or emptiness: enthusiastic promises of "Let's do lunch" that never fully materialize. In Peter Plagens's 1972 critical review of Banham's book (in which he pans the author and book for accurately capturing the clichés of Los Angeles but mistaking them for the whole truth), Plagens offers a darker and seedier image of LA: "L.A. is an elusive place: all flesh and no soul, all building and no architecture, all property and no land, all electricity and no light, all billboards and nothing to say, all ideas and no principles."[3] This too is façade, interwoven with the soul of the city.

Façade is an integral element of Los Angeles's placehood that has been a part of the city since before Disneyland and even before Hollywood. Today, façades are constantly yet surprisingly encountered when moving around the city. Façade as a material signifier of a reality otherwise promises a world to be explored even as it cannot be fully entered.

ENCOUNTERING FAÇADE

The quintessential LA façade is that of a studio back lot[4] or a theme park. Beautiful, intricate exteriors mask the construction scaffolding that prop up these fantasies of elsewhere. Upon leaving the studio or park, one might expect to also be leaving behind these façades, but they are present throughout the city. Stumbling upon such façades was a routine delight I experienced in my explorations of LA.

In July, there was a heat wave. It was a dry heat and so I still tried to get out for morning runs around my neighborhood, often taking a wide loop that traced the cream-colored walls of 20th Century Fox studios. One day during this brutal stretch of heat, I ran along Santa Monica Boulevard toward Beverly Hills. The famous, uncharacteristically tall hotels—the Beverly Hilton and Waldorf Astoria—offered more shade on this path than my usual route. I decided to turn down Rodeo Drive, curious about this iconic stretch of conspicuous consumption. I was about to turn back home when I spotted what appeared to be a rare pedestrian block. As I approached, the concrete sidewalk gave way to cobblestone street and there were elegant lampposts adorned with hanging potted plants. I felt like I was on a studio set outfitted to depict "quaint European street." At the other end of the short pedestrian walk (lined with high-end stores and an outdoor café), there was a grand staircase leading back down to the cement sidewalk and

2.2 The cobblestoned pedestrian walkway of Via Rodeo. Photograph taken in March 2022 by the author.

a fountain, as if Rome's Trevi fountain was right next to its Spanish Steps. Puzzled, I descended from Europe back to California.

When I returned home and googled "Rodeo Drive European street," I easily found a marketing website that invited me to walk along "Via Rodeo" and "Indulge [myself] with a luxury shopping experience along this European inspired walkway."[5] Also on this website, the interested location scout would learn that they welcome film crews to take advantage of the cobblestone street that is "brimming with European charm."[6] This shopping plaza was built in 1990 and proudly advertises its twenty-six architecturally unique storefronts, each inspired by a different European style. This particular façade lends itself to multiple readings: it allows the shopper momentary relief from LA's traffic, the luxury brands on display remind the window shopper of the wealth enjoyed by many of the city's residents, and of course this is a grown-up's version of Disney's Main Street, U.S.A. as this imagined European pastiche is far cleaner and orderly than any actual street on the continent. With each step, one experiences a shifting of place and time, though the where and the when evoked by these façades correlate neither to geography nor history.

THEME PARK LA

I began keeping an informal inventory of the façades I encountered. On Westwood Boulevard, in a neighborhood nicknamed Tehrangeles or Little Persia, a restaurant called Taste of Tehran is in a small complex alongside a Persian bakery and a sushi restaurant. The façade of this building has arched windows and an exterior made to appear weathered, painted such that it looks like there are patches of exposed brick where the plaster has chipped away. It announces itself as an old building, belonging in a desert in the Middle East rather than in the desert of Southern California. On the same side of the street, separated by a parking lot, the adjacent building has a similar façade. However, one end has been redressed in vibrant colors. A terra-cotta roof slopes down to create an area for outdoor seating; a Day of the Dead mural paints over the faux exposed brick for this taco stand. These westside façades are contemporary instantiations of a "theme-ing" of Los Angeles that occurred all over town in the early decades of the twentieth century, creating tourist attractions that were erected in response to nostalgia for fading colonial histories and also reflective of increasing immigrant populations.[7]

By the 1910s, it was already local LA custom to map one landscape onto another, as production companies converted streets and parts of town into proxies for the Old West. As Thom Andersen analyzes in the documentary *Los Angeles Plays Itself*, production crews took advantage of the fact that in the early days of the film industry, LA lacked its contemporary iconicity and thus could be anywhere.[8] A 1927 "location map" of California created by Paramount Pictures labeled different regions of the state as global stand-ins. Clustered around LA are places that could be used for filming movies set in or along the coast of Spain, Wales, the South Sea, Holland, and the Long Island Sound.[9] Silent filmmaker Thomas Ince bought up a tract of land in Santa Monica and built a studio with various exterior stages, creating the possibility of one place to become multiple. As a contemporary observed, "The tepees sat cheek-by-jowl with a fake Swiss landscape, a Japanese village, a Puritan settlement, mansions and cottages."[10] But even before the movie industry came to town, entrepreneurs already capitalized on the chameleon quality of LA. Inceville, as it was informally called, was established just north of where, a decade earlier, developer Abbot Kinney engineered a series of canals to create Venice, Italy, in California. While early Hollywood did eventually use the canals for films set in Italy, it was originally intended—like Via Rodeo—as a transportive tourist attraction.

Throughout the 1920s and 1930s, Venice was joined by other areas of the growing city that promised tourists exotic escapes. Nostalgic visionary Christine Sterling, for example, led a campaign to preserve one of the few remaining pueblo buildings in the ever more populous downtown. On Olvera Street, an original adobe was surrounded by a reconstructed streetscape meant to evoke a Mexican village and create, as architectural historian Josi Ward describes in language that could just as easily be applied to virtual reality, "an immersive experience in which visitors would be overcome by a tangible sense of the past."[11] When, in the 1930s, the city displaced the Chinese community and demolished their homes and businesses to make way for Union Station, two new Chinese-themed districts were created. Sterling oversaw the creation of China City as a complement to her work on Olvera Street, hiring a set designer from Paramount as artistic director for the project who in turn decorated China City with former set pieces from the 1937 movie adaptation of *The Good Earth*.[12] The Chinese and Chinese-Americans whose businesses were located in China City were asked to dress in traditional clothing and some took Anglo tourists around in rickshaws. While this project was directed by a white woman and her white collaborators, LA's Chinese community simultaneously financed and oversaw an even more architecturally elaborate installation, called New Chinatown, spearheaded by Chinese American engineer Peter SooHoo. Dismayed by Sterling's project and its failure to consult the Chinese community, New Chinatown distinguished itself by claiming authenticity. Instead of movie sets, the architecture included ornamentation produced by hand carving one-hundred-year-old imported wood, inlaid with "genuine Chinese gold." Stores sold silks imported from China and the restaurants served "real Chinese foods." In the press release drafted by SooHoo extoling these features, China City's movie set aesthetic was implicitly disparaged: "this New Chinatown . . . will give the tourists a first and lasting impression of things truly Chinese."[13]

China City burned down in the 1950s, but New Chinatown,[14] Olvera Street, and the Venice Canals remain popular LA attractions. While LA is not alone in having themed districts—pagoda-lined Chinatowns exist in cities around the world—the ubiquity of such districts as well as fantastical façades peppered throughout the city create a notable density of these architectural fantasies.[15]

LA's architectural façades are invitations to imagine being elsewhere. However, as façade implies, one can never fully enter this reality otherwise. Exotic façades are often gateways to the mundane—diner booths, a coffee shop, an apartment building, a gas station. Even at the movie studio or theme park, it is not a rich world but rather scaffolding that lies on the other side of the façade. These façades, some of which stretch back a century or more, are seamlessly woven into the fabric of the city. To be in LA is to move between these façades, to be presented with constant temptations of immersion in other worlds.

Fantasies of Reality Otherwise Set in Los Angeles

I am not the first visitor to LA who found the city's façades playfully inspiring. Previous theorists have found this eclectic built environment to be a bellwether for emergent forms of reality. Umberto Eco and Jean Baudrillard articulate LA as a manifestation of the *hyperreal* that they found to be characteristic of the condition of postmodernity.[16] Edward Soja builds on this work as well as Henri Lefebvre's spatial theories to label LA a thirdspace, which he defines as a *real-and-imagined* place. My own fieldwork experience in Los Angeles prompts me to consider how the *unreal* shapes contemporary discourse and desire. The hyperreal, the real-and-imagined, the unreal are, like façades, examples of reality otherwise. If today reality feels as though it is becoming undone, fracturing, or morphing into something else, Los Angeles has been a place to consider changes in reality for at least a half century. Perhaps those of us intrigued by the fantasy of LA slip into exceptional or romantic thinking about the city. Is LA "really" a place where new kinds of reality can be first detected, a (rightly) skeptical reader might ask. It is at the very least a place fantasized as such. As Baudrillard writes, "The irresistible rise of the simulacrum is something you can simply feel here [in California] without the slightest effort."[17]

THE HYPERREAL

Umberto Eco's essay "Travels in Hyperreality" begins with describing his encounter with what, in the early 1970s, was the closest thing to today's virtual reality: holography. After noting that this new visual science and spectacle has been used by NASA, medical professionals, and artists (the same can be said of VR), Eco remarks that "Holography could prosper only in America." This is because it is "a country obsessed with realism."[18] Eco's essay puzzles through why the "taste of America" is one where "[t]he 'completely real' becomes identified with the 'completely fake.' Absolute unreality is offered as real presence."[19] This taste (or perhaps terroir) permeates the country such that this "hyperreality" is what connects all cultural outputs, from commercial entertainment to artistic movements to religious evangelism. Eco's travels take him on a circumscribed trip across the country, though he spends the most time in Los Angeles. As he drives from San Francisco to LA, he surveys the various scenes on display in the handful of wax museums that mark this journey. Noting how historical figures like Marie Antoinette intermix with fictional ones like Alice in Wonderland, he describes the wax museum's dedicated detailing of figurines as a disorientating erasure of "the logical distinction between Real World and Possible Worlds . . . for everything must equal reality even if, as in these [fictional] cases, reality was fantasy."[20] In Southern California, he encounters other markers of the hyperreal—Sea World, Hearst Castle, the Getty Villa, and of course the "absolutely fake cities" of Disneyland and Knott's Berry Farm. Disneyland, for Eco, represents the desire for (and consequence of) "a fantasy more real than reality . . . and afterwards reality will always be inferior to it."[21]

In "The Precession of Simulacra," Jean Baudrillard similarly theorizes the implication of living in a historical moment when phenomena of hyperreality and simulation "threatens the difference between the 'true' and the 'false,' the 'real' and the 'imaginary.'"[22] Here again, Disneyland and Los Angeles are invoked as the quintessence of the present condition. In the essay, Baudrillard describes four phases of the image as it evolves from reflecting reality to masking reality to masking the absence of reality and finally to an image that has no relation to reality (pure simulacrum). Disneyland is the third kind; it masks the fact that *it* is reality: "Disneyland is presented as imaginary in order to make us believe that the rest is real, whereas all of Los Angeles and the America that surrounds it are no longer real, but belong to the hyperreal. . . . The imaginary of Disneyland is neither true nor false, it is a deterrence machine set up in order to rejuvenate the fiction of the real in the opposite camp."[23]

In Baudrillard's formulation, Disneyland emphasizes how, at some point, Los Angeles became no longer real. Yet given the theme-ing of the city that began in the first years of the twentieth century, Walt Disney's innovation was not a material instantiation of the hyperreal that then spread out to the surrounding geography as Baudrillard intimates. Rather, Disney condensed and commodified the façades already prevalent in LA's cityscape. The theme park gathered into a single place an experience by which a visitor could, as the plaque at the entrance to the park reads, "Leave today and enter the world of yesterday, tomorrow, and fantasy." Since the park's opening in 1955, it is not that Los Angeles has come to mimic the hyperreality of Disneyland but rather Disneyland was built in LA's already fantastical image.

For Baudrillard and Eco, Los Angeles helped articulate and illustrate the hyperreal and its agnosticism between real and fake. In deconstructing this binary, they mobilized the hyperreal as a new form of reality. The hyperreal was a diagnosis of the present and, for both, Los Angeles was a key place where they found the hyperreal to be emergent.

THE REAL-AND-IMAGINED

If the hyperreal invites a collapse of categories, Edward Soja proposed his concept of thirdspace—a mode of spatial thinking that holds together the real-and-imagined—as a more actionable theory, and one that similarly begins in Los Angeles. Soja was a central member of the LA school of urbanism and has been spotted in the literature driving around Orange County with fellow theorists of LA and riding in elevators with Jean Baudrillard at the Bonaventure Hotel, an LA landmark made famous in Fredric

2.3 Inside the "bewildering immersion" of the Bonaventure. Photograph taken in April 2022 by the author.

Jameson's account of it as a "postmodern hyperspace" yielding "bewildering immersion."[24] As reflected in the title of the last book he published, *My Los Angeles*, Soja's writing reflects a prideful (and at times joyous) affiliation with the city and its multiple realities.

Soja's concept of "thirdspace" is a "both/and" approach to critical theory. He does not think one must be *either* a modern *or* a postmodern theorist, nor that one must *either* accept *or* deconstruct a binary. Instead, Soja invites readers to consider "an-Other set of choices."[25] As a critical spatiality, thirdspace draws on both the "'real' material world" of what he calls firstspace and the "'imagined' representations" of this reality (secondspace), offering an-Other possibility of seeing place as simultaneously real-and-imagined.[26] This terminology captures a change in spatial thinking that began in the 1960s and is most clearly articulated in the writing of Henri Lefebvre, but also in, for example, Michel Foucault's concept of heterotopias.[27] Importantly, a thirdspace is not a kind of place but a capacious way of looking at space, one that acknowledges the inability to fully know and represent a place. Thirdspace is both/and: real-and-imagined, modern-and-postmodern, as well as a rearticulation of earlier theories and a new way to apply them.

For Soja, the hyperreal is a kind of thirdspace. Alongside the hyperreal, Soja names (in the 1990s) virtual reality and cyberspace as other recent lexical terms that draw "our attention to the fact that reality is no longer what it used to be."[28] His concern with Baudrillard's theorizing of the hyperreal is not the concept itself but rather his pushing the concept to the extreme such that it loses any political potency (and this is more broadly Soja's critique of postmodern theories). On the other hand, Eco stops too soon in his use of hyperreality, relegating it to the theme park instead of noting how it permeates everyday living. Soja insists that one must recognize "the hyperreality of everyday life" and act from within to bring forth political change.[29]

Thus, for Soja, Los Angeles is ground zero for understanding the very real consequences of hyperreality as it expands across Southern California and beyond. In the 1990s, he described one such consequence as the emergence of a "scamscape" in Orange County, which enabled financial fraud by people who could no longer distinguish between real and imagined and thus saw their deceitful actions as acceptable. Soja could also sense the implications of the confluence of real-and-imagined for politics, writing in 1996 of the spin doctors who determine what is to be revealed to the voter, and in 2014 of the "politically biased television news broadcasters" who, with others, scorn the "'reality-based community.'"[30] Soja died in 2015 and so did not live to see the rise of a literal reality TV president and the further political fracturing of media that has prompted conversations about a reality crisis. But Soja saw the implications that the real-and-imagined spatiality he detected in Los Angeles would have on the country and the world, as well as the devastation of failing to mount an appropriately radical political response. From Los Angeles, he saw that reality was becoming something else, observed VR as somehow affiliated with these changes, and urged for political action that could rise to the hyperreality of it all.

THE UNREAL

Hyperreality and the real-and-imagined character of thirdspace attempted to name a sea change theorists felt to be occurring in the last decades of the twentieth century, a wavering of a steady sense of reality upon which modern epistemologies had been built. In some respects, the contemporary moment still feels very much of a piece with the concerns that underlie these realities that demand an-Other way of thinking. The distinction is that with today's "fake news" and "alternative facts," the hyperreal subtext has become text. And precisely because the hyperreal is now part of the common vernacular—because the hyperreal has itself become a mask that conceals reality's absence—other realities continue to proliferate. What happens when hyperreality and real-and-imagined spatialities no longer diagnose an ineffable zeitgeist but are actively produced and marketed *as* the zeitgeist? It all becomes a bit unreal, and this is seen as clearly in LA as anywhere else.

Consider a marketing report by JWT Intelligence (now Wunderman Thompson) released in the spring of 2016, titled *Unreality: Next-Gen Fantasy, Utopias, and Unquantified Landscapes in a World of Hyper-Digital Realism*.[31] This glossy, thirty-four-page document intersperses beautifully surreal images with text that reads somewhere between sales pitch and vibes. As Devon Powers notes in her study of the history and contemporary business practices of trend forecasters like Wunderman Thompson, trend spotting (which is simultaneously trend producing) is cultural analysis that is then spun into a compelling story to provide concrete directions by which companies can capture consumer interest.[32] A trend report not only provides examples of diverse consumer products and interests, but then also articulates a theory of *why* these are the products du jour. And in so doing, the report ensures the propagation and proliferation of this trend. For the trend of *Unreality*, the report diagnoses nothing less than the cultural reaction to hyperreality and contemporary digital living. The text on the first page reads:

> We live in a state of hyperreality.[33] As we navigate through the stress and mundanity of our everyday existence and parallel online lives, we are increasingly turning to unreality as a form of escape and a way to search for other kinds of freedom, truth and meaning. What emerges is an appreciation for magic and spirituality, the knowingly unreal, and the intangible aspects of our lives that defy big data and the ultratransparency of the web.
>
> The digital world has created a precociously wise and cynical generation to whom "unknowing" is becoming increasingly attractive. For millennials struggling to make sense of their place in the world there is a world that doesn't make sense—but it doesn't matter because it is not real. Unreality is the natural antidote to the increasingly clichéd themes of honesty and authenticity, and appeals to those who want something beyond the evident and explainable.
>
> The digital age has created an always-on generation, for whom the desire to switch off means finding an alternative reality. When hyperbole is stratospheric, where is there that's beyond awesome? Another world, but one that doesn't actually exist.

The report goes on to knit together Norwegian slow TV, Burning Man, an Airbnb that is a 3-D replica of the bedroom Van Gogh painted in Arles, crystals and astrology and sound baths, fairy tales, Snapchat filters, meditation retreats, THC tinctures, and of course immersive experiences and virtual reality. Despite the generalizing in the text above and the eclecticism of the assembled products, the report captures the potent simultaneity of an individual feeling information overload while they also contribute to this information economy by constantly performing a curated version of their life on social media. Here, the hyperreal indexes the oppressive condition of being real-and-virtual that culminates in a desire to escape to the purely fantastical and epistemologically other realm of the unreal. In other words, the unreal (in this report) is a counterreality to the hyperreal. The trend report celebrates the unreal and notes the boredom with which honesty and authenticity are perceived, yet fails to forecast the political consequences, experienced just a few months later during the 2016 presidential election, of such an orientation.

As I described in the introduction, shortly after arriving in Los Angeles I went on a Paramount studio tour and heard the description from *The Errand Boy* of Hollywood as a "land of the real and unreal." Taken with this phrase, I began mentally tagging experiences that felt otherwise as "unreal." I would frame fieldwork encounters I couldn't fully make sense of as occurring "in the land of the unreal." The term allowed me to think about VR's blurring of "virtual" and "reality" as an unreality that might also characterize so many aspects of the Trump presidency as well as LA's façades and also consumer experiences that I encountered for the first time in LA that, as captured by the trend report, blurred the fantastical with the everyday. My field notes include links to meetups that began with a sound bath and concluded with a panel discussion on VR and Bitcoin, mentions of friends and interlocutors periodically disappearing on silent meditation retreats, bewildered accountings of how friendly conversations turned into palm or tarot readings, and conversations had with others about the Costar astrology app.[34] As worldbuilding made frequent appearances in my notes alongside these other observations, I began to see how it, too, signaled the desire for an alternative reality—the creation of, to quote the *Unreality* trend report, "another world, but one that doesn't actually exist."

I didn't encounter this report until well after fieldwork, and so while living in LA I was doing my own ethnographic knitting together of things that felt of a piece with virtual reality. When I did read the report, I admit I felt a little foolish—perhaps I was not "discovering" the unreal but instead the unreal was being actively (if disguisedly) marketed at me to be consumed and, on the pages of this very book, reproduced. This report also made me realize that while I had first become attuned to the unreal in LA, the trends I had labeled as such had since dispersed well beyond the city. Following fieldwork, I observed with interest the growing presence of astrology and tarot both among my East Coast friends and in local shops. I similarly clocked how academic conversations in anthropology increasingly embraced speculative methods, including wordbuilding, making space for scholarship that moves, as the *Unreality* report details, "beyond the evident and explainable."

But the unreal is more than just a collection of oddities. It marks the erosion of the illusion of a singular reality. This fragmentation can spark fantastical escapes as well as political, cultural, and epistemological crises. The unreal stuck with me after leaving LA because it helpfully connected my fieldwork with these broader trends. The unreal underscored how one reason speculation appealed to many academics was its refusal of a sin-

2.4 At a café in West Hollywood, patrons are implicitly asked to tag their visit with "#ifyouwerehere." When I read this, I had an experience of being interpolated whereby I identified as the "you," creating a moment when another world (in which I wasn't at the café) fleetingly existed. This was a casual encounter with the unreal that accompanied ordering a latte. Photograph taken in April 2018 by the author.

gular and fully knowable world. In my own thinking—evidenced in how I chose to organize this book—the unreal directed my energies away from describing "the real world" and instead figured fantasy as the reality most revealing. Speculative and unreal approaches have felt like an "aha moment" for academics, as we thought we had freed ourselves from certain disciplinary constraints. And yet, when I encountered the trend report I could not help but wonder how marketing forces wend their way into the ivory tower. As Powers writes, trend forecasters are not passively observing and documenting the world, but aspire "to shape how others view their surroundings, to advocate for how the world could be."[35]

The unreal patterned my experience and writing about both VR and Los Angeles, a technology and place that are themselves examples of unreality. This is an ouroboros that I cannot straighten out. The unreal, the hyperreal, the real-and-imagined—these are all fantasies of reality otherwise that emerge from thinking with (and from) Los Angeles.

It All Comes Together in VR

Is there something about LA that makes it particularly suited for creating VR—as a medium and as an industry?[36] Is there a technological terroir that shapes thinking and conversations about VR? If, as Hugo observed, LA has always been about fantasy, does VR have a better chance at achieving its fantastical potential in LA than elsewhere? My contention is that the fantasies of LA and the fantasies of VR reflect and enhance one another. Whether this will lead to commercial success is a future yet to be realized. But for now, let me draw out how LA's fantasy of place, which invites realities otherwise, can frame thinking about VR.

VR AS REALITY OTHERWISE

"Disneyland," Eco writes, "tells us that technology can give us more reality than nature can."[37] He contrasts a boat tour he took on the Mississippi River with Disneyland's Jungle Cruise. In Mississippi there was the possibility of seeing "real" crocodiles, but none broke the water's surface. In Disneyland, animatronic animal sightings are always guaranteed. This hyperreality is pushed even further for Eco when contemplating the human animatronics that people Pirates of the Caribbean, which opened in 1967. Eco muses that this ride succeeds in "breaking down the wall of the second dimension, creating not a movie, which is illusion, but total theater, and not with anthropomorphized animals, but with human beings."[38] Imagineers crafted the insult-spewing pirates by observing the expression of actors—almost an analog version of today's performance capture techniques. "Humans could do no better," Eco continues, "but the more important thing is precisely the fact that these are not humans and we know they're not. The pleasure of imitation, as the ancients knew, is one of the most innate in the human spirit . . . we also enjoy the conviction that imitation has reached its apex and afterwards reality will always be inferior to it."[39]

Many of today's virtual reality boosters frame the technology as a hyperreality (though not using this language) in the sense Eco alludes to in his discussion of Disneyland; it is hyper—more than—reality itself. It is a technology that promises "more reality" than otherwise possible. Nikhil, a master's student at USC whom I first met during a visit to a VR company where he was interning, was someone with whom I frequently crossed paths throughout fieldwork, and he was always game to discuss VR's potential. We found ourselves having lunch together on the Warner Bros.

studio lot one day when we were both attending a popular immersive entertainment conference/festival. Nikhil shared an insight he recently had about VR. He described a VR experience that he and a friend did that allowed the user to wander around the seaside cliffs of Malibu. Nikhil noted that in VR, his friend was very adventurous, wandering right up to the edge of the cliff. A few weeks later, he and the same friend visited the actual Malibu cliff that they had previously only explored virtually. His friend, Nikhil explained, was much more tentative—he sat on a bench to enjoy the scenery, keeping a safe distance from the steep cliff's edge. VR, Nikhil concluded, allows people to be more adventurous. His friend could experience "more reality" in virtual Malibu than in actual Malibu.

VR is also imagined as paving the way for the ultimate blending of real-and-imagined. Back in Beverly Hills, several months after the transportive run on which I encountered the façade of Via Rodeo, I attended the Infinity Film Festival. The festival, for which 2018 was its inaugural year, advertised itself as "the premier festival for Hollywood and Silicon Valley," celebrating, as marketing material then read, "storytelling advanced by technology." One of the keynote speakers was Ted Schilowitz, a futurist (his official title) at Paramount. Schilowitz painted a picture for the audience in which virtual and augmented realities allow for the ultimate blending of reality and fiction. For Schilowitz, this was an exciting future—one in which the story world of the screen would be integrated into our surroundings—a "total theater" to quote Eco's description of an immersive theme park ride. What happens, he asked the audience, when everything in the environment—and here he gestured to the auditorium we were sitting in—becomes part of the story? What happens when the (real) room is involved in a story and thus becomes a fiction? Schilowitz connected this desire for immersion to the theme park and showed a clip from the 1990s of Michael Eisner promoting Disney's first foray into virtual reality—a magic carpet amusement ride. Eisner was talking to the camera from what he called Disney's virtual reality studio. Computer screens and analog editing bays lined the wall behind him, and Eisner sat down and pulled on a VR headset that "allows you to step into the world of *Aladdin* on a magic carpet ride." As Eisner explained how VR works—how you can look all around—we saw the digital palace around which Eisner directed the digital magic carpet. "You control when you return to the real world," Eisner concluded as he took off the headset. But instead of the VR studio, he was himself now in the virtual world of *Aladdin*. Eisner shrugged. "Oh well. Welcome to the wonderful world of Disney." It is this confusion of the virtual and actual worlds that Schilowitz saw as the future to which today's VR and AR are still leading. Eventually, we won't have to wear boxy headsets and our digital sensorial experiences will extend beyond the screen such that the only world is a world that integrates the real-and-imagined.

Just as I detailed the realities otherwise used to describe LA, these brief examples—to which I could add a litany of others—illustrate how the same descriptions are used for VR. Just as the theme-ing of LA ebbed into Disneyland and hyperreality flowed back out, VR similarly swims in these currents such that patterns of thinking and being ripple between the place and the technology.

VR AS FAÇADE

As Eco writes, the animatronic pirates are pleasurable because the theme park goer knows they are uncanny imitations. That is also the pleasure of movie sets on studio lots and storefront façades that imitate elsewhere even as the consumer knows their feet are planted in Los Angeles. I love the fantasy that façades offer—an imagination of being whisked away to an elsewhere. Façades differ as to how far into the world a visitor can become immersed. On Via Rodeo, one can enter the shops, but the European charm does not persist past the threshold. In Pirates of the Caribbean, one can look all around and find exquisite detail but must stay seated in the rowboat that lazily but precisely takes a visitor through the world. More recent theme park attractions allow for further exploration of other realities. At Universal Studios' Wizarding World of Harry Potter, the magically inclined can purchase a bespoke wand and, if standing in the right place and waving the wand just so, aspiring Hermiones and Rons can make a flower in a window display bloom.[40]

Each of these façades facilitates a different level of immersion, promising a whole world but limiting how deeply one can explore. VR experiences are also façades as they invite immersion into a seemingly rich world even as exploration is ultimately limited. In some VR experiences, exploration of the world is limited to looking all around (like Pirates). "Room scale" experiences can be explored with one's body and, like the Wizarding World, there are designated points of interaction. VR designers are still learning the language of the medium and experimenting with how to balance the illusion that the user is fully in the world with the limitations of processing power or storytelling that necessitate guided exploration.

Returning to Beverly Hills and the Infinity Film Festival, after hearing Schilowitz's talk and the inspiration he drew from Disney's experimentation with VR in the 1990s, I sought out a display where I could do a VR experience produced by contemporary Disney animators. Disney's interest in VR has lain dormant since Aladdin's Magic Carpet Ride, and like other entertainment studios, they have been hesitant to invest in contemporary VR as it has yet to prove market success (more on this in the next chapter). One animator, Jeff Gipson, convinced the studio to let him experiment with the medium and in 2018 he and a team developed and premiered the VR animated short, *Cycles*. I had heard about *Cycles* at the computer graphics conference Special Interest Group on Computer Graphics and Interactive Techniques (SIGGRAPH) a few months earlier, where the piece made its debut. It was praised as a moving and well-executed experience, but the buzz made the line to don a headset and see *Cycles* prohibitively long. In Beverly Hills at this new and sparsely attended festival, I was able to see the piece and chat with Gipson about his experience working in VR.

Cycles is set in the living room of a house, and, as a room scale experience, I am able to walk to different parts of the animated setting as desired. It becomes clear that I am watching scenes unfold over time in this living room—newlyweds moving in, having a baby, the joys and frustrations of parenting, the sorrow of death, and alongside these emotional transformations there are also physical transformations as the living room is redecorated and trees (visible through windows) grow taller in the backyard. There is no dialogue, but a clear sense of relations and emotional interactions between characters as they move through the room. As the characters grow older, they also come closer—and so as the experience unfolds, I get a better sense of who these people are in both attitude and appearance. The last beat of the experience allows the user to look in a mirror. I was startled to see that staring back at me was an older woman's face. I now understood who *I* was in this VR experience; these were *my* memories that just flashed in front of my eyes as I was preparing to move out of my home.

After viewing the experience, I asked Gipson about the production process. He said that his team was given only a few months to go from concept to execution—a feasibility study before the studio would commit to investing any more in VR.[41] Gipson explained that they were able to pull the story together so quickly because this is his family's story—the old woman at the end was his grandmother and this is made to look like his grandparents' house. I asked Gipson about one of the more unique user interactions in the piece: as I turned my body to look at different parts of the living room, the color would sometimes fade to grayscale, encouraging me to look elsewhere—usually back at the characters—so that the color returned. Gipson explained that this was a narrative strategy for getting the user to look at where the action was happening. Because you are free to look anywhere in VR, there is the risk of "missing" what the director intends you to see. He added that such a fade is also the way memories based on photographs work—you see the two-dimensional snapshot but not always the full three-dimensional world that surrounds it.

This fading technique is a reminder that while VR invites one to imagine that they are fully immersed in a reality otherwise, it remains a façade that is ultimately propped up by invisible scaffolding. Immersion is promised but never completely achieved. Movement is ultimately constrained to a few feet given the affordances of the technology and physical space and, in *Cycles*, one's gaze is passively directed (by the grayscale fading technique) to preserve the integrity of the storytelling. Even in more open-ended experiences, where the story is nonlinear and there is greater interactivity with the virtual objects, there remains a limit to immersion. This is what the concept of façade can remind us about VR, that the complex and absorbing exterior masks the incompleteness of the world.

I offer this not as a criticism of VR nor as an argument in favor of an even greater pursuit of realism. Rather, I use the concept of façade to more carefully think through *what* a VR experience is and can be. This will be all the more important when, in chapter 4, discussion turns to the fantasy of being and claims that VR can produce better people. If, instead of thinking of VR as a medium that affords complete immersion in a world, it is understood as an engagement with façade, perhaps a different fantasy potential of VR will emerge. After all, façades are not designed to deceive but rather to capitalize on, borrowing Eco's phrase, the "pleasure of imitation"—one does not mistake being in Chinatown for being in China. Rather, façades winkingly enroll the viewer in play. Façades are an invitation to imagine being in other worlds. In the Wizarding World of Harry Potter, the façade is so exquisitely elaborate that the windows on Diagon Alley can be brought to life with the flick of a wand. It is a thrilling delight but, at least as an adult visitor, you do not mistake yourself for being a witch or wizard. It is the fleeting enjoyment of a reality otherwise.

Describing VR as a façade allows for more precision when considering the kind of worlds it creates and the activities it affords. VR cannot offer an actual visit somewhere else or the experience of being someone else but, like façade, it can facilitate imagination and the excitement and pleasure that come with disrupting assumed flows of place, time, and identity.

Conclusion

Just as Baudrillard noted that one simply *feels* the simulacrum in California, in LA one *feels* the logics of VR. It is part of how one moves about and experiences the city; it is vernacular. Both LA and VR suspend inhabitants in a land of the real and unreal, physical and fantastical, actual and virtual.

Even on days that I spent away from my VR interlocutors, the simple act of being in LA taught me about the technology. On such "days off," I would often walk over to the Century City Mall, a few blocks from my apartment. I would pass the 76 gas station, at which plaster columns made to look like palm tree trunks supported roofs adorned with terra-cotta tiles that shaded the fuel pumps. A little patch of greenery at the traffic light was an island oasis, all of which transformed getting gas into a themed experience. The mall itself was open air with any number of places to sit and read or write. There was an Eataly as well as an outpost of my favorite coffee shop in Philadelphia, La Colombe, allowing my tastebuds to facilitate travel far away from this place. The stores assembled at this mall fascinated me. They were brick-and-mortar instantiations of e-commerce businesses that I otherwise only knew from podcast advertisements. These ads filled my ears with celebrations of business models that "cut out the middleman" through internet-enabled mail order commerce. Here, though, the virtual became real. I could browse Bonobos, Untuck-It, MeUndies, Warby Parker, and, the queen of them all, Amazon. It seemed that all of these pioneers of digital retail celebrated their victories in marketing innovation by . . . opening a storefront in a mall. It was also at this mall where a pop-up VR installation called *Alien Zoo* dipped its toe in the waters to test the viability of a VR LBE. It was whispered that Steven Spielberg was funding this venture and the experience itself had the narrative beats of *Jurassic Park*, but swap out dinosaurs for aliens, and rather than the movie's protagonists, it was we VR participants who had the misfortune of what was supposed to be a safe tour of galactic fauna gone perilously wrong. The pop-up opened in February 2018 and, as my research drew to a close, a permanent installation at the mall was about to debut with plans for expanding beyond LA. Even though I wasn't directly engaging with the VR community, sitting in this mall I could feel the unreality of it all.

During one of my excursions to the mall, I was reading through a set of essays published in 1997 under the title *CyberArts: Explorations in Art and Technology*. LA-based artists Kit Galloway and Sherrie Rabinowitz contributed an essay about their Santa Monica performance space, Electronic Café International.[42] Coming from art and performance backgrounds, their desire was to embolden people to experiment with connecting remotely as a way of facilitating community building and cultural exchange. In passing, they mentioned a project they mounted in 1980 called *Hole-in-Space*, which hacked together video, sound, and telecommunications satellites to create a virtual portal between Lincoln Center in New York City and (here I nearly dropped the book I was reading) the Century City Mall in LA. In a world before FaceTime and Zoom—practically before email—for three consecutive nights pedestrians in either city might stumble upon a crowd staring into and shouting at a TV screen where another crowd on the other side of the country responded. This real-time interaction at a distance was novel and delighted the crowd. They played charades (the New Yorkers pantomimed Joan Didion's "Slouching Towards Bethlehem"), flirted, sang, shouted playful insults, and bicoastal families made plans on the second and third nights, after word of mouth spread, for virtual reunions. In an archive video documenting this installation, passersby are asked to make sense of what they are seeing. A woman hanging back in the crowd of people in Los Angeles is asked by an offscreen interviewer if she knows what's going on. She is smiling and shakes her head no. The interviewer explains that the people on the screen are in New York. "They're in New York?" the woman asks, amused, looking at the screen. "I'm in Los Angeles, right?" she says with a laugh. "Are you?" provokes the interviewer. And the woman responds with an unsteady laugh, "Yes."[43] This pleasurable disorientation was summarized by a journalist at the *Los Angeles Herald Examiner*, explaining how the "lines between imagination and reality were blurred almost to distinction [sic]."[44]

Such blurring typifies LA's fantasy of place as well as VR. To be clear, I'm not suggesting that VR is only a product of LA. Studying it from different places reveals different facets of the technology and the community striving to build a financially viable and global industry.[45] At the same time, I can imagine no place better than LA from which to understand the fluidity with which VR plays with reality. LA has always been about fantasy, and it is in such a location where the fantasy of VR is both *not* out of place but also in many ways made real.

3

TINSELTOWN AND TECHNOLOGY
PRODUCING VIRTUAL REALITY IN THE DREAM FACTORY

If, as I have detailed in the previous two chapters, the ubiquity of fantasy and the mutability of reality that shapes LA's histories, industries, and experiences is suited to VR's own unreal qualities, why hasn't the technology triumphed? Why couldn't LA make VR happen? Particularly in 2018, the VR industry was at a bit of a standstill, waiting for . . . something. Better content? Better headsets? The community wasn't sure. All they knew was that the fantasy of VR as a transformative technology had not yet been achieved. But, what if part of the reason for VR's stall was itself a product of LA's technological terroir? Despite commonly held assumptions that "technology" is a universal and unitary concept, it is still crafted and cultivated by people in specific, local contexts. These local practices and knowledges, which produce divergent and nuanced understandings of technology, are obscured by the myth of technology as somehow outside of culture. Even given my training and research interests, it took me a few months of fieldwork to realize that technology meant something different in LA, that the practices of technological development and innovation that I was attending to—that were being described and labeled as such by my interlocutors—were different

3.1 The iconic sign, photographed by the author in March 2022, from the manicured gardens of the restaurant Yamashiro (itself a façade of a Japanese estate, built in the early 1910s).

from what I might have been focused on were I to have conducted my fieldwork in Silicon Valley. Despite these differences, when folks from Silicon Valley met with folks in LA, it was assumed the technology about which they were talking was the same thing, universally defined and understood. While technology's local flavor created the opportunity to expand the voices contributing to VR's development—the fantasy of representation that will be explored in part III—it also produced a certain amount of frustration and friction when the local logics for how to advance a technology did not yield anticipated outcomes. The closer I got to Hollywood, the more I could feel this friction.

This is partly because we are not accustomed to thinking about technology alongside entertainment. They are imagined to have different geographies of power (Silicon Valley vs. Hollywood); different models of celebrity (Steve Jobs vs. Brad Pitt); different associated expertise (engineer vs. actor); and even different scholarly traditions (STS, history of technology vs. film and media studies).[1] To be sure, plenty has been written about the relationship between technology and film, as scholars have explored how scientific and technological developments shape cinematic stories,[2] how cinema shapes collective sentiment about technology,[3] and they have detailed the multitude of technological innovations (and inventors/technicians) that have changed storytelling techniques, from Edison's Black Maria to "the talkies" to computer-generated imagery (CGI).[4] Even the first (and one of the few) anthropologists to study the movie industry could not escape the centrality of technology as both metaphor and mechanism. Hortense Powdermaker[5] titled her 1950 book after one of the most significant technological innovations of the early twentieth century: the assembly line. In *Hollywood, the Dream Factory*, she derided the movie business for assuming that the same process of mass production that produced a can of beans could be suitable for the daydreams Hollywood is charged with creating.[6]

What happens, Powdermaker asked, when "an ancient and popular art, storytelling," comes "into direct contact with a modern technology"? Summarizing classic anthropological ideas, she observed that new technologies can either be integrated with traditional knowledge, can run parallel and not affect one another, or can be in conflict. For Hollywood, Powdermaker asserted, the introduction of a technological mindset to the making of movies was an example of conflict.[7] If Powdermaker was critical of the industrialization and assembly-line mentality,[8] she also recognized that certain individual visual and sonic technologies might reengage the artistry lost in mass production. While Powdermaker noted that each new production technology inevitably changed the social structure of the industry, often dispersing creative power (and thus weakening the ability to make an original film), she nonetheless found a glimmer of hope in the director who could leverage these very same technologies and push the possibilities of cinematic storytelling. Such achievements, according to Powdermaker, were "in spite of the system, rather than because of it."[9] While a technological ethos might be in conflict with artistry, there are individual technologies that warrant praise.

In the seventy years since Powdermaker's assessment, not only has there been an overhaul in studio and labor structures,[10] but technology has become even more central to the entertainment industry. The rise of multimedia and user-generated content, as well as companies like Netflix and Amazon expanding from content delivery platforms to production studios,[11] necessitate refined understandings of the technology and entertainment nexus.[12] Charles Acland's *American Blockbuster* elaborates on how the genre of blockbuster movie both encourages and is enabled by a "culture of perpetual technological change."[13] A "technological tentpole," as he calls it, both depends on ever improving technologies for movie production and celebrates a culture of gizmos and gadgets (as in the James Bond franchise). In other words, making blockbusters depends on technological innovation, these movies in turn celebrate constant improvement and innovation, which then feeds back into the expectation for new movie-making technologies.

Virtual reality illuminates the need for precise language when describing the complex intersections between entertainment, technology, the different communities invested in its success, and the broader publics imagined as being affected by a technology's adoption. This is particularly important at a moment when companies are releasing user-friendly applications that, drawing on machine learning and generative artificial intelligence (AI), allow for the widespread production of texts, images, and even videos that might have previously required significant artistic and technical training and expertise to create. When the Writers Guild of America (WGA) went on strike in 2023, they included in their initial negotiations constraints on how AI could be used in writers' rooms, as well as a stipulation that would prevent AI programs from being trained on WGA members' material. Alongside these immediate labor concerns, generative AI also raises the threat level of misinformation, as even informed consumers of media might no longer be able to distinguish between a soundbite clipped from a political speech versus one that was generated with these tools. These technologies, in other words, provide an arsenal for further fomenting the "reality crisis." During my fieldwork, VR was further along in its commercialization than AI, charismatically crystalizing discussions that anticipated and worried over the dangers posed by this broader constellation of technologies and their ability to craft realistic fantasies as well as fantastical otherwise realities. To understand the emergence of these unrealities requires not only a focus on the tech industry but also, as VR helps us see, on the entertainment industry and its technological history.

From this vantage point, one can grasp the different connotations—and thus imagined potentials—of "technology." Virtual reality is both a technology that offers new ways of crafting stories and a technology *about which* stories—especially stories of the future—have often been told. Recently, VR has even become a tool for telling stories about its own imagined future. VR thus sits as comfortably alongside technologies like motion capture and CGI as it does alongside flying cars and AI robots. It is thus necessary to understand VR as both a "cinematic technology" and an "emerging technology."[14] Like motion capture, VR offers new ways of telling cinematic stories. Like AI, VR is anticipated as societally altering. While Hollywood has long been the developer of cinematic technology, Silicon Valley has been the most recent steward of emerging technology. And here lies the friction—a friction produced by different instincts about what a technology is and ought to be—that prohibited the VR community in LA from being able to diagnose why their fantasies of the industry's future were not coming to fruition.[15] As other emerging technologies, like AI, are put to cinematic use—and employed to generate alternative facts meant to persuade—VR instructs us of the importance of attending to local political economies and associated meanings of technology that extend beyond Silicon Valley in order to more fully analyze technological potentials, failures, and harms.

Brought to You in Glorious Technicolor

To explore the relationship between technology and entertainment, like Powdermaker before me I sought out the studios. In my case, I was invited by Marcie Jastrow to be a scholar-in-residence of the Technicolor Experience Center (TEC, pronounced "tech"), a small branch of the mammoth postproduction company. Jastrow was the director of TEC, and she and her staff were trying to create a business model and production ecosystem for immersive technologies, including and especially VR. In 2018, TEC was located in a small business park in Culver City, a mismatch with the body shops and storage centers that otherwise color this strip of La Cienega Boulevard. Closer to Culver City's bustling center, however, Amazon, HBO, and Sony have headquartered their studios, upgrading and expanding lots that hosted some of Los Angeles's first and most famous production companies. *The Wizard of Oz*, one of Technicolor's triumphs, was filmed on the MGM lot in Culver City—where Sony (which purchased the lot in 2004) is today located.[16] Along this same corridor, Within, one of the few VR production companies that has weathered the industry's expansions and contractions, also had its headquarters. TEC's location, in a complex that included other branches of Technicolor's postproduction subsidiaries, prefigured a future of expansion that might connect the traditional, streaming, and immersive studios.

I confess that being at TEC—at Technicolor—felt like I had successfully made it to the belly of the beast. For a notoriously litigious industry, nervous of any exposure and thus (not surprisingly) unwelcome to an anthropologist and her notebook, TEC was ethnographic gold.[17] It would be disingenuous if I didn't admit to feeling a bit of movie magic strutting into

TEC a few times a week. While Technicolor has been consolidated, sold, and repackaged several times in its century-plus-spanning history,[18] persisting as a brand long disconnected from the color processing method that made the company a household name, it was still a bit thrilling to think about how my ethnography was "now in Technicolor!" But Technicolor also gets right to the heart of this chapter; the "Tech" in the company name is an homage to MIT, where the cofounders were both alumni and professors.[19] Technicolor, which was incorporated in Maine in 1915, built its first facilities in Boston, and opened its West Coast labs in Hollywood in 1924 (as it was by then apparent that LA, not New York, would be the center of the motion picture industry).[20] It would take another fifteen years (until *The Wizard of Oz*) for Technicolor to become synonymous with "a cinematic experience larger than life, a vibrant, multihued, and highly saturated world representing an escape from reality." While audiences learned to delight in the spectacle, for producers, color could "add production value and increase box office returns" and for filmmakers, "color was a tool to enhance storytelling." However, these multiple benefits—benefits that would come to describe any number of subsequent cinematic technologies—were not easily or obviously established. In the first decades of the company, "the value of motion pictures in color was not proven, the technology was still nascent, and public demand was uncertain."[21]

The time I spent at Technicolor was this time of uncertainty for VR. It was unclear if VR held market value beyond first person shooter games, the technology was still error prone, and while there was a growing and enthusiastic community of VR boosters in LA, this excitement was not necessarily translating to Hollywood execs or a broader public. When I started my residency at TEC in the summer of 2018, the center was bustling and exciting. There were high profile projects, secret meetings and whispers about future partnerships, and a general sense that *this* was the next big thing for Technicolor. As Jastrow stated at a staff meeting that summer, "If we don't move into XR [an abbreviation here referring to virtual, augmented, and mixed reality], Technicolor will not have a future." Jastrow came to VR after having helped build infrastructure and expertise around the technical demands that accompanied the movie industry's transition from analog to digital production. Having stewarded a previous shift in cinematic technology to success, could she do the same for VR? Or would the conflict between her expertise and those that were expected to accompany an emerging technology become too great to overcome?

Talking Technology at TEC

I spent my time in residence at TEC moving through its different spaces. The facility itself was tucked away in an office park, removed from the busy boulevard and further concealed by a garden wall that ran around the modestly sized property. Beyond this wall was a narrow, ivy-lined courtyard with a few high-top tables set on the artificial grass. During lunch time, the tables were filled with the dozen or so employees at TEC, amicably talking about their weekend plans or a Netflix show. Other times, one of the producers or Jastrow's assistants might have been taking a call, working on a budget, or meeting with a potential partner in the fresh air. Through glass doors, a visitor to TEC entered directly into the showroom. They were greeted by the immersive experience director or one of the two production coordinators (at least one of whom was always sitting at the concierge desk),[22] who welcomed them and immediately asked they sign an NDA. The showroom had several immersive experiences on display, each with a different headset and auxiliary technologies. Visitors might be led around to different experiences by a production coordinator who, knowing that for many this was their first time in VR, walked them through putting on a headset and getting comfortable. Some visitors might head to the office in the back to meet with Jastrow, who spent most of the day out of sight unless she was speaking with an employee, schmoozing a client or, on occasion, letting off some steam by playing a VR game on the showroom floor.

Other visitors to TEC were there to use the virtual production stage, complete with motion- and performance-capture capabilities (also referred to as the mocap stage for short). Leaving the showroom, one passed through a less glamorous room with ten or so workstations to get to the mocap stage. In these backrooms, developers, producers, and technicians built immersive experiences in game engines and facilitated live action shoots. TEC was designed to be an end-to-end production center, capable of going from production, to postproduction, and finally to consumption back out in the showroom.

TEC invited different clients, artists, and partners to use its facilities, personnel, and expertise to experiment with and learn about VR. During my residency, one of the main projects was a partnership with HP to create a VR experience about what a human future on Mars might look and feel like. There were also several artists-in-residence who, through a partnership with Sundance Institute's New Frontier Lab (see chapter 4), spent time at TEC working on various immersive projects. While TEC only had about a half dozen full-time employees, any given day might have twice as many or more people there to work on a project. Sometimes TEC rented out the mocap stage, either for performance capture shoots or to host events. Every day I spent at TEC, it was guaranteed that I would meet someone new and learn about a different project as Jastrow experimented with establishing an expansive base upon which an immersive industry might be built.

As I will describe, Jastrow is a saleswoman, and as director of TEC, she was trying both to sell VR to the entertainment industry and to sell the entertainment industry to more traditional tech companies. As no one knew what was going to be the "killer app" for VR, Jastrow imagined TEC as a place to bring together folks with various expertise and try to find what would make VR a success. Such promiscuous experimentation meant that the conversations and presentations I observed or took part in at TEC captured the different kinds of technology that VR was imagined alongside as well as the different experts imagined as important for VR's development. TEC illustrates how, depending on context, VR was positioned as a cinematic technology (made legible by the expertise of the entertainment industry) or an emerging technology (animated by a Silicon Valley mentality).

As a cinematic technology, VR was variously imagined either as or alongside production and postproduction techniques that are employed to enrich the storytelling experience. Toward the end of my fieldwork, one of Technicolor's visual effects (VFX) subsidiaries used TEC's mocap stage to demo their "virtual production" pipeline to the major studios. As traditional films increasingly rely on performance capture (made popular by Andy Serkis's artistry)[23] and computer-generated (CG) environments, directors and actors draw more and more from their imagination when filming. A shoot might entirely be actors in motion capture suits performing in front of green screens—posing a creative problem of not quite knowing what they are acting against or in what embodied form their performance will ultimately be rendered. Virtual production platforms allow creatives to see and even manipulate the CG assets on set; work that has usually been relegated to postproduction. On the day of the demo, Karen (the head of the Technicolor subsidiary that was selling this virtual pipeline and whom I had not previously met) impressed upon me that virtual production is not VR. Sure, VR headsets are used by the director and cinematographer to decide where to place the camera, but she was selling much more than that; she was selling a production pipeline. In fact, Karen said as she leaned

3.2 VR as a cinematic technology can be placed alongside other tools for immersive storytelling, such as those pictured here that were set up for a shoot on the TEC mocap stage, including a 3-D camera and a green screen. Photograph taken in June 2018 by the author.

in with a conspiratorial whisper, cinematographers hate VR because they can't apply techniques like zoom and pan; they are deprived of their storytelling language. I probed further on this point: Why is there so much resistance in Hollywood to VR (I had observed that my colleagues at TEC were often bemoaning Technicolor's executives and other big studios dismissal of their work)? Karen diagnosed a general technophobia in the industry. Karen had worked on *Polar Express* (2004), the first animated movie to be filmed entirely with performance capture. It was a technological triumph but, Karen lamented, it was criticized for looking creepy as the animation fell into the uncanny valley. Similarly, when Jastrow described Hollywood's resistance to new technology, she emphasized that if you can't prove to the studio head that it makes money, they don't care how magical it is. In the Hollywood context, VR as a cinematic technology—whether as a tool for traditional filmmaking or itself a medium of entertainment—demonstrates its worth by strengthening both storytelling potential and the bottom line.

As an emerging technology, VR is bundled with slightly different artifacts and concerns. Both at TEC and events around town, VR, AI, and blockchain became a triumvirate of a sort that indexed both the future of entertainment but also a more general tech-saturated future. This brought VR into conversations textured by techno-optimism and cautioned by ethical concerns. Another event on TEC's mocap stage serves as a helpful illustration. At a daylong "virtual conference" on immersive technologies (virtual insofar as the talks were prerecorded and released on YouTube) sponsored by the USC-affiliated Entertainment Technology Center, the final panel was a conversation between three TEC employees and two clients/collaborators. After a day of talks that touched upon worldbuilding and VR, AR tabletop games, a VR environmental conservation project, AI and location-based entertainment, and an investment prospectus on immersive technologies, this final panel concerned "digital doubles." This panel discussed the technical process of rendering an actual human as a digital copy that could inhabit a virtual world. The slide that served as a backdrop to this conversation depicted the different components that go into making such virtual humans, including VR, software for facial rendering, and the game engines Unity and Unreal. Jake, a producer at TEC in his early thirties who studied film at both UCLA and USC before becoming interested in VR and learning the game engine workflow, chaired this panel. Though his expertise is in film and VR, this panel did not highlight VR as a cinematic technology but rather positioned it alongside other emerging technologies. As Jake teased, they'd be discussing the "weird future world we're going to live in where people are embodying virtual avatars" and there are "real mechanical robots that humans can interact with." I was aware of TEC's interest in digital doubles, as on multiple days I had sat in the back room watching Jake and Francis (also on the panel) build up a virtual version of Erika, TEC's immersive experience director. They were experimenting with the different body and facial scanning technologies to create a digital Erika that, in the near future (so it was imagined), would be powered by AI. Then, one could be in VR and interact with dErika (their portmanteau for this digital Erika) who would look, sound, and respond like the actual Erika.

The "weird future" that Jake described and was discussed throughout the panel was one in which VR and aligned emerging technologies blurred various distinctions between virtual and actual. Rick, the virtual production supervisor at TEC who oversees the mocap stage and has worked as an animator and mocap specialist for over a decade in video games and movies, reflected on the changing expertise needed to bring about realistic digital doubles. While five years ago he would have said that computer graphic artists were needed, now he's seeing how machine learning has made great strides toward realism.[24] But while such deep learning algorithms might be an unexpected solution, he observed that because such an approach is easier to use and cheaper to apply than computer animation techniques (thus outside of the control of entertainment experts), might there be nefarious applications of the technology? In the audience, I was thinking about the sudden rise of deep fakes which, in the summer of 2018, had just made it into the popular consciousness.

Rick speculated, "We could end up in a digital rights and blockchain future where I don't know what I'm looking at anymore; if it's real, if it's right."[25] Jake built on this, asking the panelists about the ethical concerns that accompany the virtual human world. The conversation pivoted to privacy and data ownership, and again blockchain was floated as a solution to authentication. VR as an emerging technology was implicated in "tech ethics" conversations, and Rick's worry over his inability to distinguish a real human from a digital double echoed concerns around Trumpism and "fake news." As VR capabilities have improved and generative AI tools have come onto the consumer market, the concerns presaged here, framed as a distant future, have become more salient for current (as of the publication of this book) debates over these technologies.

The implications of a technology—like VR—being both cinematic and emerging are subtle yet pervasive. This distinction was not made by my interlocutors, and so VR is a fitting example of a boundary object, a classic STS concept that emphasizes how collaboration can occur among communities with different expertise due, in part, to objects or concepts with flexible identities.[26] Both Silicon Valley technologists and Hollywood entertainment specialists were working on VR—imagining themselves to be pursuing similar futures—but there was a tension between these two kinds of expertise and thus a blame game occurred as folks in LA accused folks up in the Bay Area for VR's failures (and vice versa).

Significantly, while VR was at times positioned as an emerging technology (as illustrated by the panel on digital doubles), the dominant mode of understanding VR in LA was as a cinematic technology. This rendered Hollywood expertise as vital to VR's success, which, as I'll explore in chapter 7, transformed conversations about tech more generally into something otherwise. At TEC, Jastrow gathered together experts that sought to make VR a success by implementing strategies that had worked with other cinematic technologies. However, as VR is also an emerging technology (something that can't be said of most cinematic technologies) there was a set of expertise not native to Hollywood that was often absent from these strategic approaches.

From Analog to Digital . . . to Virtual?

As Powdermaker observed more than a half century ago, "New technology always precipitates changes in the method and system of production, whether it is of storytelling or agriculture."[27] Or as media theorist John Caldwell more recently noted, "Technical progress inevitably comes alongside worker anxiety and trade power struggles."[28] For cinematic technologies, the artifact alone does not change film production but is dependent on a larger network of people, things, and ideas; and depending on how the technology reshapes production, it inevitably has supporters and detractors. In the case of Technicolor, one of the significant innovations was, along with the three-strip process, the creation of a "color supervisor." Starting in the late 1920s, Natalie Kalmus created the role of color supervisor and eventually the Color Control Department (renamed the Color Advisory Service), which advised productions on the best palettes for sets, costumes, and make-up in order to achieve the colors they were hoping for in the final print (and enhance the emotional arc of the story). When a film decided they wanted to shoot in Technicolor, not only did they hire Technicolor cameras and camera operators, but they also received the service of Kalmus or one of her trainees.[29]

More recently, the transition from analog to digital occurred not simply because of the availability of digital workstations and cameras but because certain people, as Kalmus had previously done, refined the social systems in which these cinematic technologies could function. Marcie Jastrow was one such person, establishing herself as an expert in digital workflows and thus an obvious candidate for the person who might help Hollywood embrace virtual reality as the next great cinematic technology.

The transition to digital began around 1970 and stretched to the early 2010s, affecting nearly every step of the production process. This shift was fragmented, with different departments going digital at different times and for different reasons. On the vanguard was the use of computers in both the editing process and visual effects. George Lucas catalyzed both of these fronts from his unique location in San Francisco.[30] While editors—those skilled at splicing celluloid—were a bit more resistant to digital editing, within the VFX community CG was embraced and in under a decade digital effects matured from the first fully computer animated character in a film, the stained glass knight in *Young Sherlock Holmes* (1985),[31] to herds of dinosaurs in *Jurassic Park* (1993).

In the 1990s, during the height of the digital transition, Jastrow began her career in postproduction. Though only in her midtwenties, this was already her third career. A self-described "wild child," her parents guided her to different jobs when it was clear that school was not providing enough structure. Jastrow's parents met in Philadelphia, followed career opportunities to Florida (where Jastrow was born) and then to Los Angeles. In LA, her mother, Pat Lestz, was the general manager of a high-end department store, and her father, Earl Lestz, was headhunted from the retail industry to join Paramount Pictures, where he eventually became a division president. On the one hand, Jastrow is descended from Hollywood royalty (Lestz has a star on the Hollywood Walk of Fame). On the other hand, she is the daughter of parents who—as many are promised but few obtain—achieved the American dream by working hard to rise from modest means to unimaginable success.

In high school, Jastrow began working part time in retail and continued doing so while she earned an associate degree in marketing. She might have continued in retail, but her father, still a president at Paramount, had taken on a side business of bringing his brother's food franchise, Lee's Hoagie House, from Philadelphia out west. He put twenty-one-year-old Marcie in charge. In an article in the *Los Angeles Times* profiling young entrepreneurs, Marcie Lestz is photographed at the sandwich prep station wearing a Lee's T-shirt and an apron. With big hair, hoop earrings, hands on waist, and her head tilted with an indulgent smile—*I'll let you take this photo, but I really need to get back to work*—she is immediately recognizable as the woman I'd meet thirty years later. And the advice she offers other aspiring entrepreneurs is true to who she remains: take risks and make mistakes, fire anyone who doesn't respect you, but especially, "Don't be afraid to say, 'I don't understand—teach me.'"[32]

The experiment of bringing Lee's out west was a risk that failed and after the franchises were shut down, Jastrow, in her midtwenties, had retired from her second career. Jastrow worked odd sales jobs for a couple of years before becoming an assistant (the entry-level position in Hollywood) at Paramount and eventually landing in postproduction—the sector in which she would spend the bulk of her career. She left Paramount and moved between different boutique postproduction companies that were proliferating in the late '90s and early 2000s as the studio system fractured and multimedia began to dominate. Jastrow remained in sales, getting productions to hire the company she was working at for their postproduction needs. In order to be good at her job, Jastrow had to become, as she phrased it, "more technical." She saw the sea change to digital occurring, and she wanted to be on the leading edge. Taking her own advice of claiming ignorance and asking to be taught, Jastrow set to work understanding the new workflows and processes on the digital side of things so she could act as a translator between them and the creative side. Jastrow found her calling: "I was really good at taking the friction out of workflows. . . . Being technical was the smartest decision I ever made."

In the 1990s, Hollywood's digital terrain was uneven. Different pockets of postproduction were digitizing, but directors were still shooting on film and movie theaters were still projecting celluloid. The workflow was such that there were several conversions between analog and digital during the editing process (depending on which postproduction teams had transitioned to digital), and the pipeline began and ended with film for shooting and distribution. Some filmmakers began wondering what it might be like to shoot on digital from the beginning of the production process. In 1995, Sony introduced the first standard definition digital camcorder for the consumer market. Independent filmmakers were the first to adapt these video cameras for cinematic storytelling, albeit with grainy results. As assessed by the traditional celluloid community, the appearance was inferior, but the storytelling was different and intriguing. These light, unobtrusive cameras provided, as has been said of VR, a sense of presence. As the producer of an early entrant to this genre described, "Video occupies a space in your mind [because of its use in news and pornography] where you're kind of like, 'I'm here. I'm in that room with them. Oh my God, is this really happening?'"[33] For some, the degradation in visual quality was worth the benefit to storytelling. When digitally shot independents began winning prizes at festivals like Sundance, the industry noticed.

No longer presumed inferior to film, it became an aesthetic or artistic decision to shoot in digital. George Lucas again intervened and asked Sony to develop a high-definition digital camera for him to shoot *Star Wars Episode 2* (2002). In a documentary about the digital transition in film production, *Side by Side* (2012), this moment of the story is narrated as one of great tension.[34] The documentary is edited in order to associate Lucas and the digital with San Francisco (showing an exterior of his studio and noting its Bay Area location) and pitting them against traditional film (a shot of the Hollywood sign). One of the interviewees says how Lucas was seen as going against the film industry and film itself. Lucas tells Keanu Reeves, the interviewer and narrator of the documentary (whose fame is tied up with *The Matrix*, itself exemplary of utilizing new cinematic technologies to warn of the societal dangers of emerging technologies), how the industry was "saying that I was the devil incarnate, that I was gonna destroy the industry, that I was gonna destroy all their jobs. That [digital] is inferior." And yet, as digital cameras improved and directors, cinematographers, and everyone in the production and postproduction pipeline learned how to wield these new tools, shooting digital rose in prominence across the industry. The digital pipeline rebalanced who held power and as one might imagine, those who felt they were losing power were resistant to digital. As Lucas obliquely references when he mentions the critique of digital was that it would destroy jobs (indeed, traditional film labs went out of business), the larger unsettling of the labor system in Hollywood is as important as any single technological invention in understanding the transition to digital.[35]

In addition to George Lucas, another key figure in Hollywood's embrace of shooting in digital was James Cameron. Cameron is what Charles Acland has called a "technological auteur,"[36] someone who has a creative vision and demands technological innovation of his team in order to achieve it. Cameron long embraced CG (for example, *The Abyss* [1989] and *Terminator*

2 [1991]) but was keen to push forward digital cinematography, using both newly developed digital HD cameras and even, with Vince Pace, creating his own digital camera to shoot in 3-D. However, in the early 2000s—the teenage years of digital production—things were still a bit awkward. Cameron was at the vanguard of shooting in digital and by contrast most facilities still did various parts of the postproduction pipeline on film. And aside from a scattered handful of screens, most movie theaters only projected film. Jastrow, who worked with Cameron and his production team first on *Titanic* (1997) recalled that for his follow-up documentary, *Ghosts of the Abyss* (2003), Cameron wanted a new workflow—he did not want the digital footage he shot to be "laid back to tape" for any part of the editing or for transfer between postproduction units, as he felt this degraded the visual quality. Jastrow took up the challenge of designing a new workflow, understanding the creative and technical needs and ultimately combining components that already existed—digital footage, digital disk drives, digital editing suites—into a new process that did not require converting digital to tape. Jastrow developed the "digital intermediate"[37] for her company, tweaking what other postproduction companies were doing and cutting out any need to print to analog storage in order to meet Cameron's all digital vision. As a consequence, she made her company that much more competitive for future projects in an industry that was increasingly digital. She accomplished this feat because, as she recalled, "It wasn't like I was an engineer, but I was able to speak [their language] and teach them why it was important for them to come up with a better workflow."

When *Avatar* (2009) came around, Cameron desired not only a completely digital workflow, but also digital (and 3-D) projection. Digital projection was the final step in a complete transition to digital. For *Star Wars Episode 1: The Phantom Menace* (1999), shot on film but converted to digital for postproduction, Lucas convinced four movie theaters in the suburbs of LA and NYC to install digital projectors, but more widespread adoption was a slow and expensive (if only in the initial investment) transition for theaters.[38] Cameron's ambition for *Avatar* was to speed up this transition. Acland describes *Avatar* as both a blockbuster and a technological tentpole, "under which not only commodities but also media formats slid into our lives."[39] Jastrow was at this point well known by the Cameron team, and she won the contract for her company, Modern VideoFilm, to run the digital intermediate for *Avatar*.[40] Jastrow does not have an IMDB credit for *Avatar*; the expertise she provided does not fall neatly into designated production categories. But in her office at TEC hung an *Avatar* movie poster, on which Cameron had written to Jastrow, "You have redefined what's possible."

For *Avatar* and after, theaters converted to digital, and if, in 1999, there were only a handful of screens that showed *Phantom Menace* in digital, in 2019 it was only a handful of screens that projected Tarantino's *Once Upon a Time in Hollywood* on 35mm film.[41]

By the early 2010s, the digital transition was nearly complete. After *Avatar*, Jastrow again switched companies, set up the digital intermediate at her new postproduction company, and soon after they were acquired by Technicolor. Jastrow was given the title of Senior Vice President and tasked with modernizing the company's workflow. Jastrow was no longer figuring out a puzzle, but instead helping the companies she worked with catch up to the new digital reality. She described feeling bored even as her sales continued to grow and as she worked on movies that, year after year, were winning Oscars.

It was this boredom that made her receptive to a pitch from two studio VIPs who approached her at Sundance in 2015, which had become *the* place for VR since Nonny de la Peña's 2012 premiere of *Hunger in LA* (see chapter 4), and asked her to do for VR what she had done for digital cinema. Immersive tech needed someone like Jastrow, they said, who could smooth the relationship between technical and creative folks.[42] At first, she was not persuaded; she had seen some of the VR pieces at the festival that year and was not blown away. But even if the content didn't grab Jastrow, she soon became obsessed with the puzzle—could she sell VR to Hollywood? And what kind of collaborations and expertise would be needed to be successful?

Jastrow took on this challenge and Technicolor changed her title to Senior VP of Immersive Media. She left behind her clients and set out to open TEC. Once again, she was not afraid to admit that she didn't understand this new world of immersive technology and found people who responded to her plea to "teach me." Technicolor owned smaller VFX shops—MPC, The Mill, Mr. X—and also had a research and innovation branch that were already working on VR projects. Jastrow's task was to bring this work under one roof and get off the perpetual wheel of reinventions that were happening across Technicolor's subsidiaries. Jastrow understood that her task at TEC was to "Take Technicolor, which is a one-hundred-year-old company, and convince people that [the company is] worth something." She had been asked, and would do her best, "to find out what the future is." Jastrow had been part of the transition to digital. Could she lead the transition to virtual in Hollywood?

The Fictions and Frictions of VR as a Cinematic and Emerging Technology

The success of TEC, and the embrace of VR in the entertainment industry, was at a frustrating but anticipatory standstill throughout most of 2018. There was always an event on the horizon that signaled the potential breakthrough moment. There was the premiere of *Ready Player One* (March), which the community hoped would get more people excited about VR. Then there was the release of untethered headsets like the Oculus Go (April) and the launch of the much-anticipated augmented reality headset, Magic Leap One (August). The fanfare that accompanied each of these debuts—and the hope that they would lower barriers to access and entry—quickly subsided as none were accompanied by the desired sea change. Theories of blame began circulating, criticizing the headsets as still being inferior, the content bland, and even the future depicted by *Ready Player One* lame. That a bad movie and a poor headset could both be faulted for VR's lack of success hints at the dynamic created by VR being both a cinematic and emerging technology. The fictions being told about VR's future interestingly highlighted the frictions between the different expertise that Hollywood and Silicon Valley imagined as necessary for VR's success.

FICTIONS

VR is both a technology that facilitates storytelling but also a technology about which stories are told. In *Lawnmower Man* (1992), VR was linked with a military operation that could increase intelligence, melding one's mind with the internet. In *Disclosure* (1994), VR was the MacGuffin that the protagonist's company was developing.[43] And movies like *The Matrix* (1999) and *Avatar* (2009) imagined further flung futures in which one could fully embody other worlds. These movies play with the moral complexity of VR, a technology promising liberation but delivering crises of being, or regimes of oppression and deception. In the book-turned-movie *Ready Player One* (RPO), VR is more plainly imagined as an unalloyed good for humanity, a technology of human betterment that must be maintained as such by defeating a Big Tech company wishing to overcapitalize the tech. The history

3.3 Still from *Ready Player One*. The protagonist wears a VR headset in order to enter the pristine and adventurous world of the OASIS, contrasting with the surrounding trailer in which he lives.

of RPO's production demonstrates the fluidity with which VR shapeshifts between a cinematic and emerging technology.

Written by Ernest Cline and published in 2011 (when VR was considered by many to be a bygone technology), RPO is set in 2045, where the populace has bleakly endured multiple climate, economic, and social collapses.[44] Humans voluntarily escape their scorched earth by donning full body haptic suits and VR headsets through which they log into the OASIS, a virtual world of endless possibilities. The plot centers around a ragtag group of misfits who solve a series of 1980s pop culture–themed puzzles in order to save the OASIS from corporate greed. Cline cites numerous influences for the book, including classic video games, cyberpunk texts, and movies like *Star Wars*, *Lawnmower Man*, and *The Matrix*.[45] In contrast to the totalitarian and dystopian cinematic vision of VR in 1990s cinema, Cline wanted instead to depict VR as an opt-in utopia. Unsurprisingly, this fiction of VR as a benevolent and ubiquitous platform of the future (not to mention the book's reverence for the myth of the white male tinkerer) appealed to those trying to restart interest in VR in the mid-2010s. Notably, Oculus founder Palmer Luckey gifted new employees a copy of the book (a tradition that continued after Facebook acquired Oculus[46]—a rich irony given that it is a Facebook-like company that is the villain of the story), named a conference room "The OASIS," and invited Cline to a book signing at their Irvine offices. When Oculus shipped its Touch controllers in 2016, they were accompanied by an introductory experience, *First Contact*. Riddled with references to 1980s material culture, the experience was a clear homage to RPO. Cline's story, itself influenced by an earlier wave of VR development, inspired and influenced the current resurgence.

But the entertainment–technology nexus continued to ripple, as telling stories about technology often catalyze or are enabled by technological change within the entertainment industry. RPO was optioned by Warner Bros., and Spielberg ('80s nostalgia in human form) came onboard to direct. The production required live shooting (Birmingham, England, stood in for Columbus, Ohio), performance and motion capture for the scenes taking place in the CG OASIS, and, for the denouement, a scene in which a digital avatar acted in a live action scene.[47] Warner Bros. built and integrated these multiple worlds in partnership with nearly a dozen VFX companies, including Industrial Light and Magic (ILM, founded by George Lucas) and Digital Domain (cofounded by James Cameron).

Digital Domain provided Spielberg with virtual production tools similar to the system that Technicolor was, in 2018, trying to sell. Fortuitously, by the time Spielberg began shooting in 2016, Digital Domain was able to provide the cast and crew the opportunity to see the virtual world of the OASIS through newly available commercial VR headsets[48] that the crew had on hand while filming in the motion capture volume. In VR, Spielberg could location scout within the virtual set that ILM had created and try out different camera angles, adjusting in real time potential storytelling directions that, in the absence of virtual production, are sorted out in postproduction. Cast members were also invited to put on a headset and see the virtual world in which their motion capture performance would be staged.[49] While prior movies had used similar virtual camera techniques so that directors could see the CG world on a monitor, RPO was the first to bring VR to the set and thus (it is claimed) offer a more immersive engagement with the CG world. If Hollywood provided touchstones for Cline as he wrote RPO and the book inspired Luckey and Oculus employees, here the technology was leveraged behind the scenes in order to produce a blockbuster that, it was imagined, would garner more excitement and attention for the VR industry.

RPO premiered in March 2018, and in anticipation the VR community held its collective breath. Many I spoke with hoped it would draw greater attention to the technology and were deflated when the movie did not transform their industry overnight. While modestly successful and politely received, the future offered by RPO felt tame in comparison to, say, the Afrofuturism of *Black Panther*, which had premiered a few months earlier.

For RPO, VR smoothly moved between being a cinematic technology and an emerging technology. Imagining a more distant future lessened the disagreements that Hollywood and Silicon Valley might have over VR and its immediate development, allowing both communities to enjoy creating and being inspired by a story of its success. After the movie was released, the elusiveness of industry success seemed more apparent when placed in contrast to RPO. This prompted the community to ask why: Why did RPO not do more for the industry, and why was VR not yet the ubiquitous technology the movie envisioned? Outside the confines of the dream factory's sound stage, VR's multiple identities created significant friction. This was repeatedly explained to me as a conflict between LA and Silicon Valley—a rendering of the conflict that mapped different kinds of expertise onto geographical locations. While working on a VR shoot in March, before I began my affiliation with TEC, a sound engineer described a tension she discerned between hardware development in Silicon Valley and content development in Hollywood. From the perspective of an Angeleno, up north, "they" were unwilling to invest more in hardware (i.e., better headsets) until there was better content (imagined as Hollywood's domain).[50] But creators down in Los Angeles felt that they were poised to create this better content, if only they had improved hardware. The next day, the assistant director made a similar point, with added hostility. Content producers like her were being blamed for the industry's failure to launch, even though, in the AD's estimation, it was the fault of Silicon Valley.[51]

Several times while at TEC, this topic was explored in casual conversation, further elaborating on the differences between Los Angeles and San Francisco—between Hollywood and Silicon Valley—that have impeded VR's development. In one of our early chats, Jastrow critiqued Silicon Valley for not understanding that content production is about workflows and processes. Her partners up north don't get what TEC is or what it does because they don't get entertainment production. A contractor that Jastrow had brought in to run some financial analyses once observed to me that the shallow and broad network that LA is known for (and at times ridiculed for) is necessary for the way content production works—you keep a big Rolodex so that when a project comes up, you know who to call. In Silicon Valley (where this consultant spends part of her time), the networks are deep but narrow, a configuration less suitable for producing content. And when I met an investor funding VR projects at an event at TEC who had just returned from XR on the Bay—a conference held in Silicon Valley to bring together tech and entertainment[52]—the Angeleno described a feeling of mystification at what he had observed. During a pitch contest, he described how an engineer pitched a content idea that was "weird," demonstrating that this Silicon Valley guy didn't understand how Hollywood worked.

But this is not to say that content *only* exists in LA and hardware *only* in SF. The two VFX studios that used VR on the set of RPO—ILM and Digital Domain—are telling examples of different models of distribution of labor and expertise between Hollywood and Silicon Valley. Lucas founded ILM in 1975 to do the visual effects for *Star Wars*. After the first movie, Lucas moved ILM from LA to the Bay Area where his other production facilities were located, and over the next decades, as part of going digital, transitioned from practical effects (using models and painted matte backgrounds) to computer graphics. While early employees were recruited from university computer graphics programs (the strongest ones were then on the East Coast), ILM grew alongside Silicon Valley, benefiting from an exchange of expertise between the talent in entertainment and technology. In contrast, when Cameron, Stan Winston, and Scott Ross cofounded Digital Domain in 1993 as a direct competitor to ILM, they chose to headquarter the company in LA and distinguished the company's ethos as artist (as opposed to tech) centered.[53]

Digital Domain is today located around the corner from Meta's LA offices, representing another way in which geographies and expertise are not cleanly separated. If in the 1970s and 1980s, the growth of Silicon Valley was a draw for Lucas and other Hollywood digital renegades, in the 2010s, the rise of social media and the explosion of content and content creators has made LA attractive to tech companies who have set up campuses in Venice, Santa Monica, and elsewhere around town in an effort to establish Silicon Beach. During fieldwork, I would occasionally look at the kind of jobs that Facebook, Google, Amazon, and other tech companies were hiring for their LA campuses. Rather than "full stack engineer" or "developer," I saw ads for marketing, advertising, and content producers. The people I would meet around town who worked at these companies likewise had these latter job titles. As I will explore more in the final chapter of this book, the expertise of Silicon Beach—while ostensibly being LA's tech scene—was different from the expertise that dominated Silicon Valley.

What, then, are the expertise needed to make VR succeed? That VR is both a cinematic and emerging technology means that its success most likely lies in leveraging expertise from both Hollywood and Silicon Valley. However, VR was not explicitly seen as having these multiple meanings—people assumed they were talking about the same thing, and a film like RPO that easily moved between Hollywood and Silicon Valley reinforced this idea—resulting in a blame game between SF and LA that recognized a misunderstanding but couldn't find a resolution. Moreover, at a place like TEC where VR was predominantly seen as a cinematic technology, even if Jastrow was able to create an ecosystem to support this aspect of the technology, was that enough for the industry as a whole?

Conclusion

When I interviewed Jastrow about her career and experience with VR, I asked what she thought was the difference of working on this technology in LA versus San Francisco. Jastrow paused, collecting her thoughts, before offering, "We build dreams in Hollywood . . . and we understand how content is made. In San Francisco, it's very technology driven." Her own experience with the transition to digital taught her that you need to be in close proximity to where the change is happening; you need to be hands on and learn the new workflows. That's why the future of VR is in LA, because "You need to be able to be part of where content is created. . . . Silicon Valley is about building platforms and technologies of scale. And [Los Angeles] is about fantasy and fiction and nonfiction and storytelling and interactivity and pulling those worlds all together. . . . You need to have to start from somewhere. And so it's just a natural evolution to start from the entertainment industry." This is LA's fantasy of place in that it is both acknowledged as a place that produces fantasy but also that there exists a fantasy that LA, more so than other places, can make VR successful. This is fantasy leveraged in the hopes of bringing new realities into being.

Two months after this interview, Jastrow took me to lunch as my fieldwork and residency at TEC came to a close. I had already said my goodbyes to those who let me observe and engage with their work for the past six months, and this was the final farewell. At this lunch, I found out that TEC was not going to have the Hollywood ending we were all hoping for, that the conflict and frictions had defeated Jastrow. She confided in me that Technicolor was going to close TEC in the coming months. Reflecting on the past few years, Jastrow felt she had been set up to fail—that this experiment was never meant to succeed. After all, of late Jastrow had become more animated and excited as she felt she found a viable set of partners and could envision a future for VR. Just as Hugo (the trend spotter discussed in the previous chapter) surmised, this future was focused on location-based entertainment (LBE). Folks in LA were pivoting their VR projects to elaborate site-specific "activations" as they became aware that, while the first headsets were good, they were still quite expensive. In the short term, to get people interested in VR was not going to happen at home, but in public. The ecosystem that Jastrow ended up focusing on for TEC was developing and selling VR experiences catered to museums. Jastrow felt confident that this would be a success, but Technicolor refused to give her the resources she needed to realize her vision.

Jastrow had to lay off most of the TEC staff in December 2018 and January 2019. Many found work in other parts of the immersive industry, with some going to Digital Domain, ILM, and gaming companies expanding into VR. Jastrow stayed on at Technicolor as VP of Immersive until January 2020, when she became the chief marketing officer of Evercast, a platform for remote collaboration specifically targeted at media creators. In the months before the COVID-19 pandemic, Jastrow could not have known how fortuitous it was for her to pivot away from LBEs and toward remote work.[54]

Based on the central observation in this chapter—that VR is both a cinematic and emerging technology—I have my own theories as to why TEC could not catalyze the industry and why Jastrow's experience in the transition to digital was not as portable to VR as she and her colleagues had anticipated. Namely, Jastrow exclusively understood VR as a cinematic technology and while her assessment that Silicon Valley did not understand content production might have been true, it also seems plausible that Jastrow and her Hollywood collaborators failed to understand dynamics associated with the adoption of an emerging consumer technology. This further explains the enthusiasm for LBEs in LA, which, while not cinematic technologies in the way I have described them here, puts VR back in closer association with spectacles like movie theaters and theme parks that better match the local expertise.

Hollywood remains the dominant industry in LA, and it is no surprise that it shapes the technological terroir; it shapes how technology and technological innovation are imagined and approached. My intention is not to say that technology and innovation does not exist in LA or that it is in some way less than what it is in Silicon Valley, but rather to suggest that it is something different. The ethos of tech is different, and the way an artifact like VR is approached is different. But this difference is not always visible because concepts like "technology" and "VR" are presumed to have a shared and singular meaning.

The early history of Technicolor illustrates how engineering and entertainment expertise are both needed for the success of a cinematic technology. The MIT grads who founded the company developed their color technology in labs far removed from the movie industry. In the late teens, they developed a special camera for shooting in color. In the engineers' hands, this camera was a testbed for experimenting with how color was captured in different settings; it was not a tool of storytelling. In 1921, Technicolor's lead engineers took this camera out to Hollywood for several weeks of tests and hired a local cameraman to assist. The cameraman demonstrated how filmmaking was more than pointing a camera and turning the crank—that it also involved understanding lighting and staging. Whereas the engineers were able to use the camera as a proof of concept, it was the cameraman who was able to demonstrate how it could enhance storytelling.[55]

The question in front of the VR community is how to balance these expertise not only in service of storytelling but also in service of VR as an emerging technology. Recognizing that a technology's success is predicated not only on technical problem-solving but also on the social worlds through which it emerges remains a caution for VR-adjacent technologies like generative AI and machine learning. The latter are similarly mistaken for being exclusively emerging technologies even as they are also cinematic technologies, increasingly enrolled in creating content both for the big screen as they are integrated into the VFX toolkit and on the small screens of our devices when wielded by individuals.

Jastrow and I were walking back from lunch to TEC one day, and I jokingly asked her to predict what it would take for VR to succeed.

"So then what, Marcie, is the future?" I asked.

Over my laughter she responded in jest, "I don't know, Disneyland?" And with that assessment, I could sense that we were not ambling down La Cienega Boulevard, but instead strolling through the land of the unreal, with its looming Technicolor façades of promise and folly.

PART II
FANTASY OF BEING

Among the inhabitants of the fragment of Los Angeles that, as detailed throughout part I, celebrates unrealities, virtual reality found enthusiastic support. While the entertainment potential of the medium was compelling, more so were framings that positioned VR as "an empathy machine" that could assist in overcoming societal strife and inequalities. If the fantasy of place focused attention on features of LA that invite worldbuilding and experiments with reality otherwise, part II examines the fantasies conjured by the technology itself that enabled VR's "good" potentials to be articulated and pursued. The empathy machine embraced VR's fantasy of being someone else or somewhere else, suggesting that it could provide unique insight into how race, gender, class, citizenship, and other facets of identity shape one's reality. VR could facilitate understanding across difference, repairing rifts in reality and building toward a more harmonious world. This lofty promise found comfortable purchase in Los Angeles, permeated as it is by a fantasy of place long practiced in imagining better worlds.

A fantasy of being has always been central to VR's appeal. In earlier eras, such fantasies included VR facilitating immersion in a simulated world and freeing the mind from its body. Chapter 4 excavates how a fantasy of being particular to the 2010s resurgence of VR—of being in another's world and thus being empathetic to that other person—matured through the work of journalists, filmmakers, and researchers in Los Angeles. This chapter inspects the scaffolding that supports the façade of the empathy machine and also the critique that must be levied against any technology that offers an expedient fix for the ills of humanity. Just as the façades explored in chapter 2 never promise to be anything more than fantasy, considering the empathy machine as a façade is a reminder that VR's claim of human betterment is likewise a fantasy. Chapter 5, then, describes the "special affect" that, like other cinematic special effects, makes an illusion feel real; makes the experience of being another person feel like something other than fantasy. This chapter examines the work of an LA-based start-up creating VR experiences for professional caregivers who work with aging adults. This company offers a fantasy of the empathy machine otherwise: VR leveraged for an underresourced community in support of care work.

The empathy machine imaginary was at its most potent just before and during my fieldwork. Other imaginaries—Meta's metaverse, Apple's spatial computing[1]—have since recaptured VR as a tool of work and play. Companies and individuals (including those discussed in the next two chapters) are still pursuing projects centering VR's potential to do good, but the celebration of empathy at VR events and in media coverage has died down. Despite the floundering cache of the empathy machine, I still find the concept productive to think with not only because the critiques offered throughout part II have applications for other technologies pursuing "good" outcomes, but also because the empathy machine's straightforward logic of reality repair is revealing of broader modes of reasoning about the reality crisis that, in attempts to mend fractures, often create further divides.

The empathy machine implicitly acknowledges that people experience and know the world differently; that we each occupy a different reality. VR's fantasy of being provokes an emotional reaction—which has been glossed as empathy—felt in the body as well as the mind. VR advocates surmise that this emotional charge can overcome apathy, creating a recognition of a shared humanity and thus a desire to restore a shared reality. Such a logic places individual feeling and action as the solution to societal ills, emphasizing behavior change rather than institutional and structural change. And yet, it is the weakening of institutions and the elevation of the individual that many point to when explaining the reality crisis and its close association with identity politics. It thus seems far from sufficient to presume that VR's attention to individual affect can do anything other than create a further fracturing of reality.

The transformative potential of attending to different realities has, in contexts beyond VR, similarly been both celebrated and captured by the very institutions deemed to be in need of transformation. In feminist science studies, work toward disassembling universals elevated individual experience and identity as legitimate and important ways of knowing. Standpoint epistemology and situated knowledges were strategies aimed toward more equitable (and more fine-tuned) ways of knowing and being in the world; they were proposals for objectivity otherwise.[2] And yet, as anthropologist Emily Martin observed in the 1990s, elevating the epistemological role of experience also intensified identity politics and essentialist assumptions that undermined the ways of knowing and modes of justice that these theorists imagined themselves to be pursuing.[3] While identity has drawn together and empowered individuals through shared histories of struggle, those rallying around its perverse corollary—Identitarian far-right movements—have sought to maintain their dominance by revoicing some of the ugliest racial and masculinist myths.

In today's public and political discourse, we see how the very strategies that were intended to blunt the presumed universal and singular authority of the white Anglo-European male perspective are being used to reauthorize this identity's power in society. Rhetoric initially deployed to assert bodily autonomy for nonwhite or nonmale individuals—Black Lives Matter, My Body My Choice—are modified to reassert white supremacy and patriarchy—all lives matter, or "my body my choice" as a slogan for anti-vaxxers. Whereas the left has found it at times strategic to retreat from the authority of individual experience, returning to faith in institutions by, for example, advocating for "trusting science" in order to bolster a "common reality,"[4] the right has found power in further fragmenting reality, denying that these pieces can ever be put back together into a cohesive and agreed upon whole.

If observers of the reality crisis wonder how citizens in the US came to live in such different worlds structured by alternative sets of facts, VR's fantasy of being that animates the empathy machine offers a synecdoche for examining how efforts to recommit to a common truth often strengthen the forces of division. Producers of empathy experiences be-lieve in the truth of certain injustices, imagining that these abuses persist because they are not part of everyone's reality. To suggest that a VR ex-perience is the solution reifies the power of the individual knower, which both weakens the adjudicating power of institutions as well as the civic obligation to trust the testimony of others, even and especially when an experience is unthinkable and unknowable.

Empathy experiences might aspire to do good, but at what costs?

4

BEING AND THE OTHER
DISMANTLING THE FAÇADE OF THE EMPATHY MACHINE

Nonny de la Peña has a well-articulated vision for the future of storytelling. "What if I could present you a story that you would remember with your entire body, and not just with your mind?" she asked a TEDWomen audience in May 2015 during a talk in which she recounted a career spent pioneering multimedia and immersive journalism.[1] Starting in 2010, she realized that VR was a technology through which she could most effectively tell embodied stories. As de la Peña explained to the audience, with VR, "I can put you on scene in the middle of the story." As a journalist, de la Peña tells stories about events that have already happened or are unfolding. Unlike fantastical and fictional VR experiences, in the hands of reporters and documentarians, VR promises embodied access to realities experienced by others. What impact might stories that seek to capture the complexities, inequities, and dangers of the world have when the media consumer is not just *reading* the story but *feeling* the story in their body? What about experiences in which the participant is asked to imagine being in another's body? These questions animate VR's *fantasies of being* and its promised potential.

De la Peña has used VR to tell stories about poverty, racism, climate change, the refugee crisis, and other local and global injustices. Like Iñárritu's *Carne y Arena*, described in the introduction, de la Peña places you in the scene. From this emplaced position, you are asked to bear witness to an event *as if you were there*. How does it feel, such experiences ask, to be present at the moment when a horror occurs? Other VR creators take this imaginative work a step further, asking a VR experiencer to inhabit the position—even the body—not of oneself but of the person to whom the horror is occurring. How does it feel, such experiences ask, to be the victim of an injustice? I distinguish between these different positionings, describing the former as a fantasy of being some*where* and the latter as a fantasy of being some*one*. As was the case in prior chapters, to label these experiences as fantasy is not to equate them with falsehood or fiction. Rather, in the land of the unreal, fantasies work alongside truths and facts as strategies for shaping social action. Fantasies help to imagine otherwise worlds, though like the utopian fantasies explored in chapter 1, these often fail to distribute benefits widely or evenly.

VR producers and VR researchers alike suggest that the truths contained in VR's fantasies of being elicit powerful emotional responses, jolting citizens out of their comfortable existence in order to fight for societal change. Filmmaker Chris Milk popularized this sentiment in a TED talk given in March 2015 (a few months before de la Peña's) in which he described VR as "the ultimate empathy machine."[2] VR is a machine, Milk concluded his talk, "but through this machine we become more compassionate, we become more empathetic, and we become more connected. And ultimately, we become more human." Milk is claiming that VR will make better humans who, through compassion and empathy, will be able to overcome the divergent realities that prevent knowing another and their world. This is a technological fix for humanity and for a fractured reality.[3]

The "we" in Milk's talk is clear—VR is for people of privilege to imagine being without. VR experiences variously ask a Western audience to empathize with non-Western refugees, men to empathize with women who face sexual harassment, and white Americans to empathize with Black Americans who daily encounter structural racism. This distinction between the "we" of the VR experiencer and "the other" who has agreed to share their experience is more pronounced in experiences that require embodying this other. In experiences that offer the fantasy of being someone else, there is a risk of erasing this other such that the machine to make us more human comes at the expense of another's dehumanization.

This chapter follows how projects that desire to be in service of liberal politics can, as observed in the introduction to part II, also inadvertently create the conditions for their undoing. This is particularly evident in how the body figures into conversations about VR and empathy. The body, it will be seen, is central both to earlier cyberfeminist critiques of the virtual and to promises about VR's unique affordances. However, in suggesting that VR provides access to others' embodied experiences, it devalues the very bodies (and their situated knowledges) that are the subjects of empathy experiences. The logic of the empathy machine preserves the power of embodied experience but, in claiming that VR's power lies in its engagement with the body, it simultaneously commodifies and purports to make available the otherwise inaccessible experience of being someone else. There is thus a sharp edge between the intersectional politics of embodied knowledges and their co-optation.

The critiques to be made about VR's empathic claims are significant, and this chapter will build upon this abundant literature. Assumptions about who gets to be a knower and who is rendered as knowable cleave along familiar racial divisions. In addition, this chapter also explains how empathy came to dominate the discourse (highlighting the significant role played by Angelenos) and underscores the social work performed by this vision. Drawing on the concept of façade developed in chapter 2, I frame "VR as empathy machine" as a façade that invites the participant to imagine a world of human betterment that can never be fully entered. Throughout this chapter, I attend to the scaffolding that simultaneously props up and is concealed by this façade.

As already described, façades enliven Los Angeles's cityscape and breathe magic into movie sets and theme parks. Façades enable fantasies of being elsewhere, but precisely because they are so obviously out of place—a Chinatown in an American city or a place of fiction like Hogwarts made architecturally real—these façades don't promise anything other than fantasy. To describe VR as a façade is a helpful reminder that VR experiences, even those based on actual events, remain fantasies. This is not to say that such experiences can't be meaningful or impactful, but that being somewhere or someone else in VR is a different kind of experience than actual being. The façade of the empathy machine obfuscates this distinction such that people, upon removing a headset, claim to now know what it's like to be an other. If architectural façades playfully invite imaginations of being otherwise, empathy experiences extend the same invitation but with a tone of sincerity that masks the fantasy.

I begin this chapter by returning to the history of VR that I started telling in chapter 1. Here, my intention is to distinguish the fantasies of being that enable today's empathy machine from previous imaginations of VR's promise and potential. I then elaborate on the career of Nonny de la Peña, who was a crucial catalyst for the resurgence of VR—both infrastructurally and conceptually. If these two sections describe the scaffolding that undergirds the empathy machine façade, the final section explores the social work of this façade: so compelling is this desire for a technology to be good that it conceals from the community its potential racial harms.

VR's Fantasies of Being

Fantasies of being have always been central to VR. In its earliest technical imagining, VR offered a fantasy of being in a simulated world. This is a cybernetic fantasy, fittingly first articulated by Ivan Sutherland, a student of Claude Shannon, who received his PhD from MIT in 1963. In a 1,200-word essay titled "The Ultimate Display," first published in an information processing journal in 1965, Sutherland imagines the future of computer interfaces, concluding with what he considers would be the ultimate display (and what many have since referenced as a description of virtual reality). The ultimate display is a "looking glass into a mathematical wonderland," an opportunity to explore "concepts not realizable in the physical world" but only in the computational world. Sutherland first describes the displays and interfaces that engineers are working toward, well predicting that computers will soon be able to display graphics, that "typewriters" will be the standard interface, and a "light pen" will enable one to drag objects around. But Sutherland is caught in the romance of a wonderland, and thus presents a different direction that computing could take: one centered around what he calls a kinesthetic display (or, what we might today call an immersive display) that could work in conjunction with sound and smell interfaces. He imagines a display in which one's body both directs and responds to the computer. Being embodied in a simulated world would, in turn, provide the user with an ability to know that which was otherwise unknowable: "By working with such displays of mathematical phenomena we can learn to know them as well as we know our own natural world."

The ultimate display is a fantasy of being completely embodied in the simulated world: "A chair displayed in such a room would be good enough to sit in. Handcuffs displayed in such a room would be confining, and a bullet displayed in such a room would be fatal."[4] In pursuit of this ultimate display, Sutherland and colleagues built the first head-mounted display (HMD) a few years later while he was at Harvard. The hardware then required

4.1 At a permanent VR entertainment center in the Century City Mall, a mini-museum of VR's history includes this photography display of VR headsets from the past. In the center is Sutherland's Sword of Damocles and, to its right, Fisher's NASA VIEW. Photograph taken in April 2022 by the author.

to place one in a simulation was so cumbersome and the display so heavy, that they called their contraption the Sword of Damocles as it had to be suspended from the ceiling to counterbalance its heft. Wearing the Sword of Damocles, one could see a 3-D rendered wireframe room and, moving one's head, see the different walls (marked with the cardinal directions to distinguish one wall from another). Following this project, Sutherland sensed that achieving the ultimate display was a ways off and moved on to other research areas. The Sword of Damocles was an appropriately mythic proof of concept that never fully receded from engineers' imaginations and inspired subsequent decades of work to build a system that could bring one more fully (and comfortably) inside a simulation.

In the 1980s and 1990s, more HMDs were built and tracked gloves provided rudimentary interfaces for interacting with and exploring low-resolution virtual worlds. Despite the continued focus on embodiment and feeling present in VR, fantasies of being during this period morphed into the fantasy of a freed mind achieving its potential. This is a consequence of VR becoming entangled with a broader set of ideas and innovations such that *virtual reality* as a signifier of an immersive, HMD-enabled experience gave way to an imaginary of *virtual realities*, which included VR experiences, but also activities as diverse as sending an email, logging onto a bulletin board service, or roleplaying in a virtual world. Particularly in the '80s and early '90s, "virtual reality," "virtuality," and "cyberspace" became interchangeable concepts.[5] This interwoven set of experiences and terminology impacted VR's conceptual and material development, as well as its attending fantasies of being.

In particular, the cyberpunk of William Gibson,[6] an aesthetic and philosophical orientation realized in the Wachowskis' *Matrix* films, offered a fantasy of being premised on a severed connection between mind and body.[7] Allucquére Rosanne (Sandy) Stone, drawing on ethnographic work with 1980s VR engineers as well as more casual denizens of early online worlds, articulates the significance of Gibson's *Neuromancer*, in which "cyberspace" was envisioned, noting how "it triggered a conceptual revolution among the scattered workers who had been doing virtual reality research for years. . . . Gibson's novel and the technological and social imaginary that it articulated enabled the researchers in virtual reality—or, under the new dispensation, cyberspace—to recognize and organize themselves as a community."[8] Gibson contrasted cyberspace with the disdainful "meatspace" inhabited by our physical bodies. In this imaginary, one didn't put on a headset, but rather "jacked in" to cyberspace, bypassing the body so that the mind could be unburdened of fleshy limitations. "Free your mind," Morpheus instructs Neo in *The Matrix* before impossibly leaping between skyscrapers. In these fictional cyberspaces, a bullet could still kill you (there remained a link between mind and body), but the body was otherwise inconsequential.

VR evangelists of the 1990s hyped this disconnection between mind and body. "Suddenly I don't have a body anymore," begins John Perry Barlow's essay "Being in Nothingness" (following a quote from *Neuromancer*) published in the cyberenthusiast periodical *Mondo 2000*. Barlow makes this claim even though the opening passage is a very physical and embodied description of his learning how to use a DataGlove made by VPL Research to grip a virtual object.[9] In hyperbolically denying his body, Barlow aligns his VR experience with the fantastical Gibsonian vision of being a mind in a world of information. This aspiration for disembodiment traveled between the various virtualities of the time, shoring up this fantasy and making it all the more potent for VR. This was the popular understanding of (and advertising for) the internet in the 1990s. "On the internet, nobody knows you're a dog," reads the 1993 *New Yorker* cartoon depicting a dog sitting at a PC, explaining to a puppy pal that his online persona is disconnected from his canine body. On the internet, there is no race or gender or age, "only minds," proclaims a 1997 commercial for the telecommunication company MCI.[10]

This fantasy of the freed mind floated back from science fiction and popular imaginaries and embedded in late twentieth-century theories of the virtual. In this context, the freed mind was a worry stone for cyber theorists; even when the fantasy was accepted, it was not assumed to be an unalloyed good. For example, Michael Heim's influential 1993 book, *The Metaphysics of Virtual Reality* (which is about cyberspace more generally), describes how cyberworlds "pull the user away from the internal bioenergies that run our primary body. The interface belongs to minds that love to represent."[11] Precisely because humans are embodied creatures, Heim does not see this as automatically liberating but potentially, riffing off of Gibson, "an infinite cage." As he writes later in the book, "We are more equal on the net because we can either ignore or create the body that appears in cyberspace. But in another sense, the quality of the human encounter narrows."[12] Artist and theorist Simon Penny similarly sees VR (and in this essay he *is* writing about VR specifically, not cyberspace in general) as impoverished. The virtual body is merely a body image that is lacking in the sensorially rich experiences that come with embodiment. "Virtual reality leaves the meat body on the chair. It is a confirmation of, rather than a liberation from, Cartesian dualism. Virtual reality is thus about dislocation and disassociation. . . . One does not take one's body into virtual reality, one leaves it at the door."[13] Media studies scholar Anne Balsamo likewise affirms the "*conceptual* denial of the body" that renders it "excess baggage." Balsamo goes on to argue that this presumed disembodiment obfuscates the (male) bodily desires and assumptions that in fact structure virtual worlds. Thus the (white, able-bodied) male experience becomes the naturalized and default experience of VR.[14]

Balsamo, like other feminist theorists at the time, sought to trace the power structures that enabled such fantasies of disembodiment. Still others pushed further, questioning this very claim of the freed mind and seeking a material regrounding for understanding virtual reality. N. Katherine Hayles's genealogical tracing of virtual realities back to cybernetics allows her to dispel the illusion that had allowed "virtuality to displace materiality" by reconnecting the "virtual world of information" to the human sensorium and showing how, in fact, virtuality "has its basis in the very materiality it would deny."[15] Stone similarly seeks to understand the origin of this illusion. She acknowledges the identity experimentation that occurs in cyberspace that might suggest a disconnection between mind and body. But Stone also grounds this disembodiment in a particular male fantasy borne of Silicon Valley, *Neuromancer*-reading engineers.[16] Thus, Stone cautions the reader not to mistake the fantasy for the reality: "No matter how virtual the subject may become, there is always a body attached."[17]

Feminist scholars working to recenter the body in analyses of the virtual had difficulty making their arguments stick precisely because of the diversity of experiences that virtual realities came to stand for in the 1990s and early 2000s.[18] With the deflation of the commercial VR market, most people's experience of the virtual came through the desktop computer. Ever more graphically rich virtual worlds proliferated, as did the growth of email, the World Wide Web, and attending internet applications. People dialed into cyberspace, primarily navigating it (as Sutherland anticipated) with keyboard and mouse. While this was no doubt a tactile experience, it was not embodied, allowing technologists to continue promising a race-less, genderless, and thus bodiless virtuality.

Crucially, however, when VR reemerged in the 2010s, it could do so with a focus on headset-facilitated experiences and without being conflated with the dated concept of "cyberspace."[19] In a world of digital natives, the experience of VR is easily distinguishable from the experience of the internet. This era of VR is marked by an engaged body, be it through a swiveling of the head or moving one's self fully through the world. With high-fidelity graphics and body position tracking, the first people who tried prototypes of what would become the Oculus Rift VR headset in the early 2010s did not have to overhype the technology—it was an experience (however mediated) of being elsewhere. The fantasy of the mind freed from the passive body of the previous decades could be replaced by the fantasies of being fully embodied and engaged. In contrast to *The Matrix*, in the 2018 movie *Ready Player One* the characters suit up rather than jack in. Through headsets, haptic suits, and stationary treadmills, the protagonists' avatars move in sync with their physical bodies, in contrast to the suspended animation of the protagonists' physical bodies in *The Matrix*. The body was no longer something to be discarded or transcended, but necessary for virtual being. Significantly, the virtual world was depicted as a place of emotional growth in *Ready Player One*, and this growth (in the form of budding romances and friendships) could be fully realized in the actual world. This imagination by which embodiment catalyzes emotional change is the logic that underpins claims that VR can make a better human. Recall the prompt from Nonny de la Peña's TED talk: "What if I could present you a story that you would remember with your entire body, and not just with your mind?" The body is figured as a gateway toward feeling present in a VR experience which in turn fosters personal growth and awareness. Thus, Sutherland's "ultimate display" had morphed into "the ultimate empathy machine."

The fantasies of being somewhere and being someone else, as this brief history has shown, are not the only fantasies that could accompany VR nor are they in any way naturally emergent from the technology. The work done by the VR community to build these fantasies is the scaffolding that the façade of the empathy machine comes to conceal. The next section follows the career of de la Peña, through which we see the construction of this scaffolding more clearly. De la Peña brought research findings about immersion and presence out of the laboratory, wove in the language of empathy, and presented this fantasy to her fellow storytellers in Hollywood.

Bringing VR Out of the Laboratory

Given the different fantasies of being that characterize last century's VR versus the present moment, I find thinking with Nonny de la Peña's ideas about the virtual instructive because she spans temporal and institutional divides. She has spoken about having been interested in VR ever since reading journalist Howard Rheingold's breathless account of the technology in the 1990s, an account that leans into the bodily transcendent cyberpunk of it all.[20] And while de la Peña is primarily a journalist and storyteller, she has also spent time in academic labs to develop her own theory of the virtual that undergirds her work, earning a PhD from the University of Southern California's School of Cinematic Arts in 2019 after a decade of affiliation and collaboration. In 2021, she was appointed as the founding director of Arizona State University's Narrative and Emerging Media program, headquartered in LA. De la Peña is well known in the VR community, was acknowledged by Iñárritu as being "the real VR pioneer" when he received a special Oscar for *Carne y Arena*,[21] has received substantial press coverage and, in 2022, was honored with a legacy Peabody Award when the institution created a Digital and Interactive Storytelling category. Despite these accolades, she is not one of the big financial winners of this moment of VR (she has spoken publicly about discrimination she faced as a woman when fundraising for her VR production studio), and her formative role in the development of both technology and storytelling technique was, until recently, understated. While she is called honorifically "the godmother of

VR," this suggests a supervisory role instead of that of an innovator.[22] In placing de la Peña's Los Angeles–based career at the center of my telling of VR's recent history, I emphasize her importance in laying the groundwork for both the infrastructure of today's VR as well as translating laboratory research into language more readily accessible by her nonacademic peers. In the same way that the façade of the empathy machine conceals the work that goes into constructing fantasies of being, "the empathy machine" as a charismatic phrase coined by and most associated with Chris Milk has also concealed de la Peña's role in bringing the idea of empathy out of the academic laboratory and into the field of Hollywood storytelling.

THE DUALITY OF PRESENCE

De la Peña grew up in a Mexican American household in Los Angeles, attended Harvard as an undergrad, and upon graduating began her career as a print journalist in the 1980s. Throughout the 1980s and 1990s, her media portfolio expanded to include photography, documentary film, and television. After 9/11, she began investigating the ramifications of the PATRIOT Act, including the detention and abuses at Guantánamo Bay. These military prisons proved a challenge for reporters. How could one provide what war journalist Martha Gellhorn described as "a view from the ground" when reporters themselves were denied entry? De la Peña often quotes this phrase by Gellhorn as what motivated her to develop an "immersive journalism" that strives to offer "first-person experiences of the events or situation described in news stories."[23] De la Peña's reporting on Guantánamo Bay led to her first attempt at immersive journalism. *Gone Gitmo* was a 2007 collaboration with LA-based digital media artist and scholar Peggy Weil in which they re-created (based on interviews with former prisoners and scant available photographs) the holding cells of the prison in the virtual world *Second Life*. Residents of *Second Life* could be transported to the prison—an impossibility in the physical world—and explore via their avatar the space and associated stories. Storytelling through a desktop computer in *Second Life* was a step toward immersive journalism, but didn't quite achieve, in de la Peña's assessment, that view from the ground. However, the VR that she read about in Rheingold's book promised greater immersion. If she wanted to experiment with the commercially dormant technology, she needed to find an academic lab that would let her work with their expensive setup. Fortunately, Mel Slater, a leading VR researcher in Barcelona, invited de la Peña to collaborate.

When de la Peña began working with Slater, he and his lab, codirected by Maria Sanchez-Vives, had for over a decade been studying, from a psychological and neurological perspective, the interconnections between virtual reality, embodiment, and the feeling of presence.[24] Their research seeks to understand the conditions under which a participant might—as de la Peña desired—feel present in a virtual world. And further, researchers were investigating why and how this feeling of presence might cause participants to react—both physically and mentally—to a virtual circumstance "as if they were really there." Slater argues that an impactful VR experience is one in which the participant has a sensation of "being there" where the scene is unfolding (what he calls the place illusion [PI]) combined with an illusion that they are somehow involved in the virtual scene (the plausibility illusion [Psi]). The former is achieved when head and body movements are tracked and the virtual environment responds as one would expect (when I turn my head, I see a different part of the scene). The plausibility illusion occurs when the virtual environment or its inhabitant in some way responds to the presence of the participant. "If you are there (PI) and what appears to be happening is really happening (Psi), *then it is happening to you!* Hence you are likely to respond as if it were real."[25]

Recall in the introduction to this book my recounting of Iñárritu's *Carne y Arena* and how the most impactful moment occurred at the end, when I was no longer an invisible witness but "seen" by the border agent who pointed his gun at me and demanded that I get on my knees. This plausibility illusion, combined with the place illusion of being able to move through the virtual scene, elicited a feeling of presence and even an emotional reaction of feeling uneasy and perhaps even threatened. I found this unusual and unexpected experience to be powerful.

In calling the conditions for these feelings and reactions "illusions," Slater signals that feeling present in a virtual world is not a delusion; participants do not forget their physical location. De la Peña has elaborated on the power of simultaneously being present in the virtual world and knowing your body remains in the actual world, calling this phenomenon a "duality of presence." As she writes in her dissertation, "Rather than imagining they have been transported to a virtual space, completely disconnected from their real body, instead viewers experience something more akin to a split in consciousness. They feel as if they can be in two places at once."[26] The illusion of being elsewhere is not the fantasy of a freed mind. Rather, in de la Peña's duality of presence, the body anchors consciousness in the physical world even as it extends into the virtual world.[27]

VR is curious and compelling precisely because one is aware that the fantasy of being elsewhere occurs while also being embodied in physical space. A VR experience has meaning—whether it's some generic coolness or an emotionally impactful story—precisely because the user knows they are not *actually* there. Anthropologist Tom Boellstorff flags this Deleuzean meaning of "the virtual" as its most significant: "'virtual' connotes approaching the actual *without arriving there*. This gap between virtual and actual is critical."[28] In Boellstorff's writing about virtual worlds, this gap is signified by "online" and "offline," but for immersive VR, this gap is de la Peña's duality of presence.

FROM LABORATORY TO FESTIVAL

After initial experiments with Slater's lab,[29] de la Peña continued to refine her practice back in Los Angeles. There, de la Peña found herself collaborating with the people she had read about in Rheingold's book that had kickstarted her journey more than a decade ago. Joining first as a research fellow in the journalism school at USC and eventually migrating over to the School of Cinematic Arts (from which she ultimately received her PhD), de la Peña began working in Mark Bolas's Mixed Reality lab. Bolas is mentioned briefly in Rheingold's book when he's describing "homebrew VR" projects. Bolas was a master's student at Stanford in the late 1980s and had approached researchers at NASA Ames Research Center to see if he could use their VR system for his research. Scott Fisher and his team had recently built the first immersive VR system with feedback between tracked head, hand movement, and the virtual environment (see chapter 1). Fisher served as an advisor for Bolas's degree and continued to collaborate with Bolas and his cofounded company Fakespace. Fisher, who had moved to USC, recruited Bolas to join him and together they brought the story and history of VR from Silicon Valley to the not-yet-christened Silicon Beach.[30]

By the time de la Peña arrived at USC in the early 2010s with her idea for immersive journalism, Bolas, Fisher, and other collaborators had developed and were using the Wide5 VR system, which cost a hefty $50K.[31] She began working with this device as an intern in Bolas's lab, learning how to combine 3-D computer graphics with audio collected in the field to bring a viewer into a journalistic story. In her first VR piece, titled *Hunger in LA*, de la Peña used audio recorded in line at a food bank when a man fell to the ground and entered a diabetic coma. This audio played over a digital recreation of the scene (in what, even at the time, was not particularly

4.2 The unofficial motto of USC's School of Cinematic Arts, from which de la Peña earned her PhD, is "Reality ends here." During the construction of SCA's new campus, this was translated into the Latin, "Limes Regiones Rerum," and adorns an archway that leads into the central courtyard. The campus itself was made possible by a donation in 2006 from alumnus George Lucas. The motto is a fitting guide for cinema in general and VR more specifically. Photograph taken in April 2022 by the author.

high-fidelity CG). A viewer of this experience is transported to this virtual-ized event through the VR headset and can move freely through the scene; they can crouch down and be next to the man or retreat into the crowd. The viewer cannot interact with characters or intervene in the action, but is in-stead an unseen virtual witness. The final message of the piece is that one in six adults and one in five children in the US are hungry and this need is overwhelming the food banks.

Significantly, *Hunger in LA* was shown at the New Frontier exhibition at the Sundance Film Festival in 2012. Shari Frilot began curating New Frontier in 2007, creating an experimental space to showcase media in-stallations that reengaged with cinema as an embodied and participatory experience. Before joining Sundance, Frilot worked in the queer and exper-imental film festival circuit, wishing to correct for her own marginalized experience as a Black lesbian filmmaker in order to better showcase work by those with intersectional identities. Frilot's curatorial work exploded expectations and formalisms, torqueing given definitions of identity cate-gories and challenging norms of engaging with cinema and art. Interested in work that resisted queer cinema's capture by the glossy mainstream, Frilot increasingly curated works that were multimedia and experimented with new cinematic and computing technologies. Expanding from these foundations, Frilot features work at New Frontier that characterizes what she calls a "'physical cinema,' a framing of the cinematic that calls upon the body to dynamically participate in the process of making meaning from the work."[32] Frilot had been following de la Peña's work since *Gone Gitmo* and, when de la Peña invited her to come see *Hunger in LA* at USC, it became Frilot's first VR experience. She, like many others, was emotionally over-whelmed by the experience of feeling present at the line outside the food bank. As effectively as any piece she had curated for New Frontier, VR en-gaged her body in order to tell an impactful story. Frilot invited de la Peña to show *Hunger* as the first VR piece at Sundance—or any film festival—and it has since become the premier festival for showcasing VR.

To bring VR out of the laboratory and to the festival—and to an en-tirely new audience focused on innovations in storytelling rather than optics—de la Peña had to work with Bolas and his lab to build a more por-table headset, as Bolas wasn't about to lend out the expensive Wide5 sys-tem. Another lab intern, who wasn't yet twenty when *Hunger* premiered at Sundance, had an intense interest in head-mounted displays and hacked together sufficient hardware, while Bolas and other lab members worked on the software and integration. Several months after Sundance, the intern, Palmer Luckey (himself a native Southern Californian) founded Oculus VR and Kickstarted the Rift, an HMD design based on the hardware hack he developed for de la Peña.[33] In March 2014, Facebook acquired Oculus for a few billion dollars, thus catalyzing the VR hype cycle in which my research has taken place.[34]

But in 2012, Luckey was the intern who slept on de la Peña's hotel floor in Park City and was just one member of the team that made *Hunger in LA* the success that it was, and made VR a thing of interest to the Hollywood crowd. In an interview conducted at Sundance in 2012 and published in *Fast Company*, de la Peña reflected on the overall reaction—people crying,[35] asking how they can learn more, showing concern for the man with diabetes. "That was my goal. Take a story about people who are hungry, who I felt were invisible, and make them visible in a way that was so compelling that people would really get what the fuck was going on out there. So that works. And it works in a way that has blown my mind."[36] While it might be tempting to write about VR's presence at New Frontier as a paradigm shift—and certainly it significantly increased the media attention directed at this segment of Sundance—the kind of emotional impact that *Hunger* seemed to have on its audience was the anticipated result of Frilot's physical cinema. As she described before ever having experienced VR, physical cinema moves the viewer in a different kind of way than traditional cinema. "Your body is moving within the context of the work, completing the story with the information that the body has. The body's movement is consummating the work, and calls the body to react in different ways." Roya Rastegar, writing about Frilot's curatorial practice and noting her tendency to showcase social justice–oriented pieces, summarizes, "By calling on our bodies to be part of the cinematic experience, we actively generate meaning through our interactions with the screen. In other words, curating physical cinema requires the audience to *move in order to be moved*."[37] The immersive journalism that de la Peña was producing fit seamlessly into the theoretical framework that Frilot had been cultivating and curating; this was a superposition of idea and execution that propagated with force in Hollywood and beyond.

Rheingold's history of VR in the 1980s and 1990s centers the work of white male innovators and in the contemporary moment, white male spokespeople like Palmer Luckey or Chris Milk were well cast to star in the sequel of this story. And while one can insist on telling VR's recent history through the familiar beats of white male tinkerers and Silicon Valley investors, this misses the role played by women of color and the entertainment industry. Through this focus, a different set of stories come to light. Frilot's curatorial practice has long sought to subvert given categories, and in bringing VR to Sundance she brought something often coded as an *emerging* technology into an explicitly *cinematic* space (see chapter 3). The emphasis that both Frilot and de la Peña placed on storytelling and the body additionally made VR legible as a site for feminist praxis, as will be further explored in part III. And significant to bolstering this aspect of VR was its association with empathy, allowing the community in LA to imagine VR as a "new" and transformative industry whose success would be found through featuring diverse voices.

THE EMERGENCE OF EMPATHY

Following the 2012 Sundance Film Festival, visitors would come visit de la Peña at USC to see *Hunger in LA* and chat with her about VR and its potential. In this space, rather than extolling VR's commercial potential as a gaming platform or revisiting the prior century's consensual hallucination of cyberspace, the focus was on VR as a compelling and affective storytelling vehicle. *Empathy* emerged as the term that circulated most widely from these discussions, distinguishing the VR of the 2010s from the VR of the previous decades. Empathy has a variety of psychological and colloquial meanings, usually suggesting a projective, emotional experience. Despite sounding like an "old" word, *empathy* was introduced to the English language in the early twentieth century by experimental psychologist Edward Titchener as a translation of the German term *einfühlung*, which literally means "feeling oneself into."[38] In the context of VR, there are two kinds of "feeling into," or projection, that get conflated with one another but have distinct implications to any critical engagement with VR as empathy machine. These different tacit meanings of empathy map onto the two fantasies of being already introduced. Empathy could indicate the experience of projecting one's self into the virtual world, resulting in a fantasy of being elsewhere that is nonetheless felt in one's physical body. Alternatively, it could indicate the experience of projecting one's self into another's virtual body, resulting in a more literal embodied fantasy of being someone else. When empathy is used to describe VR, these distinct experiences are often collapsed and confused.

I've already discussed some of the VR research, particularly coming out of Slater's lab as well as de la Peña's duality of presence, that aligns with the first meaning of empathy. However, the second meaning is premised not only on the ability to be present in a virtual world, but to feel embodied in a virtual avatar. The fungibility of the bounds of our body has long fascinated researchers in psychology. Famously, the "rubber hand illusion" suggested that participants could come to feel a sense of body ownership over an artificial hand that was removed in space from their physical hand.[39] Slater and other researchers investigated the circumstances under which one could feel ownership over a virtual body.[40] In these experiments, the focus was on achieving the illusion of ownership, and not the significance of the identity of the virtual body nor the impact of ownership.[41] Subsequent researchers, however, were able to build on the ownership studies and turn to these latter issues. Significantly, Jeremy Bailenson at Stanford began studying the effects of different virtual embodiments on behavior—if you were embodied as a taller avatar, would you negotiate more aggressively?[42] Could embodying another age, race, or gender change your assumptions about others? In Bailenson's early publications, he used the language of *perspective-taking* rather than empathy, even though an early article title, "Walk a Mile in Digital Shoes," implied empathy's colloquial definition.[43] Bailenson's lab studied a diverse set of behavioral and learning implications that stemmed from VR. In 2014, the lab ramped up their perspective-taking research and began using the language of empathy.[44]

As this research matured, de la Peña continued to produce VR pieces on a wide range of topics (domestic violence, police brutality, the refugee crisis), researching and recreating scenes of conflict in CG, often with audio recordings from the event. As with *Hunger*, the potential impact of the pieces came not from embodying an avatar, but rather from projecting oneself into the story as a witness. Like Frilot's physical cinema, these were stories to be felt in the body as well as the mind. De la Peña explained this to podcaster Kent Bye in an interview at the first Silicon Valley VR (SVVR) Conference and Expo in May 2014. De la Peña was one of the few women in attendance and the only woman invited to speak (Palmer Luckey was one of the widely advertised panelists).[45] Bye was launching what would become the popular and prolific *Voices of VR* podcast, a rich archive of interviews that continues today. In the interview, de la Peña gives a description of her work to date, emphasizing the nearly indescribable feeling that comes with being elsewhere. After she tells Bye about the intense audience reactions to her VR pieces at a recent festival and how this is illustrative of the power of the medium, he introduces the language of empathy to the conversation,[46] asking why empathy is stronger in VR. De la Peña responds, "It may be that once you feel like you're there, that the experience is felt through your whole body rather than just seen through your ocular system . . . you seem to *feel* the story as much as to think it."[47] This is empathy derived from the experience of feeling oneself into the world; the fantasy of being elsewhere.

And yet, in packaging this feeling of being elsewhere as empathy, it became easily conflated with feeling oneself into another's body, the fantasy of being someone else. We see this slippage in an interview for the same podcast (also recorded at svvr) with usc undergrad (and cofounder of the popular vrla Meetup, modeled after svvr) Cosmo Scharf. When Bye asks if Scharf is familiar with de la Peña's work (both were affiliated with usc), Scharf volunteers that he's fascinated with how she is using "vr as a tool for generating empathy." He remarks on the power of place, that "when you are in vr you're not watching something. You're in it." But then Scharf invokes the classic metaphor of empathy: "When you can be placed virtually in someone else's shoes and you can look around as if you are someone else regardless of who that is, you feel what they are going to feel."[48]

By the following year, the nuance with which de la Peña described vr's affective potential (emphasizing being somewhere else rather than being someone else) was erased by Chris Milk's grand claim that vr was an empathy machine. As mentioned at the start of the chapter, both de la Peña and Milk gave TED talks in 2015. Milk, one of the many people who began to work with vr after visiting de la Peña at usc in order to see *Hunger* (at the urging of Frilot),[49] was featured on the TED mainstage in March and de la Peña at TEDWomen in May. De la Peña used her talk to situate vr as the future of journalism, finally achieving her vision of placing someone at the scene of a story. She described for the audience the significance of the duality of presence and explained how this projective experience allowed her "to tap into these feelings of empathy." Creators must be cautious, she warned, and follow best journalistic practices to ensure these stories have integrity.

In contrast to de la Peña's measured discussion about empathy and vr's role in the *future of journalism*, Milk situated vr as the *future of humanity*. Milk's debut vr work was not cg but rather what is called 360° video (shot with specially fashioned digital cameras that capture a sphere of action). As a live-action documentary, the viewer experiences the fantasy of being somewhere as the action unfolds around them, able to move their head to observe different parts of the environment even as their body remains fixed in place. Milk directed the piece such that the viewer is often directly addressed by the subjects of the documentary. Milk explained in his talk that vr provides the experience of being in another world—of being with the people of this other world—which allowed one to feel their "humanity in a deeper way." This connection between humans—a connection that Milk claimed VR could achieve but traditional film could not—led Milk to conclude his TED talk by provocatively describing VR as the ultimate empathy machine through which "we become more human."[50]

I provide these different touchstones—psychology research, podcast interviews, TED talks—not to argue *who* first linked VR and empathy but rather to illustrate *how* by the end of 2015 this zeitgeist had permeated the community, popular discourse, and much of the early critical academic reactions to today's VR.[51] VR as empathy machine became the most visible (and enticing) façade. This façade is scaffolded by the work of researchers and storytellers. Importantly, de la Peña transformed VR from a laboratory tool for studying presence to a storytelling tool for eliciting emotion through an embodied experience of being at the scene of an event. The empathy machine conceals this work, but also projects a grander fantasy of human betterment that collapses the different kinds of projective experiences and fantasies of being that have been and are being created.

Humanity and Its Others

By the time I arrived in LA in 2018, the VR community had empathy machine fatigue. In public presentations, it was sometimes brought up to dazzle or intrigue an audience, but the limits of empathy were also probed. What good is empathy, asked one VR producer on a film festival panel, if it doesn't translate into action? What good is empathy, asked a CEO on a start-up panel, if it doesn't help raise venture capital (VC) money? In private conversations, interlocutors would dismiss empathy as a gimmick. Multiple people confided in me that those who are the most vocal about VR's empathic powers when communicating to the public are also the most critical behind closed doors.[52]

The community critique of empathy that I observed centered on the overuse or imprecision of the word; it was not skepticism about the greater good inherent in VR. The community thus seemed agnostic to the disproportionate amount of empathy experiences that reinforced racial othering, a concern that was glaringly apparent to many outsiders.[53] Perhaps because the VR community was invested in telling a positive story about its diverse workforce (see part III), this allowed assumptions about the identity of VR users to remain unexamined. But implicit in these experiences is an imagination of *who* needs empathy. White people need to have more empathy for those who look different from them, Americans need it for those far away, men for women, the rich for the poor. In other words, because empathy is presumed to be lacking by those with societal power and because these experiences are made for those lacking empathy, the presumed viewer is exactly the audience to whom media and new technologies have often catered.

What, then, of the unintended audience? Journalist Priscilla Ward, upon seeing de la Peña's *One Dark Night*, about the killing of Trayvon Martin, at the Tribeca Film Festival in 2015, describes the potentially traumatizing effect the piece could have on Black viewers: "New technology may work to agitate empathy in white people, but at the same time, it can pick at Black America's wounds, wounds that haven't yet healed."[54] Media studies scholar Lisa Nakamura quotes from Ward's article in her critique of VR empathy experiences. Nakamura draws attention to the epistemological and labor asymmetries in these experiences. "[T]he idea [is] that you cannot trust marginalized people when they speak their own truth or describe their own suffering, but you have to experience it for yourself through digital representation, to know that it is true."[55] And it is also these marginalized people who provide the narration or found audio on which these experiences are built. "The empathy of racially marginalized women is figured as an emotional resource for white viewers . . . [enabling] a fantasy of virtuous empathy on the part of the viewer."[56] Nakamura is primarily drawing from examples of VR experiences like de la Peña's where one is a witness, fantasies of being somewhere else rather than someone else.[57] But she can see experiences on the horizon where the participant is asked to take on someone else's body, predicting the damage that might accompany a white person occupying the body of "an other who might not even own their own body."[58] Media theorist Grant Bollmer similarly elaborates on the destructive capacity of "absorbing another's body and experience into one's own." He concludes that empathy "denies the existence of the Other; empathy only acknowledges the Other insofar as it can be assimilated into the same."[59]

At stake in these critiques is the question of whose humanity matters and perhaps even who gets to be human. This is the question that has been doggedly attached to the very concept of "race" as it has been weaponized time and again in order to elevate certain ways of being and knowing—certain realities—over others. Historically, a denial of reality—a denial of being fully human—was accompanied by a denial of interiority and subjectivity that justified slavery, genocide, and even the first decades of anthropological research by which non-Western subjects were transformed by Western scientists into objects of study. The storytellers producing empathy experiences would unequivocally denounce assumptions of racial inferiority or superiority. And yet, these experiences are premised on this very denial of interiority. Fantasies of being someone else assume that being in the embodied position of another is the same as being another. This assumes that exteriority—what is happening in the scene—drives experience. The interiority of being Black (and the lifetime that informs what this means) is rendered less significant.

By deconstructing the façade of the empathy machine, we see that the fantasy of human betterment conceals the simultaneous work of dehumanization. VR might be a machine that makes "us" more human, but only by making "them" less so. Significantly, while VR creators might claim that VR affords a copresence with those for whom we are meant to feel empathy, this is an experience performed in the absence of another human. W. E. B. Du Bois, writing about segregation, described the difficulty of seeing another's humanity when interaction is prohibited: "In a world where it means so much to take a man by the hand and sit beside him, to look frankly into his eyes and feel his heart beating with red blood; in a world where a social cigar or a cup of tea together means more than legislative halls and magazine articles and speeches—one can imagine the consequences of the almost utter absence of such social amenities between estranged races, whose separation extends even to parks and streetcars."[60] In Milk's TED talk, when he is describing the impact of his VR experience about a young female refugee, he explains that you are not watching a film but instead "you're sitting there with her. When you look down, you're sitting on the same ground that she's sitting on. And because of that, you feel her humanity in a deeper way. You empathize with her in a deeper way." But Du Bois is making a distinction between an actual encounter (a cup of tea together) and a mediated encounter (articles and speeches). Milk is mistaking the latter for the former. The white viewer is allowed the fantasy of sitting beside the other, but it remains only the self who is present; the other has been made virtual and thus always segregated from the actual. Theorist Sherry Turkle notes the damage done through VR in absenting actual human interaction: "The *feeling* of being in conversation becomes conversation enough."[61]

De la Peña's goal has always been journalistic: How can you place the viewer at the scene of the story so that they care more about the stories that, when just headlines, can be ignored? This is not to say her work is free from criticism. Indeed, Susan Sontag's meditation on war photography condemns the false sense of proximity that such photographs (and we can extend this to VR) offer. A sympathetic reaction "proclaims our innocence" and masks "how our privileges are located in the same map as their suffering, and may—in ways we might prefer not to imagine—be linked to their suffering."[62] As described in chapter 2, navigating to sites in LA where one could experience VR empathy experiences—the museum, the festival— occurred quite literally on the same map of so much suffering, but through highway routes that had been carefully insulated from excessive witnessing of this suffering. I'd additionally like to suggest that as empathy experiences strive to be ever more affective—creating a heightened fictional scenario or asking the viewer to play a character in the story—additional potential harms proliferate. Allow me to offer a description of my own experience of a VR piece in which I was asked to take on the perspective of an other, before turning to Saidiya Hartman's elaboration on the dehumanization that accompanies such empathy attempts.

THE ERASURE OF THE OTHER THROUGH THE FANTASY OF BEING SOMEONE ELSE

I was at the Technicolor Experience Center (TEC, see chapter 3) one afternoon, when a production team came through to show off a nearly finished project. They were hoping TEC would add it to the dozen or so experiences that they showcase to visitors. Toward the end of the visit, I was invited to try the experience. The HMD had a sensor attached that tracked my hand movements; when I was in the experience, I could look down and see a pair of hands moving as mine were, but altered in appearance to look not like a white woman's hands but the hands of a Black child. This is a technique frequently used to achieve the illusion of body ownership in VR experiences. I was seated throughout the experience, which was live action, except for my hands and a static CG avatar I could see when looking down. I was sitting in the passenger seat of a car and my avatar was dressed like a little kid. Looking out the window, the sun was shining, and looking to my left, a man (presumably "my" father) was driving and chatting happily. This jovial moment between father and son was disrupted by the blare of a police siren and the dad's face suddenly became somber as he advised his son to stay calm and remember everything he's been taught. After the dad brings the car to a stop, white officers approach, one each at the passenger's and driver's window. The questioning escalates rapidly and without cause the father is pulled out of the car. Through the windshield I see the father slammed down on the car's hood. As the pat down gets more aggressive, the second officer, hand on gun, shifts his gaze between me and the father. A sound of ears ringing crescendos to dominate the soundscape and the experience ends.[63]

This piece, inspired by Philando Castile's murder by police in front of his partner and her daughter, is part of a VR series called *The Messy Truth*, produced by Van Jones, a Black CNN correspondent, and directed by Elijah Allan-Blitz, a white filmmaker. The series won a Lumiere Award for social justice in 2019 and an Emmy in the new category of Outstanding Original Interactive Program in 2020.[64] During a red-carpet interview before the Lumiere ceremony, Jones described how he and Allan-Blitz were "trying to use virtual reality to create empathy across all kinds of divisions of race, of class, of political ideology." This empathy is achieved, Jones explained, by not just hearing about an experience, but going through it. "We have these experiences based on our bodies. It's hard to have empathy when you haven't gone through the experience. We want to use VR to put you in a different body. . . . Hopefully we'll understand each other a little better."[65]

Indeed, this piece is one of the more affecting (and disturbing) VR experiences I have done. The acting is excellent[66] and the director's decision to surround the viewer by cops—placing one at each window—creates a disorientation and sense of overwhelm. Not knowing if the piece will "go there" and actually show a murder adds to the anxiety of viewing the piece. I was stunned and came out of the headset with my heart beating fast and, quite honestly, near tears.[67] But I am not anywhere closer to understanding what it is like to be Black in America. Rather, I have a better sense of how I would feel were cops to pull me over (which, of course, they are less likely to do because of my gender and skin color). Indeed, precisely because I am embodied as the child and therefore not witness to his reaction, I am foreclosed from understanding the experience of this young boy. The boy's being—his voice, his face, his trauma—is erased, replaced by my own. This erasure is more devastating than the piece itself.

I am not the first to look to Saidiya Hartman's discussion on the erasure that attends empathy when trying to reckon with VR as an empathy machine.[68] In her 1997 book *Scenes of Subjection*, Hartman opens her analysis of empathy by describing the letters of a white abolitionist, John Rankin, that describe the inhumanity of slavery in minute detail "to rouse the sensibility of those indifferent to slavery by exhibiting the suffering of the enslaved and facilitating an identification between those free and those enslaved."[69] In one letter, Rankin conducts a thought experiment by which he imagines himself, his wife, and his child enslaved and being whipped. Pen and paper become his empathy machine, arousing in Rankin "the strongest feelings of resentment." Hartman assesses Rankin's identification as an enslaved person as "complicated, unsettling, and disturbing . . . this flight of imagination and slipping into the captive's body unlatches a Pandora's box and, surprisingly, what comes to the fore is the difficulty and slipperiness of empathy."[70] She continues, "Empathy in important respects confounds Rankin's efforts to identify with the enslaved because in making the slave's suffering his own, Rankin begins to feel for himself rather than for those whom this exercise in imagination presumably is designed to reach." Hartman makes the argument that Rankin's very ability to embody a Black person, despite being motivated by good intentions, only serves to reinforce "the captive body as a vessel for the uses, thoughts, and feelings of others."[71] In arguing that Rankin's empathy experiment is enabled by the very logics of chattel slavery that he is intending to write against, Hartman places this abolitionist work in the same lineage as blackface and minstrelsy, which "restaged the seizure and possession of the black body for the other's use and enjoyment."[72]

Throughout this chapter, I have been describing a logic of VR by which the embodied experience of being somewhere (or someone) else is believed to access an emotional truth: de la Peña describes the power of feeling a story with one's entire body, Frilot's physical cinema requires moving to be moved, Iñárritu (as quoted in the introduction) claims the body does not lie and that is why VR is so powerful. Hartman is pointing out that this relationship between body and truth is an assumption made by those in privileged positions. However, the enslaved body—presented to white witnesses as happy-go-lucky, content in captivity—dissembles. In analyzing John Brown's *Slave Life in Georgia*, Hartman notes how he attunes "the reader to the difference between the apparent and the actual, narrating the repression of the 'real' that occurs by way of this costuming of the contented slave." The body of the enslaved person was weaponized against them, possessed and instrumentalized by the owner.[73] The relationship between embodiment and truth is likewise corrupted.

Just as Hartman places Rankin's empathy in the same lineage as minstrelsy, and both as a reassertion of white power over Black bodies, so too are we forced to ask if VR—particularly a piece like *The Messy Truth* that centers Black suffering—similarly dehumanizes despite striving to cultivate empathy. That Hartman focuses on an abolitionist reminds us that good intentions do not necessarily yield good actions. "This is not to suggest that empathy can be discarded or that Rankin's desire to exist in the place of the other can be dismissed as a narcissistic exercise," she writes, "but rather to highlight the dangers of a too-easy intimacy, the consideration of the self that occurs at the expense of the slave's suffering, and the violence of identification."[74] The enslaved person was denied her full humanity; her exterior appearance was taken for her whole self. In order for VR to offer a "too-easy intimacy," the Black body must be hollowed out to make room for the white empathizer.

Conclusion

Between the abolitionist and the VR producer, there has been a slew of other activists, journalists, and storytellers intrigued by the imagined benefit that might come from a white person temporarily inhabiting Black skin. The misunderstandings of both race and racism in these projects also plague the empathy machine. Writer and critic Namwali Serpell has emphasized the confounding essentialist logic in journalistic and fictional accounts of race transformation by which "Race is somehow both surface and depth, construct and essence, transmutable yet fixed . . . a fantasy and a reality."[75] Race is mistaken for something exclusively of the soul and the skin, failing to understand race as a social and cultural formation that "can only happen in time, over time, and through time."[76] A ten-minute VR experience might reveal *something*, but not what it is like to be another.

The very impulse behind VR and other experiments in imagining oneself into another's body obfuscate the ways in which racism is a structural and institutional problem, not just an individual and moral failing. Alisha Gaines makes this point in her book, *Black for A Day*, which analyzes the work of white journalists who darkened their skin and went to the Jim Crow South in order to provide their white readers a glimpse of being an other. Racism is implicitly understood as something that individual insight can remedy. Gaines argues that this belief came to dominate because of an influential 1944 study written by the Swedish economist Gunnar Myrdal, which found "the American dilemma" to be rooted in individual prejudice, catalyzing structural inequalities. If you address the prejudice, Myrdal encouraged, the inequalities will be resolved. This placed the burden on the individual, rather than the system, for creating change.[77]

VR further focuses attention on presumptions about the body's role in shaping a moral knower. Not only does this pull attention away from structural failures, but it ironically and unfortunately often reaffirms the power structures the storyteller strives to topple.[78] Reflective of broader trends in the reality crisis, embodied knowledges have been lifted from their origins in intersectional projects and captured by efforts aimed at weakening institutional authority. And at the same time, in creating the illusion that these partial standpoints are available to other knowers, these same projects have also, despite aiming to illustrate the value of diverse ways of knowing, allowed the fantasy of a universal knower to persist. VR allowed privileged voices to reenter conversations about social justice in which they had been asked to yield the floor. This was exemplified at an event I attended, noting why and for what purpose a speaker invoked the façade of the empathy machine.

The Impact of Immersive Reality was the theme for a mixer held in March 2018, well attended despite competing with the opening night of *Ready Player One*. Several VR experiences were being demoed, raising awareness about factory farming, the opioid epidemic, testicular cancer, and climate change. The audience eventually gathered for a panel discussion intended to be an even-handed conversation on VR's positive and negative impacts. A few weeks earlier, news broke that Cambridge Analytica illegally used "private" Facebook user data for targeted advertising. Keeping the fact that the largest investor in VR was caught in a moral and political scandal in mind, the host began the panel—which included independent VR producers as well as employees of Google and Vice media—with a reminder that tech isn't inherently good. "With the advent and introduction of any technology," the host observed, "[there are] immediate troubling issues that arise. . . . What are some of the social issues that you foresee coming out of [immersive media]?" The first two panelists responded with the worry that VR might replace meaningful encounters with the natural world. However, the panelist from Vice rejected the question, asking why this conversation has to be so negative. Why can't the panel instead talk about "the sense of empathy" and community building that VR might be able to foster? This comment successfully reoriented the rest of the panel conversation around positioning VR as a "good technology" that can avoid the pitfalls of previous "bad tech" by conscientiously choosing to tell diverse stories.

It is perhaps telling that the panelist that dismissed the negativity of the host's question was a young, white man who, in comparison to his fellow panelists, was a relative newcomer to the VR industry. In fact, several times during the panel, he was called out by members of the audience (near to the point of heckling) for his lack of expertise. But it is also this archetype of the mediocre white male to whom the fantasy of being someone else promises a restoration of authority. To restate this more generously, progressive white men who take seriously their role as an ally—to women, to people of color—have recently been asked to step back and listen to the experiences of those for whom they'd like to advocate (and, likewise, white women desiring to be in community and alliance with POC, straight people advocating for queer rights, etc.). They (the societally advantaged, but I'm also specifically turning back to liberal white men) have been told that their privilege prevents them from understanding other people's experiences of being in the world. But the empathy machine promises access to these very embodied experiences that, not having had, keeps them on the outskirts of the conversation.[79] This is one additional reason that Chris Milk, rather than Nonny de la Peña, was a fitting messenger for articulating VR's potential. In his hands, the empathy machine gives those who might identify with Milk a technological fix that reauthorizes their voice in racial and feminist discourse.

In a chapter on white male vulnerability in *The Souls of Cyberfolk*, Thomas Foster argues that in cyberpunk fiction, scenes of white men becoming cyborgs are often depicted as traumatic.[80] This trauma enables a sympathetic reassertion of the white male as the unmarked universal human, a position that has been challenged by feminist and antiracist movements. Foster analyzes Billy Idol's 1993 music video "Shock to the System," inspired by the police beating of Rodney King and the uprising in LA that followed the acquittal of the police officers.[81] "Shock to the System" was on the album *Cyberpunk*, a sonic exploration of the *Neuromancer* universe. In the music video, Idol (who is white) is first the videographer of a police beating, then becomes himself a victim of police brutality, and finally, as his camera merges with his self (the lens becoming his eye) becomes a cyborg and stands up against the police, allowing the uprising to flourish. The story arcs from "a hysterical representation of a vulnerable white male body deprived of the ability to retain the integrity of its ego boundaries or its physical form and toward a fortified, armored corporeality that aggressively reasserts those boundaries and recontains the crisis in white masculinity that his transformation dramatized."[82] The video is also ostensibly a call for racial justice, which illustrates for Foster how the white reckoning with slavery and colonialism's injustices is often done through this empathic perspective taking (this is my language, not Foster's), which erases the need to acknowledge one's complicity with structural racism (cf Sontag), thus defanging history.

The façade of the empathy machine situates VR as an easy fix to a multitude of problems. To be *otherwise* promises to transcend human differences and attending prejudices. For people who want to be better and want to live in a better world, VR offers such a fantasy. I chose to center my research on those in the VR community who were involved in this project of betterment because it is a laudable endeavor. This project is not without its flaws, however, and "the empathy machine" has come to represent the potential pitfalls precisely because it obscures the complexity required to produce this façade and thus fails to adequately reckon with associated ethics and norms. In the next chapter, I continue to explore VR's fantasy of being someone else, discussing a company that centers an ethic of care and strives to shift assumptions about who this fantasy is for and toward what purpose it ought to be directed.

5

SPECIAL AFFECT
AN EMPATHY MACHINE
OTHERWISE

Can the empathy machine be otherwise? What happens when the fantasy of being another is detached from the generic aspiration for human betterment or a salve for the guilt of privilege and instead made available as a support for those who are themselves underresourced and already working with communities overlooked by society? This is the vision that founder Carrie Shaw has for her company, Embodied Labs (EL), which makes VR experiences for professional caregivers who work with aging adults. Virtual reality is here imagined as a tool for helping younger and more able-bodied caregivers better grasp the physical, social, and psychological difficulties faced by their elderly clients. The work of Shaw and her colleagues—both in how they are developing their fledgling company and creating VR experiences—opens up a space to consider who else might benefit from VR and its fantasies.

Six months after I met Shaw, we drove an hour north of LA into Antelope Valley. This desert valley is yet another location proximal to LA that has stood in for an elsewhere (see chapter 2), frequently used as a film set for Westerns in the 1970s. We were not scouting locations, but this fantasy of a place that can become another is a fitting backdrop for the visit we were making to meet with caregivers and hear their first impressions of EL's VR experiences of being another. Our destination was a local branch of a national in-home senior care organization that had purchased a subscription to EL's content library as well as several VR headsets so that their staff could access as desired and needed these virtual reality experiences. During this trip, Shaw and I were meeting with the three experienced caregivers who administered this branch: Maggie and Francesca, two white women in their fifties or sixties, and Elaine, a Black woman in her thirties. These three women would be responsible for introducing the virtual reality experiences to their network of care workers.

In contrast to most of the other VR events I attended throughout fieldwork, where VR's users (both actual and projected) skewed young and, to a slightly lesser extent, white and male, Shaw always brought me into spaces where the technology was being differently used and imagined. The lead administrator, Maggie, explained how until two years ago their office had "absolutely no technology." The first innovation was to implement an electronic scheduler to replace pen and paper. As we talked about and handled the VR gear, all three women were gentle and cautious—not used to working with an emerging technology—but at the same time enthusiastic. Maggie explained how she saw this as the future and wants to be part of a profession and organization that embraces change. She was so excited to receive the VR equipment that she did all of the available experiences in advance of our visit. Maggie expressed surprise at how moved she was and how amazing it is that EL provides "an experience of embodying someone else."

Shaw facilitated a workshop for these women that went over the history and approach of Embodied Labs, the role VR can play in caregiving, an introduction to the technology, and support on how the women could themselves facilitate workshops using EL materials. Shaw communicated how EL is different from other simulation training because it doesn't reduce a disease to its symptoms.[1] Rather, it brings you into another person's world, telling a story and providing an aesthetic experience meant to represent a full life, thus offering an experience of being someone else that is otherwise impossible. Each "lab," as EL calls their experiences, is named for the central fictional character in the story who is an elderly person facing a challenge: disease progression, conflict with family, or changing life circumstances. Labs capture how families and professional care teams both affect and are affected by an aging senior. Like *The Messy Truth* experience described in the previous chapter, EL's VR experiences are 360° video with added CG effects, including hand tracking such that one embodies (and feels embodied as) the (fictional) elderly person at the heart of the narrative. In explaining to the care workers why VR is more effective than other training approaches, Shaw stated a central belief of the VR community that

5.1 Carrie Shaw sets up a VR experience for a demo. The experience begins with the VR experiencer realizing that their hand movements are being tracked in VR. This is the first step of feeling embodied. Photograph taken in April 2018 by the author.

I have also heard Nonny de la Peña and others assert: in physically embodying the experience, "you trick your brain into living 'real' experiences," and so you are also creating a memory around it. This is a way of learning, she mused, fundamentally different from reading or watching a video. "I learn things I couldn't learn any other way," Shaw emphasized.

Maggie, Francesca, and Elaine were all eager to talk about the experiences they had done and tell us how they felt it could improve their work. Elaine said how in *The Beatriz Lab*—an experience in which she embodied a Latina woman with Alzheimer's—there is one scene in which family members are shouting and getting angry over a decision they are making about Beatriz's treatment. Elaine's experience of this scene was utter confusion; she couldn't understand what was happening and it made her realize that in her own caring for patients with Alzheimer's, she ought to make sure to speak calmly and not too loudly. Francesca nodded in agreement, saying she felt frustration during that scene because "they weren't communicating with me," using the first-person pronoun to emphasize how, in that moment, she felt that she was Beatriz.

Maggie attempted to summarize the overall impact of EL, explaining how it draws attention to the very different worlds we all inhabit. We assume we understand another person's experience, but we each inhabit our own reality. Maggie hypothesized that those who are willing to embrace this idea will benefit the most from these experiences.[2] Maggie went on to describe how profound it was for her to see the world through another's eyes. She discussed her experience of *The Clay Lab* and embodying an older white man who is a Korean War veteran and dying from lung cancer. The experience is about end-of-life decision-making and Maggie, herself a survivor of cancer, explained, "I was so overcome by emotion, it was unreal." And yet, she added, "My thoughts were very real." She thought about her own death and how her family would respond and whether she has prepared them. "I didn't expect . . ." she trails off. "But it was—it was real."[3] The extent to which Maggie, Elaine, and Francesca were able to embody Clay or Beatriz was unreal because it provided an extraordinary way of experiencing another's reality which, in turn, prompted these workers to think about how unreal it was that their reality differed so radically from those for whom they care. It was through this fantasy of being that they were able to imagine not only an other's world, but also another world: an otherwise way of engaging with their care work. While concerns raised in the last chapter about how this form of embodiment might inadvertently erase another's subjectivity persist, that these caregivers are already in community with those represented in the experiences exposes how VR harbors not only a fantasy of being another but also a fantasy of being better able to care for another.

Unsettling the Empathy Machine

The concept of "care" has been an illuminating analytic in feminist STS.[4] While analyses of care often focus on the devalued labor of women, particularly women economically or racially marginalized, scholars have also experimented with how care can refocus our approaches to understanding science and technology more generally.[5] Maria Puig de la Bellacasa proposes approaching the politics of knowledge as matters of care.[6] This is a reorientation of Bruno Latour's replacement of matters of fact with matters of concern. Latour's "matters of concern" are a response to what he considers misreadings of STS as antiscience, rather than analyses that strive to portray science as more messy, complex, and human than scientists who praise their work as being unbiased might prefer.[7] As Puig de la Bellacasa interprets Latour, matters of concern were meant to "enrich and affirm [the] reality" of scientific matters of fact while continuing to show the richness of human and nonhuman relations.[8] Matters of care, then, are meant to further intensify how affect and ethics are also implicated in technoscientific endeavors—it is not enough to passively show concern, one must also enact care. To posit the need to care for people and things is to acknowledge that there is a possible world better than the uncared for one. Pursuing an "as well as possible" world through care is an inherently speculative endeavor for Puig de la Bellacasa.[9] Care is thus of a piece with the other fantasies discussed in this book that facilitate imagining the other worlds that might be possible.[10]

Michelle Murphy importantly punctures this fantasy of care, cautioning that care needs unsettling; it is "noninnocent."[11] Precisely because in common parlance care, like VR empathy experiences, is treated as an unalloyed good, care work deployed in an effort to relieve suffering can sometimes exacerbate inequalities.[12] As Murphy writes, "There is an ongoing temptation within feminist scholarship to view positive affect and care as a route to emancipated science and alternative knowledge-making without critically examining the ways positive feelings, sympathy, and other forms of attachment can work with and through the grain of hegemonic structures, rather than against them."[13] Indeed, in the previous chapter, empathy (imagined as an alternative way of knowing an-Other) was "unsettled" by illustrating the forms of privilege that it reproduces and by drawing attention to the insufficiency of focusing on individual improvement in the face of structural inequalities. Murphy's intention is not to discard care but, as Puig de la Bellacasa summarizes of her own critical project, to reclaim care "not from its impurities but rather from tendencies to smooth out its asperities."[14]

If it takes work to see care itself as noninnocent, scholars more readily approach care technologies with skepticism. Robotic companions designed for the elderly, for example, are criticized as not being able to care in the same way as a human.[15] Such a technology replaces rather than augments human labor. Neda Atanasoski and Kalindi Vora, in *Surrogate Humanity*, offer the concept of technoliberalism as the "fantasy that as machines, algorithms, and artificial intelligence take over the dull, dirty, repetitive, and even reproductive labor performed by racialized, gendered, and colonized workers in the past, the full humanity of the (already) human subject will be freed for creative capacities."[16] But, the authors argue, the technologies positioned to replace human labor continue to replicate the racial, gender, and colonial logics that deny humanity for all. The example of a companion robot makes clear that in this purportedly harmonious future, certain humans (family members who feel burdened by their elders) will continue to matter more than others. Atanasoski and Vora emphasize that even when technologies that can replace specific kinds of labor do not yet exist, façades proliferate of purportedly automated platforms that are instead concealing underlying human labor. This contributes "to the seeming inevitability of the domestic realm as an atomized and apparently autonomous economy where the support of life is an individual, rather than social, concern."[17]

This argument reinforces the need to unsettle technologies that claim to cultivate care. My contention is not that technology *can't* be implemented in care contexts but, following Atanasoski and Vora, one way to ascertain unintended harms is to examine which technologies seek to conceal or replace human labor and which might instead aspire to augment or support such labor. This opens up the possibility of multiple kinds of empathy machines. The empathy machine imagined by Chris Milk is not without merit and has leveraged VR experiences focused on humanitarian causes as a successful means of soliciting donations or supporting a community that is struggling. But this empathy machine offers more than just a promise of awareness or increased aid; as Milk stated, it is also a promise to make us more human. It does so, as discussed in the previous chapter, by eliminating the need to *be* with another. As ethnographer Lilly Irani's research on the work and rhetoric of innovation as applied to development projects demonstrates, empathy is productively traded between entrepreneurs and stakeholders "by keeping *representations of people* nearby while keeping actual demands from people far away."[18] VR empathy experiences are often as much (if not more) about individual betterment as they are about collective betterment. There are also VR experiences that more explicitly seek to replace human care work. Embodied Labs is not the only VR company in the aging market, and one competitor has been developing a library of VR experiences curated for senior citizens in care facilities. This company, like the companion robot, offers a technological curative, suggesting a lessened need for human care and attention.

But can a different empathy machine exist? Can VR be care-fully implemented? Embodied Labs—focused on assisting with, not replacing, the human (albeit still gendered and racialized) work of care—differently enacts the fantasy of being at the heart of VR.[19] Throughout this chapter, I heed the call to treat care as noninnocent while not foreclosing the possibility that a company like Embodied Labs might indeed be able to forge an empathy machine otherwise that meets a specific community need. After providing the "founder's story" for Embodied Labs, I explore various facets of the company that complicate how to think about care, affect, and value in the context of a virtual reality start-up. By following the entire process of creating a VR experience, I describe the "special affect" that produces a fantasy of being. While this same trick is used in many empathy experiences, I am interested in how different contexts inform its impact. In the end, Embodied Labs is a company and had to figure out if their otherwise imagination of who VR might serve could square with investor demands. What was the value of this special affect and for whom? Could a small start-up in an unconventional tech market succeed where Hollywood had stalled?

The Pitch

Embodied Labs was founded in August 2016 in Chicago by Carrie Shaw, Tom Leahy, Erin Washington, and Ryan Lebar (who left the company in 2017). In 2018, a year after moving the company to LA, they had around fifty customers and stayed financially afloat through subscriptions from these clients, angel investors, and competition winnings (in 2018, they won the grand prize from the Bill and Melinda Gates Global XR in Education Challenge). I met Shaw in March 2018 after she responded to a post I made on the Women in VR Facebook group looking for folks in the community willing to share their work with me. At that meeting, she invited me to participate in a VR shoot they were doing over the next week for the lab they were currently producing and to hang out with her and Leahy, the two LA-based employees, as they worked out of two cramped, adjoining rooms that constituted the Embodied Labs headquarters. The office was located in the back of a film production company, itself located on the fourteenth floor of a tall office building on Wilshire Boulevard. Though a modest headquarters, for us three LA transplants, this space was an exciting reminder of where we were. Through the thin walls we could often hear the sounds of explosions as a sound editor worked on a scene, and from the window the iconic Hollywood sign was just visible.

Shaw is the CEO and face of Embodied Labs. Like other people in her position, she uses a personal narrative when pitching her company and their product.[20] She publicly pitched Embodied Labs for the first time, shortly after incorporating, at a 2016 event for fledgling tech companies to attract early stage investors. She disclosed to the audience that ten years ago, when she was eighteen, her mother was diagnosed with early onset Alzheimer's. After graduating from college, she moved back home to help her father care for her mom. Shaw was responsible for hiring and working with the home health aides. From her own caregiving, Shaw knew her mom had a visual impairment that affected how she ate and performed other basic activities. After struggling to convey this perceptual condition to new aides, she joked to the audience that she made a "high-tech wearable," and here she put on a pair of plastic safety glasses that had been hanging around her neck. The goggles that Shaw modeled for the audience were partially covered with blue masking tape, simulating for the wearer her mother's partial field of view. The audience laughed, charmed by Shaw whose pitching demeanor, while it has the "vision" statements one expects from this genre, avoids the aloofness that is often a trademark of the entrepreneur. Rather, Shaw projects a quiet self-confidence that enrolls the audience in partnership. The downside of these safety goggles, Shaw explained, was that they only simulated one aspect of a more complex disease. Shaw then positioned VR as the inevitable evolution of the desire to provide caregivers holistic access to a patient's lived experience. After demonstrating the upgrade—from safety goggles to VR goggles—and showing the audience what it looks like inside a lab by putting on a headset and projecting her point of view onto the screen, Shaw concluded with the value proposition. Embodied Labs posits that "having a shared experience with their patient" can transform a caregiver from a "sympathetic provider" to one who can "truly empathize" with their patient, becoming a "more effective and efficient" worker.

The beats of this pitch are familiar, as during my time in LA I saw Shaw present a similar version of this talk several times. The framing has changed a bit, as has some of the language, but the story about her mother and her own experience as a caregiver remains central. Shaw told me that she gave this first pitch just days after her mother's funeral, but watching the recording, I couldn't tell. I do agree with Shaw's diagnosis that she looks young and different from the image of a female entrepreneur that she has cultivated since the company moved to LA in June 2017. When Shaw pitches today, she usually wears a black leather jacket and pulls back her hair into a French braid. While Shaw acknowledges that she *was* young (she was twenty-eight at founding, the second oldest of her cofounders), she also puzzles through why this should matter. After all, she was still older than a lot of the men who were pitching their companies.

As I got to know Shaw, I learned more of her story than what gets folded into this founding tale.[21] Like Nonny de la Peña and Marcie Jastrow, earlier life and career moves can be neatly lined up to make it seem inevitable that each woman would play the role she has in the VR community. But Shaw's experiences are more unexpected. Unlike de la Peña's long fascination with VR or Jastrow's experience in digital cinema, it was Shaw's experiences of being on the science fair circuit as a kid, taking a gap semester away from college to work on an organic farm in Costa Rica, joining the Peace Corps after college and teaching community health in the Dominican Republic, studying to become a medical illustrator, and of course being a caregiver for her mother—intensely at the beginning of her disease, but from a distance as it progressed—that shapes how Shaw approaches VR's fantasy of being.

In the summer of 2017, Shaw, Leahy, and Embodied Labs relocated to Los Angeles. Shaw offers two reasons for this move. First was that it seemed clear that LA was the place where content was being produced. But also, Shaw was an active member of the Women in VR Facebook group and observed that many of the events posted on that page were happening in LA. This is also what brought me to LA. This virtual community promised a vibrant, actual community in Southern California, and both of us yielded to the fantasy of place that seemed to await us in LA.

The Product

Shaw spent 2018 hustling—pitching potential investors, running workshops with clients, speaking at conferences, developing partnerships—and rarely got to enjoy being in LA as she was so often out of town. Tom Leahy and I would often be in the office by ourselves, working companionably in silence until one of us, usually Leahy, would bring up a topic from which a philosophical query would unfold. Leahy was only a few years out of undergrad, and I felt like most of our conversations could have occurred late at night in a dorm room, under the influence of some substance or another. We would talk about the nature of reality, how we imagine concepts in our mind's eye, how to push the technical limits of VR. Always Leahy was figuring out how this technology allows us to think otherwise about the world. He would show me visual tricks meant to demonstrate how flexible our perceptual systems are: putting me in a headset and then changing the image from being projected as a sphere to instead an oblong shape, stretching and warping the scene. When I asked him what his favorite aspect of developing VR was, he mentioned these experiments in tinkering, marveling at how effective they are. "You can't escape the effect," he told me. Creating a special effect was a metaphor Leahy offered for creating a VR experience. "It's basically like real-time special effects done in a game engine," he described. "It's an early form of a different kind of special effects." This is a fitting metaphor for VR given how, as described in chapter 3, the technology's Hollywood story can be sutured to the digital transition catalyzed by the visual effects industry.[22] Building on Leahy's description, I suggest that the experience of embodying another is a *special affect*, one facilitated by the 360° camera: the charismatic technology at the heart of a live-action VR shoot.[23] Like care, this special affect is noninnocent; a special affect does not automatically create understanding (or harm), and thus must be understood in context. After explaining how a special affect is produced—both how the broader VR community thinks about the 360° camera as well as how this was enacted on the Embodied Labs' shoot for *The Clay Lab*—I will further consider the affective economies, a concept proposed by feminist scholar Sara Ahmed, in which special affects circulate.

"WHO IS THE CAMERA?"

360° video (as opposed to a fully CG experience) has a slightly lower barrier to entry, making it particularly desirable to newer VR creators. To shoot their first VR piece (part of Shaw's master's thesis while studying biomedical visualization at the University of Illinois–Chicago), she and Leahy (then an undergraduate computer science major) DIYed a 360° camera out of GoPro cameras and a 3-D printer (this was a common hack for folks experimenting with VR in the early 2010s and making content for the developer version of the Oculus headset before its commercial launch). Many of the people I met in LA, particularly those who migrated to VR from traditional film, began by creating 360° experiences even if they ended up working on more complex CG projects.

The 360° camera is a cinematic technology that induces a sociality central to achieving VR's special affect. The camera is personified by filmmakers, impelling a particular kind of action and performance by not only actors but also the consumer of a VR piece. VR filmmakers ask, "Who is the camera?" LA-based French filmmaker Céline Tricart well describes this in a podcast interview. Tricart starts by reminding the listeners of the essence of a VR experience: "You're present. . . . You're a physical presence. That's what VR is about. It's about being physically present in the story. . . . So, when you design your story . . . I ask myself, 'Who am I?' 'Who is the camera?'" (And here she is conflating "I" with simultaneously herself as director, a future VR viewer, and the camera.) "Where would I place my physical presence in that scene? Where would I put my physical body?" If the filmmaker can understand "this is not a camera *capturing*, this is a real human being *being* there," then they are ready to start making a VR film.[24]

I witnessed this way of thinking about the camera again while attending VR Day at the University of Southern California. There, a panel of three 360° filmmakers tried to get the audience in the mindset of thinking differently about the camera when it came to VR. The panel moderator described how a traditional 360° approach for capturing the experience of the panel would be to put the camera right in front of the stage. The viewer could see everything going on, panelists and audience, from a central location. But, in this setup, the camera is not part of the scene. One of the panelists jumped in and said how she would place a 360° camera onstage in a fourth chair as if the camera were another panelist. She could even direct some comments to the camera and bring the camera/panelist/VR experiencer into the scene as much as possible. The third panelist agreed, saying that such a setup gives the experiencer a perspective and a personality. He advised the audience of student filmmakers to think of the camera as a character.

This is foundational to cinematic VR and is also key to understanding how one performs for the 360° camera. I spoke with one actress, Maria, who told me about her experience of auditioning for the first Embodied Labs project shot in LA. Maria played the daughter in *The Beatriz Lab*, and her audition was the first time she acted with a 360° camera. When she arrived to read her lines, she hadn't realized that the audition she was going on was for an immersive project. She laughed, recalling how she showed up for the audition and instead of being introduced to a scene partner, she was introduced to the 360° camera. "Meet your mom!" Maria recalled the director saying, in reference to the camera.

The move to LA enabled Shaw and Leahy to retire their makeshift GoPro rig and hire experienced directors of photography who brought to set newly marketed high-end 360° cameras. The 360° camera used on *The Clay Lab* was a star-shaped black box the size of a head of lettuce. On each of the six points of the star was a fisheye lens, capturing the scene in every direction. Notably, as with any 360° camera, there is no eyepiece to look

5.2 A 360° camera on a tripod, capturing a perspective of floating above the ground. Photograph taken in March 2018 by the author.

through. To see as the camera does, one uses a phone or tablet to act as both viewfinder and remote trigger. Additionally, as the name suggests, a 360° camera films in all directions at once, creating not a flat image but rather a sphere in which a viewer is centrally placed at the position of the camera. There is no behind the scenes on a VR shoot. For a crew and director to be out of the shot, they must be in a different room or concealed by the environment. If you can see the camera, the camera can see you.

SHOOTING AND SHAPING CLAY

On the first day of *The Clay Lab* shoot, I arrived at a residential house in Altadena at 6:00 a.m. We had fourteen hours to transform the house into a set appropriate for the shoot, to film several scenes, and then transform it back so that the family who was renting it to us for the day would never know the difference (though they of course had given us permission to make these temporary changes). By 7:00 a.m., the bedroom was ready for the director of photography (DP) to come in and set up the shot. It was then that I also got to "meet" Clay—to see the camera that would be playing this pivotal role.

On a traditional movie set, camera angles and movements are established, lights are rigged and hung. On a 360° set, the camera usually stays still (for fear of inducing nausea in the viewer) and the lighting has to come from natural sources in the room. Since the camera is all seeing, the DP can't simply hang a light so that it shines becomingly on an actor's face.

For this scene, the DP placed the camera in bed, where Clay is spending his last days under the care of hospice nurses. It was daytime, so the room was well lit by natural light, and the DP had requested a floor lamp to be placed next to Clay to serve as both prop and additional light source. At 10:00 a.m., we started shooting. Since there is no "behind the scenes" at a 360° shoot, the half dozen of us crew members crowded into a small hallway that was also filled with the furniture we had pushed out of the bedroom to make room for the actors.

The director couldn't watch the scene in the room, but rather looked at the DP's iPad, which showed Clay's (i.e., the 360° camera's) perspective. In the first take, the actors—all new to acting in 360°—talked to the pillow, not the camera hovering a half foot above the pillow. The director called cut from the hallway and went into the room to talk to the actors, reminding them to talk to the camera/Clay—to look directly at it/him. The actress playing a nurse said that it was freaky to look right at the camera (often a taboo of traditional film acting), and the director chuckled and said that it was also freaky to look at a dying person. "Use that," he directed.

As the shoot continued, the actors became more comfortable with the camera as a scene partner. For each new scene, we thought about what Clay was going through at that moment in the script—was it early on and so maybe he had more energy and was sitting upright, or was this toward the end of the script, when he was dying and likely lying flat? The camera position was accordingly adjusted, and the actors modified the level of concern as they delivered their lines to the 360° camera—to Clay.

By the time we wrapped for the day, it was dark and we were bone tired. We returned the house to its former state and, before we drove away, the DP poured everyone a shot of tequila, delivered in plastic cups that he kept tucked away in his truck. The woman in charge of feeding the cast and crew all day—a friend of Shaw's who was between jobs—distributed ice cream pops that she had been storing in a freezer bag.

The shoot lasted for several more days, and the work then turned to editing together the footage, mixing the spatial audio, importing the audio-visual components into a game engine, and adding CG elements, including the hand-tracking aspect of the experience. I showed up at the Embodied Labs office a few weeks after this process had begun, and Leahy—who does most of the postproduction—was eager to show me a rough cut and get my feedback. I watched the fifteen-minute-long experience and made mental notes of moments that didn't quite feel right. In a scene that takes place in a hospital room, I commented that Clay felt too tall. Leahy agreed, lamenting that while they would be able to adjust the height a bit, there was only so much he could do because this was live action, not animation. He explained that this was one of the first scenes they shot and they were still learning who Clay was, and so the camera was placed too high. With notes in hand, Leahy returned to his work. When I saw the piece again a week later—with the CG effects all added—I did feel a bit more like I was embodying Clay. When I looked down, my hands were aged and I could hear the raspiness of my/Clay's breath. In the final scene, lying flat in bed and waiting for death, the visual field becomes dim and distorted; I found it harder to see my/Clay's wife clearly.

SPECIAL AFFECT

The 360° camera facilitates a special affect[25] that atemporally links the actors' performances and my viewing of the VR experience such that I am convincingly embodied as the character the 360° camera is playing. To parse this striking affective relationship, I draw a parallel with what in visual effects lingo is called a *composite shot*—a shot that combines elements that have been asynchronously filmed or composed in different media (film versus animation) and composited to appear as a unified, synchronous scene.[26] In a predigital age, a simple composite shot from a film like *Who Framed Roger Rabbit* required several components that would be layered together for the final celluloid print. In the scenes where Detective Eddie Valiant is in Toontown, actor Bob Hoskins was filmed in front of a blue screen. This was in turn used to create a Valiant-shaped black cutout layered onto the animated film. Hoskin's live-action performance was then composited in, creating the illusion of Valiant's immersion in the animated suburb of Los Angeles. Instead of combining live-action and animation, in VR the composite shot is comprised of the 360° scene and the VR participant. The camera becomes that which is masked out to layer in the viewer. Whereas a scene from *Who Framed Roger Rabbit* is finished once it is "in the can" and shipped to theaters, it is only the act of doing a VR experience that completes the composite shot. As with a special effect in which Detective Valiant is made to seem present with any number of Looney Tunes, VR's special affect creates the illusion for the viewer of presence in the scene and being present with others. And it is that experience of *being with* that lends credence to the fantasy of *being someone else*.

In *The Clay Lab*, there are several scenes in which I/Clay hold a cell phone which (as is the conceit of the story) I use to communicate with my family because I have lost my ability to speak due to the lung cancer. As a plot device, it allows me insight into what I, as Clay, am thinking. While I was going through the final version of the experience (and knowing that I was being observed by Leahy, who awaited my final assessment), I found myself self-consciously (even performatively) holding the cell phone such that my virtual scene partner could also read the text. In a scene with my daughters and a hospice representative, I held the phone so that my daughter and I could both read the screen. Having observed this scene being shot, I recalled how the actress took a few takes to get the right timing and gaze interaction of looking down (to an empty spot where plausibly someone doing the experience might be holding the animated cell phone) to read the text aloud and looking at the camera to give a supportive response. As the camera/as Clay, I now also looked down at my phone and after a beat (that I knew was coming from watching her performance during the shoot) decided to meet the daughter's gaze. I made eye contact with her—a gesture that often signifies connection.

Special affect bolsters the fantasy by which this embodied being—inhabiting another's world and enacting their relationships—translates into understanding and empathy. As the previous chapter demonstrated, this special affect is noninnocent and can lead to harm if thought is not given to audience as well as outcome. How, then, to evaluate the effect of a special affect? In Murphy's call to unsettle care, they draw on Sara Ahmed's concept of "affective economies" to think through how an affect like care (or, in this case, empathy) is not something that emerges from some inner state of the individual, but rather circulates—and, like capital, thus accumulates—among bodies, things, and ideas. Because of the social nature of affect, emotions are not inherently good or bad but rather a product of their historical and material circumstances. If, as Murphy writes (still drawing on Ahmed), "the value of certain affects . . . are the accumulated effects of patterns of circulation" that do "particular kinds of work arranging social relations," then how specific special affects circulate—*The Clay Lab* versus *The Messy Truth*—is key to understanding the work that they do and the benefit or harm they might bring.[27] One could take circulation very literally to emphasize, as I've already intimated, the importance of Embodied Labs' VR experiences being created for care workers who are already in a social world with those whom they are supposed to be empathizing. But Ahmed's concept of affective economies also demands a macro-level assessment of the other affects with which empathy circulates to further understand the work a special affect does.

Ahmed describes how "the accumulation of affective value shapes the surfaces of bodies and worlds."[28] Writing in 2004 with the figure of the terrorist and refugee in mind, she is specifically interested in how fear and hate circulate and gain traction specifically by drawing boundaries between the white, Western "us" and a nonwhite, non-Western "them." Fear affectively draws together the international terrorist seeking to do harm with the refugee seeking to escape harm, both relegated to outside the bounds of "our" world/nation and thus both equally unwanted. "Emotions work," Ahmed argues, "by sticking figures together."[29] Special affect is a material instantiation of this compositing work, drawing together bodies that do not actually exist in the same place and time—the terrorist and asylum seeker, myself and Clay's daughter.

Significantly, special affect and the empathy it hopes to elicit circulate as a *response* to the affective economy of fear that Ahmed articulates. In 2006, then Senator Barack Obama observed an "empathy deficit" (purposely making an economic analogy) among US citizens, lamenting how American culture devalued "the ability to put ourselves in someone else's shoes; to see the world through those who are different from us."[30] If fear and hate drew robust borders between an us and a them, empathy was positioned as the affect needed to overcome these divisions. The empathy machine and the histories told in the previous chapter emerged from and accrued value in this affective economy. As empathy circulated in the aftermath of Obama's speech, it sought to stick together the bodies that the affective economy of hate had drawn boundaries between. The illusion produced by the special affect of VR that composites a viewer into the scene is the feeling of being in another's shoes; this is a sticking together in the hopes of inducing empathy.

It is within this affective economy that we again must ask if there can be an empathy machine otherwise. Put another way, special affect is necessarily a *trick*, but a trick that VR innovators have come to see as real because it has become second nature to treat the camera as a cast member. Can this trick ever be more than a deception? Lilly Irani's analysis of how empathy is used by designers to attract investment or buy-in for development projects concludes with skepticism: "Empathy was not an understanding of the other. It was the *feeling* of understanding the other—a feeling more stable as a memory rather than as the reality of the lives of others."[31] While this echoes the claim Shaw made to the caregivers we met with, she offered VR's ability to create a memory as something that might supplement—rather than replace—other resources by which these workers come to know their clients. Embodied Labs certainly leans into special affect's ability to translate the illusion of being someone else into a fantasy of greater understanding. But in this context, it is a fantasy that centers community and care rather than individual affect and moral improvement.[32] Special affect might suggest a deeper knowing, but it does not deceive that this is all that is needed to care for another. It is one strategy among many.

That empathy has come to be seen as a magical, standalone cure-all has made several people in the VR community, including Shaw, uncomfortable with its prominence. In particular, as Shaw sought investors and customers, she found that the inability to measure the existence or impact of empathy hindered her ability to articulate why care facilities should adopt VR. Empathy did not, Shaw found, have market value. Embodied Labs needed to refine their "value proposition," the tangible benefit they claimed to offer a customer. In so doing, Shaw and her team settled on how, in order to make an empathy machine otherwise, they had to reject the category of empathy.

The Value Proposition

In 2018, when the VR industry was neither booming nor a complete bust, many of my interlocutors struggled with articulating the *value* offered by VR. During a visit I made to Nonny de la Peña's studio, a business development consultant was helping the team articulate the value proposition for a volumetric VR journalism platform they were about to launch. Over at Technicolor, Marcie Jastrow's principal job was convincing the company heads that VR had entertainment value, and she tried various strategies for defining a market. At Embodied Labs, in addition to drawing up term sheets for potential investors and projecting their estimated worth, the company also worked to define their value in the affective economy of care.

During my first meeting with Shaw, she described how her understanding of VR was influenced by academic research, citing Jeremy Bailenson's work on empathy and Skip Rizzo's medical research on VR as PTSD therapy. These academic ideas, she was discovering, do not translate to the business world.[33] Empathy, she explained, doesn't work in a pitch. Shaw and I frequently returned to this topic, often with Shaw expressing frustration about how empathy might be nice to have, but no one is willing to pay for it. "It makes it hard to assign value," she once exclaimed. Sure, she went on, it was great that Chris Milk was able to use empathy to get people interested in VR, "but the empathy machine stuff has been really destructive to making [VR] a viable business." While in her first pitch in 2016 Shaw used the language of empathy, by 2018 that word was purposely absent from her public presentations. Instead, Shaw and the Embodied Labs team worked to craft value propositions that were both measurable and meaningful to their clients.

On a phone call in May with cofounder Erin Washington and their business development advisor (both of whom lived on the East Coast), Shaw described how, as they have grown, her pitch was feeling clunky. Through client feedback, the company had also learned more about why the caregivers found the labs useful, and Shaw wanted to figure out how to incorporate the clients' language into the company's marketing materials. Their advisor suggested refining the company's value propositions, often a necessary step at this stage of a company's life cycle. Washington shared a document she had been working on, puzzling through how Embodied Labs can be positioned as a solution, bridging a problem with an outcome. On this document, Washington listed potential techniques, solutions, and outcomes they might want to highlight: storytelling, advocacy, training, empowerment, and empathy. The advisor helped Shaw and Washington formulate a general value proposition that they could then plug in different problems and solutions to craft multiple persuasive ways of articulating the company's purpose. Importantly, they all agreed that the value propositions should be independent of needing to define the value of VR. People still don't understand the technology, the advisor cautioned, and so their company needs to stand apart.

A few weeks later, Embodied Labs hosted a retreat that included the cofounders, an employee who flew down from San Francisco, a summer intern, and several trusted collaborators. Most of the day was devoted to continuing the work of developing these value propositions. The business advisor joined via Zoom after the first brainstorming session and observed that the value propositions we had drafted bifurcated between solutions oriented around technology, platforms, or services versus those that centered storytelling and community. Articulating this distinction was helpful, as Shaw wanted the latter to be what they emphasized, showing how VR could create shared experiences that might change employee cultures at care facilities. The room buzzed with excitement as this conversation began to make clear a grander vision for this company beyond simply using VR as empathy training. In fact, Washington brought up that she was not sure "training" even belonged in their value proposition. She disliked how it operates on a deficit model, implying that there are skills missing. Shaw agreed, drawing a connection to the phrase *empathy machine* which also seemed to make an accusation of a lack or absence (a fair assessment insofar as the empathy machine can be seen as a solution to Obama's stated empathy deficit). As this conversation progressed, the team kept returning to how their VR experiences were less about individual betterment, but rather about community growth. Framed this way, the team understood VR not as "fixing" caregivers, but rather providing a shared set of experiences and stories to support and strengthen their professional community. They transformed VR from the technoliberal idea (to bring back the language proposed by Atanasoski and Vora) of a machine fashioned for an individual's pursuit of becoming more human and into a shared resource for fostering community.

In addition to the language of empathy, Shaw also worried that the phrase *virtual reality* misled the value she saw her company providing. While at an aging conference in August, Shaw reported that the audience was critical of "fake" training experiences that mischaracterize ailments of aging. Shaw agreed with this critique and worried whether the "virtual" in virtual reality might be equated with this kind of "fake"ness. She posted on the company Slack, "Virtual is the wrong word. We are creating more reality. . . . We're actually trying to build real experiences for the purpose of having more reality. Expand reality. Give people more life experiences to learn from. . . . More reality can be created if it's done the right way." Here again is the hyperreality encountered in chapter 2. But in this context, hyperness—this "more than" aspiration—potentially repositions VR as additive rather than substitutive.

Shortly after the company retreat, Shaw gave a talk at the Augmented World Expo in front of a sizable audience, describing the company as well as some of the internal research they had done about the efficacy of their labs in medical education programs and care facilities. After telling the story about her mother and showing the safety goggles with blue masking tape, Shaw put up a slide titled "Value Proposition." The slide captured the language that had emerged throughout the past month of conversations. It read, "Embodied Labs creates immersive VR experiences about key issues in aging care that drive: improved outcomes in caregiving, positive company culture shift, lower staff turnover, better family caregiver outreach, education, and support." Significantly, empathy was nowhere on this slide nor in Shaw's talk.

Conclusion

Care is a collective, relational endeavor and this communality serves as a reminder of why empathy has value in the first place. Empathy matters not as individual affect, but as a catalyst by which the individual might find additional ways of relating to and caring for one's community. The special affect of VR is non-innocent because it can replace the act of being in community with the feeling of having already been present with others. If in the last chapter I wrote generally about how the empathy machine is a façade, here more specifically is a concern that the mechanizing of empathy masks the active need to care.

We care because we want to live in a world that is cared for; we want to bring forth what Puig de la Bellacasa calls an "as well as possible" world. Care is thus a method of worldbuilding, bridging the now with a future. In chapter 1, I introduced worldbuilding, noting how in LA it has transcended fictional and cinematic storytelling, becoming a method for envisioning desirable civic futures. The fantasy of being shifts the focus from a world of the future to the world of another, with the assumption being that the future, better world is one in which these others are cared for. In the specific context of elderly care, these other worlds are not symptomatic of a politically fractured reality nor a radically different lived reality due to one's race or gender. While one may embody a person with a different identity in an Embodied Labs' experience, there remains a common reality at the center of these experiences: we are all going to age, we are all going to die. For these VR experiences, then, the worldbuilding is simultaneously about supporting professional caregivers and their clients in the present but also about creating this ethic of care such that, by the time one ages into the world of the elderly, it will be care-filled.

Imagining care as worldbuilding for a better world extends beyond the VR context, illustrated in a striking essay by medical anthropologist Arthur Kleinman. In writing about being a caregiver for his wife, who had Alzheimer's, Kleinman presages the language of the empathy machine years before VR's re-emergence. He describes caregiving for a loved one as hard, both emotionally and physically. But he also describes it as a practice that makes us "more human." "It is a practice of empathetic imagination, responsibility, witnessing, and solidarity with those in great need. It is a moral practice that makes caregivers, and at times even the care-receivers, more present and thereby fully human." Following a Chinese belief, Kleinman notes how in becoming more human we also "humanise the world."[34] This is one logic of the empathy machine: individual affect converts to doing good and thus bringing about a better world. But often for VR, unlike Kleinman's experience, empathy happens in isolation from others and in *both* cases it seems overly optimistic to assume that this conversion inevitably happens.

In wondering if there could be an empathy machine otherwise, this chapter has more closely examined the ways in which VR could be more integrated into communities of care. This is necessarily a less fantastical implementation of VR than experiences that grab headlines by offering to bridge racial divides or impact the refugee crisis. Shaw's decision to exclude the language of empathy from her Embodied Labs pitch distanced the work she saw her company doing from some of the other projects in the space that she viewed with skepticism. In a conversation we had toward the end of my research, she returned to the value of empathy, a conundrum she had been contemplating all year. "Why should we be empathetic?" she pondered. This question was multi-valanced. She was in part voicing some frustration about what is expected of her as a female founder of a company in the caregiving space. Even as an entrepreneur, she is expected to be empathetic in a way that her male counterparts are not. But in this question is a more pointed (if unintentional critique) of her own company. Why should caregivers be empathetic? Even if the language has been removed from the value propositions, it is still a tacit outcome of each lab. Puig de la Bellacasa more directly troubles the relationship between care and affect, writing, "There are situations when care work involves a removal of the affective—we ask, then, why would a paid care worker have to involve affection in her work? This is crucial because we have to consider how care can turn into moral pressure for workers who might rightfully want to preserve their affective engagement from exploitations of waged labor. But if maintenance does not involve some affective involvement . . . is it still care?"[35] When Shaw and I met with the caregivers at the facility in Antelope Valley, Maggie worried that these VR experiences might open the emotional floodgates for some professional caregivers, perhaps even triggering something like PTSD. Francesca agreed and Maggie further explained that caregivers try very hard to control their emotions, not because they are unfeeling but because they have a job to do. When Shaw asked "Why should we be empathic" I don't think she was imagining these caregivers. In other words, she was not imagining what caregiving would look like if the labor of these workers was differently understood, valued, and compensated. Instead, within the current system of care work, Embodied Labs more modestly sought to offer support. While Embodied Labs offers an empathy machine otherwise, the worldbuilding that the company is doing is not a radical vision for care otherwise.

This more modest world, however, was one that investors were willing to underwrite. In January 2020, Embodied Labs successfully closed their seed round of venture capital fundraising. A few months later, the COVID-19 pandemic disrupted everyone's world and proved particularly devastating for the elderly, both those at care facilities and those living independently. Embodied Labs has made it through this unsettling time, and the content they have recently created has shifted accordingly. In response to the pandemic, they created a lab on social isolation and have also launched multiple experiences in which caregivers have the opportunity to not only embody the person they are caring for but also a nurse or an aide who is experiencing a difficult situation or burnout and is thus also in need of care. These more recent developments expand beyond the fantasy of being another to include fantasies for oneself and the better world that selfcare might bring about.

In the press release announcing the closing of the seed funding round, investors described the company as "innovative," "transformative," "a quantum leap," noting the significance of applying a high-tech solution to a "traditionally tech-phobic" industry.[36] But there was another dimension to this triumph. Shaw herself noted in the press release her excitement that the investors demonstrated expertise in, among other things, "female empowerment." The final quote from an angel investor reciprocated the sentiment, praising the "Female-driven innovation and influence" exemplified by Shaw and Embodied Labs. This hints at the third fantasy that has been in the background of the chapters thus far: that precisely because of LA's fantasy of place and VR's fantasy of being, it was not only possible but imperative to conjure a fantasy of representation by which women and underrepresented voices were central to VR's success. In the final part of this book, I will explore how and why the VR community in LA sought to bring forth an industry otherwise.

PART III
FANTASY OF REPRE- SENTATION

In 2018, Hollywood and Silicon Valley were both under public scrutiny as commentators processed revelations of abusive, exploitative, and unethical behaviors. In Hollywood, the news of producer Harvey Weinstein's sexual predation led to a cascade of similar accusations across the entertainment industry and beyond. In Silicon Valley, calls for addressing gendered mistreatment in the workforce were drowned out by a louder insistence that tech companies reckon with their role in the toxicity and privacy violations plaguing social networks and algorithm-driven products. #MeToo posts flooded these networks at the same time that "techlash" was coined to name the growing negative assessment of Facebook, Google, and other Silicon Valley giants. Though a push for VR to be an inclusive industry had begun a few years earlier, in LA during my fieldwork this resolve was intensified precisely because of the conversations spurred by #MeToo and the techlash. The fantasy of representation that was being offered—and that will be explored in this book's final part—was a fantasy that, in contrast to entertainment and tech, the VR community could enact how an equitable industry and technology might come into being.

#MeToo and the techlash served as cultural resources that VR folks in LA drew on when justifying why their industry ought to be different. They are also additional points of connection between VR and the reality crisis. #MeToo and the techlash index differences in lived experiences and the media infrastructures that have fragmented and shaped which and whose experiences and ideas we consume. Given their mutual flourishing in 2018, one can speculate as to the extent to which frustrations with the inability to hold Trump accountable for his misuses of power and alleged harassments prompted the voicings of abuse in these other sectors. While the harms caused by the sexual predations central to #MeToo are in no way equivalent to those that provoked the techlash, both conversations sought to end the gaslighting that made victims of harassment or skeptics of tech's inherent beneficence feel as though they occupied a different reality. They signaled desires for other realities to be acknowledged with a hoped-for outcome of inaugurating different, better futures.

Similarly, the unreal—the analytic I offer for capturing extraordinary ways of experiencing and comprehending reality—signals not only crisis but also opportunity. The crises that come from reckoning with reality's fracturing additionally surface reality's malleability and thus the opportunity to imagine otherwise worlds. To be in the land of the unreal is to be in a landscape textured by multiple and conflicting realities where fantasy serves as a strategy for reshaping the world. Part I explored long-standing practices of Angelenos who engaged with fantasy for both on-screen and off-screen conjurings of other worlds. Part II proffered fantasies that responded to a fractured reality with attempts to bridge divides. The fantasy of being, a feature of the VR experience, was positioned as providing insight into other realities that, after completing the experience, could inspire change. In part III, the fantasy of representation is also in service of better futures, but it animates the community assembled around VR rather than the technology itself. Instead of reality repair being figured through the circulation of VR experiences, creating an inclusive VR industry was imagined to be reparative insofar as it responded to the calls for reform issued by #MeToo and the techlash. Though examined at different scales and in different ways throughout the three parts of this book, I have sought to tease out a common tendency by which the unreal invites fantasies that play with reality's plasticity in order to articulate better worlds. The noir has always been close at hand as, in each case, vigilance is needed to avoid the recapture of these fantasies by the worlds and structures they are hoping to unsettle.

The two chapters in part III focus specifically on the fantasy that women ought to be leading VR. This conviction is spurred not only by a sense that "the time has come" for industry change and female empowerment, but also from a belief that a feminine outlook leads to the creation of impactful VR experiences. Chapter 6 explores how these pragmatic and intuitive logics reinforce the idea that female leadership best guarantees VR's success. While noting some of the VR community's triumphs in empowering women, this chapter also approaches the essentialist logic undergirding parts of this fantasy with caution. Chapter 7 shows how the fantasies of place, being, and representation, working together, constitute a worldbuilding project that summons an inclusive future by redefining what "tech" is and thus who gets to be a tech worker. In these chapters, I present the fantasies of the women in LA's VR community as well as their concerns, enumerating the social work these fantasies do at the level of the individual and the community.

These chapters further highlight the importance of understanding VR's fantasy of representation as not only responsive to temporal currents like #MeToo and the techlash, but also, returning to the framework from part I, as a product of place, possessing a local technological terroir despite appeals to the universality of digital and virtual spaces. The desire for female leadership was prominent in LA, but in other locations where VR similarly inspired a fantasy of representation, it cleaved along different identity axes. Illuminatingly, Jessica Dickson, in her ethnographic study of the South African film industry, observes that in the mid-2010s, some filmmakers from South Africa and other countries on the continent imagined themselves as VR's potential leaders. In both LA and South Africa, the sentiment (to be explored in depth in chapter 7) was similar: because this was a "new" technology, anyone could become an expert and thus be at the forefront of a cutting-edge field. At last, it seemed, there was an opportunity for those historically disadvantaged due to race, gender, or nationality to become leaders. This fantasy is complex and heterogeneous, and in the South African context, as Dickson analyzes, at times reinforces hegemonic assumptions about "the West and the Rest" while also providing, for some, the ability to construct "'new narratives' for envisioning futures beyond a white Eurocentric modernism."[1] The tension between reinforcing normative assumptions and advocating for radical change is common between these different fantasies of representation (and part II's fantasies of being) even as they are formed in response to distinct local political urgencies.

In both of these contexts, the fantasy of representation is wrapped up in the assertion that VR is a "good" technology, a claim that, as I state in the introduction, demands both skepticism and focus on the social action it catalyzes. The meaning of "the good" expands here to include both the empathy machine's "goodness" as well as the "good" demographics of a diverse workforce. In other words, returning to the categorical language introduced in chapter 3, VR's potential to do good is figured both through how it is implemented as a cinematic technology and through the demographic empowerment that comes from being associated with an emerging technology. Conversations about representation and VR in LA thus refracted between the importance of telling meaningful stories that showcase a multitude of lived realities and the importance of having a diverse workforce. Similarly, in the South African context, as Dickson describes, VR's potential goodness stemmed from both its potential to tell "disruptive" stories[2] about Africa and to elevate the voices of African filmmakers.

These mutual fantasies of the good do not run in parallel, but come to reinforce each other: VR's good workforce will produce good content that will be able to turn those who engage with this content into good humans. And all of these fantasies are compelling precisely because of the systemic violations that catalyzed the techlash and #MeToo, as well as the overall frustration of living in a world that feels not particularly good and hopelessly divided. As much as VR was hyped and made desirable due to its software and hardware capabilities, it was also desirable because it animated fantasies of a good and better world. The fantasy of representation and the belief in the goodness of VR became a potent alternative to #MeToo and the techlash. At a moment when change was being demanded, VR offered the fantasy that it could be otherwise.

6

VR'S FEMININE MYSTIQUE
A TECHNOLOGY OF THE #METOO MOMENT

In June, after a day of working out of the Embodied Labs office, Carrie Shaw and I cruised down Olympic Boulevard at sunset from mid-Wilshire to a not-yet-but-almost-happening neighborhood in west LA. Shaw had met with several investors that week and while we spoke briefly of the frustrations she was facing—including the challenges of being a woman in these pitch meetings and getting venture capitalists to care about the aging population—we distracted ourselves with nonwork stuff. We chatted about our Myers–Briggs personalities and, as we were both still relatively new to LA, reflected on the joys and strangenesses of the city.

We were heading to a meetup for women in VR hosted at a new branch of The Riveter, a Seattle-based coworking company. This was their first location in LA, and they were inviting different communities into the space to share their vision of catering to companies and projects that are either led by women or otherwise demonstrated gender diversity. During my year in LA, I attended events in a half-dozen different coworking spaces, each with their own design aesthetic and mission. The Riveter was crisp and white, with glass partitions for breakout spaces and enamel desks on wheels that could be endlessly reconfigured. The refreshments were healthier than what was usually served at these events, including a proper salad to go along with hummus, cheese, and wine. There were about forty to fifty attendees (three quarters of whom were women) and, halfway through fieldwork, I saw many familiar faces. Julie Young and Jenn Duong, founders of the Women in VR Facebook group, were both in attendance, as were other women I met through that group, at a programming class I took, and through Embodied Labs. Each of these women were differently navigating the VR industry, and during this chapter and the next, we'll hear more about their careers, aspirations, and difficulties. While folks networked and caught up, some stepped into breakout rooms to try VR experiences that were being demoed; one was a trailer for a longer experience about Marie Antoinette, and the other was about abortion. When my friend came out of the abortion experience, after making sure we were out of earshot of the woman running the demo (and likely its creator), she confided in me that she couldn't tell whether the experience was pro- or antichoice, but maybe that was the point?

Young was the emcee for the evening, and eventually interrupted the mingling to request that we take our seats for a panel discussion on entrepreneurship. She had invited five women who started (and received funding for) companies in the VR/AR space. The companies ranged from content production to location-based entertainment to workforce sexual harassment training. We learned little about these companies, but more about the women's experience as company leaders and working in a space like VR that fluctuates with such volatility. Young began the panel discussion with the wry observation that despite the fact that everyone on stage was in their twenties or early thirties, as people who have been working in VR for a few years, they were considered veterans of the industry. Indeed, the woman on stage who was well known in the community for having raised one of the largest funding rounds remarked that she woke up one day in November 2016 knowing nothing about VR but having a vision for her company. As previous chapters have discussed, however, VR is not new and as the evening went on, the panelists chipped away at this façade, first referencing the work of Nonny de la Peña as being "here before us" and then acknowledging that the only reason it is so easy to enter VR today is because of previous decades of work in the defense, aerospace, and healthcare industries.

Though much of the conversation was about the industry, strategies for being successful, and what exciting developments were coming down the pipeline, there were also moments for reflecting on gender. One woman remarked that she began her company because she was tired of the male dominance at the tech companies she had worked at. She wanted to be in charge. Now that she is running a company and pitching to investors, she has observed that when men pitch, they act as though they have the most amazing idea and it needs to be funded. Women, on the other hand, are more modest and come in with ideas seeking to "make the world a better place." As the panelists knew (and as Shaw and I had discussed on the ride over), there is a significant disparity between VC funding for female- versus male-led ventures, and the panelist who made this observation suggested the need for a middle ground between these two approaches; men have the "right attitude" and women have the "right empathy," and she insisted that men and women need to develop pitches with both attitude and empathy.

This panel and the conversation on gender and VR were like many I had attended. But what made this event memorable was an announcement that came at the beginning of the evening. Though this was the first Riveter location in LA, the head of marketing of the company announced at this event that they had recently closed on a second LA location in Marina del Rey, the former LA headquarters of a company known as Upload. There were cheers and whoops in the audience at this announcement. How fitting, she went on, that the space is being taken over by a "female forward coworking space. . . . You know the story, and you know what needs to happen in that space now."

The story of Upload can be glossed as a triumph of the #MeToo movement for the VR community. This chapter focuses on the fantasy of representation that imagines women as having a significant role to play in VR's development. The downfall of Upload, which I'll discuss in more detail, felt for many to be an important step toward realizing this fantasy. Many women shared with me that they were attracted to VR because it is new and would allow them to ascend to positions of leadership more quickly than in other industries.[1] Whether VR will be a progressive industry with gender parity remains to be seen; however, lessons drawn from the history of technology do not paint a promising picture. Women have frequently been written out of stories about technology development, or their importance has been marginalized.[2] The history of computing in particular is a story of how a new field rose in prestige and men took control and ownership of work that was at first deemed menial and thus left to women. Further, as computers became ubiquitous, the precise (if repetitive) task of making circuit boards was skillfully carried out by women of color, first in factories in the US and today in China where several investigations have revealed human rights violations.[3] This labor structure is no doubt one of the conditions by which today's consumer VR headsets are able to be affordably priced.

Most of the big winners of the current VR wave are men or large corporations. And yet, the fantasy persists that VR could be different; that the history being made today could diverge from what has unfolded in the past. During my fieldwork, I discerned two conversations concerning women's role in VR. The first, which began before but gained momentum in the aftermath of the 2017 #MeToo moment and the resulting #TimesUp campaign (launched by women in Hollywood in 2018), was that it was finally time in society writ large for women to lead. The Women in VR Facebook group started in November 2015 and is the most successful of several networking platforms that helped create visibility for women creators, enthusiasts, and their allies. In addition to this sociological or structural conversation, there was an ontological one. There were several ways in which virtual reality was being constructed as inherently feminine (and, importantly, this does not necessarily mean feminist) such that women were its natural stewards. This construction has its roots in 1980s and 1990s cyberfeminism, reinforcing the subtle point made during the panel that today's VR is structured by work and conversations of previous decades. This chapter explores these two conversations, how they reinforce each other, and the gender trouble that accompanies essentializing claims of affinity between technology and gender. In the next chapter, I will explore an undercurrent in the conversations regarding women in VR that offers an alternative to the story of gender and technology told in this chapter: perhaps the fantasy of women in tech more broadly can be realized if we change what "tech" means and whose expertise matters.

When discussing my research with people unfamiliar with the VR space, they would often ask me whether women were "really" leading. After all, it seemed kind of unreal that a technology associated in pop culture with the masculine and the military would appeal so strongly to women. Indeed, this is what is revealing about the unreal: it signals not only the hazards of conflicting realities but also their ability to invite fantasies of hopeful futures. The fantasy of representation gives shape to an otherwise world where women lead technological innovation and those who threaten careers with their abuse are held accountable. The fantasy performs social work, even as the conditions to which it reacts remain ongoing. As realities multiply, there are fleeting moments when the otherwise comes into being. This fantasy quickly dissipates, revealing the world as it has always been.

VR's #MeToo Moment

Another woman in the audience at the Riveter event, Carla, was my project partner in a VR class we took during the first few months of 2018 at the infamous Upload's LA headquarters. An anthropologist ought to learn the language of the community they are living with, and so I enrolled in a class that would teach me the basics of building VR experiences in the Unity game engine. Taking the class also allowed me a perspective outside of the established companies I worked with in regards to the ease or difficulty with which one can enter the VR industry. Carla was in her twenties, came to LA for film school, and is passionate about supporting women in the workforce. She was employed in a leadership position at a coworking space that provided in-house daycare; it was an experiment in helping women work, indeed be entrepreneurs, even while their children were young. The company was in flux, and she was still searching for a career. Carla grew up in the US Virgin Islands and has always felt behind when it comes to technology. She compared her technical ability to her brother-in-law's, who taught himself to code in high school. This wasn't a possibility for Carla. She didn't have her own computer until college, not because her family couldn't afford it but because that kind of connectivity wasn't the norm where she grew up. Despite this perceived disadvantage, she was always interested in science and technology and when she learned about VR (after seeing demos at street festivals in LA), she became excited that there was a new medium that combined her love of storytelling with technology. Linking it to her current professional interests, she told me that part of VR's appeal was also that it would satisfy her desire "to be another lady in tech in some way." Carla genuinely enjoyed doing VR and would often get to class early or come in during office hours and try out different VR games and experiences (few of us taking the class had a VR setup at home, as not only were the headsets expensive but they also needed to be tethered to pricey gaming computers). She was the woman at the Riveter event who tried out the demos and reported back to me on their quality. Carla saw the class at Upload as a first step toward a future career in VR, even though in 2018 there were far fewer opportunities than a year or two earlier. Whereas some members of my class made resolutions that by year's end they would be employed at a VR company, Carla was content to be engaged and aware of industry happenings.

THE PROMISE OF ACCESS

Most of us who enrolled in the VR development class were outsiders: assistants, animators, actors, engineers, educators, high school and college students, all pursuing a new passion or hoping for a career change. Being in the Upload space—a two-story open office layout, with a hint of the tech bro vibe (a conference table, but instead of chairs, swings!) but otherwise sleek and shiny—made one feel like part of the club. As we arrived for class on Tuesday evenings, companies that worked there during the day would be packing up, or maybe sticking around for a beer, and were happy to talk about the VR game or 360° film project they were working on. On nights when class wasn't being held, there were meetups, talks, or demos hosted in the space. Upload never felt particularly crowded, and as the class progressed there were fewer events and fewer people around. In contrast to the decline that we could all observe, the message on the first day of the course was that we should congratulate ourselves for being in the right place at the right time. Our lead instructor delivered a message from Upload's founder: "As a pioneer in this new medium, it's important to remember how much responsibility we have. VR has incredible power over the human mind, experience, and perception . . . and the impact you're having should always be considered. It's an honor to build this future with all of you."

Carla, myself, and a few others did our best to take advantage of the space and the knowledge of our instructors. We would come in on weekends and during office hours to work on homework, our final projects, and help each other out in learning the basics of Unity and working with VR. Two weeks before the course's conclusion and the "demo day," where we would share our projects with friends, family, and "industry leaders," Upload's CFO came to class to announce that Upload was "getting out of the physical space business" and the office would be closing at the end of the month. Students were given the chance to ask questions, and many expressed frustration that some of the promises of the class—a discount membership to the coworking space, guarantee of an industry internship—were not being honored. One student offered his condolences and delicately asked what this closure portends for the VR industry writ large? The CFO admitted that when Upload was founded, the VR market was hot. This simply wasn't the case anymore. With that, he handed class over to our instructor, who tried to paint a sunnier picture—did we all see that "Unity developer" was just listed as one of ten growth jobs?

Following the session at which this announcement was made, Carla and I decided to meet at Upload over the weekend to finish up our project and, despite this wrinkle, do our best to deliver a polished experience for the demo day. We were greeted with an unusual scene at Upload. Racks of clothes were being wheeled in, models were walking around in partial makeup, producers were shouting angrily into cell phones. We looked at each other with confusion, and slinked up to the classroom to get in a few hours of work. As we left, the space was more chaotic, clearly being transformed into a fashion show. Two programmers, who rented office space at Upload and were also trying to squeeze in a weekend work session, looked tired and out of place. When Carla and I returned the next morning for more project work, the normally neat and tidy office was trashed from the previous night's event. Most of the Upload staff had been fired or preemptively left immediately following the announcement that the space was closing, and it showed. The class concluded with everyone feeling deflated. Only eight teams presented at the demo day, and while it felt celebratory and we were proud of ourselves, most of my classmates expressed a frustration that the next steps of breaking into the VR industry were unclear. The one connection they had, Upload, officially shuttered its doors shortly after the course ended.

VIOLATIONS

When I signed up for this class in fall 2017, a few months before I began fieldwork, I had vaguely remembered reading that Upload's founders were being sued for sexual harassment. However, I was in the middle of my first semester teaching at a new university and was not paying as close attention to the community as I ought to have been leading up to fieldwork. I had seen that one of the women I met during preliminary fieldwork, Jacki Ford Morie, had joined Upload as the Vice President of Education. I respected her work and her role in the community and did not therefore perform my due diligence with regards to vetting Upload. I admit that I was eager to see Upload as a neutral site, given that it was the only place in LA I had found that offered a basic skills class in VR development. In hindsight, I regret giving tuition money to Upload and providing any kind of legitimacy

6.1 The Upload office shuts down. Photograph taken in March 2018 by the author.

that might have come with an Ivy League professor being in their space. But I do feel fortunate to have met so many wonderful students in the class who, as outsiders, did not (as far as I could tell) know Upload's backstory.

During the first few months of fieldwork, while I was taking the class and meeting with people in the VR community, it became clear that I had violated a taboo in affiliating with Upload. Lunches with potential collaborators that had been going well instantly turned cold when I mentioned that I was taking a development class at Upload. Whereas I thought I was flashing credentials ("I'm learning your language"), I was violating a norm. I would leave such meetings confused, knowing that there would be no follow up. By late February, my fieldnotes had taken on an air of conspiracy—was word spreading that the anthropologist interested in women in VR was consorting with Upload? Is that why no one was returning my emails? At this point, I had searched through the Facebook group archives and understood how polarizing the Upload case was and how betrayed the community felt by the continued failure of the cofounders (whose words, on the first night of class, preached of responsibility) to properly own up to their past actions and therefore were undeserving of support even if they were on the surface making amends.

To take a step back, Upload was founded in 2014 by two men in their midtwenties. It raised several million dollars of VC money and opened an office in Silicon Valley in 2016 that held events and workshops catering to the growing VR community. In 2017, Upload opened its second office in LA, and this became the company's new headquarters. When the LA office opened, the VR community (men and women) were excited and supportive.[4] However, in the summer of 2017, a female San Francisco employee sued Upload for sexual harassment. By this point, the San Francisco office, managed as it was by young men who suddenly saw wealthy futures, had become known for wild parties where attendees could slip into a "kink room" for additional fun.[5] The fantasy that I encountered in LA, that VR could be a different kind of industry, was shattered in Upload's SF office, which seemed to be charting the typical path of other tech companies. The "move fast and break things" mentality was leaving victims in its wake. In September 2017, the *New York Times* reported that the lawsuit had been settled. The article's title read, "Lurid Lawsuit's Quiet End Leaves Silicon Valley Start-Up Barely Dented."[6] The reporter lamented that sexual harassment seems to have become standard in the tech industry, with few facing its consequences. The coda of the article reported that Upload brought on a woman to serve as chief operating officer, who noted with melancholy in the article that as a woman in Silicon Valley, she only gets such a job offer when a company is in trouble. Her office, noted the reporter, was in what used to be the kink room.

As far as I could tell, there was no kink room in the LA Upload building, and the few events I attended outside of class were far tamer than those described in the article. I did notice that most of the Upload staff were young women, and as such they were always cleaning up the space and setting out the food for the mostly (but not exclusively) male clients; these were hardly optics that signaled equality. I had one unsavory encounter at Upload in March, just before the company's collapse. I was attending office hours one evening and on my way to the classroom, two guys were setting up for a shoot. I didn't recognize them, but one was sprawled on a couch and asked if I "wanted to be in it." What was "it," I asked, and he said, "Talking about your first sexual experience." I passed.

I found this situation extraordinary (and offensive) given Upload's PR precarity and the recent conversations in Hollywood that had made the implicit winks about "the casting couch" into an explicit conversation about harassment and assault. A month after the article detailing Upload's quiet settlement of the sexual harassment case was published in the *Times*, the paper reported a bombshell by Jodi Kantor and Megan Twohey (corroborated and elaborated upon by Ronan Farrow at the *New Yorker*) on the abuses and sexual misconduct of Hollywood producer Harvey Weinstein.[7] This catalyzed the celebrity-driven arm of the #MeToo movement, as actors asked for all people who have been sexually harassed or assaulted to post "Me Too" on social media to illustrate the scope of the problem.[8] This campaign ignited in LA but quickly became symbolic of national and global inequities that women and other vulnerable populations face in the workplace.[9] On January 1, 2018, in response to Weinstein and the #MeToo movement, women in Hollywood unveiled their Time's Up campaign. This shifted the conversation from highlighting the prevalence of abusers to actively working toward gender parity in studios and talent agencies.

#MeToo provided a language for linking individual harassment cases with an industry-wide problem. This framework strengthened the VR community's campaign against Upload, with people voicing distrust in Upload's efforts of reform. The woman who had been hired as the new chief operating officer and a face of this reform resigned just weeks after she was quoted in the *Times* article, and Upload was being kept financially afloat by a personal investment from Palmer Luckey, founder of Oculus who himself had been ostracized from the VR community for voicing racist opinions representative of radical right politics.[10] In April 2018, just after my class concluded, both the LA and San Francisco Upload offices closed. And at the June 2018 Riveter event, the women in VR community rejoiced in the irony of the space's takeover.

The Upload case, which at first seemed to suggest that VR was just like any other tech industry in that sexual harassment suits would barely leave a dent in the face of the overwhelming promises of VC wealth, had leveraged community sentiment and the #MeToo movement to bolster the conviction that VR could be a different kind of industry. This was an industry where sexual harassers were not welcome. Contrary to the *New York Times* article, VR would not tolerate business as usual. This strand of the conversation about women in VR rested on a belief that it was time for change in the workforce more broadly. Both Hollywood and tech were old industries, and gender hierarchies were deeply engrained. But perhaps, as the fantasy goes, sitting as it does between entertainment and tech, nimble in its newness, VR could be a different kind of industry. For the young, hopeful VR workers I met in class or I heard speaking on panels, there was a reluctance to let go of the idea that the technology could be different. Even women with longer histories in the field remained optimistic; if VR seems to be forever on the brink of emergence, so too was the hope of female leadership. In tracing back the longer history of women in VR, we see that this fantasy of representation is bolstered by a claim that VR in specific is a technology best understood and utilized by women.

Women and the Machine

One of the few women who remained affiliated with Upload until the end was Jacki Ford Morie. Morie is respected and beloved by the LA women in the VR community, and many were hurt when she announced accepting the position of VP of Education at Upload. Even when we spoke toward the end of my fieldwork, after Upload had collapsed, she remained supportive of one of the founders who she felt genuinely cared about VR education. She also remains supportive of (if wounded by) women she had mentored who turned their backs on her for this affiliation. Unlike some of the people who, like Morie, were involved in VR's prior waves, she remains bullish about the technology and genuinely excited by all the new interest. Further, she wants women to remain involved as the feminine perspective is necessary, Morie claims, for VR to be truly innovative and enduring.

The few times I visited Morie at her house, it was clear that she was a cultivator. Her plants were thriving, her cats numerous and purring, and family members flowed through the house asking Morie for this or that. On one occasion, I was invited over to give a talk at her VR Salon, an occasional happening that she hosts with the hopes of enriching LA's VR community by bringing together those who are newly excited about the technology and those, like herself, who have worked with the medium in its earlier days. Morie's research and artistic work in VR (she has two master's degrees as well as a PhD that all inform her current thinking about the medium) are themselves significant, but of interest here is also her cultivation of the narrative that women are best suited for creating impactful VR experiences and thus they ought to have a leading role in VR. This claim is bolstered through both Morie's philosophical musings on VR as well as reintroducing work by women in the 1980s and '90s into VR's history. In July 2015 (several months before the Women in VR Facebook group was established), she wrote an article about the history of women in VR. It was published by VRScout, a popular LA-based media company founded in 2014 that covers all things VR, hosts podcasts, and holds community events. She introduced readers to several women who, in previous decades, produced significant VR works and yet are largely overlooked when telling VR's male-centric history.[11]

The prominence of women in VR as early as the late '80s and '90s was an unexpected finding of Morie's PhD dissertation, completed in 2007. The thesis is a reflection on artistic practices used for creating fully immersive VR experiences. She was a senior research scientist at the University of Southern California's Institute for Creative Technologies (see chapter 1) while doing her degree remotely at the University of East London. Morie told me in an interview that she did her dissertation "thinking VR was dead." It was a way to summarize the work she had done over the last two decades before moving on to whatever would be next. As part of her research, she wanted to create a historical record of the VR artistic works that had been created since the 1980s. Many were not documented, but Morie catalogued about one hundred. She was surprised to note that nearly two-thirds of these pieces were created by women. "I knew all my women friends who did VR," she told me, "but I didn't realize in the grand scheme of things how prominent they were."

Women, unsurprisingly, have been scrubbed from VR's history. During the 1990s, when a dozen or so popular books about the medium were released, fueling the hype, women were rarely mentioned. Even though Jaron

Lanier, who coined the phrase *virtual reality*, observes the significance of women in his 2017 memoir *Dawn of the New Everything*, he nonetheless fails to see their role as VR creators. In Silicon Valley in the 1980s, several women were nicknamed "Grand Networking Females" (GNF) and, as Lanier narrates, were the original LinkedIn, responsible for placing programmers and engineers at both fledgling and established tech companies. He remarks that Coco Conn, an LA-based "GNF," "was probably at least half responsible for connecting the VR scene of the 1980s."[12] Lanier is making an earnest effort to include these hidden figures in his account, but in elevating the importance of women's "soft skills" for the tech industry, he also denies their role as innovators.[13]

Most narratives of VR's history focus on the hardware development or the military investment and thus the overt masculinity of such enterprises. As media theorist June Deery observed in 1994, the root of *virtual*, "vir," is an Indo-European root for *man* and can also be found in words of strength (*virility*) and goodness (*virtue*). Deery writes, "In [VR's] present applications it is easier to see strength and prowess than obvious goodness. Simulated military attacks and violent video games are some of the first and most popular applications of this new technology."[14] It is precisely this history of VR that Morie is seeking to counter in her focus on the people who were producing VR art, downplaying virility in favor of virtue. These early VR artists (both men and women) faced significant challenges. VR setups were expensive and unwieldy, located primarily in laboratories. Morie observes in her thesis (based in part on her own experience of creating with VR in the 1990s) that artists working in these labs were often shunned by other artists because the labs, and therefore the art, were military funded.[15] Nor was it easy for artists to gain access to such labs. Even when they succeeded, the work produced could not be seen by a wide audience. Margaret Dolinsky, an artist who has worked in immersive CAVE environments as well as VR, explained in 2014 on the cusp of the release of commercial headsets, how even if you were able to get access to a lab "and get an art piece going, it's really difficult to set up a time and place where people can come through and see it. . . . You can just hear about it. . . . And I think that when people don't have accessibility to the medium, it really limits the conversation about it."[16] Dolinsky is one of several artists Morie credits with pushing the limits of the medium. Dolinsky was able to maintain an artistic practice in VR as a university professor. Other creators from the 1990s received funding from The Banff Center in Alberta.[17] When this funding stream dried up, however, artists lost access to the technology and ceased producing VR art (though many found other ways to persist in their interests).[18]

A WOMAN'S TOUCH?

In her thesis and subsequent articles, Morie offered (what she admitted to me are "half-baked") intuitions to explain the role women have played in experimenting with VR's expressive and artistic potential. Morie does not deny that men were also creating VR art in the '90s, but attributes a "feminine approach" to the most significant work produced during this period. "This approach seems well suited to immersive environments as it incorporates aspects of inclusion, wholeness, and a blending of the body and the spirit."[19] She draws on feminist theorist Hélène Cixous, who notes that the pen in all its phallic connotation has made writing a masculine medium. Morie counters: "If a text is inherently male, then a virtual environment is inherently female" in that it cultivates possibilities for becoming as does a woman when birthing a child.[20] In our interview, she clarified this connection: "You can't author a child. And I think letting go of that, that premier-author mode of creation in VR—by creating a space where [the experiencer] completes the work—that it is the perfect medium for women." Wrapped up in this claim that VR is the ideal *l'écriture féminine* are also assertions (made throughout Morie's dissertation) that truly impactful VR is fully immersive and interactive; it allows an experient (Morie's term) to explore an open world and, unlike 360° video, does not insist on expressing a single story from a single perspective.[21]

This idea that VR is "naturally" suited for women captured the imagination of many women in the space. Morie is not credited for bringing this idea into the field, though given the informal ways ideas travel in LA's VR community—especially ideas that affirm a belief about the technology— it is plausible that women close to her picked up this idea and repeated it to others. As the claim moved further from Morie's research, a woman's natural affinity for VR was no longer expressed as a hypothesis or a theory; it was shared as a fact about VR. In 2021, I heard this "fact" expressed on a podcast during which two female "tech futurists" were discussing how VR, unlike other tech sectors, had more gender parity. One of the futurists mused that maybe this was because VR was suited to open-ended storytelling and women are more comfortable with this uncertainty; they are not as fixated on controlling the story as their male counterparts.[22]

A few years before this podcast was recorded, I was having tea with three women (an artist, an actress, and a producer; all were working in VR) to talk about an educational venture they were beginning. In this conversation, women's leadership in VR served to naturalize VR as an empathy machine, which in turn reinforced women's role in the industry. The producer, Jasmine, was eager to share her gloss on the industry with an anthropologist and offer her explanation as to why women were VR's "natural" leaders. Women, she explained to me, have an innate ability to create VR as "we" are more empathetic. This is the mindset one needs to have if you are making impactful VR. The actress, Ashley, agreed (and I could tell this was a conversation the two of them had had many times). Ashley shifted from the affective skill women bring to VR and drew an evolutionary affinity between women and VR. Men are hunters, Ashley told me. They can't help that they are predisposed to looking straight ahead. But women are gatherers and have a habit of looking all around. VR, as a fully immersive medium, requires such behavior. Both because of an aptitude for empathy and a physical way of being in the world—of looking all around oneself that by this reasoning emerges from previous women's work as gatherers—women create better VR experiences. This is slightly different from Morie's explanation that women are holistic and collaborative creators, or the podcaster's suggestion that women are comfortable with uncertainty, but regardless of the reasoning, women are positioned as VR's natural stewards.

This is not the first new technology that has been praised as a path toward women's empowerment (nor the first one to appeal to gender essentialism and a singular "woman's" experience). Notably, as digital and networked activity became ubiquitous in the '80s and '90s (at the same time that VR was making its first commercialization attempt), cyberfeminism emerged as a genre of scholarship and an accompanying social and artistic movement. In some of the foundational works for theorists in this genre, for example N. Katherine Hayles's *How We Became Posthuman* or Donna Haraway's "A Cyborg Manifesto," there was a fantasy of co-opting the new digital technologies for feminist ends. As Haraway observed, cyborgs are "the illegitimate offspring of militarism and patriarchal capitalism. . . . [They] are often exceedingly unfaithful to their origins."[23] Haraway and Hayles were both in search of figures of transcendence that could lead to postgender or posthuman futures: figures that were not femin*ine* but rather femin*ist*. For Hayles, virtual reality was exciting because it was visual confirmation that "a world of information exists parallel to the 'real world.'"[24] VR in specific and what she called "virtuality" more generally drew attention to the invis-

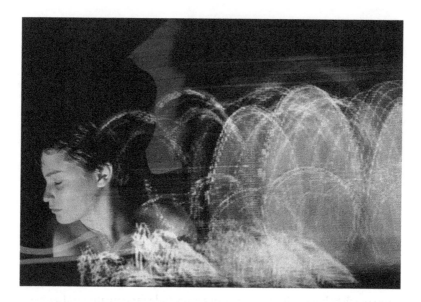

6.2 "Das Energi." Part of Morie's 1984 mixed media MFA, titled "Integrated Fantasies." Courtesy of Jacki Ford Morie.

ible networks of information increasingly patterning the conditions of life in the late twentieth century. Hayles and Haraway both took figures of the military–industrial complex and demanded that scholars reject their explicit symbolism and instead acknowledge how they represent new modes of being across virtual and physical worlds and this could be inspiring rather than constraining.

In the early 1990s, it might have felt like VR and the internet were developing at the same pace and part of a common future in which we might all be using VR to enter William Gibson's (deeply masculine) "cyberspace."[25] "The virtual" was thus a capacious category that rarely distinguished between the virtual of VR and the virtual of email and chat rooms. As the internet was realized and VR floundered, in cyberfeminism and other critical media scholarship, "the virtual" narrowed in reference to online, networked experiences (sometimes more specifically called "virtual worlds").[26] As the technologies that initially inspired cyberfeminism changed, so too did its theoretical commitments. In 2009, sociologist Jessie Daniels reviewed the cyberfeminism literature of the previous decades, outlining the initial utopian hope and ambition of cyberfeminist scholars and collaborators as well as the challenges scholars now faced. The internet was initially seen by many as a site of liberation and equality, an escape from sexualized (and racialized) bodies.[27] Daniels observes that as online spaces have moved from text-based to image-based, such freedom no longer seems so straightforward. Her own studies of online chat groups show how early cyberfeminist assumptions are now much more complicated; there is no one way to "be" online, and certainly there is no one way to be a woman online. If Sadie Plant, who fleshed out and popularized "cyberfeminism," argued in the mid-1990s that "virtuality brings a fluidity to identities which once had to be fixed; and multimedia provides a new tactile environment in which women artists can find their space," Daniels notes a decade later that online gender performance need not be necessarily progressive: "Self-identified girls and women engage in practices with internet technologies to manage, transform, and control their physical bodies in ways that both resist and reinforce hierarchies of gender and race."[28]

Scholars moved away from cyberfeminism throughout the 2000s despite effort by Daniels and others to open new avenues of inquiry that were free from some of the utopianism and essentialism of earlier writing. Though Morie has some familiarity with this literature, most of the women I spoke with during fieldwork were unaware of cyberfeminism. And yet, I found community conversations to resonate and diverge with this scholarship in interesting ways. VR had the potential to be a feminist technology, but female empowerment came from different imaginations of the relationship between body and technology. Similar to the shift I detail in chapter 4, by which VR's fantasy of being in the 1990s was premised on a mind freed from the body versus a focus in the 2010s on the ability to be embodied somewhere else or as someone else, cyberfeminists initially imagined the feminist potential of "the virtual" as an escape from the *marked* body (though not from the body itself, in distinction to the fantasy of the freed mind),[29] whereas today's potential is located in VR's ability to replicate embodiment; to fuse mind and body in a post-Cartesian configuration.[30] But this is not the fantasy of being *another*. Rather, some articulate how *virtual embodied being* is how women best embody and express *themselves*. When Morie or Jasmine or Ashley gesture toward VR as a woman's technology, it is supported by a belief that women are better able to realize the potential of embodied storytelling.[31] In addition to building on cyberfeminist imaginaries of VR as a feminist technology, it is today also being positioned as a feminine technology. If a few commentators wrote in the 1990s that VR's feminist potential was in facilitating a postgender future,[32] in 2018, some celebrated the ways in which VR elevated the female above the male as she who is best suited for creating, experiencing, and innovating VR.

Conversations about women in VR seamlessly weave together ontological claims about VR as a feminine technology and structural claims that VR is an industry women can and ought to lead. While many find this coupling empowering, it is necessary to identify what this compelling fantasy obscures both in terms of whose voices are excluded and what power dynamics such essentialist claims propagate. The fantasy of representation falls prey to similar misdirections as the fantasy of being in that both present façades of better, other worlds while concealing the structures that enable the fantasies as well as the worlds that persist despite the fantasies. Most of the conversations on gender that I witnessed reinforced cisgender categories even as the community embraced queer and trans members.[33] One of my interlocutors told me that they preferred the label of "girl" to "woman," as to them "woman" signified reproduction and they had no interest in this. This perspective was in the minority as many felt "girl" was infantilizing and unprofessional. This same person felt alienated from the community as, particularly at the in-person events around LA, there was a "popular girls" vibe that made one flash back to middle school. Perhaps this is unsurprising as the kind of feminism that was often on display is what Sarah Banet-Weiser has called "popular feminism."[34] Popular feminism arises from the awareness and articulation of gender imbalance in industries like entertainment and tech. There is a naïve attitude that simply adding more women will lead to feminist futures, thus ignoring underlying structural problems. Banet-Weiser also draws out the dynamic of popularity in "popular feminism" by which white, cisgendered, heterosexual women feel most at ease with this feminist discourse. My friend who felt marginalized by the women in VR community was nonwhite and gender nonconforming; they were not "popular" in the traditional sense and thus ill at ease with the popular feminism of the community.

And while the community had created a space that encouraged public and explicit conversations about gender diversity, more encompassing intersectional conversations especially about race were largely muted and left implicit. Most of the events I attended were carefully curated to include people of color as panelists. However, narratives of being nonwhite in this industry were not discussed with the same freedom as the experience of being a woman. There were nonwhite women in leadership positions within VR, and throughout 2018, Kamal Sinclair, a Black woman who was known to the community for her role as director and cocurator of Sundance's New Frontier Lab (see chapter 4) researched and wrote a series of articles about diversity issues in VR and emerging media that went beyond gender.[35] These circulated widely and were frequently discussed online even if they were not given the same treatment in person.

The fantasy of representation encapsulated by VR as an industry that prizes gender equality not only occluded intersectional conversations, but in arguing that women were its "naturally" suited leaders weakened the potential to fulfill this fantasy. Claims of VR being inherently feminine likely sound discordant to those whose feminist commitments don't deny difference but likewise don't build claims of ability upon difference. Joan Scott persuasively argued in 1988 that in feminist theory and politics, essentializing difference naturalizes inequality: "To maintain that femininity predisposes women to certain (nurturing) jobs or (collaborative) styles of work is to naturalize complex economic and social process and, once again, to obscure the differences that have characterized women's occupational histories."[36] Even if, in this case, the essentialist claims were being used to elevate the status of women, it invited counterclaims that therefore (most) other technologies were suited for a masculine approach.

The VR community needs a different model for thinking about gender and technology. Perhaps xenofeminism, proposed by Helen Hester and her Laboria Cuboniks collaborators, could assist in refiguring the conversation.[37] Building on cyborg- and cyber-feminisms, xenofeminism wrestles with the material role technology plays in the everyday while also adopting intersectional, "antinaturalist," and "gender abolitionist" stances. In other words, rather than either essentializing gender or denying gender (as some cyborg approaches do), xenofeminism leans into the ways biology shapes embodiment. It does, however, reject the fixity of both biology and embodiment. The body is a site of technopolitical intervention through its reworking. As Hester writes, "Gender should be granted no extraordinary power. We must look for more nimble and inclusive vectors of solidarity."[38] The examples of xenofeminist technologies provided by Hester focus on the potential of reproductive or hormonal interventions that circumnavigate the medical establishment and allow people to reclaim control over the knowledge and futures of their bodies.

VR's feminist potential similarly lies in its link to embodiment. But VR's ability to explore one's own embodied fluidity cannot be conflated with the "empathy machine" drive, as previously discussed, to embody an Other.[39] Xenofeminism advocates for technological repurposing, and here one can imagine VR experiences that interrogate the very fantasy of embodiment that VR facilitates.

Conclusion

The fantasy of representation—central to the aspiration for VR to be a good industry—is complexly entwined with the fantasy of VR as a good technology. In 2018, a good industry meant one that was diverse. Compatibly, VR's goodness was attached to empathy. The perceived feminine energy emanating from both of these claims united in an overall expectation that women were VR's natural leaders. This is a compelling fantasy, and in many ways, it did good work in terms of making people like Carla feel as though they would be welcomed into this community as a "lady in tech." But in addition to the gender essentialism that plagues this fantasy, there runs the risk that it perpetuates a technological essentialism. Namely, can this fantasy persist without falling back on a belief that technology is somehow inevitably tied to good social outcomes?

In late November 2018, two weeks before I would pack up and leave LA, I returned to what used to be Upload and was now The Riveter's second LA location. The space looked mostly the same, though the VR demos were gone as was the conference table with swings for chairs. Things were a bit more polished, a bit more LA, a bit less Silicon Valley. I'd returned to this space for an event called #MeToo: How Do We Heal, which had been advertised on the Women in VR Facebook group. It was not well attended; maybe it was the time of year, maybe because people had grown exhausted of the conversation. Or maybe because it was raining, and this unusual LA weather occurrence keeps people at home. There were a dozen of us, and I only recognized one woman, whom I had met a few weeks ago at the salon at which Jacki Morie had invited me to speak.

Though the event wasn't explicitly about VR or tech, the host worked in tech and so did some of the panelists. As she explained, the idea for this event came from her participation in a "women in blockchain" conference that was held on the same day that Dr. Christine Blasey Ford testified to the harassment and abuses of (now) Supreme Court Justice Brett Kavanaugh. She saw how much Ford's testimony affected the community, how people were impassioned to keep fighting. Our host decided there needed to be more conversations about how women, particularly those working in male-dominated industries, could heal and protect themselves while also devising constructive steps to be taken as the first year of the Weinstein-catalyzed #MeToo movement drew to a close. The invited panelists all led initiatives that sought to better women's lives and perhaps could inspire those of us in the audience to create or contribute to similar projects.

Each panelist presented their company or endeavor, explaining how it facilitated healing. And because of the intimacy of the event, some of the panelists also shared their own histories of assault and abuse, and how that contributed to the work they chose to pursue. Some of the talks imagined the women in the room as the target of healing: a psychotherapist led us through a guided meditation, and an activist explained how telling one's story is therapeutic. In contrast, the tech projects were animated by the hope of helping less privileged women.[40] One panelist was a VR director, and she discussed her 360° documentary about women who escaped from being sex slaves held by ISIS and formed a resistance militia. She noted that we are all probably sick of hearing about "VR as an empathy machine." Who cares if it produces empathy if that doesn't translate into action? Her solution was to use VR's (assumed) empathetic quality for leveraging funds to support these female fighters. The final panelist explained the cryptocurrency she developed, intended to help women all over the world. If someone acquired a digital token, they could use it to "ask the blockchain for help," requesting a certain amount of money for a particular reason. The speaker made grand claims about how this token system could help topple the patriarchy. When asked how she assures that requests for money are made by those with good cause, she responded that the community does the vetting; good requests will be honored, and bad ones will fail. She said that she founded the company with good core values, and this will translate into good actors using her products. Driving home from the event (cautious on the rain-slickened roads), I thought about how it was telling that the projects that didn't employ technology were targeted at individual healing, but the high-tech solutions were figured as those that could scale up and extend past the local community to bring about global change. Women could use tech to heal the world.

Despite the VR director and the developer of the crypto fundraising platform highlighting the social apparatuses they developed to ensure that their technology would do good work in the world, there remained an assumption that their goals *required* emerging technology to succeed (that VR and crypto were the best ways to support women). Further, the crypto platform's success was premised on an unsupported belief that the blockchain was inherently democratic. Consequently, an assumption that technology leads to, and thus becomes equated with, social progress remained unperturbed in these conversations about how to heal after trauma. This assumption persists in the fantasy of representation by which VR's technological affordances (as well as its novelty) made it seem possible, perhaps inevitable, that a diverse industry could emerge. But technology's association with progress is a product of historical circumstance[41] and in practice novel technologies tend to buttress, rather than challenge, the very social norms that the #MeToo movement sought to undermine.[42]

STS scholar Christina Dunbar-Hester puts this succinctly in her book *Hacking Diversity*: "*Technology* is a fraught concept to place in a central role in a project of emancipation."[43] Dunbar-Hester's ethnography of the open technology community teases out how advocating for diversity within this community telescopes out into assumptions that a good workforce will necessarily seed outcomes that bring forth a better world. However, "assuming that diverse people cultivating diverse technologies will lead to a more egalitarian and empowering technological future" fails to critically examine and reform "how *technology itself* is implicated in projects of social sorting and domination."[44] The harms that have led to "the techlash" are not solved simply by diversifying the workforce. There are deeper structural problems that plague the tech industry, rendered invisible by the essentialist belief that technology is progressive. This is not to say that technology *can't* be implemented to good ends, but instead that this is not inevitable, as the foundations upon which the tech industry is built (capitalism, surveillance, imperialism) thwart most efforts of resistance.

Dunbar-Hester concludes her book by suggesting that technological communities that strive to build a better world—both for their community and through the things they produce—ought to do so not only through technical interventions but also through critical analyses of technology and power. Such analyses have the potential to question the very meaning of "technology," as it is a concept historically, socially, and politically shaped. My own concluding chapter will suggest that women in LA's VR scene were already engaged with a project of redefining what "technology" means and therefore who gets to be a "tech worker." They were implicitly fomenting a tech otherwise which further bolstered the fantasy of representation. But a question lingers: What further work is needed such that the fantasies emergent from the unreal are not captured by the structures they are imagined as opposing?

MAKING INNOVATION WOMEN'S WORK

STORYTELLING AND WORLDBUILDING FOR A "TECH" OTHERWISE

In August 2018, I observed a motion-capture shoot that was using the stage at the Technicolor Experience Center (TEC). I arrived with the crew at seven thirty in the morning and as wires were connected and Pelican cases unpacked, I settled into a corner and googled the VR gaming company that had rented out the stage. On their "Our Vision" page, they praised VR as being able to bring a player into the world of a game. Like so many other pitches I heard throughout the year, VR's appeal didn't stop simply at its immersiveness or entertainment value, but rather VR was positioned as *the* medium of the future because it reconnects us, as the gaming website read, to "what truly makes us human."

During this first hour of set up, I was the only woman on the sound stage. The TEC employees who run the stage calibrated the mocap cameras and explained to me the procedure for and the importance of each step. The next people to show up included a few women: a production assistant, the script supervisor, and a sound engineer. To my surprise, more women kept arriving, including a writer as well as two producers and the director. Whereas in most of my other fieldwork experiences, I purposely sought out projects that were female led, I had asked to observe this shoot simply to get a better sense of the mechanics of a performance-capture shoot for VR. I also assumed that because this was a first-person shooter game—not typically what is intended by the claims of VR connecting us to "what truly makes us human," thus stripped of the pretense of VR being a good technology that I thought might select for gender diverse teams—I'd get a glimpse at what a shoot "typically" looks like. And yet, I was again on a majority female set.

With everyone assembled, the shoot began. The director was a seasoned mocap director (the producer told me, in awe, that she has worked "on everything"), but it was her first VR shoot, and this was true for most others on set. As with the Embodied Labs shoot, basic rules of acting in VR had to be explained. The director instructed the mocap performer to deliver his lines directly to the camera (the footage would be used as reference when compositing the CG scene): "The player is the camera," she said, reminding him of VR's special affect. The actor got into the role, embracing the predatory nature of the line he delivered to the camera—to the player who is a female character in the story. The producer shivered, and she complimented him on his sleaziness. "Just call me Mr. Weinstein," he responded, and they both laughed and grimaced.

Throughout the day, as I chatted with different members of the crew, people kept repeating two observations. The first was a general excitement to be working in VR and how its newness made it feel like there were no limits. A writer reflected how amazed she was that "anything goes" and how it was cool to be at the forefront of a new medium. As folks learned the ropes of working on a VR set, they made constant comparison to traditional film and television sets, remarking on the freedom that comes when standards are relaxed and there's no presumed "right way" of doing things. The other comment made again and again was about the number of women on set. The writer described it as the "best ratio" she'd ever experienced on a set. Later, a producer made a similar comment, but emphasized to me that this is not typical, intimating that VR was special. While the director didn't comment on the gender ratio, throughout the day she struck a genial tone. There were numerous delays (as well as an actor that couldn't remember his blocking), but she laughed it off and encouraged everyone to keep going and keep doing good work (a stark contrast from a different shoot I observed on the mocap stage where the male director/lead actor was . . . not so generous with his attitude). The day was chill and much was accomplished, leading me at the end of the shoot to recall a line uttered by one of the characters marveling at the ornate (virtual) world they were in: "Is this place real?"

As I've proposed throughout this book, fantasies as much as realities deserve our critical attention. Not only are these fantasies meaningful to the members of the community that hold fast to them, but their repeated articulation grows the coalition of people who believe in the fantasy and even create the conditions for the worlds being conjured to momentarily manifest, as was the case for this mocap shoot. How, then, might these fantasies come to matter beyond the confines of this fleeting moment in VR's history? In this chapter, the fantasies of place, being, and representation interlock in order to decipher not whether VR is *really* some feminist utopia that makes better humans, but rather if the land of the unreal might instructively point toward an otherwise way of doing and being in tech.

Was the work I observed on the shoot "tech work"? Wasn't it instead content production? Certainly, a multitude of cinematic technologies were required, and a lot of data were collected that needed to be cleaned before being imported into a game engine and sent to a developer. But just because technology was present doesn't make something tech work, as we have come to understand it. And yet, throughout fieldwork, being involved in VR was synonymous with being "in tech," regardless of whether someone was writing code or writing dialogue. What are the implications of this categorical collapse?

What it meant—both in LA and for this VR community—to be a "woman in tech" is revealing.[1] I've made passing reference to this phrase throughout the book and in the previous chapter described how Carla, a former film student with no experience in computer programming, found VR appealing because she wanted to be a "lady in tech." Because VR fuses cinematic technology and emerging technology (as I elaborated on in chapter 3), Carla's expertise as a storyteller gave her the initial confidence to pursue this interest in VR and thus tech. But I also observed during fieldwork that the expansion of who claimed a "woman in tech" identity extended beyond VR. I attended a few "women in tech" events around the city expecting to learn about hardware hacks or programming triumphs and would instead be treated to insight into marketing campaigns and business models. In LA, to be a woman in tech did not seem to require being *technical*; that is, having a STEM background and applying that training in the workplace. Being a woman in tech indexed a different set of expertise. Did this in turn mean that "tech" itself had an expanded meaning?[2]

7.1 The Oculus store promotes experiences with female leads and contributors for International Women's Day, 2019.

In the first part of the book, I used the idea of technological terroir to highlight how LA informs the ways in which VR has been imagined and implemented. But, as will be explored in this chapter, the concept of "tech" also has local meanings and associations.[3] Prior to this research, my understanding of tech—and being a woman in tech—was informed by the hegemonic connotation emerging from Silicon Valley and the geographically separated but ideologically connected Cambridge, Massachusetts, the two places I lived between the ages of eighteen and twenty-eight. Though I had not lived in the Bay Area or Cambridge for several years, when I arrived in LA intent on studying the tech scene, I struggled to find conversations about tech that I could comprehend as such. My first reaction was despair: I wasn't sure how I, an anthropologist studying technology, could do the research I intended in a place where there didn't seem to be any tech. But then I realized I had stumbled into a romanticized ethnographic position: "tech" was strange here, and my task was to make it familiar. To be "in tech" in LA was different and somehow, as I began to understand, VR was instrumental to the worldbuilding project that informed this difference.

This chapter draws primarily on interviews I conducted toward the end of my fieldwork with women that I had come to know over the course of my research. With a few exceptions, these women were, at the time of the interviews, making a living from their work in VR. They occupied different positions of power, from assistants to executives, and they all had a background in media and entertainment even as they might have come to identify as a woman in tech.[4] These conversations were an opportunity for us to theorize in tandem about, among other things, what would become the central topics of this book: the VR community and how this city shaped the work being done, what it meant for VR to be perceived as a technology that could be leveraged for social good, and the gender dynamics of both VR and the tech scene in LA.

Squaring these conversations with my observations throughout the year, I offer in this chapter a fantasy of tech otherwise. Against the backdrop of #MeToo, the growing discomfort with the outsized influence of Big Tech, and the general feeling that reality was becoming undone and needed repair, this community wondered if there might be a different kind of future for women, for tech, and for the world. In the previous chapter, I noted that in the history of computing, women were abundant in the early years but systematically marginalized and excluded as the industry grew and gained power. This same pattern exists in the history of Hollywood, where jobs in the studio system that were originally done by women were reclassed as men's work and women's work was relegated to undercompensated and devalued tasks.[5] The kinds of expertise needed to make movies or be a computer programmer were redefined and arbitrarily deemed most suitable for men. If the twentieth-century story is of expertise being narrowed for exclusionary ends, what might it look like in the twenty-first century if expertise is instead expanded with inclusion in mind?[6] What if being a woman in tech does not require an aptitude for hacking but instead storytelling? What if one strategy for making innovation women's work is to redefine what constitutes innovation?

Such experiments were already playing out in LA during my fieldwork. A headline in *Variety* from January 2018 began "AIS Honors 13 Leading Women in Tech," with the lede reading: "In a validation of the goals of #MeToo and #TimesUp . . . the 13 women who won the Advanced Imaging Society's Distinguished Leadership Award made impassioned pleas for the inclusion of more women in science, technology, engineering, and math." Held at the Waldorf Astoria, the honorees were mostly women executives who worked at studios and postproduction companies, who themselves did not have STEM backgrounds despite being honored as women in tech. One honoree was Marcie Jastrow, the head of TEC and who (as detailed in chapter 3) had a successful career in postproduction sales before entering VR.[7] This is a different model for being a woman in tech, and one that offers a tantalizing glimpse of a tech otherwise.

Expanding Expertise

Despite VR having been around for decades, the lead-up to and its successful emergence onto the commercial market in 2016 brought many new people to the technology—as enthusiasts, consumers, and actual and aspiring workers. Importantly, it brought a kind of person who was markedly different from the VR experts that had, for years, occupied academic or defense research labs. In chapter 4, I described how Nonny de la Peña's immersive journalism (and subsequently Chris Milk's TED talk) sounded an invitation to those who wanted to believe that technology, combined with a powerful story, could make the world better. Most of the folks I met during my research were those who responded to this call, attracted to the utopian possibilities that seemed to accompany VR as a "new" technology and industry. Passionate spokespeople for VR emerged, who were able to explain the potential of this technology as well as the various paths to market. Many of the women I spoke with were surprised and appreciative that— sometimes quite quickly—they had come to be considered experts by the VR community and beyond.

Joanna Popper, who I would occasionally check in with over coffee or sushi throughout my year of research, was one such expert who knew everyone in VR and, so it seemed, most everyone else in LA. In January 2018, she had started a job at HP, working as their global head of VR specifically for location-based entertainment installations. Part of the reason she was so well connected was because her job included brokering partnerships with content producers to use HP hardware (it was Popper who introduced me to Jastrow, as TEC was one of the partnerships she had cultivated). She compared her experience of working for a hardware company in VR—and the visibility and power accompanying this position—versus working for a hardware company in television. "The industry is so new," she explained. "There's no way in television, if I was working at Samsung [marketing TVs], I'd sit down with the show runner. I'm not going to sit down with that guy and talk about the show he's making because that's not where the industry is. But this industry, those people who are the creatives and are doing the coolest stuff, which is the stuff that I love, need hardware still."[8]

Popper draws this comparison from her previous experience of working in television marketing for nearly a decade at NBC Universal, focusing on increasing the viewership and market share of Telemundo. She was based in Miami and enjoyed being in entertainment but became frustrated with some of the hierarchies that structured her professional life, both the rigid and long advancement track in television but also the gender hierarchy that she found to be particularly pronounced in Latin entertainment. When Comcast bought NBC Universal and subsequent restructuring led to her being laid off, she took the opportunity to move to the West Coast and began figuring out what to do next. In 2015, Popper was keenly aware that content streaming was a growing market, and she began splitting her time between LA and San Francisco as she conducted her job search. At first, Silicon Valley was disorienting. She didn't understand how the tech industry worked, and jobs came with different titles that did not map onto what she was familiar with from entertainment. And unlike entertainment, where the hierarchy, while arbitrary, is at least clearly laid out, Popper gleaned that though tech pretended to be a meritocracy, the power structure was just cleverly masked. Despite her feeling disconnected from tech culture—she was not a hacker, did not relish in Burning Man, did not wear hoodies—Popper landed a job at Singularity University (SU) to produce content and lead a rebranding effort.

SU proselytizes a Silicon Valley belief that technology is the (only) path toward better human futures. To spread this gospel, it offers programming for entrepreneurs and innovators to learn about emerging technologies that can be leveraged for social progress.[9] Unsurprisingly, during Popper's tenure at SU, VR was a featured technology, noted for its potential to bring about social change. Popper began meeting with folks in the Bay Area working in VR, quickly realizing that, as she described for me, it combined her "passion for content and storytelling, plus newly found appreciation for innovation and technology." When, in March 2017, an SF Women in Tech group put together a panel on VR and other related technologies, the organizer asked Popper to give a short talk about her career thus far, her thoughts on diversity in tech, and where she thought VR was heading. This was the first time Popper had been asked to speak on these topics and, even though she wasn't formally working in VR, she had been informally researching the field for the past year and felt she could speak to its challenges and potentials—at least in the context of a ten-minute talk.

By the end of April, she had spoken two more times about VR for audiences of increasing size. And by the end of the year, she had been invited to give several more talks, including in Mexico and Ireland. She had become a thought leader for VR and a spokesperson advocating for diversity in tech, all while being somewhat of an outsider to both industries. However, Popper also ended the year with a job offer from HP to move to LA and work squarely in VR.

As Popper reflected on this moment in her career, she acknowledged that her interest in VR—not much more than a year old—had led to more prestigious invitations than her eight years in television. She then joyfully described a memorable boat cruise she took with Marcie Jastrow and Shari Frilot (the curator of Sundance's New Frontier) in Venice during the eponymous film festival. All three were invited guests and they were celebrating each other on the canal, shouting how much they loved VR. This excitement, Popper speculated, came from an unspoken realization that had they still been working in TV or VFX or experimental cinema, they probably wouldn't have been invited. Popper clarified that this isn't to say that VR is an easy industry—in fact she imagines that they are all "too early." But it's nonetheless a place where she and others have found more of a voice than they might have otherwise.

For women earlier in their careers, VR was attractive because it was a way to avoid the entertainment industry's rigid hierarchy that depended on an exploitative "dues paying" period at the start of one's career. At TEC, I was chatting with a producer one day at lunch who was usually locked away working on a secret project. Misty was in her midtwenties and found VR to be an easier field in which to claim expertise and be taken seriously. Victoria, an immersive sound designer whom I met on an Embodied Labs shoot on a separate occasion, made a similar point when describing her decision to try for a career in VR upon graduating from college in December 2016. Both Misty and Victoria learned during their undergraduate educations (in animation and film production, respectively) that men dominated. Misty particularly noted that the VFX crowd was a boy's club well versed in the history of the field and if you didn't already have this knowledge (which came not from the classroom, but from adolescent obsession), it was hard to break in. But in VR, Misty glossed, no one was an expert yet, and that was appealing.

If it was perceived that there were few experts because of VR's relative newness, then this also meant that there was the potential to redefine what counted as expertise. VR was thus imagined as not having boundaries or hierarchies or rules; VR did not need to be structured like traditional tech or entertainment companies. Erika, who was the immersive experience coordinator at TEC and ran much of the facility's day-to-day operations, moved to LA to be part of the VR industry after having experienced the medium for the first time while working as a venue coordinator for Sundance in 2016. Her first job in LA was working for Frilot to help curate New Frontier for the 2017 festival. Jastrow then hired her to help open TEC. Erika was initially hired as Jastrow's executive assistant, a typical entry-level job in entertainment that, for some people including Jastrow, leads to a more prestigious position. Assistants who don't burn out and quit might hold their position for up to a decade (an observation that a VR producer I met in passing provided as the reason why she switched from traditional film to VR, where she could be a producer right away).[10] It's telling, then, that Erika asked (and Jastrow agreed) for a title change when TEC opened. While there were still several employees at TEC who did the work normally assigned to assistants, no one held the title, bolstering the fantasy that VR could be different even while masking the labor exploitation that persisted.[11]

VR's newness was attractive to men and women alike. But for women, it resonated differently. Erika captured this difference when I asked her what she thought about the preponderance of women in VR: "I think a lot of the storytellers and creators I met through Sundance came from traditional media. So a lot of writers or filmmakers saw this new medium where there wasn't these preconceived notions or boundaries or footsteps to follow in. And they pivoted to that." For someone who might have felt constrained or limited or pigeonholed in traditional media—conditions more likely to be experienced by those who are underrepresented—VR seemed to offer different career opportunities. Rather than being in the shadow of an established industry, in VR one could more easily experiment, more quickly gain visibility, and perhaps also more persuasively make a case for why their talent and perspective constituted expertise.

Expertise and Empowerment

VR's appeal lay not only in its opportunity to circumvent hierarchy and claim expertise, but also to do so in a domain—tech—where simply existing as a woman is an act of change making. For folks in VR, this contributed to the desirability of claiming a woman in tech identity. Tech's cultural cache comes in part from a belief in the difficulty of STEM work—that one has to have a particular kind of intelligence for that work. And repeatedly, this kind of intelligence has been attributed to men. For example, in 2005 Harvard President Larry Summers publicly referenced studies that claimed men were more likely to be mathematical savants; in 2017 a Google engineer circulated a memo about the biological differences between men and women to explain the gender gap in tech and leadership.[12] In one sense, VR was empowering because—by the nature of it being both a cinematic and emerging technology—women could apply their skills from entertainment to VR and thus affiliate as a tech worker, a position that they might have felt to be otherwise out of reach. This was most clearly demonstrated in my interactions with Ashley and Jasmine, the actor and producer who, as previously discussed, described VR as a feminine medium because it spoke to women's "gathering" and holistic nature (and as I noted last chapter, this essentialist thinking is as troubling as the statements by Summers and in the Google memo). Ashley, like Popper, rapidly became seen as an "expert" after having helped launch a VR experience based on a popular television franchise.[13] This was in 2015, when, as Ashley described, "Nobody was really talking about VR. Yet, after that experience, and being female, I became somebody that could sit on a panel and talk about virtual reality." This amused her, because six months previous she didn't know anything, but now she was looked to as an expert. "All of a sudden, I became an expert in something that I'm not an expert in," and people began hiring her to help launch their VR titles. Ashley understood that she had a new power acquired by being in close proximity to a trendy technology. In a sense, Ashley felt she found a loophole—because VR was both new and had the shimmer of being an emerging technology, the skills she was able to quickly acquire could be transferred to other people who might, in turn, enjoy a success similar to her own. She was particularly interested in teaching VR development to girls who might otherwise not have a path toward college or employment.[14]

Jasmine, who was working with Ashley to realize this vision of teaching school-aged girls the basics of VR, had herself the experience of feeling empowered by working with "tech." On one occasion, when I accompanied Jasmine to observe the work she was doing with a pilot class of girls, she had just returned from a trip to DC where she and other organizations were meeting with congresspeople to share ideas about education technologies. She told me how she was nervous about this event, but once she got in the room, she quickly realized how much better Ashley and her approach was than some of the other projects on display. Jasmine, who had studied fine arts in college, proudly spoke on behalf of women in tech, and while most of the congresspeople showed little interest, there were a few with whom she exchanged cards. She took these cards out of her wallet, showing them to me and saying how this gave her hope that maybe the vision she and Ashley were fostering in LA might spread beyond the city.

Being a "woman in tech," however, is neither an easy nor stable identity. Victoria, the immersive sound engineer I met through Embodied Labs, identified as a woman though she presented as androgynous. She had thought about her gender performance at length, noting that audio is a male-dominated specialty, and she experienced a shift in how men interacted with her when she cut her hair short. Being androgynous presenting, she observed, "Helps me in tech and in audio." When I asked her to describe what it means for her to identify as a woman in tech, she acknowledged, "It's become kind of a catch phrase." At the same time, "We're reclaiming a space or trying to take up space in something that's not very welcoming. . . . Learning to code or learning a new skill, it's like 'Alright, I'm entering into this hostile environment where I know all the stats are against me . . . I know it's going to be a challenge. But I want to do it anyways.' So I think people wear it as a badge of honor. We're challenging the norm; we're accomplishing things." I also heard from several others that even if they felt a bit uncomfortable claiming the title of "woman in tech," they nonetheless felt it was important to, echoing Victoria, "take up space" and show other women that people who look like them are putting on VR headsets and engaging with the industry. Joanna Popper, who is fashionable and extroverted, considered it important for people to see her in a headset. "It's not only for men. It's not only for some stereotype woman. Come as you are. It's not like you have to not be you to be in tech."

While having to prove oneself as a woman might be motivating for some, Carrie Shaw, the CEO of Embodied Labs, found the fundraising challenges faced by women in tech to be frustrating and filled with expectations as to the kind of company women founders ought to be starting. Shaw speculated that (male) investors were most interested in funding women-led companies that addressed female issues like sexual harassment or reproductive choice so that the investors could not only support women but simultaneously claim they were supporting progressive women's causes. She and other women in the VR space whose companies were not "pink," Shaw observed, faced steeper funding challenges. Several months later, Shaw came to me with a revelation that perhaps her company was a pink company. Care work, she acknowledged, is traditionally considered women's work. But rather than this being something she might be able to leverage in her pitch to VCs, this just made her realize that not just any woman's issue is attractive to investors—it has to be the right kind of issue.

Despite these frustrations, Shaw was committed to being, as Popper exemplified, true to herself. She was able to maintain this conviction in part because, as 2018 progressed and she won a prestigious prize from the Gates Foundation, she realized that she was increasingly being recognized as a thought leader in VR. While she continued to get feedback from (male) mentors and potential investors that she was not the "typical CEO" (neither masculine nor bold nor direct enough), she was increasingly able to compartmentalize this feedback and be the CEO she desired. Come as you are; take up space; be a woman in tech not in order to conform to the industry but rather to push it forward.

VR for Multiple Goods

Being a woman in tech was desirable for those I spoke with because it was an active step toward diversifying a workforce.[15] Advocates for diversity in tech and entertainment have demonstrated that an inclusive team leads to better outcomes, both in terms of products and finances.[16] Diversity, then, is both a goal for bettering an individual's experience and also a means for broader improvement. This was expressed by Popper in a media interview: "It's important that this industry is built by a representative group. There's an opportunity to create a technology that's best for all of us."[17] VR's goodness is thus enacted at multiple levels. For Popper, VR allowed her to combine her passions in media, technology, and activism. Advocating for an inclusive workforce, marching in political protests, and supporting the creation of diverse VR content were, for Popper, all part of the same mission. As she expressed it to me, everyone ought to be working toward building "a world where there's humanity and kindness and treating each other well."

As discussed in the previous chapter's conclusion, this idea that VR is a good industry reinforces and is reinforced by VR's status as a good technology. I warned how this powerful coupling accepts an ideology that improved technology in and of itself means improved social progress.[18] This is in fact one reason women I spoke with mentioned for why they were so excited by VR's potential. For those already pursuing good causes, incorporating a technology (VR) could elevate and help the cause.

Ashley described how her first job in VR taught her that "tech makes things possible." She was interested in experimenting with whether, in applying tech to her nonprofit work (using VR experiences to solicit donations), she could leverage that spirit into social change. For Shaw, in bringing VR to elderly care, she has demonstrated how a technological solution can generate attention and resources. Similarly, Popper quickly recognized that both tech and media *inspire*, and "VR brought these two together" in order to "bring positive messages." In these cases, women were able to symbolically capitalize on technology's association with social progress.

I don't read these strategies as cynical, but rather borne from a genuine and passionate belief in VR's ability to do good in the world. As I've said, many women were drawn to the technology precisely because they were introduced to it not as a gaming platform but as an engine of social change. Ashley's first experience, like many, was *Clouds over Sidra*, about the Syrian refugee crisis; at Sundance, Erika first tried a VR experience that allowed her to embody a dragonfly and "experience" its fragile ecosystem. I was surprised to find out how passionately Erika believed in VR's ability to do good. Over the many months of working with her at TEC, I had come to see her as deeply knowledgeable about VR but assumed that the enthusiasm she exuded when showing potential partners around was part of the skill she had at doing her job. She startled both of us when, during our interview, she began crying when trying to articulate why she found VR to be so meaningful.[19] It establishes an emotional connection, Erika postulated, that is needed by a society that has become numb. The tears started flowing as she described the terrible state of the world, mentioning the shooter that killed eleven people at a synagogue in Pittsburgh earlier that week. What if "we could put Trump or anyone from the NRA—" The sentence ended, interrupted by a sob, but I knew that Erika was wondering if someone could be put into VR and see the world as she did, could things be different; could society heal? After regaining composure, with her tears replaced by anger, she continued, "It's such a fucked-up world right now. And I think that if people could take a fucking moment and watch a VR piece for human rights or for immigrants or for birth control or for fucking women's rights—If you can show these fucking people seeing the world through someone else's eyes, that's just . . ." Erika's sentence completed itself in the silence, implying, That's just powerful; that could make a difference.

Erika believed in the goodness of VR, but *not* because it was a technology and therefore symbolic of progress. She was one of the few people I met who did not see herself as a "woman in tech" and rather understood VR's power as coming from its adjacency with entertainment. As with the tech industry, there is also a deterministic ideal of media and storytelling being inherently good endeavors. But here, too, structural issues plague the industry and, as with a technology, there are plenty of examples of harms coming from media and its spread. But this is again why such a strong fantasy has developed around VR being a good technology and a good industry. Precisely because it is between tech and entertainment, VR becomes a site upon which to focus the mutual aspirations of building a good world that the structures undergirding the entertainment and tech industries make impossible.

Storytelling as Technology

VR, then, is a locus of imagining an industry otherwise that can produce a technology otherwise, which can hopefully bring about a world otherwise. This fantasy work was able to gain traction in LA because "tech" had a different, local meaning that expanded who could be part of making VR successful. This expansion made room for storytelling as a form of technological innovation.

In my interview with Victoria, she recalled being pleasantly surprised upon moving to LA that there was a tech scene, something she associated more with Silicon Valley or Seattle. "The cool part about tech in LA," she explained, "is that it inherently merges with entertainment. . . . They influence each other in a positive way." To her, it is no surprise that VR is prolific in LA because it "inherently has a storytelling component to it." Victoria reprised the sentiment that VR's newness makes it an exciting field to be in. "It's kind of like the early days of computing where there are no rules. And so we're making the rules as we go. . . . So everyone's an inventor. Everyone's bringing their unique perspective to the table to see how we can better tell stories." Victoria, without hesitating, coupled being an inventor with being a storyteller. She was not making the claim (as some of my other interlocutors had) of an inherent predisposition that women had for storytelling that gave them an advantage in VR. Indeed, storytelling is supremely *male* in Hollywood. But in VR, Victoria and others found a less hierarchical space that allowed them to apply their storytelling expertise in service of invention. What I take away as instructive from Victoria's observation is that *any* expansion of what tech work means might have the potential of increasing diversity. If the current pipeline for being a female tech worker is, as has been endlessly observed, leaky, the fantastical work that VR does in yoking together storytelling and invention proposes an alternative route to becoming a woman in tech.

When media scholar Janet Murray imagined in the 1990s who might crack the code of telling compelling stories with digital media, she sensed on the horizon "a new kind of storyteller, one who is half hacker, half bard."[20] At that time, writers and directors were already doing work in traditional media that pushed "against the boundaries of linear storytelling."[21] The storyteller's impulse preceded technological capabilities, but the computer held new possibility. Murray thus anticipated the "computer scientist as storyteller," noting a convergence between traditional and new media. "While dramatic and written narrative traditions have moved closer to the computer and computer-based entertainments have become more storylike, computer science itself is moving into domains that were previously the province of creative artists."[22] Exemplary of the computer scientist as storyteller was the VR researcher, shifting their work from military to entertainment applications. As Jacki Morie documented in her dissertation (and life experience), the VR lab became a space of collaboration between artist and researcher.[23] In the 1990s, one could pose a question about the future of narrative—would it be driven by the engineer turned storyteller or the storyteller turned engineer?

This directionality might seem inconsequential, but the way in which storytelling is positioned vis-à-vis technology spills over into questions of power and expertise that lie at the heart of the fantasies offered in this chapter. Here, again, there seems to be a split between how this relationship is today figured in Silicon Valley versus Los Angeles. In Silicon Valley, storytelling drives technological innovation and this, in turn, is the key to building a better world. Ethnographer Lilly Irani explores how this reasoning works in the context of an India-based design firm that worked on and provided support for development projects. At that firm, filmic storytelling was a powerful tool used to solicit investors, generate emotional buy-in, and incite "low-commitment future talk."[24] Irani traces this trend in design work to an influential 1996 report by a researcher at Apple titled *Design as Storytelling*. In this context, storytelling becomes a step in technical ideation that leads to design and engineering work to solve a perceived problem.[25] Storytelling is in service of technological development.

In Los Angeles, there was a slightly different logic at work. Storytelling, unsurprisingly, was at the center and technology at the periphery.

Storytelling was not an intermediary to creating a technology that could change the world; it was itself the technology that changed the world. This is seen in Alex McDowell's worldbuilding practice (discussed in chapter 1), widely embraced by the VR community. McDowell titled a 2019 essay "Storytelling Shapes the Future," enthusing (a similar claim that Murray had made twenty years earlier) how new technologies could finally unlock the full potential of the narrative arts. He no longer saw storytelling (as he had during his training in traditional film) as a "factory-line Victorian industrial process"[26]—a dream factory—but instead as a nonlinear enterprise fueled by immersive technology: "A new form, one that can powerfully change the world."[27] Reading McDowell's meditation on worldbuilding as an engine for progress, storytelling comes to look a lot like technology.

And this is where I begin to feel ambivalent or even nervous about this fantasy. Making innovation women's work happens, I have argued, because storytelling is recast as tech work. In VR, women without STEM backgrounds found that, as storytellers, they had expertise that mattered for this emerging industry; they found success and power they thought themselves otherwise unable to achieve. This is the scaffolding of the fantasy of VR as a good industry producing a good technology that might help bring about a better world. And, importantly, this was perceived from within the community I spent time with as an alternative to Big Tech, as better than the way of doing tech in Silicon Valley. And yet, if one of the foundational flaws of the tech industry is its unmitigated belief that technology in and of itself can solve problems—the "technological fix" as snake oil—as storytelling becomes technical, is there not then a danger of a "narrative fix" that posits how a powerful story might be enough to solve a problem? As I've been suggesting, the technology and entertainment industries have similar structural issues, and VR—even as it exists between the two—cannot hope to be an alternative if it accepts the same ideological presuppositions. Expanding representation and challenging the meaning of "tech" can lead to radical change, but only if the emergent forms of doing and innovating can avoid being recaptured by the systems to which VR is imagined as being an alternative.

While storytelling as technological innovation might facilitate taking the first steps toward tech otherwise, it seems likely that, given the close affinity of these imaginaries, it might too easily be tamed by the existing currents of power. Shifting contexts, however, we are given an example of how storytelling *can* radically disrupt current ways of being and knowing. As race and gender scholar Katherine McKittrick notes in her book *Dear*

Science and Other Stories, most critical projects that seek to disrupt the logics of technoscience inevitably get trapped in a loop. McKittrick is writing about the interrelations of race and science, observing that the important work of enumerating the continued prevalence of scientific racism and the role of scientific thought in racial formations remain captured by the colonial first principle of the scientific project: a presumption of Black people as less-than-human. In seeking a critical theory that centers Black liveliness, McKittrick looks to creative practices including storytelling as theory building that invites a "scientifically creative frame, that unfolds into a different future."[28] Her framework renegotiates the relationship between art and science to center other ways of knowing and creating futures. "The story," McKittrick writes, "opens the door to curiosity; the reams of evidence dissipate as we tell the world differently, with a creative precision. The story asks that we live with the difficult and frustrating ways of knowing different."[29] Storytelling *can* be innovation, *can* be technology, *can* be radical, *can* be world changing. But what's needed are stories that more aggressively challenge what it means to be good, to be a woman, to be a world.

Conclusion

We *ought* to be working toward better worlds. Here, in late capitalism, in early Anthropocene, in perpetual colonialism, we need fantasies to propel us forward, to inspire us to think otherwise. We speculate, we innovate, we try, we fail. In *Staying with the Trouble*, Donna Haraway suggests, perhaps too conservatively, that we work toward "modest possibilities of partial recuperation." To find her way, she looks "for real stories that are also speculative fabulations and speculative realisms."[30] While Haraway looks to multispecies stories, this book has turned back to the cyborg; human–machine entanglements emergent from "militarism and patriarchal capitalism," but that can be, as Haraway promised, "unfaithful to their origins."[31] In LA, with VR, I found fantasies offering modest possibilities. I found a community who believed, as Haraway writes, that "It matters what stories make worlds, what worlds make stories."[32] The recursive project flowed like this:

> Women were telling a story about representation
> that made the world of women in VR

that told a story
about building better worlds.

It was a story about tech being different
that created a world
in which storytelling was innovation.

There was an amplifying feedback loop between storytelling and world-building, and VR was caught up in these reverberations as a propulsive force. This made space for a conversation about tech in LA—not a radical conversation, but the start of a conversation otherwise. The women I spoke with saw different careers and futures for themselves. They saw the possibility to change what a tech industry looked like and support a technology that they felt could convey a powerful message.

I mentioned at the start of this chapter that the women whom I chose to voice the particular fantasies explored in this chapter were making a living working in VR—the fantasies were working for them. These women were also by and large LA transplants, members of the creative class who should not be read as representative Angelenos but rather denizens of the fragment of LA that has been the ethnographic focus of this book, a very partial representation of a much more diverse and sprawling city. Even within this fragment, there is a larger range of experiences than those profiled here. I met and spoke to other women who had far more precarious livelihoods—who were working odd or unpleasant or exploitative jobs while pursuing and hoping for a career in VR. And yet, these fantasies held sway.

Angie, who is Latina and grew up in LA, responded to one of my early calls to meet with members of the VR community. She quickly discerned that I was mostly being exposed to only one facet of LA and generously offered to be my guide to what she considered the real LA. Throughout the year, we would meet in her neighborhood on the Eastside and hang out there or head Downtown so she could show me her favorite spots. Angie was cool and smart and passionate and dreamed of something more. She first introduced herself to me by explaining that she was interested in "the social implications of immersive reality across class boundaries" and though we never spoke about it explicitly, I got the sense that she understood her own foray into this world as an experiment in crossing class (and other) boundaries, crossing between the real LA and the unreal LA of Hollywood and tech. She spoke of the importance of having diverse people in the industry, referencing one of the leaders of the community in LA who was a non–college-educated, queer woman of color. This made Angie feel welcome, and she wanted to do the same for others. Angie initially became involved in immersive technology after working for a company that was using AR, VR, and holograms at live music events. She entered, along with her colleagues, a hackathon and this made her more engaged with the immersive community. Angie parted ways with the company, but continued to work on an AR game on her own—doing the design and storytelling while finding a developer to help with the execution. In 2018, she had been underemployed in the tech world for a couple of years, but she nonetheless found it to be exhilarating—fast moving and filled with possibility. The possibility of tech was what had kept her involved, even as opportunities seemed to vanish. Angie continued to believe that tech would be her way toward a different station in life. This conviction led her to start a tech club at a public charter school in South LA where her partner taught.

Shortly after I completed fieldwork, Angie sent me a text to see if we were going to get together again. In a flurry of end-of-research activity (perhaps also having been caught up in the fantasies and unreality of LA), I had neglected to say goodbye. I felt terrible, especially because over the last few months Angie's spirits had been on the decline—a failed job search, her tech club floundering. As we texted, she confessed to feeling "disengaged from anything relating to 'women in tech/xr.'" She felt abandoned by the community, wondering if it even existed anymore. I was curious what she meant by the community not existing, and Angie replied cynically, "I just think the idea of it being a true community was kind of BS and superficial to begin with. It feels like it was much more of a show riding on momentum than a genuine network." For Angie, the fantasy had been revealed as façade, and her reality increasingly diverged from those still striving toward the otherwise. The women in VR community wasn't perfect, and other people throughout the year expressed frustration with "popularity" dynamics and not feeling that the language of empowerment stretched very far beyond the inner circle. Angie concluded the text exchange: "I'm shedding my identity as a 'woman in xr.' I've never identified as a woman anyway ¯_(ツ)_/¯."

Does the idea of a woman tech worker do good work? My interlocutors were conflicted. Not only did Angie express misgivings about the label and the community, but others confided that they thought the "woman in VR" label downgraded potential projects. Given the concerted effort that had been made to elevate female-created content, could this backfire and lead to its dismissal? Would people assume that a VR experience was only successful because it was created by a woman, thus receiving an unearned signal boost? As one woman told me in an interview, "The amount of focus in VR/AR about gender is a problem." The fantasy of a diverse industry is welcome; it's a story that conjures a world worth working toward. But perhaps the approach taken by the VR community was too blunt, and identifying as a woman in VR or a woman in tech did more to naturalize gender differences than imagine a world more radically equitable.

So we're left with the fantasy of fantasy. The kind of otherwise world we ought to be imagining is not yet clear, much less what we need to do to get there. Speculative experiments will continue, possible worlds will proliferate, but which ones will be "good," and who will get to enjoy these worlds otherwise?

EPILOGUE

It is always a risky prospect to write a book about emerging technology, especially as an academic. The process of research and writing, done while attending to other tasks demanded by our jobs, happens over a stretch of time often longer than a typical product cycle or hype cycle. Having started this research in 2015, I watched the enthusiasm for VR crest and fall several times, observing sharp shifts in the imagination of VR's potential for ubiquity or likelihood of obsolescence. Those of us writing about such volatile things, industries, and communities worry whether, when our work finally makes it into the world, it will have any relevance. In my case, the elapse of time turned out to be a gift. It wasn't until "the reality crisis" came into focus in 2020 and 2021 that I could see how the questions the VR community explicitly asks about the possibility of understanding the world from another's subjectivity were implicitly at the heart of an ongoing cultural and political worry.

This book is organized around the fantasies that mobilized VR at a specific time in a specific place. I always knew these fantasies would be memories by the time this book made it into the world. It seemed inevitable that the more idealistic aspirations of the empathy machine and Hollywood's gambit that they could steer the development of VR would likely be eclipsed once Big Tech companies took back any control they might have ceded during the nascent stages of commercialization (including deference to concerns about diversity) and voiced their own fantasies. This happened first in 2021 with Zuckerberg's fantasy of "the metaverse" and again in 2023 when Apple CEO Tim Cook announced that his company would release a headset and usher in the era of "spatial computing."

From the biggest companies in Silicon Valley, one might expect novel visions for the future of immersive technology. But both the metaverse and spatial computing are plucked from previous eras' fantasies, even if the CEOs wielding these terms implied they were offering new futures. The metaverse is borrowed from cyberpunk fiction of the previous century. Neal Stephenson used the term in his 1992 Los Angeles–set novel *Snow Crash* to describe the virtual world that the small percentage of the global population wealthy enough to own a computer and VR goggles could access as an escape from the dystopian physical world. In the metaverse, the same activities carried out in the physical world—work, play, love, war— are meaningfully pursued. And many of the same inequalities are replicated, except for a few software savants that are able to hack their way into metaverse prosperity. In *Snow Crash*, the metaverse is a single platform, like the internet, that facilitates all virtual experiences. Companies and individuals can develop their own enterprises in the virtual world, but it is a common virtual reality. This is similar to how, in *Ready Player One*, the OASIS is figured as the only virtual platform that everyone inhabits, and (in the plot of that book and movie) it is why the control of the OASIS is feverishly pursued without concern for cost or human lives.

The metaverse gained traction as a branding strategy throughout 2021, rallying interest around a future in which VR and augmented reality (AR) headsets are omnipresent technologies, blurring the distinction between virtual and physical worlds. When Zuckerberg announced he was changing Facebook's name to Meta, signaling its commitment to the metaverse, it seemed like this might be game over for any radical or alternative vision of VR. Like the evil Big Tech company in *Ready Player One*, Meta's willingness to invest abundant resources in this vision would mean that it would own (figuratively and literally) this future. But much had changed between when Zuckerberg launched Facebook in 2004 and the renaming of Meta in 2021. Most significantly, social media and Facebook had become a primary target of the techlash that had been brewing for several years. Zuckerberg was no longer hailed as a boy genius and instead reviled as a robotic, soulless profit-seeker. Critiques of Zuckerberg's Meta vision were swiftly penned and harshly worded.[1]

Given this cultural rejection of the metaverse, it was somewhat surprising that Apple also entered the fray. In the announcement of the Vision Pro headset, the words "virtual reality" and "metaverse" were carefully avoided, suggesting instead that the fantasy of spatial computing would take headsets in a different direction. While spatial computing might have sounded new to some, it, too, has a decades long history and was frequently discussed during my fieldwork in reference to the AR company Magic Leap. Though Apple might wish for its product to be distinct and distant from Meta's, both converge on integrated virtual and physical worlds, where the screen is no longer in our pocket or on our wrist, but attached to our face and made essential (should these companies achieve their fantasies) for accessing the world as it might be.

Confronted with these futures, we can reappraise the flickering flame that was "the empathy machine." VR's resurgence in the mid-2010s was helped along by widespread interest in the fantasy of a good technology. The empathy machine is what initially drew me to this research as I, along with others, knew to be suspicious of a technology that promised a fix for humanity's ills. As I conducted fieldwork, however, I learned that many of the people who were building empathy projects were doing so with more care than I expected and were learning from the critiques being made. When I virtually attended Sundance New Frontier in 2021 and 2022, I noted that the experiences meant to bring viewers with privilege into the worlds of others were being conceptualized and led by those whom the VR pieces were about—a corrective from the first generation of empathy experiences. This is not to say that the critique "worked," but rather that, as it became clear that the empathy machine was not going to create wealth, the biggest offenders left in search of greener futures. Notably, Chris Milk, the strawman many of us pulled at with our empathy critiques, left behind the idea of making better humans and developed instead a VR exercise app to make fitter humans. During Zuckerberg's grand unveiling of the metaverse, it was announced that Meta purchased Milk's company—a payday attributable entirely to the success of the fitness app and not the "VR for Good" arm of the company.

Neither the metaverse nor spatial computing will be where the fantasy of VR culminates, leaving us to wonder what the next imaginary to emerge might be. There are lessons to be learned from the empathy machine which, in its best version, reached toward a technology otherwise. It was a project of imagining how VR could be something other than a gaming device, a social networking platform, or a screen to be worn at all times. It wondered what *else* the fantasy of being might offer. What I personally find unsettling about Big Tech's VR visions is that they foreclose the otherwise by collapsing multiple visions of VR and technological futures back onto the dominant imaginary that will keep in power those already at the top. This is a vision to refuse, insisting that it can and should be otherwise.

A Paradox of Unreality

Imagining this otherwise is challenging, particularly in the time of the unreal when reality has fragmented and multiplied. The return to a unified commons is appealing not only for those who stand to financially benefit from such a monopoly, but also for those who desire a resolution to the chaos wrought by the reality crisis. This yields a *paradox of unreality* by which attempts to heal a fractured reality through the reassertion of a commons invariably reinforce the conditions that led to the fracturing in the first place. An episode of *The Voices of* VR podcast hosted by Kent Bye and released in late January 2021 illustrates the slipperiness of this paradox. Bye was interviewing a "VR industry defector," Fox Buchele, who was fired as a VR developer and, as a consequence, left the industry, citing a culture of "toxic positivity."[2] The conversation fascinatingly juxtaposed sentiment about VR with sentiment about US politics, demonstrating how those who might resist a monolithic VR future governed by Big Tech continue to imagine VR as a commons that can heal the rifts in the United States.

Buchele's dissatisfaction with the VR industry is directly related, in his narrative, to the Trump administration. In 2017 he was hired at a well-known Austin-based VR company that he greatly respected; it felt like a family, and he liked and wanted to be liked by his colleagues. In the early days of the Trump administration, it was hard for someone like Buchele to let the outrages of Trumpism go unremarked upon. There was a "Politics" channel on the company Slack in which he participated. Like many liberals reacting to the Trump administration, the vibe of this channel was outrage and despair. Company leaders decided this was damaging morale and shut down the channel. Buchele still spoke with his colleagues about politics in the company break rooms at the office, but this, too, was seen as a source of negativity and, for the sake of the company, employees were asked to stop discussing politics at work. Buchele acquiesced and internalized a broader lesson that negativity was, in general, counter to the emergence of VR as a successful industry—this is what he identified as the culture of toxic positivity. Not only did he self-censor himself when it came to politics (both at his company and on social media), but he also self-censored any critique he might have about a VR project or the direction of the industry. He learned both tacitly and through punitive measures that he could either support the direction envisioned by those in power (both at his company and in the industry) or he could remain silent. Bye, an astute social theorist, observed the replication of US politics in VR industry politics, describing how a "shadow projection of the thing they were avoiding talking about—authoritarian politics—gets embodied [in the company]."

Toward the end of the podcast, Buchele returned to the point about toxic positivity and how it silences and isolates those who wish to articulate an alternative vision for VR. Bye thanked him for breaking the taboo and speaking out, noting the narrative façade mounted by VR: "The reality is actually a lot different than the stories we tell about it." Bye offered an understanding of the VR industry as unreal—as comprised of multiple, conflicting realities. However, it is not as easy as Bye makes it seem to access some "actual reality" of this industry, as the stories and the fantasies are themselves doing real work. And having entered the land of the unreal, Bye then quickly and fluidly linked the VR industry back to the unreality of US politics. With a half chuckle indicating amusement or amazement at this connection, he observed how this VR industry problem is of a piece with the "existential story of our day" in which "we have different reality bubbles of fragmentation of our culture that we're trying to get onto the same page of what actual reality is." Bye was referencing the January 6 riots at the Capitol building that occurred only weeks earlier as well as the reality bubbles occupied by those waiting for COVID-19 vaccines versus those viewing the pandemic as a hoax.

Both Bye and Buchele felt the political urgency of this unreality, wondering how these bubbles could be remerged through a common consensus of what is and isn't real. Bye pivoted back to VR, "Maybe that's one potential for VR, is to provide these experiences—these cultural artifacts—that we can connect about." But even as he imagined the "radical empathy of tolerance" that VR might be able to facilitate, he recalled Karl Popper's paradox of tolerance. Tolerance of the intolerant, as the paradox goes, leads to the disappearance of tolerance. A tolerant society, Popper wrote, must defend "in the name of tolerance, the right not to tolerate the intolerant."[3] This is a paradox indeed, and Buchele and Bye both sensed that US democracy was at an impasse in that both sides lacked any tolerance for the other—both were deeply convinced that their reality was the actual reality. Buchele despaired that finding a point of reality that can be agreed upon feels impossible. Bye, more optimistic, proposed "entertainment and games and experiences that we share could be one of those points. Culture and art and stories. That's where I put my hope."

And here is the paradox of unreality. Buchele and Bye both lamented the monoculture of the VR industry. Buchele suggested that toxic positivity keeps alternative visions of VR and its future from emerging. In his final reflection at the end of the episode, Bye reinforced the importance of diversity and inclusion (by which he meant the involvement of people of color, underrepresented voices, and "people with divergent perspective of what the future of VR should be") for the health of the VR industry. And yet, when faced with the expansive problem of US democracy, VR was imagined as something that might bring divergent reality bubbles back together. The VR industry's strength would come only with multiple visions, and yet VR as a salve to the reality crisis would come from offering a unifying experience.

In confronting a fractured reality, the instinct is to make it whole once more—to rebuild the commons, to repair reality. But is that actually how a better world will come to be? Throughout this book, I've used the unreal to capture the feeling that reality is multiplying and becoming something else. In reaction to this ineffable shift, fantasy and other marginalized modes of reasoning about the world come into prevalence and facilitate the imagining of technology otherwise, futures otherwise, and worlds otherwise. In writing from a US context, the unreal seems "new." But anthropologist Arturo Escobar, in concert with others writing about Latin and South American Indigenous ontologies, argues that singular reality is an illusion masking what he calls the pluriverse: an unreality that preexists the Western "real." The pluriverse captures the Indigenous idea of life as something always becoming and inherently relational, but also expresses a world of many worlds. Earth as a single world with a single reality is a fiction of the West. Thus, a pluriversal politics presumes that "another world is possible because another real and another possible are possible."[4] Rejecting the "belief in a single reality means developing another, entirely different understanding of what change and transformation are, and thus of what politics can be."[5]

The paradox of the unreal, in the American context, captures how the reality crisis has demanded that leftist politics reinvest in a notion of singular reality (evidenced by the yard signs reading "In this house, we believe science is real") to the detriment of holding open a space for otherwise imaginings of the world. I agree with Bye and Buchele that VR's future will be more exciting if it allows for different fantasies of technology and the tech industry. I part ways in a belief that *experiencing* VR will become a common touchstone—a radical empathy machine of tolerance—that reunites humanity. Resisting this commonality of VR seems essential to resisting Big Tech's fantasies for the future of immersive technology. Not only should we insist that any metaverse be a pluriverse, but we must also nurture multiple fantasies of what a future that freely mixes the actual and the virtual might look like—including fantasies in which VR and AR remain marginal media. There can be better technologies and better worlds. But these can't exist in the reality Big Tech has built. We need a tech otherwise.

NOTES

Prologue

1   Raz, "Screen Time."

2   Media outlets not only covered these "good" VR projects, but also produced their own. As one example, in November 2015 the *New York Times* created a VR experience following the terrorist attacks in Paris. The experience covered the ensuing vigils in order to "bring our audience to the streets of Paris in the most visceral way we could." Solomon and Davis, "Finding Hope."

3   While Trumpism made more visible the mechanisms for undermining trust in institutions, the weaponization of such strategies began well before Trump's presidency. See, for example, Oreskes and Conway, *Merchants of Doubt*.

4   Lithwick, "Stop Trying to Understand." This statement from October 2018 was in reaction to a week of domestic terrorism catalyzed by Trumpism and, as the journalist argued, hate spewed on social media. These attacks included the thwarting of a plan to send pipe bombs to prominent Trump critics, the murder at the hands of a white nationalist of a Black man and woman who were grocery shopping, and the murder of eleven members of Pittsburgh's Tree of Life synagogue. Prior to this mass murder, the gunman posted on social media that he was taking a stand against those who tolerate "invaders," referring to the congregation's outreach work with South American migrants and refugees. Alerting his followers to the danger of this "caravan" of migrants was Trump's primary campaign strategy in the lead up to the 2018 midterm election.

5   Slate, "The Greatest Deliberative Body."

6   Bernstein and Marritz, "Warnings."

7   Biden, "Remarks."

8   Warzel, "The Pro-Trump Movement." See also Roose, "How the Biden Administration."

9   Whistleblower Frances Haugen released a trove of private papers that documented how the platform "sows division and undermines democracy

in pursuit of breakneck growth and 'astronomical profits.'" Chappell, "The Facebook Papers." See Vaidhyanathan, *Antisocial Media.*

10 Zuckerberg, "I Wanted to Share a Note."

11 Zuckerberg, "Facebook Connect 2021."

Introduction

1 Oscars, "Alejandro González Iñárritu." For an anthropological account of oceanic submersion as a mediated way of knowing, see Helmreich "An Anthropologist Underwater."

2 Anthropologist Jason De León has pursued a variety of multimodal methods to convey the experience of border crossing, including photography. In explaining why he included photographs of people's faces (instead of obscuring their identity as ethnographers working with at-risk communities often do in order to ensure anonymity), he notes the desires of his interlocutors to be seen as people. As one migrant explained to De León, "I want you to put photos that show our reality. That is better. That way people can see what happens. The realness." Words and pictures do for De León what VR does for Iñárritu: "Maybe the photos and stories revealed in the following pages will somehow help those of us who will never know the desperation required to head into the desert or the sorrow that accompanies losing someone to this process get a little closer to 'the realness.'" De León, *The Land of Open Graves*, 19.

3 Gunning, "An Aesthetic of Astonishment," observes that the startled audience did not believe a train was in the theater (as the magic of cinema is sometimes naïvely glossed) but rather they experienced a pleasurable awareness of the illusionistic capacity of the new medium. Murray draws on the Lumière example (and Gunning's analysis) to remind readers that "there is no reason to believe that VR is more likely to deceive us than older media forms, which were once described as equally magical." See Murray "Virtual/Reality," 24.

4 Chagollan, "Iñárritu's 'Lumiére Moment.'"

5 Wynter, "Unsettling the Coloniality of Being."

6 For critiques of tech for good projects deployed in "humanitarian" contexts, see Ames, *The Charisma Machine*; Madianou, "Nonhuman Humanitarianism"; Henriksen and Richey, "Google's Tech Philanthropy."

7 This logic is not unique to VR. See Giridharadas, *Winners Take All.* There are some VR for Good projects that are about getting VR headsets into classrooms or underresourced communities, but the VR for Good that I most frequently encountered in research were experiences, like *Carne y Arena* targeted at making a privileged person aware of social inequities.

8 Yee and Bailenson, "The Proteus Effect." Additional research has nuanced these claims. For example, Jeremy Bailenson's lab has also found that embodying a Black avatar didn't increase empathy, but actually reinforced stereotypes. See Groom, Bailenson, and Nass, "The Influence of Racial Embodiment." A few years later, Mel Slater's lab ran a similar experiment and reported reduced bias. See Peck et al., "Putting Yourself in the Skin." Bailenson suggested in his book that the different experimental findings could be attributed to Slater's VR system having better tracking. Bailenson, *Experience on Demand*, 90.

9 Milk, "How Virtual Reality Can Create the Ultimate Empathy Machine." As stated by Milk in a keynote conversation during the 2020 Games for Change conference, this is a riff on film critic Roger Ebert's claim that film itself is "the most powerful empathy machine in all the arts." Ebert, "Ebert's Walk of Fame Remarks."

10 In later chapters, I will more fully explore the critique of the empathy machine as enumerated by these scholars and others: Nakamura, "Feeling Good about Feeling Bad"; Roquet, "Empathy for the Game Master"; Bollmer and Guinness, "Empathy and Nausea"; Glabau, "Imagination, Whiteness, and the Future."

11 Magalhães and Couldry, "Giving by Taking Away," 343. See also Madianou, "Nonhuman Humanitarianism." Rider, "Volunteering the Valley," argues that even when tech workers volunteer for civic technology projects precisely because they are disillusioned by their day jobs, they nevertheless "export the moral orders structuring their workplaces— judgments about what makes a good worker, project, technology, and organization—into civic groups." This can lead to well-meaning efforts that "actively reinforce the epistemic, cultural, and economic power of Big Tech firms—even when technologists are openly critical of the industry," 6.

12 Marx, "Does Improved Technology"; Madianou, "Technological Futures."

13 Scholars studying Los Angeles's dominant cultural product, cinema, have also operationalized fantasy as an analytic. Many draw on Freud and Lacan, for example, McGowan, *The Real Gaze*; Meiri and Kohen-Raz, *Traversing the Fantasy*; Metz, *The Imaginary Signifier*. Žižek, *Looking Awry*, uses film and other media to introduce Lacan's ideas. Fantasy has also been analyzed as a literary and cinematic genre. See Sobchack, *Screening Space*; Saler, *As If*; Hassler-Forest, *Science Fiction, Fantasy, and Politics*.

14 McGowan, *The Real Gaze*, 23.

15 McGowan, "Lost on Mulholland Drive," 80. McGowan's article, which is an analysis of *Mulholland Drive* and thus fittingly reflexive about Hollywood as a creator of fantasy, concludes by suggesting that Hollywood's

failure, and this extends to the populace more widely, is failing to commit fully to fantasy in order to achieve its radical potential. "Subjects today have remained too removed from fantasy, resisting the experience toward which it compels them. But *Mulholland Drive* calls us to fully immerse ourselves in fantasy, to abandon ourselves in its logic. Only in this way can we experience fantasy's privileged path to the Real," 86. However, as I discuss toward the beginning of this introduction, fantasy is a double-edged sword that could as easily lead to "the Real" as a complete rejection of that real. Fantasy facilitates "experiences otherwise unthinkable," but it does not determine the morality of these experiences.

16   Nusselder, *Interface Fantasy*. For other applications of Lacan to computing, see Žižek, "Cyberspace," and Dean, "The Real Internet," for a critique.

17   Brandt and Messeri, "Imagining Feminist Futures."

18   As will be discussed further in chapter 6, Alyssa Milano, who first tweeted #MeToo in response to the Weinstein revelations, quickly acknowledged that activist Tarana Burke had been using "Me Too" for a decade to shed light on the harassment experienced by girls and women of color.

19   Berlant, *Cruel Optimism*, 11. Thanks are due to Michelle Venetucci for pointing out this connection.

20   Soja, *My Los Angeles*, 86.

21   Soja, *My Los Angeles*, 107.

22   Soja, *My Los Angeles*, 108.

23   Soja, *My Los Angeles*, 87.

24   Cohan analyzes the opening of *The Errand Boy* as part of a discussion about the genre of "backstudio pictures." Significantly, "Within the studio the engineering, technology, and artifice of acting are openly exposed." The narrator of *The Errand Boy* explains that what follows is not a documentary (as one would hardly expect from a Jerry Lewis picture), and so Cohan concludes that despite a prologue that suggests it is taking the viewer inside Hollywood, "the 'real' Hollywood remains inaccessible . . . insofar as the industry's operation by top management is still closed off to outsiders." See Cohan, *Hollywood by Hollywood*, 67. Andersen's documentary *Los Angeles Plays Itself* further explores the representational folds by which the movie industry in turn masks and reveals the kind of place that it is.

25   Davidson, *The Real and the Unreal*, 4.

26   Rosten, *Hollywood*, 34–35.

27   Two "Theorizing the Contemporary" series, published by the journal *Cultural Anthropology*, summarize this "speculative turn" in anthropology: Anderson et al., "Introduction: Speculative Anthropologies"; Mc-

Tighe and Raschig, "Introduction: An Otherwise Anthropology." There is precedence within the discipline for retreating from "the real" at moments of heightened political conflict, as evidenced by the turn to surrealism that inspired theorists and anthropologists following the crises of WWI and the global depression of the 1930s. See Fischer, "Culture and Cultural Analysis as Experimental Systems," 21–23. A speculative turn is also at work in other disciplines, including STS. See, among others, Haraway, *Simians, Cyborgs, and Women* and *Staying with the Trouble*; Benjamin, "Racial Fictions"; and Radin, "The Speculative Present." In the field of critical design, see Dunne and Raby, *Speculative Everything*; Chin, "Using Fiction"; Forlano and Mathew, "From Design Fiction"; and Galloway and Caudwell, "Speculative Design as Research Method." In the social sciences more generally, see contributors to Wilkie, Savransky, and Rosengarten, eds., *Speculative Research*; as well as Cortiel et al., eds., *Practices of Speculation*. Applying speculation to historical methods, Saidiya Hartman, *Wayward Lives, Beautiful Experiments*, uses speculation as a method for filling in the gaps of an archive that has left out Black women. Bahng, *Migrant Futures*, contrasts speculative finance with speculative fiction in understanding how postcapital worlds are imagined.

28 Wolf-Meyer, *Theory for the World*, 15. See also Appadurai, *The Future as Cultural Fact*; Bryant and Knight, *The Anthropology of the Future*; Salazar et al., *Anthropologies and Futures*; and Valentine and Hassoun, "Uncommon Futures."

29 Jobson, "The Case," 261. For some, any attempt to save anthropology from its history is a futile endeavor given the field's colonial past and the ways in which this history has propagated legacies of racism and elitism that continue to harm scholars in many of the discipline's storied institutions. See Todd, "The Decolonial Turn 2.0."

30 Gupta, "Decolonizing U.S. Anthropology."

31 Pandian, *A Possible Anthropology*, 4.

32 Latour, *Science in Action*, 93.

33 Mol, "Ontological Politics," 95.

34 Barad, "Posthumanist Performativity," 817.

35 Oreskes and Conway, *Merchants of Doubt*; Sismondo, "Post-Truth?"; Latour, *Down to Earth*; Radin, "Alternative Facts."

36 Kofman, "Bruno Latour."

37 This point is made by Woolgar and Lezaun, "The Wrong Bin Bag," during a disciplinary conversation about the "turn" in STS from focusing on epistemology to ontology. Relevant for the preceding discussion, Sismondo revisits this phrase to reject claims that STS is complicit in the post-truth era of the Trump presidency. "It could be otherwise" does not suggest "that 'it could easily be otherwise'; instead [STS arguments] point to other possible infrastructures, efforts, ingenuity and

validation structures. That doesn't look at all like post-truth. A Twitter account alone does not make what we have been calling knowledge." Sismondo, "Post-Truth?," 3. "The otherwise" is also a theoretical resource for Povinelli, "Routes/Worlds" and *Geontologies*.

38 Noble, *Algorithms of Oppression*; Benjamin, *Race after Technology*; Mullaney et al., *Your Computer Is on Fire*.

39 Craig and Cunningham, *Social Media Entertainment*. For the rise of episodic, scripted content delivered over streaming platforms, see Christian, *Open TV*.

40 Elliott, "Silicon Is Just Sand."

41 To be clear, while the tech community hailed the success of Snap, residents of Venice saw their community change drastically as the company expanded and others, seeking to match the unicorn success, moved in. As had happened in the Bay Area, property prices skyrocketed, diversity decreased, and the unhoused population, long a fixture of Venice Beach, was displaced. Snap Inc. eventually relocated to Santa Monica (in part due to protests from Venice Beach residents). Hernandez, "Snapchat's Disappearing Act."

42 Elliott, "Silicon Is Just Sand." See also Bowles, "The Battle over 'Silicon Beach.'"

43 King, *Virtual Memory*, 11–12.

44 Bergson, *Mind-Energy*; Deleuze, *Difference and Repetition*. See also Massumi, *Parables for the Virtual*, and Grosz, *Time Travels*.

45 Levy, *Becoming Virtual*; Grosz, *Architecture from the Outside*; Shields, *The Virtual*.

46 Friedberg, *Window Shopping* and *The Virtual Window*; King, *Virtual Memory*.

47 Boellstorff, *Coming of Age in Second Life*. Chalmers, *Reality+*, also makes this argument from a metaphysical perspective. Nardi, "Virtuality," while not denying that the virtual is real finds utility in maintaining virtual in opposition to the real as it follows the linguistic habits of gamers and other virtual consumers.

48 Boellstorff, "For Whom the Ontology Turns."

49 Boellstorff et al., *Ethnography and Virtual Worlds*.

50 Pink et al., *Digital Ethnography*.

51 Coleman, "Ethnographic Approaches to Digital Media."

Part I. Fantasy of Place

1 A similar intention animates Roquet's book, *The Immersive Enclosure*. VR, he argues, is neither uniquely American nor a placeless technology. In studying VR from Japan, as Roquet does, desires for VR to cultivate private spaces of perception and exploration come into focus.

2   With apologies to New York.

3   My thanks to Nicole Hemmer who, in the summer of 2017, proposed this phrase as we sipped wine in Charlottesville and talked about our respective research projects.

4   To reference just a few recent ethnographies, Emily Wanderer, *The Life of a Pest*, explores how the meaning of "biosecurity" is different in Mexico in comparison to US connotations. Lilly Irani, *Chasing Innovation*, makes a similar argument about the expanded meaning of "innovation" in the Indian context. See also Pollock, *Synthesizing Hope*. While these studies focus on the production of technoscience, Miller et al., *How the World Changed*, analyze how local use of the same technology varies widely.

5   Mavhunga, *What Do Science, Technology, and Innovation Mean from Africa?*; Liboiron, *Pollution Is Colonialism*.

6   ESTS Editorial Collective, "Provincializing STS Scholarship Landscape." This approach is, of course, indebted to Chakrabarty, *Provincializing Europe*.

7   Loukissas, *All Data Are Local*. See also Schwartz and Halegoua, "The Spatial Self"; Kraemer, "Locating Emerging Media"; and Halegoua, *The Digital City*, for other approaches to how new media and place co-construct each other.

8   Trubek, *The Taste of Place*.

9   Paxson, *The Life of Cheese*. The way in which Paxson flips terroir from being something that describes taste to something that is being produced by tastemakers resonates with Appadurai's rethinking of locality as something produced by both communities and ethnographers as opposed to that which is the setting for cultural and anthropological work. See Appadurai, *Modernity at Large*, particularly his chapter "The Production of Locality."

10   As is posited by the milieux of innovation framework, proposed by Castells and Hall, *Technopoles of the World*.

11   Marwick, "Silicon Valley." Similarly, Angela VandenBroek's ethnography of the Stockholm tech scene notes how a particular kind of pitch strategy that gained prominence in Silicon Valley (which she calls "hype storytelling") had to be actively taught and learned in Stockholm, where cultural norms lead to pitches more humble than what has become expected by investors. VandenBroek, "A Very Lengthy Swedish Introduction." In contrast, Isenberg, "The Big Idea," has argued that entrepreneurial ecosystems should not seek to imitate Silicon Valley but rather build on their own local strengths.

12   Barbrook and Cameron, "The Californian Ideology," 45. See also Turner, *From Counterculture to Cyberculture* and "Burning Man at Google."

13   Barbrook and Cameron, "The Californian Ideology," 62.

1. Desert of the Unreal

1   Caro, "A Debate Club."

2   The belief that LA was "far from the entrenched attitudes and rigid power hierarchies of the hidebound East" frames writer Gary Krist's group biography of early twentieth century Los Angeles innovators, *The Mirage Factory*, 9. Journalist Neal Gabler has argued that, in a similar fashion, Eastern European Jews recognized that there was less social hierarchy out west and, should they desire to rise to the highest echelon of US society, they could not do so on the East Coast. The first studios in Los Angeles were founded by American Jews creating, as Gabler titles his book, *An Empire of Their Own*.

3   Kilston, *Sun Seekers*, 9.

4   McWilliams, *Southern California Country*, 21.

5   Davis, *City of Quartz*, 23.

6   Kilston, *Sun Seekers*, 14. This book also delves into the fantasy of place, drawing connections between nineteenth-century theories of medicine that emphasize the curative practices of place. Kilston draws connection between these founding myths and continued healthful practices followed and popularized by Angelenos.

7   Le Guin, "A Non-Euclidean View," 162.

8   Le Guin, "A Non-Euclidean View," 178.

9   For a brief history on the different reasons Native Americans migrated to the Los Angeles region, see Akins and Bauer, "Native Spaces."

10   Raab, "Political Ecology."

11   Kun and Pulido, "Introduction," 9.

12   Kun and Pulido, "Introduction," 9.

13   Anderson, "City Called Heaven," 337.

14   Du Bois, "Colored California," 192–93.

15   Du Bois, "Colored California," 193–94.

16   Scott, *Technopolis*. Much has been said, particularly by the LA School of Urbanism, about the post-Ford and postmodern character of LA's urban and industrial development. For texts exemplifying the LA School, see the articles published in *Environment and Planning D: Society and Space* 4(3); Scott and Soja, *The City*; and Dear and Flusty, "Postmodern Urbanism." Some urban theorists have critiqued the LA School for their boosterish stance (Beauregard, "City of Superlatives"). My thanks to Abby Spinak for pointing me toward this article.

17   I learned of this camouflage project from reading a memoir by LA writer D. J. Waldie, *Holy Land*, 25.

18   See Andersson, *The Future of the World*, for a history and analysis of the emergence of future research following World War II. Andersson makes the point that in the early decades of the Cold War there were

rivaling modes of engaging the future—as either a rational science of prediction devoid of utopian aims or pronouncements on the moral character of society. Futurists drew from "eclectic repertoires and fuzzy boundaries between rationality and speculation, science and art," 7. I highlight Disney and Kahn as futurists relevant for VR's history because they embraced the spectacle, illustrating a kind of future that was being practiced and imagined in LA. See also Wurgaft, "The Future of Futurism," and his assessment of the differences between today's Silicon Valley futurism and the Cold War futurism of Los Angeles.

19   This is from a quote by Imagineer Tony Baxter: "If the Magic Kingdom is fantasy made real, EPCOT is reality made fantastic," Iwerks, "What Would Walt Do?" Thanks to Kalindi Vora for this viewing suggestion. In 2022, the Disney corporation announced a new venture, "Storyliving," that are retirement communities infused with the magic of Disney.

20   Ghamari-Tabrizi, "The Worlds of Herman Kahn," 38–39.

21   Ghamari-Tabrizi, "The Worlds of Herman Kahn," 75–76.

22   Rosten was freelancing at RAND, perhaps employed both because of his storytelling prowess but also his training as a sociologist. Rosten penned the first sociological study of Hollywood in 1941 and, failing to find a professorship, became a writer in Hollywood. I encountered this connection between Rosten and Kahn in Wurgaft's essay, "The Future of Futurism," who himself cites Kleiner, The Age of Heretics. Kleiner notes that this story comes directly from Rosten.

23   Which is not to say that military and fiction/fantasy/entertainment only mix in Los Angeles. Bahng offers an example of science fiction writers being invited to a DOD meeting in DC to take part in a Homeland Security conference on science and technology. She notes that this meeting is part of the longer tradition of scenario planning. See Bahng, Migrant Futures, 52. See also Lakoff, "The Generic Biothreat."

24   Light, From Warfare to Welfare.

25   Didion, "Trouble in Lakewood." See also Faludi, "Girls Have All the Power."

26   Rheingold, Virtual Reality, 206.

27   Furness shared this anecdote while giving a talk I attended at the Institute of Electrical and Electronics Engineers (IEEE) VR conference in 2016. He was being honored with a VR Career Award.

28   Foley, "Interfaces for Advanced Computing."

29   Laboratory research continued at multiple institutions, significantly Fred Brooks's team at the University of North Carolina–Chapel Hill. At the University of Virginia, where I would first encounter virtual reality, Randy Pausch and Denny Proffitt collaborated on VR research (Pausch also collaborated with Disney Imagineers to evaluate the storytelling efficacy of an Aladdin VR experience they piloted in EPCOT in the 1990s) until Pausch moved to Carnegie Mellon to continue his work.

30   National Research Council, *Modeling and Simulation*, 4.

31   See Molotch, "L.A. as Design Product," 240–41.

32   See Brandt, "War, Trauma, and Technologies," for an ethnographic analysis of VR PTSD therapy at USC's Institute for Creative Technologies. See also Suchman, "Configuring the Other," which describes ICT's counterinsurgency simulation, FlatWorld. Suchman attends carefully to the "military–entertainment complex," noting how the expertise of the entertainment industry is used to create an immersive theater of war.

33   Klein, *The History of Forgetting*.

34   Pacleb, "Hauntings of a Different Kind," 10.

35   J.R.R. Tolkien's Middle Earth is retrospectively described as worldbuilding. For a more contemporary example, N. K. Jemisin gives workshops on her worldbuilding method, employed in her celebrated *Broken Earth* trilogy and other writing.

36   See Jenkins, *Convergence Culture*; and Wolf, *Building Imaginary Worlds*.

37   See McDowell, "Storytelling Shapes the Future," 105. The first film that McDowell was a production designer for was *Lawnmower Man*, a 1992 film in which the military uses VR to enhance human intelligence.

38   McDowell, "Storytelling Shapes the Future," 107.

39   Underkoffler, "Pointing to the Future."

40   McDowell and von Stackelberg, "What in the World," 30.

41   McDowell, "Storytelling Shapes the Future," 108. Importantly, McDowell's conception of worldbuilding is different in both form and practice from the more radical potential of transmedia worldbuilding as described by Dan Hassler-Forest, *Science Fiction, Fantasy, and Politics*. Hassler-Forest articulates the political potential of story worlds that are collaboratively constructed not only by Hollywood and consulted experts, but also by fans. Such decentralized worldbuilding not only immerses but also engages fans as themselves worldbuilders who might imagine alternative futures for their own communities. McDowell's work doesn't question assumptions of capitalism and empire whereas Hassler-Forest's analysis explores transmedia projects that imagine alternatives—even as they are the product of the very forces they critique. Worldbuilding's politics are multiple, depending on the narratives, practitioners, and communities involved.

42   That the ideal of peace often conceals violence and war is explored in Idris, *War for Peace*.

43   Klein, *History of Forgetting*, 62.

44   Starosielski, *Media Hot and Cold*, details the various ways in which hot and cold are used by theorists including Lévi-Strauss, McLuhan, and others to describe the relationship between technology, including media technology, and culture. Starosielski's book more generally

moves beyond media in order to apply media theory to the cultural dimensions of temperature.

45 Le Guin, "A Non-Euclidean View," 177.

2. Realities Otherwise

1 Pine and Gilmore, "Welcome to the Experience Economy."

2 Banham, *Los Angeles*.

3 Plagens, "Los Angeles."

4 Though not located in LA, Lucas's Skywalker Ranch exemplifies this fantasy. The buildings that comprise this studio, built starting in the 1980s, are meant to look like nineteenth and early twentieth-century settler estates. Electrical wiring and the parking garage are all concealed underground so as not to disturb this façade. As Connor has noted, the Skywalker Ranch is a product of the same intricate world-building that Lucas applied to *Star Wars*. Lucas himself described Skywalker Ranch as the "part of the *Star Wars* universe which juts up above the top layer of the myth, into the real world." Quoted in Connor, "The Nature of the Firm," 244.

5 Thanks to Peter Messeri for pointing out the irony of my immediate reliance on Google for virtually validating what had been a somewhat inscrutable encounter in the physical world. It became a "real" experience for me when I found the website that affirmed my architectural reading.

6 One show that shot on location, Showtime's *House of Lies*, used it not as a set for Europe but rather as representative of the iconicity of LA itself. The third season's finale ends in a drive-by shooting with Via Rodeo serving as the backdrop. Some viewers were upset at both the realism of the shooting and that it was filmed not far from where Christopher Wallace (The Notorious B.I.G.) had been murdered, also in a drive-by. Madden Toby, "'House of Lies.'"

7 Westwood Village, just north of the façades described, was built up as a shopping district in the 1920s to mimic a Mediterranean town.

8 Andersen, *Los Angeles Plays Itself*. Thanks go to Stefan Helmreich for suggesting this film.

9 This map is an internet curiosity (thanks, Bron Szerszinsky, for tweeting it at me), but was printed in Tino Balio's primary source reader, *The American Film Industry*, 202.

10 Quoted in Krist, *The Mirage Factory*, 110.

11 Ward, "Dreams of Oriental Romance," 23.

12 Ward, "Dreams of Oriental Romance," 29. See also Staszak, who observes that China City was a prime example of a Baudrillardian

simulacrum, as it was "a copy of something that did not even exist," "An Oriental Town," 158. It was also in China City where many Chinese American extras and actors lived. When casting a film, scouts would often go to China City to recruit members of the Chinese community for crowd scenes. Producers would also shop the stores for props. See Lui, *Inside Los Angeles Chinatown*.

13   Letter detailing New Chinatown, 1938, mssSooHoo, box 2, folder 7, Peter SooHoo, Sr. papers, Pacific Rim, Huntington Digital Library, https://hdl.huntington.org/digital/collection/p16003coll12/id/2367/rec /78.

14   New Chinatown "played" old Chinatown in the eponymous 1974 movie. *Chinatown* is set in 1937, and the pagodas of New Chinatown serve as establishing shots. However, China City and New Chinatown didn't open until 1938, after the movie's action has concluded. The movie plays on the stereotypes of old Chinatown as a seedy area of disrepute (not the sanitized tourist destination of New Chinatown). There is also a scene filmed along the Venice Canals, playing themselves.

15   The prime comparison to Los Angeles would be Las Vegas. In Vegas, all of the façades are spectacle. My contention is that in LA, while the spectacle exists, many façades have been more seamlessly folded into the quotidian act of being in and moving through the city.

16   Eco, *Travels in Hyperreality*; Baudrillard, *Simulacra and Simulation*. And of course, Fredric Jameson's extended meditation on Downtown LA's Bonaventure hotel similarly illustrates the city as metaphor for such theorizing. See Jameson, *Postmodernism*.

17   Baudrillard, *America*, 104.

18   Eco, *Travels in Hyperreality*, 4.

19   Eco, *Travels in Hyperreality*, 7.

20   Eco, *Travels in Hyperreality*, 14–15. On the Warner Bros. studio tour, one of the stops is "the archive" where props and replicas from movies are on display. There is a whole Harry Potter section, including a silicone model of Dobby, the house elf, that, though not used during filming, was on set to help actors imagine their invisible scene partner. One of the people on the tour exclaimed, "He looks so real!" and this is certainly a comment on the reality of fantasy, as Dobby was a CG creation of a fictional creature.

21   Eco, *Travels in Hyperreality*, 45–46.

22   Baudrillard, *Simulacra and Simulation*, 3. As is well known, *The Matrix*, a touchstone movie for many in the VR community, is riddled with references to Baudrillard. Neo keeps his contraband hardware in a hollowed-out copy of *Simulacra and Simulation*. Morpheus quotes Baudrillard when revealing the scorched earth to Neo, solemnly stating, "Welcome to the desert of the real." Baudrillard has taken issue with

this citation, as the desert of the real was meant to indicate the inability to distinguish between the real and its representation—a distinction that is quite clear in *The Matrix*. Whereas the movie is a fight to maintain a separation between the real and the virtual, Baudrillard expresses more interest in a film like *Minority Report* that dwells on the inextricable codependence of reality and virtuality. Baudrillard, "The Matrix Decoded"; see also Merrin, *Baudrillard and the Media*.

23 Baudrillard, *Simulacra and Simulation*, 12–13.

24 Soja, *Thirdspace*, 196; Jameson, *Postmodernism*, 43.

25 Soja, *Thirdspace*, 5. Soja notes that the capitalization of "Other" preserves Henri Lefevre's spatial trialectic, as he wrote of "l'Autre."

26 Soja, *Thirdspace*, 6.

27 Lefebvre, *The Production of Space*; Foucault, "Of Other Spaces."

28 Soja, *Thirdspace*, 240.

29 Soja, *Thirdspace*, 279.

30 Soja, *Thirdspace*, 278; Soja, *My Los Angeles*, 2.

31 The report is available at https://www.wundermanthompson.com /insight/unreality.

32 Powers, *On Trend*.

33 This invocation of hyperreality is both vague and most certainly a misinterpretation of Baudrillard (and who can blame). But I find its presence fascinating—as if the hyperreal so obviously exists that the next, more hidden thing needs to be drawn out.

34 In Martin's *Haunted*, an ethnography of Hollywood and the Hong Kong entertainment industry, she traces the theme of enchantment through these spaces, observing how Hollywood has long been attracted to New Age spiritual practices.

35 Powers, *On Trend*, 92.

36 This section title is a play on a chapter title from Soja's *Postmodern Geographies*. He titled the penultimate chapter "It All Comes Together in Los Angeles," which was itself a riff on what was then the masthead of the *Los Angeles Times*. With the motto retired, this phrase is now most associated with Soja. Fittingly for this book, the *Times* slogan changed in 2019 to "The State of What's Next."

37 Eco, *Travels in Hyperreality*, 44.

38 Eco, *Travels in Hyperreality*, 45.

39 Eco, *Travels in Hyperreality*, 46.

40 I went to Universal Studios with my parents when they visited me during fieldwork. Later, when I was first working on the argument of this chapter and trying to explain it to my mother, Ellen Musikant, she reminded me of these windows.

41 Disney has repeatedly dipped its feet in VR but never fully committed. It has dabbled in VR shorts, like *Cycles*. It created a metaverse unit, only

to subsequently lay off the whole team. When Apple signaled its ambition to enter the fray with its Vision Pro headset at its World Wide Development Conference in 2023, CEO Bob Iger appeared on stage to announce that Disney Plus would be bundled into this product.

42 Galloway and Rabinowitz, "Welcome to 'Electronic Cafe International.'"

43 Archival footage can be found on YouTube, however not posted by the artists: https://www.youtube.com/channel/UCfFufZfQ87lStZXaiOGfxBA.

44 This blurb is from the artists' website, Galloway and Rabinowitz, "Hole-in-Space Project Credits."

45 For example, Otsuki, "Human and Machine in Formation," and Roquet, "The Body Shop" and *The Immersive Enclosure*, are both scholars of contemporary Japanese culture and their writing about VR highlights its overlap with robotics and telepresence. Given the central role that robots play in Japan (see Robertson, *Robo Sapiens Japanicus*), writing from that context brings out a different and fascinating set of associations that are less visible in LA.

3. Tinseltown and Technology

1 In the introduction of *Engineering Hollywood*, published in 2021, Marzola notes that historians of technology have paid little attention to Hollywood, and film historians are often deterministic in their treatment of technology. Marzola's project is to span these disciplines, and her focus on the figure of the engineer in early Hollywood is an informative approach.

2 Of particular note is work by Frank, "Lab Coats in the Dream Factory," and Kirby, *Lab Coats in Hollywood*, both of whom conducted ethnographic and interview-based research with science consultants in Hollywood. Kirby additionally argues that movies can act as "diegetic prototypes" that argue for certain technological futures.

3 Sobchack, "Science Fiction Film."

4 Salt, *Film Style and Technology*; Crafton, *The Talkies*; Higgins, *Harnessing the Technicolor Rainbow*; Telotte, *The Mouse Machine*; Prince, *Digital Visual Effects in Cinema*; Whissel, *Spectacular Digital Effects*; Jones, *Spaces Mapped and Monstrous*; Marzola, *Engineering Hollywood*. More reflexively, film studies scholars have begun asking how cinema's transition to digital changes the discipline itself, demanding attention be paid to technological change. See Hidalgo, *Technology and Film Scholarship*.

5 While the first anthropologist, Powdermaker was not Hollywood's first social scientist. Leo Rosten published a deeply researched sociological monograph in 1941 titled *Hollywood: The Movie Colony, The Movie Makers*. Rosten is one of my favorite minor characters in this book, having al-

ready appeared in the introduction, noting how fantasy permeates reality for the movie makers, and in the first chapter, offering "scenario" as a descriptor to the lads at RAND. Rosten was also Margaret Mead's brother-in-law, and in the acknowledgments to *Hollywood* he thanks both Mead and Gregory Bateson for reading drafts of his study. Rosten, unlike Powdermaker, was less of an idealist and more of a realist with regards to their mutual subject of interest. While Rosten was critical, he did not see a lurking evil in Hollywood that Powdermaker did. Notably, Rosten in addition to having a PhD and writing several academic books and articles, found his financial success as a fiction writer, screen writer, and chronicler of the Yiddish language. Powdermaker does not reference Rosten's book, possibly because she did not respect his having "gone native" or because he let Hollywood off too easily. Or perhaps because of what might have been a less than kind relationship between Powdermaker and Mead (which Ortner briefly excavates in "Powdermaker's Anthropology"). Powdermaker also makes no acknowledgment of Rosten in her memoir, going so far as to state, "As far as I knew, no comparable research existed to serve as a model for the study of Hollywood." See *Stranger and Friend*, 213. Powdermaker does praise *New Yorker* journalist Lillian Ross for her long-form reporting on the making of the movie *The Red Badge of Courage*—published after *Hollywood*—observing that Ross had been a more successful participant observer than Powdermaker herself. *Stranger and Friend*, 230.

6   Powdermaker, *Hollywood, the Dream Factory*, 288–89. "The dream factory" offers a similar semiotic contradiction as Horkheimer and Adorno's "culture industry," the phrase used to title an essay written after the two German Jewish thinkers had fled Germany and were living in Los Angeles. Additionally, at least two writers prior to Powdermaker also called Hollywood a "dream factory" in order to make a similar critique. Soviet writer Ilya Ehrenburg wrote a fictional satire of Paramount Pictures in Russian in 1931 that he titled *The Dream Factory* (Фабрика снов). When he later visited the United States and wrote about his trip for readers back home, he noted: "I was reminded again of the book I wrote many years ago about the cinema 'dream factory.' The American's desire to forget and divert himself by day-dreaming in the evening has given birth to a vast industry; in Hollywood mass dreams are turned out just as skillfully and quickly as tinned meat in Chicago." See Ehrenburg, "Ilya Ehrenburg's America," 572. Writer and activist James Rorty penned an article in the magazine *Forum and Century* in 1935 titled "Dream Factory," in which he criticized Hollywood for eschewing art and proletariat concerns heightened by the Depression and instead manufacturing trifles for the youth. Ehrenburg, Rorty, and Powdermaker are all developing a Marxist critique, building on concerns of Hollywood censorship

at the time and lamenting that cinema is no longer properly artistic. If in the 1930s and 1940s, "the dream factory" was a derisive nickname when wielded by cultural critics, in the 1910s and 1920s, in the immediate shadow of Ford's success, Hollywood studios gladly compared their work to factories in the hopes of emphasizing their sound and profitable business models to potential investors. See Marzola, *Engineering Hollywood*, 8.

7   Powdermaker, *Hollywood, the Dream Factory*, 39.

8   In Sherry Ortner's *Not Hollywood*, she explores a different kind of dream—the American Dream—arguing that the emergence of the independent film industry (and the content of many such films) occurs in the wake of the ravages of neoliberalism and the degradation of the American Dream both as myth and (for some) reality. Additionally, Ortner outlines how, to some extent, the independent film scene understands itself as an alternative to the dream factory.

9   Powdermaker, *Hollywood, the Dream Factory*, 204.

10 Ortner, however, notes that the film set itself remains Fordist even if the studios have been changed by neoliberalism. *Not Hollywood*, 199–200. For other analyses of the political economy of Hollywood after the "vertical disintegration" of the studio system, see Christopherson and Storper, "The City as Studio"; Storper and Christopherson, "Flexible Specialization"; and Scott, *On Hollywood*. For film as a global endeavor, see Miller et al., *Global Hollywood 2*; Christopherson, "Behind the Scenes"; and Kokas, *Hollywood Made in China*.

11 Jenkins, *Convergence Culture*; Rose, *The Art of Immersion*; McDonald and Smith-Rowsey, *The Netflix Effect*; Craig and Cunningham, *Social Media Entertainment*; Bacon, *Transmedia Cultures*.

12 Not only did chapter 1 illustrate how entertainment and the aerospace industry have always been entangled in Los Angeles, but the origins of Silicon Valley also owe a debt to Hollywood. Hewlett-Packard's first client was Disney, who bought several audio oscilloscopes for *Fantasia* in 1939. This sale helped the new company move out of their storied garage.

13 Acland, *American Blockbuster*, 45.

14 John Thornton Caldwell, in *Production Culture*, complicates thinking about cinematic technologies, noting that they are not simply instrumental machines that make meaning but are themselves machines invested with meaning by the community that operates them. Even as Caldwell pushes toward a Latourian understanding of technologies involved in movie production, he does not suggest (as I do) that it might be further instructive to think about cinematic technologies as a distinct kind of technology.

15 While I'm interested in offering social, institutional, and cultural reasons for VR's failure to launch, the medium itself might be incompatible with cinematic aesthetics. See, for example, Sandifer, "Out of the Screen," for an applicable analysis of why 3-D has gone through cycles of hype and disappointment similar to VR.

16 In 2021, Amazon purchased MGM for $8.45 billion.

17 See Ortner, "Access," for a methodological reflection on her own ethnographic difficulty in gaining access to Hollywood. Because VR was not (quite) Hollywood (riffing on Ortner's consequent study of independent film, *Not Hollywood*), my access issues were not (quite) the same. Especially because VR had not yet "made it," the director of TEC welcomed my presence as she felt I (and my Yale credentials) legitimated the work she was doing. While I was thus able to get into Hollywood's periphery, where I *was* denied access (or where it was clear that while I would have been tolerated, I wasn't wholeheartedly welcomed) was to the few established production companies exclusively focused on VR.

18 The most recent acquisition was in 2000 by the French multinational media company Thomson SARL. Thomson embraced the Technicolor name, rebranding their corporate entity.

19 Layton and Pierce, *The Dawn of Technicolor*, 42. I received both my undergraduate and graduate degrees from MIT, which contributed to my warm feelings toward this affiliation.

20 As Marzola further notes, it was precisely the relocation of companies like Technicolor to Los Angeles that further solidified the region's stronghold on cinema production. See *Engineering Hollywood*, 44.

21 Layton and Pierce, *The Dawn of Technicolor*, 19. Murray argues in her book *Bright Signals* that color TV underwent a similarly slow process of adoption. Like cinema (and VR), it promised the viewer greater immersion, but it took twenty years from when color was introduced for it to transcend novelty and challenge the black-and-white standard of TV.

22 In other Hollywood contexts, these would be considered "assistants"—the entry-level position in the film industry. See also Hill, "Hollywood Assistanting."

23 See Allison, "More than a Man," for an analysis of realism in Serkis's performance.

24 Recall that this event occurred in 2018. While generative AI apps would not be released to the public for several more years, Rick and others in his position were well aware of these developments. I myself sat in on several private demos during fieldwork, as companies pitched their AI tools to Hollywood chief technology officers.

25 Rick's quote is an example of a recurring theme that I noted throughout fieldwork around "the blockchain" that I found fascinating, especially in

the post-truth moment. While Rick was hinting at a dystopian block-chain future, it was more common for blockchain to be invoked as a shorthand for promising a more sturdy reality that today's unreal-ity has undone. However, few people I spoke with who expressed this excitement about blockchain were able to explain to me in any mean-ingful way how it worked (though of course there are some people who understand it and have found meaningful applications). Blockchain (as I encountered it during fieldwork) strikes me as an ironic reclamation of truth and reality through mysterious mechanisms.

26   Star and Griesemer, "Institutional Ecology."

27   Powdermaker, *Hollywood*, 39. In her memoir, Powdermaker writes that it was at the behest of her publisher that she added analogies between Hollywood and "primitive societies." In retrospect, Powdermaker felt that they are out of place and weakened the book. In general, Powder-maker considered *Hollywood* to be her least successful book (by scien-tific standards) as she was not a full participant observer and could not manage the overall dislike she had for the Hollywood community. See Powdermaker, *Stranger and Friend*, 229–30.

28   Caldwell, *Production Culture*, 184.

29   Layton and Pierce, *The Dawn of Technicolor*, 232. See also Street, "Colour Consciousness," for more on Natalie Kalmus's theory of "color con-sciousness" but also an argument about how Technicolor had a differ-ent feel in British productions as opposed to Hollywood. Pandian notes that, as was also the case for *The Wizard of Oz*, in Tamil cinema, Tech-nicolor was first used for scenes and stories depicting worlds apart. "Fantasy's colors are portals into another world, composing an alter-nate universe with a nature of its own," *Reel World*, 125. Color, then, is not only a question of aesthetics, but also plays a role in defining the limits of imagination and, as demonstrated by Rossi, *The Republic of Color*, a means of social reform and control.

30   Lucas was from Modesto, California, just outside of the Bay Area. Though he went to USC and lived briefly in Los Angeles, he itched to leave Hollywood. With Francis Ford Coppola (who today resides in Napa), they founded American Zoetrope in San Francisco in 1969. Lucas proudly claims that he has never made a movie in Los Angeles. See Hartlaub, "George Lucas." Connor, "The Nature of the Firm," analyzes what I am tempted to call the "cinematic terroir" of Lucasfilm and the influence of the Bay Area, including the frontier imagination and viti-culture, on the studio Lucas built.

31   The knight was animated by the Pixar division of Lucas's VFX studio, Industrial Light and Magic (ILM). A year after *Young Sherlock Holmes*, this division was sold to Steve Jobs and Pixar Animation Studios was founded.

32 Applegate, "Entrepreneurs Find," C3.

33 Kenneally, *Side by Side*.

34 Thanks here are due to my brother, Jason Messeri, who has worked in film production since the early 2000s. He shared with me his experience of working through the digital transition, referred me to the documentary, *Side by Side*, and fact checked parts of this chapter for me.

35 Caldwell details various ways different cinematic technologies have changed labor relations. For example, directors of photography lost a significant amount of control in the transition to digital and many lamented this shift. See Caldwell, *Production Culture*, 179–84. See also Deuze, *Media Work*; Curtin and Vanderhoef, "Vanishing Piece of the Pi"; and Curtin and Sanson, *Precarious Creativity*. Chung, *Media Heterotopias*, traces the changing labor relations of the digital workflow beyond Hollywood, showing how these flows are increasingly transnational and invisible (a configuration Chung terms *spectral effects*). At TEC, much of the animation work was carried out by a team in Bangalore, India. I once referred to this as outsourcing and got reprimanded—these are Technicolor employees, I was corrected, based at a different branch. Thanks to folks on Twitter who chimed in with thoughts and sources on the relationship between labor and the transition to digital: @amcomiskey, @iycrtylph, @fleming77, @therourke, @profJohnEllis, @Art HouseDirectr, @shannonmattern, @clancynewyork, @bestqualitycrab, @harbinger, @elainemgan, @jippykelly.

36 Acland, *American Blockbuster*, 237. See also Turnock, *Plastic Reality*, for an accounting of the special effects industry in the 1970s and 1980s and her argument for thinking about early blockbusters of this period as having an auteur aesthetic.

37 The digital intermediate (DI) was introduced to postproduction in the late 1990s. Though productions were still shooting in film, the DI referred to the process for converting celluloid to a digital file in order to perform digital corrections to the image. This was an intermediate, because the movie would then be converted back to film for theater distribution. See Prince, *Digital Visual Effects*. In the case of Jastrow's work with Cameron, because the whole workflow was digital there was not technically an "intermediate," but Jastrow was applying the principles of other, newly developing DIs to this project.

38 Revkin, "Showing in Theaters."

39 Acland, *American Blockbuster*, 261. Acland further reflects on the metonymic relationship between *Avatar*'s plot and Cameron's technological impulse: "The Na'vi are not merely representations of an ancient and superstitious worldview; they offer an image of a superior technological system. Pandora is worth defending, then, as an example of perfect synergy across beings and devices, with integration a racial,

environmental, and technological concept simultaneously. . . . [*Avatar*] by the end sneaks in the true colonists, those hybrid avatars. The technological game-changing film is a tale of full acceptance and assimilation . . . with an even more advanced game-changing technological system," 263.

40 The sociological importance of continuity between technical crews across films has been observed by Deuze in *Media Work* and Acland has specifically noted that this holds true for Cameron. See Acland, *American Blockbuster*, 250–51.

41 See also Bordwell, *Pandora's Digital Box*, for an account of the changeover from film to digital projection. The brief history I offer here is necessarily incomplete. Sound, picture editing, and even the use of digital dailies each have their own interesting story and ramifications in this conversion to digital. See, for example, Dhir, "The Modern Entertainment Marketplace," for an analysis of how the editing process has changed. Television also underwent a digital transition, shaped by different technologies and narratives. Connor offers a reflexive analysis of this transition, drawing on *Lost* as a striking allegory of an industry dealing with both changing production technologies and the rise of online fandom. *Hollywood Math and Aftermath*, chapter 6.

42 Not discussed here are other cinematic technologies (for example the Steadicam or the Probe lens) that Caldwell notes demonstrated "proto-VR" tendencies and satisfied an "immersive urge" that he suggests began as early as the 1990s, during the previous VR wave. *Production Culture*, 167.

43 My thanks are due to Joanna Radin who joined me for 1990s movie nights as we explored cinematic commonalities between my work and her research on Michael Crichton. We were both scarred by a screening of *Strange Days*, a 1995 film directed by Kathryn Bigelow and written by James Cameron that depicted VR as an illicit substance, heavily trafficked in a dystopic LA at the end of the millennium. The less said, the better. For the curious, see Chan, *Virtual Reality*, who discusses both *Strange Days* and other cinematic depictions of VR in the 1980s and 1990s.

44 Cline, *Ready Player One*.

45 Cline, "Foreword by Ernest Cline," ix–xvi.

46 D'Onfro, "Facebook Gives Its Oculus Employees."

47 In one climactic scene, the protagonists are in the OASIS and have to solve a puzzle set in the hotel from Kubrick's *The Shining*. I attended a talk at SIGGRAPH in 2018 by the VFX supervisor of RPO as he explained how they created a digital model of the hotel and then rendered it to look as though it was a celluloid shot. While the scene looks as though the avatars are wandering through a brick-and-mortar hotel, the whole scene is digital.

48 Both HTC and Oculus released their first commercial headsets in spring 2016, a few months before the RPO shoot began.

49 "HTC Vive x Ready Player One"; Parisi, "'Ready Player One.'"

50 Scott, in his economic history of Hollywood, similarly draws attention to a geographic distribution of expertise (and consequent disputes). As Hollywood established itself in the first decades of the twentieth century, it differentiated itself from other movie centers by focusing on content and audience. This was in contrast to an East Coast model based on patenting sophisticated equipment. See *On Hollywood*, 17–21. Technicolor resisted moving its headquarters, originally in Boston, to Los Angeles because it thought it advantageous to be near technical and financial centers. With regard to VR, Hollywood continues to have a content-centered model in contrast to Silicon Valley's technology-centered model.

51 VR is not alone in acting as a boundary object between entertainment and technology, between Hollywood and Silicon Valley. Craig and Cunningham analyze content producers who create entertainment for social media platforms (YouTube, Instagram, etc.). In chapter 1 of their book, *Social Media Entertainment*, they explore a "clash of industrial cultures" between "NoCal" and "SoCal," 22. Similar to the conflict emergent from VR being both a cinematic technology and an emerging technology, social media entertainment is caught between understandings of platforms as both content delivery systems and networked communication systems.

52 During the opening keynote of XR on the Bay, the convener of the conference described the motivation for the event: "The realization is that technology empowers artists and artists empower technology. And for the longest time, the technology community has existed in Silicon Valley and a creative community has existed in Hollywood. And those cultures have not had a chance to get to know each other." See Ward, Chabin, and Miranda, "Jonathan Miranda @ XR Day on the Bay."

53 Acland, *American Blockbuster*, 243.

54 In 2022, Jastrow left Evercast and joined the Shiba Inu web3 company (which began as a crypto meme coin) as the Metaverse Advisor.

55 Layton and Pierce, *The Dawn of Technicolor*, 90–91.

Part II. Fantasy of Being

1 The imaginaries of the metaverse and spatial computing existed before Meta and Apple made the terms part of their marketing strategy.

2 Harding, *The Science Question in Feminism*; Haraway, "Situated Knowledges."

3 Martin, "Meeting Polemics."

4 Wynter, in her analysis of Fanon, argues that what it means to be human is not a universal phenomenon, but rather one that is culturally and historical contingent. Not everyone has equal access to *being* human. If there is anything we might call a "common reality," Wynter argues, it is "our varied cultural modes of being/experiencing ourselves as human." The political appeal to a common reality as well as the VR experiences that will be described in the following chapters presume (falsely, according to Wynter) that there is a common experience of being human. Wynter, "Towards the Sociogenic Principle," 60.

4. Being and the Other

1 De la Peña, "The Future of News?" TEDWomen is an annual TED event "about the power of women and girls to be creators and change makers."
2 Milk, "How Virtual Reality Can Create."
3 Virtual and digital technologies often hold an (unfulfilled) promise of bettering humanity. Bill Gates offered this early vision of the internet: "We are all created equal in the virtual world and we can use this equality to help address some of the sociological problems that society has yet to solve in the physical world." Quoted in Chun, *Control and Freedom*, 130. But the actual story of the internet is the story of sociological problems getting reinforced in the digital world. See, among many others, Nakamura, *Cybertypes*, and Noble, *Algorithms of Oppression*. Ames, in *The Charisma Machine*, chronicles how One Laptop per Child, another digital intervention with aspirations of solving a "sociological problem," fell short of its utopian promises.
4 Sutherland, "The Ultimate Display," 508.
5 Rogers makes a similar point, noting that in the 1990s VR began to stand for not only HMD technologies, but any mediated experience that promised immersion, " 'Taking the Plunge,' " 142. Thus, reading both popular and scholarly work from the 1980s and 1990s can be disorienting as authors treated subsets of the terms VR, *virtual, cyberspace, internet,* and *online* as interchangeable in variable and promiscuous ways. A collection of essays edited by Markley, titled *Virtual Realities and their Discontents* and published in 1996, includes references to VR systems, but places them in fluid connection to cyberspace and similar imaginaries. By the early 2000s, these terms begin to desegregate, at least in academic writing. Boellstorff distinguishes the goggled experience of virtual reality from the virtual worlds he writes about, but *virtual, cyber,* and *online* are for him equivalent terms, *Coming of Age in Second Life*, 17. Presciently, Markley warned that for VR to achieve the hype its many

promoters state, it must resist "being collapsed into 'cyberspace'—the naive, totalizing incarnation of Western tendencies to privilege mind over materiality," "Boundaries," 57.

6   As has been ubiquitously noted, Gibson coined *cyberspace* in his 1982 short story "Burning Chrome" and fleshed out the concept in *Neuromancer* and its sequels.

7   Zoë Sophia points to several female sci-fi authors who were offering cyborg stories that challenged the bounds of body and machine before Gibson, "Virtual Corporeality," 16.

8   Stone, "Will the Real Body," 98–99.

9   Barlow, "Being in Nothingness."

10 Chun offers an analysis of this commercial and more generally critically excavates the fantasy of the mind freed of the body. "Significantly, this rewriting of the internet as emancipatory, as 'freeing' oneself from one's body, also naturalizes racism. The logic framing MCI's commercial reduces to what *they* can't see, can't hurt *you* . . . this formulation effectively conceals individual and institutional responsibility from discrimination, positing discrimination as a problem that the discriminated must solve," *Control and Freedom*, 132. See also Nakamura, "Where Do You Want," 25.

11 Heim, *The Metaphysics of Virtual Reality*, 80.

12 Heim, *The Metaphysics of Virtual Reality*, 100.

13 Penny, "Virtual Bodybuilding," 20.

14 Balsamo, *Technologies of the Gendered Body*, 123, 125.

15 Hayles, "Boundary Disputes," 13. See also Hayles, *How We Became Posthuman*. Similarly, Chan, *Virtual Reality* (writing between VR hype cycles), focuses her analysis on the embodiment always already present in representations of VR and virtual worlds even as it is denied.

16 Stone, "Will the Real Body." Grosz, *Architecture from the Outside*, similarly observes how the fantasy of disembodiment is linked to the fantasy of mastery at a distance.

17 Stone, "Will the Real Body," 111. While this chapter by Stone questions the fantasy of the freed mind, her other writing, *The War of Desire and Technology at the Close of the Mechanical Age*, has been critiqued by Nelson, "Introduction: Future Texts," for treating the body as something to be transcended through online identity play. This fails to ask *who* is able to engage in such imagination (and acknowledge that people of color might not so easily free their bodies from historical contingency). For other writing on dis/embodiment and VR, see Murray and Sixsmith, "The Corporeal Body."

18 Such arguments also inevitably reinforced a Cartesian duality even as they wrote against the mind/body split. Hayles, "Flesh and Metal,"

makes this critique of her own work and Richardson and Harper, "Corporeal Virtuality," make this critique of Stone.

19　*Cyberspace* was not a term I encountered with any regularity during fieldwork. Searching my field notes returned only one instance of "cyberspace," invoked during a talk given at a hackathon in which I participated. In a room of tired, mostly Gen Z participants, a Gen X speaker talked about how he saw potential for VR in his work as an IT security consultant as it enabled his clients to "'see' cyberspace" so that they could better understand his technological offerings. Starting in 2021, however, *the metaverse*—a term from Stephenson's 1992 cyberpunk novel, *Snow Crash*—began dominating discourse and conflating conversations about VR with what have become known as Web3 technologies (many of which are blockchain-based).

20　Bye, "Nonny de la Peña."

21　Oscars, "Alejandro González Iñárritu Accepts a Special Oscar."

22　De la Peña was first referred to as "the godmother of VR" in an article on *Engadget* in January 2015, see Volpe, "The Godmother of Virtual Reality." A curator of Sundance New Frontiers, Kamal Sinclair, had noticed that despite growing media interest in VR, women weren't getting as much press as the male VR innovators. In 2015, Sinclair and her colleagues made a concerted effort to talk up de la Peña's work to the press. One of the outcomes was this *Engadget* article. De la Peña supposes that she got labeled "godmother" because the interviewer saw how she had encouraged and nurtured so many of the big names that were emerging in the industry. See Sinclair, "Use the Amplification Strategy," and De la Peña and Furness, "VWS Fireside Chat #13."

23　De la Peña et al., "Immersive Journalism," 291.

24　Slater and Wilbur, "A Framework for Immersive"; Sanchez-Vives and Slater, "From Presence to Consciousness," to reference only a couple of the lab's most cited work on this topic.

25　Slater, "Place Illusion and Plausibility," 3554.

26　De la Peña, "Inventing Immersive Journalism."

27　Murray, in a measured critique of overblown claims about VR's potential (especially in academic research) notes that some of the thrill of VR is exactly because you can never fully forget where you are even as you can cognitively appreciate how "real" the virtual setting feels. See Murray, "Virtual/Reality," 19.

28　Boellstorff, *Coming of Age in Second Life*, 19.

29　De la Peña et al., "Immersive Journalism."

30　Fisher sponsored my visiting affiliation with USC's School of Cinematic Arts (SCA) while I was doing fieldwork. I sat in with a class that he and Perry Hoberman were teaching, for which Mark Bolas (now at Microsoft) was the "industry client." While I am here only making passing reference to Fisher and Bolas, their influence in the development of VR, past and present, cannot be overstated. While my exposure to VR at USC was entirely through SCA, Bolas's lab was also in the military-funded Institute for Creative Technologies (see chapter 1). Because, as will be explained, de la Peña was working with Bolas's VR setup, she too was initially affiliated with the Institute for Creative Technologies.

31 This HMD was developed jointly between Fakespace and USC. Funding came from the Office of Naval Research.

32 Rastegar, "Curating 'Physical Cinema.'" See also Rastegar, "A Cosmic Demonstration."

33 This version of the origin story of Oculus was told by de la Peña during a conversation with Tom Furness at an event in the VR social world *AltSpace* in November 2020, "VWS Fireside Chat #13." At this same event, she also connected the development of Google Cardboard to *Hunger*. When she was asked to show the piece at Google, USC researcher Perry Hoberman helped put together kits based on the Fov2Go display for smartphones that he, Bolas, Luckey, and others had developed in February 2012 for the IEEE VR conference. This, like all of the VR projects coming out of USC, was an open-source product and Google Cardboard, released in 2014, was based on this design.

34 Frilot says in a podcast interview how, having met Luckey through de la Peña, she would often suggest to artists (including Chris Milk) that were working in immersive media to get their hands on an Oculus development kit, putting them in touch with Luckey; see Bye, "Sundance's Shari Frilot." Oculus was the headset of choice at New Frontier for many years. For more of Frilot's reflections on VR's aesthetics and potential, see Frilot and King, "Virtual Reality."

35 Lisa Nakamura, "Feeling Good about Feeling Bad," has critiqued how tears serve as a proof of concept of a sort for VR; evidence that it "works" and makes an impact.

36 Goodman, "Hunger in L.A." As already alluded to, one of the people who saw de la Peña's work and became interested in VR was Iñárritu. *Carne y Arena* plays with this idea of invisibility in its subtitle ("Virtually Present, Physically Invisible") in a way reminiscent of how de la Peña here describes the power of making those who are invisible (undernourished people, immigrants) to a certain audience, visible.

37 Rastegar, "Curating 'Physical Cinema.'"

38 For a history of empathy, see Lanzoni, *Empathy*. For ambiguity over the historical development of the definition as it pertains to VR, see Bollmer, "Empathy Machines."

39 Botvinick and Cohen, "Rubber Hands 'Feel' Touch." IJsselsteijn, de Kort, and Haans, "Is This My Hand," and Slater et al., "Towards a Digital Body," have both replicated this illusion in VR. For a history of illusion

in perceptual psychology research, including VR replications of illusion, see Messeri, "Realities of Illusion."

40 Slater et al., "Inducing Illusory Ownership."

41 The initial collaboration between Slater and de la Peña deviates from this pattern, as they had participants embody a prisoner who was in a "stress position."

42 Yee and Bailenson, "The Proteus Effect."

43 Yee and Bailenson, "Walk a Mile."

44 Banakou et al., "Virtual Body Ownership," interrogate assumptions that often shape laboratory research on VR and its role in producing empathy or reducing bias. If a situation is negative, virtual embodiment of someone else might actually increase rather than decrease implicit bias.

45 De la Peña wasn't even listed as a speaker in the first press releases for the conference, James, "The Faces of SVVR."

46 Bye, "Nonny de la Peña." I mention that Bye introduces this language, because it's not clear to me that "empathy" was, at this point, central to how de la Peña spoke about VR. Certainly, the word was already associated with her work. A review of *Hunger in LA* published on the tech news site *The Verge* was titled "Digital Empathy: How 'Hunger in Los Angeles' Broke My Heart in a Virtual World," see Bishop, "Digital Empathy." But "empathy" was only used in the title, not by de la Peña, who was interviewed for the piece. By 2015, however, she was using this term. An interview in *Engadget* (another tech news site) quotes de la Peña as explaining that VR "is such a visceral empathy generator." See Volpe, "The Godmother of Virtual Reality."

47 Bye, "Nonny de la Peña."

48 Bye, "Cosmo Scharf on VR Storytelling."

49 Bye, "Sundance's Shari Frilot."

50 Milk, "How Virtual Reality Can Create."

51 Illustrative of these critiques are Turkle, "Empathy Machines"; Hassan, "Digitality, Virtual Reality and the 'Empathy Machine'"; Bollmer, "Empathy Machines"; and Nakamura, "Feeling Good about Feeling Bad." Empathy as part of the process of human-centered design has also been critiqued (similarly to how VR as empathy machine has been critiqued) by Irani, *Chasing Innovation*. Benjamin links the critique of VR and HCD in chapter 5 of *Race after Technology*. Bloom in *Against Empathy* offers a general critique of empathy, arguing instead for what he calls rational compassion when it comes to large-scale decision-making. Serpell, "The Banality of Empathy," questions the broader claim that any media (VR included) impels empathy. And Paul proposes a "Paradox of Empathy" by which open-mindedness holds epistemic danger.

52 The overuse of *empathy machine* is apparent in an article from 2017 that reports fatigue from VR creators of the phrase. See Robertson, "VR Was Sold as an 'Empathy Machine.'" This was not a rejection of the idea of VR as impactful, but rather an exhaustion of the clichéd language.

53 This is not to say the racial critique was not also coming from the community. But as a white person who was known to be interested in gender (as opposed to specifically race) and VR, it is also possible I was not invited to nor welcome at these conversations. And while, in 2018, I didn't witness much in the way of a racial critique from within the industry, there is some evidence of it coming from aligned industries, for example a game designer who astutely called out VR as not an empathy machine but an appropriation machine. See Yang, "If You Walk in Someone Else's Shoes."

54 Ward, "Black Pain."

55 Nakamura, "Feeling Good about Feeling Bad," 53. Or, as Chin writes, "Your empathy, it is not you feeling what I feel, it is you inventing what I feel so you can feel good," "Using Fiction," 485.

56 Nakamura, "Feeling Good about Feeling Bad," 57.

57 Most critiques of VR as empathy machine do not distinguish between the different fantasies of being that I outline in this chapter. One exception is Kamau, "Rooms Full of Mirrors," who is slightly less critical of VR experiences that ask the viewer to take a witnessing perspective. These experiences "allow viewers to imagine what it would be like to be in those environments but unencumbered by a body, letting them have it both ways: They experience a new perspective without having to surrender their own." For Kamau, the embodied VR experiences are more problematic for reasons similar to those outlined by Nakamura.

58 Nakamura, "Feeling Good about Feeling Bad," 51.

59 Bollmer, "Empathy Machines," 71. See also Nash, "Virtual Reality Witness."

60 Du Bois, *The Souls of Black Folk*, 150. In 1996, Tal wrote in *Wired*, "Life Behind the Screen," that cybertheorists ought to look to Black thought, particularly Du Bois's notion of double consciousness, as they discussed the "multiple identities, fragmented personae, and liminality" that cyberspace was thought to offer but that has long shaped Black Americans' experience. See also Nelson, "Introduction: Future Texts," where Tal is cited, for further critique of how Blackness gets constructed in opposition to the freedom promised by the internet and technological progress.

61 Turkle, "Empathy Machines," 26. Hollan, "Being There," observes that while empathy is often discussed as unidirectional (an attribute of the empathizer), it is an intersubjective experience. One can only empathize

if "the other" is allowing themselves to be known. This is another way of articulating Turkle's concern—the absenting of the other despite the illusion of their presence—while also highlighting the impoverished understanding of empathy that undergirds these experiences.

62 Sontag, *Regarding the Pain of Others*, 102–103.

63 A version of this piece is available on YouTube without the digital avatar and hand tracking. If the viewer looks down, one sees an empty car seat instead of a child's body; see Allan-Blitz, "Messy Truth in VR."

64 The Lumiere Awards are the flagship event of the Advanced Imaging Society. Founded in 2009 by Disney, DreamWorks, and other VFX-oriented studios, the AIS was originally founded to promote 3-D cinema, but has branched out to recognize other achievements in cinematic technology, including immersive technology. See Roettgers, "Van Jones Talks."

65 "Van Jones, Lumiere Awards Winner."

66 The father is played by Winston Duke, best known for playing M'Baku in *Black Panther* and *Avenger* movies. Brie Larson, also of the Marvel Cinematic Universe, stars in the second episode, about sexual harassment.

67 Thinking back on this experience, I wonder at this response. Were these tears meant as proof to myself that I felt, that I understood? As Chin reprimands, "Is that a tear in your eye? Don't look to me to justify your goodness as you reach toward me across the digital divide. Has your empathy filled my belly?," "Using Fiction," 486.

68 Nakamura, "Feeling Good about Feeling Bad," draws on Hartman in her critique of VR. Hartman is also referenced by those writing about empathy in design practices and technology more generally. Bennett and Rosner, "The Promise of Empathy," draw on Hartman in their critique for how empathy as used in human-centered design creates distance (not closeness) between designer and potential user. Chun, *Control and Freedom*, 136, uses Hartman to analyze circulated fantasies of equality that instead reproduce unequal subjectivity. See also Rosane, "Empathy Machines."

69 Hartman, *Scenes of Subjection*, 18.

70 Hartman, *Scenes of Subjection*, 18.

71 Hartman, *Scenes of Subjection*, 19.

72 Hartman, *Scenes of Subjection*, 31–32.

73 Hartman, *Scenes of Subjection*, 39.

74 Hartman, *Scenes of Subjection*, 20.

75 Serpell, "Race Off," 58.

76 Serpell, "Race Off," 72.

77 Gaines, *Black for a Day*, 10.

78 Gaines draws on bell hooks's essay "Eating the Other," in which hooks states: "Certainly from the standpoint of white supremacist capital-

ist patriarchy, the hope is that desires for the 'primitive' or fantasies about the Other can be continually exploited, and that such exploitation will occur in a manner that reinscribes and maintains the *status quo*," 22. Hooks was not writing about empathy experiences, but rather was interested in why late '80s and early '90s mass culture had become so multicultural, containing traces of a desire to know and be with the Other. In one reading, this could be interpreted as a challenge to white supremacy; there could be liberatory potential. But hooks cautions this ought not be accepted without criticism for exactly the reason that she saw more reason to worry that this desire reasserted rather than toppled dominant power structures.

79   I thank my friend and colleague Molly Crocket for this insight.

80   Foster, *The Souls of Cyberfolk*. Foster's focus on race allows him to read cyborgs differently than cyberfeminists who, in his accounting, have focused on gender to the exclusion of race. See chapter 6 in this book for more on cyberfeminism.

81   The director of the music video, Brett Leonard, also directed the VR thriller *Lawnmower Man* for which Alex McDowell (see chapter 1) was production designer.

82   Foster, *The Souls of Cyberfolk*, 183.

5. Special Affect

1   Analog simulation training, particularly of physical disabilities, are a mainstay of medical education and other outreach efforts. Like VR, these simulations hope to instill empathy and understanding in the user. Also like VR, simulations that reduce *being disabled* to having limited mobility or otherwise different ability have been heavily critiqued by the disability community and scholars. For example, "[disability] simulations require participants to personally experience an artificially manufactured version of disability rather than having them imagine the problems that people with disabilities actually confront," Nario-Redmond, Gospodinov, and Cobb, "Crip for a Day," 2. Embodied Labs' aspiration is, as Shaw explains, to move away from this model and toward one that more fully captures another's world. While a VR experience is still only a matter of minutes—and thus can't capture complex structural barriers nor the experience of *living* with disability—Embodied Labs imagines it as a support resource, complementing the experience and education caregivers already draw from. This is not to say that this company completely avoids the problems of stereotype that plague other VR experiences. But the unique context of this implementation makes some of the previous studies on simulations (which depend on undergraduates

as test subjects) less applicable. Embodied Labs has self-assessed the efficacy of their products for caregivers, and one research team studied the implementation of their VR experiences in a medical school curriculum. See Elzie and Shaia, "A Pilot Study."

2   This point is echoed by STS scholars Martin, Myers, and Viseu who write, "A person who cares must first be willing and available *to be moved by* this other [object or phenomenon]," "The Politics of Care," 635. In other words, VR does not automatically elicit an emotional reaction, but the degree of affective response is always an outcome of the person and how they choose to relate to the technology.

3   This reaction highlights an important distinction between first-person perspective-taking activities that ask the participant to imagine themselves (as themselves) in a situation versus activities that ask the participant to imagine themselves as someone else in a situation. Embodied Labs produces VR experiences in the latter category. In a study of first-person perspective-taking situations facilitated through imagination (as opposed to VR), Batson, Early, and Salvarani, "Perspective Taking," found that when the participant was asked to imagine themself in a traumatic situation, the empathetic perspective taking is potentially distressing. But when asked to take on the perspective of another person in the same situation, a similarly empathic response was measured without the distress. Maggie might have more easily slipped into imagining herself, rather than Clay, in the scenario because the experience was so close to her own.

4   "Care" is also widely researched in anthropology, especially as it pertains to aging. See, for example, Buch, "Anthropology of Aging and Care." As my focus is not on caring practices but rather on how a specific technology filters imaginations of care, I primarily orient around the STS literature.

5   In the contexts of science and technology, the analytic of care sheds light on what, at first blush, appear to be opposites. Wanderer, *The Life of a Pest*, demonstrates how a "care of the pest" in invasive species research is essential to constructing knowledge. In the case of tech companies, Seaver, "Care and Scale," notes how care and scale are in practice redefined in order to feel that, despite being seemingly at odds, both have been achieved.

6   Puig de la Bellacasa, "Matters of Care in Technoscience" and *Matters of Care*.

7   Latour, "Why Has Critique."

8   Puig de la Bellacasa, "Matters of Care in Technoscience," 89.

9   Puig de la Bellacasa, *Matters of Care*, 60.

10   See also Hobart and Kneese, "Radical Care."

11   Murphy, "Unsettling Care."

12   Ticktin, *Casualties of Care Immigration*.

13   Murphy, "Unsettling Care," 719.

14   Puig de la Bellacasa, *Matters of Care*, 11.

15   Turkle, *Alone Together*. As a counterpoint, the introduction to a special issue of the *International Journal of Cultural Studies* observes that the isolation wrought by the COVID-19 pandemic illustrated how instrumental media technologies are for doing care work, especially at a distance, Gibson, Hjorth, and Choi, "Caring Media Futures." See also Pols, *Care at a Distance*. Zeavin, *The Distance Cure*, excavates the ethics of the infrastructure that underly teletherapy.

16   Atanasoski and Vora, *Surrogate Humanity*, 4.

17   Atanasoski and Vora, *Surrogate Humanity*, 90.

18   Irani, *Chasing Innovation*, 168.

19   Shaw and her cofounders let me into almost every aspect of company life, a generous transparency especially for a start-up (there were certain topics that Shaw and I discussed that we agreed I would not write about, but this rarely had to do with anything that would change the analysis of this chapter). While this kind of access can sometimes reveal unseemly undertakings, the more I learned about Embodied Labs, the more my admiration grew. This chapter thus presents a favorable depiction of the company, but I acknowledge that there are other ways of interpreting EL's mission. Thinking again about the arguments presented in *Surrogate Humanity*, one could hypothesize that, by introducing VR to care workers, the technology creates a high-tech façade that elevates technological potential over human potential through augmentation. This could render care work itself as high tech even as it remains fully human, which could in turn mask over the continued devaluing (especially in terms of wages) of care workers. For this analysis, one would need to better understand Embodied Labs' impact in care facilities, and while the company has partnered with researchers who report positive impacts, such evaluative research remains preliminary. My own research was primarily with the company, and so my analysis is on the fantasy offered by Embodied Labs, not the actuality of its implementation.

20   Beginning a pitch with a personal story is a practice *de rigueur* for today's VC culture. Before this pitch, Embodied Labs had participated in an accelerator where they had the opportunity to develop and hone this make-or-break five-minute summary of the company's origin, mission, and financial payoff. I am curious about how the personal narrative became the center of the pitch—not a generic "someone's" problem, but a specific "my" problem. I posed this question over on Twitter, and while I leave this detour for someone else to take up, @mckelveyf noted how the podcast *StartUp* illustrates the conventional wisdom of a

founder-centered pitch. Also thanks to @bratton, @CHarblay, @shannonmattern, @fstflofscholars, @nooshinsamimi, @richardson__m_a, @onthemasspike, @MelanieKiechle, and @NassimParvin for suggesting directions in which to take this question.

21   When I interviewed Shaw in the fall of 2018 and she filled in the details of her journey, she mentioned that she usually doesn't talk about her pre–Embodied Lab experiences (aside from her mother's illness). In more recent talks she has given, however, she has fleshed out her journey, including parts that in 2018 she was still leaving out.

22   In the entertainment industry, *special effects* refer to effects (like pyrotechnics) that can be filmed in the same manner as live action. *Visual effects* refer to shots that require special means for filming or editing. CG are technically visual effects, not special effects. Leahy uses the colloquial connotation of *special effect*, and I will continue that usage in my proposal of special affect.

23   The charisma of the camera is a feature of traditional sets as well. Martin describes the camera as an "evocative apparatus," one that is "an active, even predatory presence" on set, *Haunted*, 168–69.

24   Probst, Abes, and Tricart, "VRScout Creator Spotlight."

25   Affect has been significantly discussed and theorized in cinema studies, inquiring into the alchemy by which the passive reception of image, sound, and story transforms into an emotional, visceral, and even embodied reaction. If affect is conventionally attributed to (and studied in the context of) quieter movies—the blockbuster's opposite—Isaacs, *The Orientation of Future Cinema*, has focused on the "spectacle affect" of VFX-heavy movies, specifically the work of James Cameron. While I am not directly engaging with the cinematic approach to affect in this section, "special affect" is an intentional allusion to the history of digital effects discussed in chapter 3, and Isaacs's analysis nicely deepens this connection. Indeed, even more could be said specifically about *Avatar*, in which the wheelchair-bound white, male colonizer protagonist embodies the hyper able-bodied Other, cultivating so much empathy that he decides to "go native." Isaacs argues in reference to *Avatar* that "the body is the primary site through which spectacle cinema manifests affectively," 230.

26   For an extended discussion of compositing as a technique of simulation that connects the façades of the Potemkin villages with cinematic special effects with virtual reality, see Manovich, *Language of New Media*, 136–60.

27   Murphy, "Unsettling Care," 723.

28   Ahmed, "Affective Economies," 121.

29   Ahmed, "Affective Economies," 119.

30   Obama, "Obama to Graduates." While writing the first draft of this chapter in November 2020, I noted with interest the frequency with

which the media commented upon Biden's empathy in the lead up to and following the presidential election. Biden's empathy came to summarize the most stark difference between him and Trump, who embodied the empathy deficit Obama described.

31 Irani, *Chasing Innovation*, 170.

32 While most of Embodied Labs' clients are elderly care organizations, they also have partnerships with several medical schools. Perhaps unintentionally, what Embodied Labs is offering fits well into a shift that has occurred in medical training over the past few decades in which "technologies of affect," as Underman calls them, have become more prominent. These technologies, which include simulated patients, "seek to measure, harness, and manage the affective capacities of medical students. . . . These technologies seek to discipline affect in order to produce medical experts who can more effectively govern the conduct of their patients," *Feeling Medicine*, 60. While caregivers, rather than students, are the primary audience for Embodied Labs' VR experiences (and it is with those users in mind that the company has created most of its content), this is another affective economy in which the product circulates.

33 Translating ideas from academic to corporate settings requires significant tweaking. Bailenson cofounded the company Strivr with a Stanford student after testing out VR as a tool for training college football players. Here, too, empathy was dismissed in favor of a value proposition of using the first-person perspective for more effective training.

34 Kleinman, "Caregiving," 293.

35 Puig de la Bellacasa, *Matters of Care*, 5. Buch's study of home care workers in Chicago, "Senses of Care," further explores how the embodied work required by caregivers in order to support the personhood of those they are charged to care for heightens social hierarchies, thus reinforcing expectations that some people's sense of self matters more than others. Care, it can be said again, is noninnocent. Also of note here is Puig de la Bellacasa's use of the word *maintenance* to set up a mode of care that doesn't require affect. She then situates her analysis between care as affect and care as maintenance, exploring this push and pull. For more on maintenance and/as care, see Mattern, "Maintenance and Care."

36 Embodied Labs, "Embodied Labs."

Part III. Fantasy of Representation

1 Dickson, "Making Virtual Reality Film," 196.

2 Dickson writes that VR was imagined as being able to "disrupt teleological narratives about Africa that placed it either ahead of or behind

persistent Euro-modern measures of progress," "Making Virtual Reality Film," 184.

6. VR's Feminine Mystique

1   Female exoplanet astronomers who I worked with in my previous research shared similar observations, adding that they were allowed to take risks that their male colleagues were discouraged from as their research potentials were seen as inherently lower. See Messeri, *Placing Outer Space*. One woman I met in LA explained that if she were a man, it would make career sense to work up the chain of command in the entertainment industry because there was more of a guarantee that putting in the effort would yield a successful career. As a woman, there was no such tacit agreement and so being in VR was no more or less risky than being in traditional film. I imagine not all men would agree with this assessment nor would they feel that their futures were secure.

2   See Abbate, *Recoding Gender*; Hicks, *Programmed Inequality* and "Sexism is a Feature"; Light, "When Computers Were Women"; and Misa, *Gender Codes*.

3   Flanagan and Booth, *Reload*; Fusco, "At Your Service"; Nakamura, "Indigenous Circuits."

4   Following the lawsuit and fallout between Upload and the women in VR community, several people reframed these early partnerships as manipulation on the part of Upload to promote their brand as female friendly.

5   See Chang, *Brotopia*, and Wiener, *Uncanny Valley*, for similar accounts of the toxic masculinity shaping corporate life in Silicon Valley.

6   Streitfeld, "Lurid Lawsuit's Quiet End."

7   For the original reporting, see Kantor and Twohey, "Harvey Weinstein," and Farrow, "From Aggressive Overtures." As soon as this reporting broke, conversations on the Women in VR Facebook group about Upload were reframed in the context of Weinstein and #MeToo. Kantor and Twohey elaborated on their reporting in *She Said*, in which they describe the investigations of harassment in Silicon Valley that complemented the Weinstein case.

8   Alyssa Milano, who tweeted this call to arms, quickly acknowledged that activist Tarana Burke had been using "Me Too" for a decade to shed light on the harassment experienced by girls and women of color.

9   Martin, "Anthropology's Prophecy," further shows how Hollywood's culture of patriarchy expands beyond the United States, traveling along global production and distribution networks. In analyzing the globality of #MeToo in entertainment, Martin also revisits Powdermaker and her

midcentury descriptions of the toxic male personalities that dominated the studios.

10   Matney, "Upload Exec Tasked" and "VR Startup Upload Shuts Down." On Luckey's alt-right affiliation see Collins and Resnick, "Palmer Luckey," and Roquet, "Empathy for the Game Master."

11   Morie, "Why Yes, Virginia."

12   Lanier, *Dawn of the New Everything*, 117. Coco Conn was more than a connector; she was also an entrepreneur and producer. A *Wired* article from 1994 serves as a nice reminder that, despite these bona fides, coverage of Conn's work also included mention of her husband, her children, and her appearance. See Guglielmo, "Coco's Channel."

13   Lanier's discussion of gender in Silicon Valley simultaneously apologizes for not being more inclusive to women, acknowledging the role played by these networkers, but also strangely underplays the role of people like Ann Lasko-Harvill, an early employee of his company VPL with whom he has several patents. She was an artist and so despite (like Morie) also contributing technical work, it seems that even Lanier does not view her in the same way as he does the more classically trained (male) engineers on his team.

14   Deery, "Ectopic and Utopic Reproduction," 44.

15   Morie, "Meaning and Emplacement," 22–23.

16   Morie, Laurel, and Dolinsky, "When VR Really Hits the Streets."

17   For example, Brenda Laurel and Char Davies.

18   Laurel says how she turned to critical theory, writing about the potential of the medium rather than actively creating. See Morie, Laurel, and Dolinsky, "When VR Really Hits the Streets." For more on Banff's support of VR, see Morie, "Female Artists and the VR Crucible."

19   Morie, "Meaning and Emplacement," 80.

20   Morie, "Meaning and Emplacement," 82. Sadie Plant, "On the Matrix," made a similar point a decade earlier, noting that *matrix* (a cyberspace term popularized by sci-fi writer William Gibson) is Latin for "womb."

21   Plant, "On the Matrix," observed in the mid-1990s that beyond VR art in specific, women were part of the cutting-edge growth of the digital arts.

22   Hackl, "LeaderING and Incentivizing Curiosity."

23   Haraway, *Simians, Cyborgs, and Women*, 151.

24   Hayles, *How We Became Posthuman*, 14.

25   While it seemed during fieldwork that twenty-first century VR had shed these 1980s cyberpunk associations, in 2021 Neal Stephenson's "metaverse" terminology (from his 1992 book *Snow Crash*) took marketing hold.

26   The *Journal of Virtual World Research*, for example, was founded in 2008.

27 For just a few examples, see Balsamo, *Technologies of the Gendered Body*; Cherny and Weise, *Wired Women*; and Stone, *The War of Desire*.

28 Plant, "On the Matrix," 325; Daniels, "Rethinking Cyberfeminism(s)," 117. Early cyberfeminist conversations were also dominated by white, elite women. Alice Marwick, "None of This Is New (Media)," makes this point while historicizing different eras of online feminism.

29 For example, du Preez, *Gendered Bodies and New Technologies*, argues that embodiment has always been central to cyberfeminism.

30 Morie, "Meaning and Emplacement." In an article published after *How We Became Posthuman*, Hayles recognized that despite her best intentions to think in a post-Cartesian mode, her theories reaffirmed certain dualities. This article tries a slightly different approach to rework some of her initial ideas in a more radical collapse of the binary between mind and body. See Hayles, "Flesh and Metal."

31 This claim is despite many studies that show how headsets assume a white male user and thus are more likely to cause cybersickness in women, Stanney, Fidopiastis, and Foster, "Virtual Reality Is Sexist." There has also been much said about how HMDs mess up people's hair, especially women with long hair or people with textured or curly hair (i.e., Black men and women), Minor, "Virtual Reality."

32 Deery, "Ectopic and Utopic Reproduction"; Lasko-Harvill, "Identity and Mask."

33 An article about a transgender person's experience of VR was also posted in the Facebook group but did not spark any conversation, Osworth, "I Thought I Understood."

34 Banet-Weiser, *Empowered*.

35 Sinclair, "Making a New Reality." Sinclair wrote the original posts, and in 2019 Jessica Clark and Carrie McLaren updated the research and made it a downloadable ebook.

36 Scott, "Deconstructing Equality-versus-Difference," 47.

37 Hester, *Xenofeminism*. My thanks to Danya Glabau who, when I wrote to her asking how she was puzzling through conversations on gender and VR, pointed me to Hester.

38 Hester, *Xenofeminism*, 32.

39 In a 1993 interview conducted with the trans scholar Sandy Stone for *Mondo 2000*, when one of the interviewers mentioned how VR allows for a man to experience sex as a woman, Stone pushed back forcefully. VR cannot provide this experience. "When you say a man experiences sex different from a woman experiencing sex, people are trained and socialized to experience sex differently, and that means that as a man you can *never* experience sex as a woman, unless you were socialized as a woman." The interviewer tried to defend his claim, insisting that this is the whole point of gender switch in VR, saying, "You're a man,

but you can be a woman." Stone interrupted, "It's bullshit! All bullshit, folks! . . . unless you're willing to take the time to realize how asymmetrical gender works, how asymmetrical socialization works, you can never understand what it is to be on the other side of the line." Lebkowsky, Nathan, and MacKenzie, "Bait and Switch," 56.

40 This is an instantiation of the long-critiqued ambition of Western feminism to intervene on behalf of the monolithic "Third World Woman." Rather than an expression of allyship or feminist praxis, such projects reassert colonial hierarchies of knowledge and power. See Mohanty, "Under Western Eyes."

41 Marx, "Technology."

42 That technologies reinforce norms was canonically documented by Winner, "Do Artifacts Have Politics?," and more recently by Noble, *Algorithms of Oppression*. As Ames has argued, this is especially true of "charismatic technologies," a fitting description of both VR and blockchain. See Ames, *The Charisma Machine*.

43 Dunbar-Hester, *Hacking Diversity*, 6.

44 Dunbar-Hester, *Hacking Diversity*, 22.

7. Making Innovation Women's Work

1 For an analysis of the label "women in tech" in the centers of the tech industry (i.e., Silicon Valley and its global counterparts), see Hardey, *The Culture of Women in Tech*.

2 An expansion of the meaning of "tech" can be seen in other contexts. Marwick, "Silicon Valley," notes in passing that the online mattress retailer company Casper considers itself a tech company in order to capitalize on ideas of innovation and disruption often associated with the word *tech*. I am proposing that in the case of VR, the changing meaning of *tech* can be attributed, in part, to a geographic grounding of where a particular conversation is happening. I further examine the consequences that emerge from such a change in meaning.

3 I am grateful for a conversation I had with Laura Hertzfeld in May 2018 for planting the seed of this inquiry. Hertzfeld works at the intersection of immersive technology, art, and journalism. She has been based in LA since the early 2000s and is well connected and informed of the work in this space. I was wondering aloud about the offices of Big Tech companies headquartered not far from where we were having lunch in Venice. What happened at these offices; was it "tech work" or content production/marketing? Hertzfeld noted that in her experience, it is quite challenging to find good programmers based in LA. We both began brainstorming how "tech" was different in LA.

4   Over the course of my year in LA, I only met a small handful of women who were developers with computer science backgrounds. I reached out to a couple of these women for interviews but received nonresponses or polite declines.

5   Hill's *Never Done* fleshes out the role that women played in the studio system, arguing that it is incorrect to say women were kicked out of the industry (as is often mythologized) but rather that they were doing secretarial and craft work that was deemed less significant than creative work. See also Hallett, *Go West, Young Women!*; Pearlman and Heftberger, "Recognising Women's Work."

6   Separate conversations with both Debbie Coen and Angela VandenBroek helped me articulate this question.

7   Caranicas, "AIS Honors 13 Leading Women in Tech."

8   Popper astutely observed that this wouldn't always be the case for VR. When color cameras were first introduced, companies like Technicolor had both cameramen and color consultants that worked with the art department and director to strategize on how best to achieve the look and emotional feel they were going for. As that technology matured, and this is the trend Popper sees for VR, Technicolor no longer needed to provide in-house experts.

9   For an ethnographic analysis of Singularity University, see Boenig-Liptsin and Hurlbut, "Technologies of Transcendence."

10   Hill, *Never Done*, shows how the current job category "assistant" is an outgrowth of feminized secretarial labor. This underpins the current exploitative working conditions for today's assistants. While no longer exclusively women, assistants' work is still undervalued, underpaid, and abusive, though it comes with a mythology of "paying one's dues," which Hill argues renders this abuse noble.

11   Burnout was still an issue in VR, especially as the funding in 2018 was sparse and the labor required to build an industry was great.

12   Jaschik, "What Larry Summers Said"; Damore, "Google's Ideological Echo Chamber." The Google memo contains a footnote that defines "tech" to mean software engineering. Both Summers and the memo draw on studies that hide behind the seeming neutrality of statistics— the standard deviation as explanatory—in order to explain the gender gap as a product of biology, not society.

13   To run a large activation required that Ashley learn, in the year before the more stable commercial headsets launched, how to troubleshoot developer HMDs. She had to understand how the hardware and software interacted so she could fix the many problems that would occur during demos.

14   This is somewhat in the model of Girls Who Code, an initiative that strives to rectify the "pipeline problem" that many use to explain why women are underrepresented in STEM. As Abbate observes, the "pipe-

line model" only reinforces the "pattern matching" outlook that tech companies often take to hiring. Girls Who Code and similar programs are not effective because this approach simply reinforces stereotypes and behaviors that have long favored white men. "The software industry is unlikely to achieve equal representation until computer work is equally *meaningful* for groups who do not necessarily share the values and priorities that currently dominate Silicon Valley," Abbate, "Coding is Not Empowerment," 266.

15 To be clear, the advantages of a push for a diverse workforce will only be enjoyed by certain women. While VR had several women of color in positions of leadership and visibility, white women were still overrepresented. Similarly, in order to take a risk and join the VR industry, one already had to have both a certain amount of economic stability, and many also had work experience they were able to leverage. In other words, this fantasy of women leading VR is not a claim that VR was making itself out as an industry that centered *equity*. Gender equality was a narrow focus that deferred the challenge of tackling other, more intractable inequities.

16 Noting that workplaces have begun to take it for granted that diversity leads to better outcomes, Smith-Doerr, Alegria, and Sacco, "How Diversity Matters," refined the conditions under which this better performance is realized. This cannot simply be "representational diversity," but full integration with nonhierarchical interactions. For how (lack of) diversity impacts technological products, see Alegria, "What Do We Mean." In entertainment, there have been plenty of reports that quantify the lack of diversity behind the camera as well as reports that speak to the importance (and profit) of on-screen representation. See Higginbotham, Zheng, and Uhls, "Beyond Checking." The Gina Davis Institute on Gender in Media (founded in 2004) is a nonprofit organization that tracks inclusion and equity markers in Hollywood. As articulated on the "About Us" page, "In order to bring about a global culture change, it is especially important that children see diverse, intersectional representations. . . . Doing good is also good for business!" To achieve diverse on-screen representation, the assumption is that diversity off the screen is needed.

17 Pressberg, "How Joanna Popper."

18 Importantly, just because this is a central belief, doesn't mean it is historically supported. See Marx, "Does Improved Technology Mean Progress?"

19 To not leave Erika hanging, I'll note that when I was conducting a different interview, *I* was the one who started crying when describing for the interviewee a particularly affecting VR experience. Both Erika and I had upsetting national events that had happened recently on our

minds, and this might have been triggered when reflecting on what, for each of us, had been a particularly vivid VR experience.

20   Murray, *Hamlet on the Holodeck*, 10.

21   Murray, *Hamlet on the Holodeck*, 35.

22   Murray, *Hamlet on the Holodeck*, 66.

23   Morie, "Meaning and Emplacement." Such art-and-technology collaborations have several precedents, as McCray explores in *Making Art Work*. He notes that in the 1960s, amidst a crest of such experiments, artists were often driving the creative vision with engineers offering support. This is the arrangement that Morie describes, even as Murray (informed by her work with MIT undergraduates) also sees the potential for engineers to drive a narratively creative enterprise.

24   Irani, *Chasing Innovation*, 165.

25   For the nonneutrality of storytelling—especially in social justice contexts—see Parvin, "Doing Justice to Stories."

26   McDowell, "Storytelling Shapes the Future," 106.

27   McDowell, "Storytelling Shapes the Future," 110.

28   McKittrick, *Dear Science and Other Stories*, 51.

29   McKittrick, *Dear Science and Other Stories*, 7.

30   Haraway, *Staying with the Trouble*, 10.

31   Haraway, "A Cyborg Manifesto," 151.

32   Haraway, *Staying with the Trouble*, 12.

Epilogue

1   Bogost, "The Metaverse Is Bad"; Zuckerman, "Hey, Facebook"; Vaidhyanathan, "You Don't Change Your Name"; Messeri, "The Man, The Myth"; Bell, "The Metaverse Is a New Word."

2   Bye, "VR Industry Defector."

3   Popper, *The Open Society*, 581. Popper wrote this book during World War II, from exile in New Zealand.

4   Escobar, *Pluriversal Politics*, ix.

5   Escobar, *Pluriversal Politics*, 3.

BIBLIOGRAPHY

Abbate, Janet. "Coding Is Not Empowerment." In *Your Computer Is on Fire*, edited by Thomas S. Mullaney, Benjamin Peters, Mar Hicks, and Kavita Philip. Cambridge, MA: MIT Press, 2020.

Abbate, Janet. *Recoding Gender: Women's Changing Participation in Computing.* Cambridge, MA: MIT Press, 2012.

Acland, Charles R. *American Blockbuster: Movies, Technology, and Wonder.* Durham, NC: Duke University Press, 2020.

Ahmed, Sara. "Affective Economies." *Social Text* 22, no. 2 (2004): 117–39. doi:10.1215/01642472–22–2_79–117.

Akins, Damon B., and William J. Bauer Jr. "Native Spaces: Los Angeles." In *We Are the Land: A History of Native California*, 262–69. Berkeley: University of California Press, 2021.

Alegria, Sharla N. "What Do We Mean by Broadening Participation? Race, Inequality, and Diversity in Tech Work." *Sociology Compass* 14, no. 6 (2020): e12793. doi:10.1111/soc4.12793.

Allan-Blitz, Elijah. "Messy Truth in VR." Magic Labs Media, 2019. https://www.youtube.com/watch?v=d-awEAkvEQE.

Allison, Tanine. "More than a Man in a Monkey Suit: Andy Serkis, Motion Capture, and Digital Realism." *Quarterly Review of Film and Video* 28, no. 4 (2011): 325–41. doi:10.1080/10509208.2010.500947.

Ames, Morgan G. *The Charisma Machine: The Life, Death, and Legacy of One Laptop per Child.* Cambridge, MA: MIT Press, 2019.

Andersen, Thom. *Los Angeles Plays Itself.* Documentary. Thom Andersen Productions, 2004.

Anderson, Susan. "A City Called Heaven: Black Enchantment and Despair in Los Angeles." In *The City: Los Angeles and Urban Theory at the End of the Twentieth Century*, edited by Allen Scott and Edward Soja. Los Angeles: University of California Press, 1996.

Andersson, Jenny. *The Future of the World: Futurology, Futurists, and the Struggle for the Post Cold War Imagination.* Oxford: Oxford University Press, 2018.

Appadurai, Arjun. *The Future as Cultural Fact: Essays on the Global Condition.* London: Verso, 2013.

Appadurai, Arjun. *Modernity at Large: Cultural Dimensions of Globalization.* Minneapolis: University of Minnesota Press, 1996.

Applegate, Jane. "Entrepreneurs Find Youth Has Its Advantages." *Los Angeles Times*, March 10, 1989.

Atanasoski, Neda, and Kalindi Vora. *Surrogate Humanity: Race, Robots, and the Politics of Technological Futures.* Durham, NC: Duke University Press, 2019.

Bacon, Simon. *Transmedia Cultures: A Companion.* New York: Peter Lang, 2021.

Bahng, Aimee. *Migrant Futures: Decolonizing Speculation in Financial Times.* Durham, NC: Duke University Press, 2018.

Bailenson, Jeremy. *Experience on Demand: What Virtual Reality Is, How It Works, and What It Can Do.* New York: W. W. Norton and Company, 2018.

Balio, Tino, ed. 1976. *The American Film Industry.* Revised edition. Madison: University of Wisconsin Press, 1985.

Balsamo, Anne. *Technologies of the Gendered Body: Reading Cyborg Women.* Durham, NC: Duke University Press, 1996.

Banakou, Domna, Alejandro Beacco, Solène Neyret, Marta Blasco-Oliver, Sofia Seinfeld, and Mel Slater. "Virtual Body Ownership and Its Consequences for Implicit Racial Bias Are Dependent on Social Context." *Royal Society Open Science* 7, no. 12 (2020): 201848. doi:10.1098/rsos.201848.

Banet-Weiser, Sarah. *Empowered: Popular Feminism and Popular Misogyny.* Durham, NC: Duke University Press, 2018.

Banham, Reyner. *Los Angeles: The Architecture of Four Ecologies.* New York: Harper and Row, 1971.

Barad, Karen. "Posthumanist Performativity: Toward an Understanding of How Matter Comes to Matter." *Signs: Journal of Women in Culture and Society* 28, no. 3 (2003): 801–31. doi:10.1086/345321.

Barbrook, Richard, and Andy Cameron. "The Californian Ideology." *Science as Culture* 6, no. 1 (1996): 44–72. doi:10.1080/09505439609526455.

Barlow, John Perry. "Being in Nothingness." *Mondo 2000*, 1990.

Batson, C. Daniel, Shannon Early, and Giovanni Salvarani. "Perspective Taking: Imagining How Another Feels versus Imaging How You Would Feel." *Personality and Social Psychology Bulletin* 23, no. 7 (1997): 751–58. doi:10.1177/0146167297237008.

Baudrillard, Jean. *America.* Translated by Chris Turner. London: Verso, 1988.

Baudrillard, Jean. "The Matrix Decoded: Le Nouvel Observateur Interview with Jean Baudrillard." Interview by Aude Lancelin, 2003. Translated by Gary Genosko and Adam Bryx, 2004. https://baudrillardstudies.ubishops.ca/the-matrix-decoded-le-nouvel-observateur-interview-with-jean-baudrillard/.

Baudrillard, Jean. *Simulacra and Simulation*. Translated by Sheila F. Glaser. Ann Arbor: University of Michigan Press, 1994.

Beauregard, Robert A. "City of Superlatives." *City and Community* 2, no. 3 (2003): 183–99. doi:10.1111/1540–6040.00049.

Bell, Genevieve. "The Metaverse Is a New Word for an Old Idea." MIT *Technology Review*, February 8, 2022. https://www.technologyreview.com/2022 /02/08/1044732/metaverse-history-snow-crash/.

Benjamin, Ruha. *Race after Technology: Abolitionist Tools for the New Jim Code*. Medford, MA: Polity Press, 2019.

Benjamin, Ruha. "Racial Fictions, Biological Facts: Expanding the Sociological Imagination through Speculative Methods." *Catalyst: Feminism, Theory, Technoscience* 2, no. 2 (2016): 1–28. doi:doi.org/10.28968 /cftt.v2i2.28798.

Bennett, Cynthia, and Daniela Rosner. "The Promise of Empathy: Design, Disability, and Knowing the 'Other.'" In *CHI 2019*, Glasgow, Scotland, UK, 2019. doi:10.1145/3290605.3300528.

Bergson, Henri. *Mind-Energy: Lectures and Essays*. Translated by H. Wildon Carr. New York: Henry Holt and Company, 1920.

Berlant, Lauren. *Cruel Optimism*. Durham, NC: Duke University Press, 2011.

Bernstein, Andrea, and Ilya Marritz. *Will Be Wild* . "Warnings." 2022. https://wondery.com/shows/will-be-wild/.

Biden, Joe. "Remarks by President Biden on Standing Up for Democracy." The White House. November 3, 2022. https://www.whitehouse.gov /briefing-room/speeches-remarks/2022/11/03/remarks-by-president -biden-on-standing-up-for-democracy/.

Bishop, Bryan. "Digital Empathy: How 'Hunger in Los Angeles' Broke My Heart in a Virtual World." *The Verge*, June 14, 2013. https://www .theverge.com/2013/6/14/4431308/digital-empathy-how-hunger-in-los -angeles-broke-my-heart-virtual-reality.

Bloom, Paul. *Against Empathy: The Case for Rational Compassion*. New York: Ecco, 2016.

Boellstorff, Tom. *Coming of Age in Second Life: An Anthropologist Explores the Virtually Human*. Princeton, NJ: Princeton University Press, 2008.

Boellstorff, Tom. "For Whom the Ontology Turns: Theorizing the Digital Real." *Current Anthropology* 57, no. 4 (2016): 387–407. doi:10.1086/687362.

Boellstorff, Tom, Bonnie Nardi, Celia Pearce, and T. L. Taylor. *Ethnography and Virtual Worlds: A Handbook of Method*. Princeton, NJ: Princeton University Press, 2012.

Boenig-Liptsin, Margarita, and J. Benjamin Hurlbut. "Technologies of Transcendence at Singularity University." In *Perfecting Human Futures: Transhuman Visions and Technological Imaginations*, edited by J. Benjamin Hurlbut and Hava Tirosh-Samuelson. Wiesbaden: Springer VS, 2016.

Bogost, Ian. "The Metaverse Is Bad." *Atlantic*, October 21, 2021. https://www
.theatlantic.com/technology/archive/2021/10/facebook-metaverse
-name-change/620449/.

Bollmer, Grant. "Empathy Machines." *Media International Australia* 165, no. 1
(2017): 63–76. doi:10.1177/1329878X17726794.

Bollmer, Grant, and Katherine Guinness. "Empathy and Nausea: Virtual
Reality and Jordan Wolfson's Real Violence." *Journal of Visual Culture* 19,
no. 1 (2020): 28–46. doi:10.1177/1470412920906261.

Bordwell, David. *Pandora's Digital Box: Films, Files, and the Future of Movies.*
Madison, WI: Irvington Way Institute Press, 2013.

Botvinick, Matthew, and Jonathan Cohen. "Rubber Hands 'Feel' Touch That
Eyes See." *Nature* 391 (February 1998): 756. doi:10.1038/35784.

Bowles, Nellie. "The Battle over 'Silicon Beach.'" *Vox*, June 10, 2014. https://
www.vox.com/2014/6/10/11627758/party-boys-and-fighting-words-the
-battle-over-silicon-beach.

Brandt, Marisa. "War, Trauma, and Technologies of the Self: The Making
of Virtual Reality Exposure Therapy." PhD diss., UC San Diego, 2013.
https://escholarship.org/uc/item/6698t67t.

Brandt, Marisa, and Lisa Messeri. "Imagining Feminist Futures on the
Small Screen: Inclusion and Care in VR Fictions." *NatureCulture* 5
(2019): 1–25.

Bryant, Rebecca, and Daniel M. Knight. *The Anthropology of the Future.* Cambridge, UK: Cambridge University Press, 2019.

Buch, Elana D. "Anthropology of Aging and Care." *Annual Review of Anthropology* 44 (October 2015): 277–93. doi:10.1146/
annurev-anthro-102214-014254.

Buch, Elana D. "Senses of Care: Embodying Inequality and Sustaining Personhood in the Home Care of Older Adults in Chicago." *American Ethnologist* 40, no. 4 (2013): 637–50. doi:10.1111/amet.12044.

Bye, Kent. "Cosmo Scharf on VR Storytelling, Insights from Filmmaking, and VR Meetups." *Voices of VR*, podcast, 2014. https://voicesofvr
.com/cosmo-scharf-on-vr-storytelling-insights-from-filmmaking-vr
-meetups/.

Bye, Kent. "Nonny de La Peña on Immersive Journalism, Empathy in VR
Storytelling, Human Rights, Virtual Identity, Diversity in VR and Collaborating with Palmer Luckey at USC." *Voices of VR*, podcast, 2014.
https://voicesofvr.com/6-nonny-de-la-pena-on-immersive-journalism
-empathy-vr-storytelling-human-rights-virtual-identity-diversity-in
-vr-collaborating-with-palmer-luckey-at-usc/.

Bye, Kent. "Sundance's Shari Frilot on the Power of VR Storytelling to See
Ourselves in a New Way." *Voices of VR*, podcast, 2017. https://voicesofvr
.com/522-sundances-shari-frilot-on-the-power-of-vr-storytelling-to
-see-ourselves-in-a-new-way/.

Bye, Kent. "VR Industry Defector Reflects on Google, Owlchemy Labs, Game Dev Culture, Stagnation of Innovation, and Toxic Positivity." *Voices of VR*, podcast, 2021. https://voicesofvr.com/974-vr-industry-defector -reflects-on-google-owlchemy-labs-game-dev-culture-stagnation-of -innovation-toxic-positivity/.

Caldwell, John Thornton. *Production Culture: Industrial Reflexivity and Critical Practice in Film and Television*. Durham, NC: Duke University Press, 2008.

Caranicas, Peter. "AIS Honors 13 Leading Women in Tech and Names 10 Winners of Its 2018 Technology Awards." *Variety*, January 16, 2018. https://variety.com/2018/artisans/awards/ais-honors-13-leading -women-in-tech-and-names-10-winners-of-its-2018-technology -awards-marvel-studios-1202666483/.

Caro, Zenka. "A Debate Club for the Galactic Age." Zenka: Strategy Lab for the Galactic Age. Accessed July 5, 2021. https://www.zenka.org/#/ye -old-futurist-union-la/.

Castells, Manuel, and Peter Hall. *Technopoles of the World: The Making of Twenty-First-Century Industrial Complexes*. London: Routledge, 1994.

Chagollan, Steve. "Iñárritu's 'Lumiére Moment.'" DGA *Quarterly*, 2018. https://www.dga.org/Craft/DGAQ/All-Articles/1801-Winter-2018 /Bleeding-Edge-Inarritu.aspx.

Chakrabarty, Dipesh. *Provincializing Europe: Postcolonial Thought and Historical Difference*. Princeton, NJ: Princeton University Press, 2000.

Chalmers, David J. *Reality+: Virtual Worlds and the Problems of Philosophy*. New York: W. W. Norton and Company, 2022.

Chan, Melanie. *Virtual Reality: Representations in Contemporary Media*. New York: Bloomsbury Academic, 2014.

Chang, Emily. *Brotopia: Breaking Up the Boys' Club of Silicon Valley*. New York: Portfolio/Penguin, 2018.

Chappell, Bill. "The Facebook Papers: What You Need to Know about the Trove of Insider Documents." NPR, October 25, 2021, sec. Technology. https://www.npr.org/2021/10/25/1049015366/the-facebook-papers -what-you-need-to-know.

Cherny, Lynn, and Elizabeth Reba Weise, eds. *Wired Women: Gender and the New Realities in Cyberspace*. Cypress, CA: Seal Press, 1996.

Chin, Elizabeth. "Using Fiction to Explore Social Facts: The Laboratory of Speculative Ethnology." In *The Routledge Companion to Digital Ethnography*, edited by Larissa Hjorth, Heather Horst, Anne Galloway, and Genevieve Bell. New York: Routledge, 2016.

Christian, Aymar Jean. *Open TV: Innovation beyond Hollywood and the Rise of Web Television*. New York: New York University Press, 2018.

Christopherson, Susan. "Behind the Scenes: How Transnational Firms Are Constructing a New International Division of Labor in Media Work." *Geoforum* 37, no. 5 (2006): 739–51. doi:10.1016/j.geoforum.2006.01.003.

Christopherson, Susan, and Michael Storper. "The City as Studio; The World as Back Lot: The Impact of Vertical Disintegration on the Location of the Motion Picture Industry." *Environment and Planning D: Society and Space* 4, no. 3 (1986): 305–20.

Chun, Wendy Hui-Kyong. *Control and Freedom: Power and Paranoia in the Age of Fiber Optics*. Cambridge, MA: MIT Press, 2006.

Chung, Hye Jean. *Media Heterotopias: Digital Effects and Material Labor in Global Film Production*. Durham, NC: Duke University Press, 2018.

Cline, Ernest. "Foreword by Ernest Cline." In *The History of the Future: Oculus, Facebook, and the Revolution That Swept Virtual Reality*, by Blake J. Harris, ix–xvi. New York: Harper Collins, 2019.

Cline, Ernest. *Ready Player One*. New York: Crown Publishers, 2011.

Cohan, Steven. *Hollywood by Hollywood: The Backstudio Picture and the Mystique of Making Movies*. Oxford: Oxford University Press, 2018.

Coleman, Gabriella. "Ethnographic Approaches to Digital Media." *Annual Review of Anthropology* 39, no. 1 (2010): 487–505.

Collins, Ben, and Gideon Resnick. "Palmer Luckey: The Facebook Near-Billionaire Secretly Funding Trump's Meme Machine." *Daily Beast*, April 13, 2017, sec. Politics. https://www.thedailybeast.com/articles /2016/09/22/palmer-luckey-the-facebook-billionaire-secretly-funding -trump-s-meme-machine.

Connor, J. D. *Hollywood Math and Aftermath: The Economic Image and the Digital Recession*. New York: Bloomsbury, 2018.

Connor, J. D. "The Nature of the Firm and the Nature of the Farm: Lucasfilm, the Campus, and the Contract." In *In the Studio*, edited by Brian R. Jacobson. Berkeley: University of California Press, 2020. doi:10.1525/9780520969896–013.

Cortiel, Jeanne, Christine Hanke, Jan Simon Hutta, and Colin Milburn, eds. *Practices of Speculation: Modeling, Embodiment, Figuration*. Bielefeld, DE: transcript Verlag, 2020. doi:10.14361/9783839447512.

Crafton, Donald. *The Talkies: American Cinema's Transition to Sound, 1926–1931*. New York: Charles Scribner's Sons, 1997.

Craig, David, and Stuart Cunningham. *Social Media Entertainment: The New Intersection of Hollywood and Silicon Valley*. New York: New York University Press, 2019.

Curtin, Michael, and Kevin Sanson, eds. *Precarious Creativity: Global Media, Local Labor*. Oakland: University of California Press, 2016.

Curtin, Michael, and John Vanderhoef. "A Vanishing Piece of the Pi: The Globalization of Visual Effects Labor." *Television and New Media* 16, no. 3 (2015): 219–39. doi:10.1177/1527476414524285.

Damore, James. "Google's Ideological Echo Chamber," 2017. https://docs .google.com/viewer?url=https%3A%2F%2Fassets.documentcloud.org% 2Fdocuments%2F3914586%2FGoogles-Ideological-Echo-Chamber.pdf.

Daniels, Jessie. "Rethinking Cyberfeminism(s): Race, Gender, and Embodiment." *Women's Studies Quarterly* 37, no. 1/2 (2009): 101–24. doi:10.1353/wsq.0.0158.

Davidson, Bill. *The Real and the Unreal*. New York: Harper and Brothers, 1961.

Davis, Mike. *City of Quartz: Excavating the Future in Los Angeles*. London: Verso, 1990.

Dean, Jodi. "The Real Internet." In *Žižek and Media Studies*, edited by M. Flisfeder and L. P. Willis. New York: Palgrave Macmillian, 2014.

Dear, Michael, and Steven Flusty. "Postmodern Urbanism." *Annals of the Association of American Geographers* 88, no. 1 (1998): 50–72.

Deery, June. "Ectopic and Utopic Reproduction: He, She and It." *Utopian Studies* 5, no. 2 (1994): 36–49.

De la Peña, Nonny. "The Future of News? Virtual Reality." Presented at TED-Women2015, May 2015. https://www.ted.com/talks/nonny_de_la_pena_the_future_of_news_virtual_reality.

De la Peña, Nonny. "Inventing Immersive Journalism: Embodiment, Realism and Presence in Nonfiction." PhD diss., University of Southern California, 2019. http://digitallibrary.usc.edu/digital/collection/p15799coll89/id/255520.

De la Peña, Nonny, and Tom Furness. "vws Fireside Chat #13: Immersive Journalism and How to Experience the World," 2020. https://www.youtube.com/watch?v=mHgrdBFdYfc&t=606s.

De la Peña, Nonny, Peggy Weil, Joan Llobera, Elias Giannopoulos, Ausiàs Pomés, Bernhard Spanlang, Doron Friedman, Maria Sanchez-Vives, and Mel Slater. "Immersive Journalism: Immersive Virtual Reality for the First-Person Experience of News." *Presence Teleoperators and Virtual Environments* 19, no. 4 (2010): 291–301. doi:10.1162/PRES_a_00005.

De León, Jason. *Land of Open Graves: Living and Dying on the Migrant Trail*. Berkeley: University of California Press, 2015.

Deleuze, Gilles. *Difference and Repetition*. Translated by Paul Patton. New York: Continuum, 2004.

Deuze, Mark. *Media Work*. Cambridge, UK: Polity Press, 2007.

Dhir, Meraj. "The Modern Entertainment Marketplace, 2000–Present: Editing." In *Editing and Special/Visual Effects*, 156–71. New Brunswick, NJ: Rutgers University Press, 2016.

Dickson, Jessica. "Making Virtual Reality Film: An Untimely View of Film Futures from (South) Africa." In *Anthropology, Film Industries, Modularity*, edited by Ramyar D. Rossoukh and Steven C. Caton. Durham, NC: Duke University Press, 2021.

Didion, Joan. "Trouble in Lakewood." *New Yorker*, July 26, 1993.

D'Onfro, Jillian. "Facebook Gives Its Oculus Employees a Dystopian Sci-Fi Book to Get Them Excited about Building the Future." *Business Insider*, July 27, 2016, sec. Tech. https://www.businessinsider.in/facebook-gives

-its-oculus-employees-a-dystopian-sci-fi-book-to-get-them-excited
-about-building-the-future/articleshow/53423878.cms.

Du Bois, W. E. B. "Colored California." *The Crisis: A Record of the Darker Races,* August 1913.

Du Bois, W. E. B. *The Souls of Black Folk.* New York: Penguin, 1996.

du Preez, Amanda. *Gendered Bodies and New Technologies: Rethinking Embodiment in a Cyber-Era.* Newcastle upon Tyne: Cambridge Scholars Publishing, 2009.

Dunbar-Hester, Christina. *Hacking Diversity: The Politics of Inclusion in Open Technology Cultures.* Princeton, NJ: Princeton University Press, 2019.

Dunne, Anthony, and Fiona Raby. *Speculative Everything: Design, Fiction, and Social Dreaming.* Cambridge, MA: MIT Press, 2013.

Ebert, Roger. "Ebert's Walk of Fame Remarks." Rogerebert.com. June 24, 2005. https://www.rogerebert.com/rogers-journal/eberts-walk-of
-fame-remarks.

Eco, Umberto. *Travels in Hyperreality.* Translated by William Weaver. San Diego: Harcourt, 1986.

Ehrenburg, Ilya. "Ilya Ehrenburg's America." *Harper's Magazine,* December 1946.

Elliott, Stephen. "Silicon Is Just Sand." *Epic Magazine.* Accessed July 2, 2021. http://epicmagazine.com/silicon-is-just-sand/.

Elzie, Carrie A., and Jacqueline Shaia. "A Pilot Study of the Impact of Virtually Embodying a Patient with a Terminal Illness." *Medical Science Educator* 31, no. 2 (2021): 665–75. doi:10.1007/s40670–021–01243–9.

Embodied Labs. "Embodied Labs Raises $3.2 Million in Seed Funding with Diverse Investors across Aging, Tech and Impact Funds." Cision PR Newswire. January 13, 2020. https://www.prnewswire.com/news-releases
/embodied-labs-raises-3–2-million-in-seed-funding-with-diverse
-investors-across-aging-tech-and-impact-funds-300986016.html.

Escobar, Arturo. *Pluriversal Politics: The Real and the Possible.* Durham, NC: Duke University Press, 2020.

ESTS Editorial Collective. "Provincializing STS Scholarship Landscape: Interview with ESTS Editorial Collective." Interview by Aybike Alkan, 2021. http://www.stsistanbul.org/2021/03/29/provincializing-sts
-scholarship-landscape-interview-with-ests-editorial-collective/.

Faludi, Susan. "Girls Have All the Power: What's Troubling Troubled Boys." In *Stiffed: The Betrayal of The American Man,* 102–52. New York: Harper Collins, 2011.

Farrow, Ronan. "From Aggressive Overtures to Sexual Assault: Harvey Weinstein's Accusers Tell Their Stories." *New Yorker,* October 10, 2017. https://
www.newyorker.com/news/news-desk/from-aggressive-overtures-to
-sexual-assault-harvey-weinsteins-accusers-tell-their-stories.

Fischer, Michael M. J. "Culture and Cultural Analysis as Experimental Systems." *Cultural Anthropology* 22, no. 1 (2007): 1–65.

Flanagan, Mary, and Austin Booth, eds. *Reload: Rethinking Women + Cyberculture*. Cambridge, MA: MIT Press, 2002.

Fogelson, Robert M. *The Fragmented Metropolis: Los Angeles, 1850–1930*. Cambridge, MA: Harvard University Press, 1967.

Foley, James D. "Interfaces for Advanced Computing." *Scientific American* 257, no. 4 (1987): 126–35.

Forlano, Laura, and Anijo Mathew. "From Design Fiction to Design Friction: Speculative and Participatory Design of Values-Embedded Urban Technology." *Journal of Urban Technology* 21, no. 4 (2014): 7–24. doi:10.108 0/10630732.2014.971525.

Foster, Thomas. *The Souls of Cyberfolk: Posthumanism as Vernacular Theory*. Minneapolis: University of Minnesota Press, 2005.

Foucault, Michel. "Of Other Spaces." Translated by Jay Miskowiec. *Diacritics* 16, no. 1 (1986): 22–27. doi:10.2307/464648.

Frank, Scott. "Lab Coats in the Dream Factory: Science and Scientists in Hollywood." PhD diss., University of Southern California, 2002. https://www.proquest.com/openview/16ae948cda02893f4f376780f4749 3af/1?pq-origsite=gscholar&cbl=18750&diss=y.

Friedberg, Anne. *The Virtual Window: From Alberti to Microsoft*. Cambridge, MA: MIT Press, 2009.

Friedberg, Anne. *Window Shopping: Cinema and the Postmodern*. Berkeley: University of California Press, 1994.

Frilot, Shari, and Homay King. "Virtual Reality in Real Time: A Conversation." *Film Quarterly* 71, no. 1 (2017): 51–58.

Fusco, Coco. "At Your Service: Latin Women in the Global Information Network." In *The Bodies That Were Not Ours: And Other Writings*, 186–201. London: Routledge, 2001.

Gabler, Neal. *An Empire of Their Own: How the Jews Invented Hollywood*. New York: Crown Publishers, Inc., 1988.

Gaines, Alisha. *Black for a Day: White Fantasies of Race and Empathy*. Chapel Hill: University of North Carolina Press, 2017.

Galloway, Anne, and Catherine Caudwell. "Speculative Design as Research Method: From Answers to Questions and 'Staying with the Trouble.'" In *Undesign: Critical Practices at the Intersection of Art and Design*, edited by Gretchen Coombs, Andrew McNamara, and Gavin Sade. New York: Routledge, 2019.

Galloway, Kit, and Sherrie Rabinowitz. "Hole-in-Space Project Credits." Telecollaborative Art Projects of Electronic Cafe International Founders. Accessed July 21, 2021. http://www.ecafe.com/getty/HIS /HIScredits.html.

Galloway, Kit, and Sherrie Rabinowitz. "Welcome to 'Electronic Cafe International': A Nice Place for Hot Coffee, Iced Tea, and Virtual Space." In *CyberArts: Exploring Art and Technology*, edited by Linda Jacobson. San Francisco: Miller Freeman, 1992.

Ghamari-Tabrizi, Sharon. *The Worlds of Herman Kahn: The Intuitive Science of Thermonuclear War*. Cambridge, MA: Harvard University Press, 2009.

Gibson, Margaret, Larissa Hjorth, and Jaz Hee-jeong Choi. "Introduction: Caring Media Futures." *International Journal of Cultural Studies* 24, no. 4 (2021): 557–66. doi:10.1177/13678779211015252.

Gibson, William. "Burning Chrome." *Omni*, July 1982.

Gibson, William. *Neuromancer*. New York: Ace Books, 1984.

Giridharadas, Anand. *Winners Take All: The Elite Charade of Changing the World*. New York: Knopf, 2018.

Glabau, Danya. "Imagination, Whiteness, and the Future of Virtual Reality," forthcoming.

Goodman, Lizzy. "'Hunger in L.A.' Immerses Viewers in an Interactive Journalism Experience (and a Food Line)." *Fast Company*, January 31, 2012. https://www.fastcompany.com/1679530/hunger-in-la-immerses -viewers-in-an-interactive-journalism-experience-and-a-food-line.

Groom, Victoria, Jeremy Bailenson, and Clifford Nass. "The Influence of Racial Embodiment on Racial Bias in Immersive Virtual Environments." *Social Influence* 4, no. 3 (2009): 231–48. doi:10.1080/15534510802643750.

Grosz, Elizabeth. *Architecture from the Outside: Essays on Virtual and Real Space*. Cambridge, MA: MIT Press, 2001.

Grosz, Elizabeth. *Time Travels: Feminism, Nature, Power*. Durham, NC: Duke University Press, 2005.

Guglielmo, Connie. "Coco's Channel." *Wired*, April 1, 1994. https://www .wired.com/1994/04/sigg-kids/.

Gunning, Tom. "An Aesthetic of Astonishment: Early Film and the (in) Credulous Spectator." *Art and Text* 34, no. 1 (1989): 31–45.

Gupta, Akhil. "Decolonizing U.S. Anthropology." Presented at the Annual Meeting of the American Anthropological Association, Baltimore, MD, November 20, 2021.

Hackl, Cathy. "LeaderING and Incentivizing Curiosity with Strategic Futurist, Nancy Giordano." *Future of the Metaverse*, podcast, 2021. https:// open.spotify.com/episode/3d0xE13iE1XyWoswnrChYJ.

Halegoua, Germaine R. *The Digital City: Media and the Social Production of Place*. New York: New York University Press, 2019.

Hallett, Hilary A. *Go West, Young Women! The Rise of Early Hollywood*. Berkeley: University of California Press, 2013.

Haraway, Donna. "A Cyborg Manifesto: Science, Technology, and Socialist-Feminism in the Late Twentieth Century." In *Simians, Cyborgs, and Women: The Reinvention of Women*, 149–82. New York: Routledge, 1991.

Haraway, Donna. *Simians, Cyborgs, and Women: The Reinvention of Nature*. New York: Routledge, 1991.

Haraway, Donna. "Situated Knowledges: The Science Question in Feminism and the Privilege of Partial Perspective." *Feminist Studies* 14, no. 3 (1988): 575–99. doi:10.2307/3178066.

Haraway, Donna. *Staying with the Trouble: Making Kin in the Chthulucene*. Durham, NC: Duke University Press, 2016.

Hardey, Mariann. *The Culture of Women in Tech: An Unsuitable Job for a Woman*. Bingley: Emerald Publishing Limited, 2019.

Harding, Sandra G. *The Science Question in Feminism*. Ithaca, NY: Cornell University Press, 1986.

Hartlaub, Peter. "George Lucas: 'Star Wars' Creator in a Valley Not Far, Far Away." *SFGATE*, April 27, 2007, sec. Entertainment. https://www.sfgate.com/entertainment/article/IN-A-VALLEY-NOT-FAR-FAR-AWAY-2599071.php.

Hartman, Saidiya. *Scenes of Subjection: Terror, Slavery, and Self-Making in Nineteenth-Century America*. New York: Oxford University Press, 1997.

Hartman, Saidiya. *Wayward Lives, Beautiful Experiments: Intimate Histories of Riotous Black Girls, Troublesome Women, and Queer Radicals*. New York: W. W. Norton and Company, 2019.

Hassan, Robert. "Digitality, Virtual Reality and the 'Empathy Machine.'" *Digital Journalism* 8, no. 2 (2020): 195–212.

Hassler-Forest, Dan. *Science Fiction, Fantasy, and Politics: Transmedia World-Building beyond Capitalism*. New York: Rowman and Littlefield International, 2016.

Hayles, N. Katherine. "Boundary Disputes: Homeostasis, Reflexivity, and the Foundations of Cybernetics." In *Virtual Realities and Their Discontents*, edited by Robert Markley. Baltimore, MD: John Hopkins University Press, 1996.

Hayles, N. Katherine. "Flesh and Metal: Reconfiguring the Mindbody in Virtual Environments." *Configurations* 10, no. 2 (2002): 297–320. doi:10.1353/con.2003.0015.

Hayles, N. Katherine. *How We Became Posthuman: Virtual Bodies in Cybernetics, Literature, and Informatics*. Chicago: University of Chicago Press, 1999.

Heim, Michael. *The Metaphysics of Virtual Reality*. New York: Oxford University Press, 1993.

Helmreich, Stefan. "An Anthropologist Underwater: Immersive Soundscapes, Submarine Cyborgs, and Transductive Ethnography." *American Ethnologist* 34, no. 4 (2008): 621–41.

Henriksen, Sofie Elbæk, and Lisa Ann Richey. "Google's Tech Philanthropy: Capitalism and Humanitarianism in the Digital Age." *Public Anthropologist* 4, no. 1 (2022): 21–50.

Hernandez, Daniel. "Snapchat's Disappearing Act Leaves Venice Beach Searching for Its Future." *New York Times*, August 23, 2019. https://www.nytimes.com/2019/08/23/style/snapchat-venice-resistance.html.

Hester, Helen. *Xenofeminism*. Cambridge, UK: Polity, 2018.

Hicks, Mar. *Programmed Inequality: How Britain Discarded Women Technologists and Lost Its Edge in Computing*. Cambridge, MA: MIT Press, 2017.

Hicks, Mar. "Sexism Is a Feature, Not a Bug." In *Your Computer Is on Fire*, edited by Thomas S. Mullaney, Benjamin Peters, Mar Hicks, and Kavita Philip. Cambridge, MA: MIT Press, 2020.

Hidalgo, Santiago, ed. *Technology and Film Scholarship: Experience, Study, Theory*. Amsterdam: Amsterdam University Press, 2018. doi:10.5117/9789089647542.

Higginbotham, Gerald D., Zhanpeng Zheng, and Yalda T. Uhls. "Beyond Checking a Box: A Lack of Authentically Inclusive Representation Has Costs at the Box Office." Center for Scholars and Storytellers. Los Angeles: UCLA, 2020.

Higgins, Scott. *Harnessing the Technicolor Rainbow: Color Design in the 1930s*. Austin, TX: University of Texas Press, 2007.

Hill, Erin. "Hollywood Assistanting." In *Production Studies: Cultural Studies of Media Industries*, 220–23. New York: Routledge, 2009.

Hill, Erin. *Never Done: A History of Women's Work in Media Production*. New Brunswick, NJ: Rutgers University Press, 2016.

Hobart, Hiʻilei Julia Kawehipuaakahaopulani, and Tamara Kneese. "Radical Care: Survival Strategies for Uncertain Times." *Social Text* 38, no. 1 (2020): 1–16. doi:10.1215/01642472-7971067.

Hollan, Douglas. "Being There: On the Imaginative Aspects of Understanding Others and Being Understood." *Ethos* 36, no. 4 (2008): 475–89. doi:10.1111/j.1548-1352.2008.00028.x.

hooks, bell. "Eating the Other." In *Black Looks: Race and Representation*, 21–39. Boston: South End Press, 1992.

Horkheimer, Max, and Theodor W. Adorno. 1947. "The Culture Industry: Enlightenment as Mass Deception." In *Dialectic of Enlightenment*, translated by John Cumming. New York: Herder and Herder, 1972.

"HTC Vive x Ready Player One—Utilizing Vive in the Filmmaking Process," 2018. https://www.youtube.com/watch?v=W_6vTqIyPmM.

Idris, Murad. *War for Peace: Genealogies of a Violent Ideal in Western and Islamic Thought*. Oxford: Oxford University Press, 2018.

IJsselsteijn, Wijnand A., Yvonne A. W. de Kort, and Antal Haans. "Is This My Hand I See before Me? The Rubber Hand Illusion in Reality, Virtual Reality, and Mixed Reality." *Presence: Teleoperators and Virtual Environments* 15, no. 4 (2006): 455–64. Doi:10.1162/pres.15.4.455.

Irani, Lilly. *Chasing Innovation: Making Entrepreneurial Citizens in Modern India*. Princeton, NJ: Princeton University Press, 2019.

Isaacs, Bruce. *The Orientation of Future Cinema: Technology, Aesthetics, Spectacle.* New York: Bloomsbury, 2013.

Isenberg, Daniel. "The Big Idea: How to Start an Entrepreneurial Revolution." *Harvard Business Review,* June 2010. https://hbr.org/2010/06/the -big-idea-how-to-start-an-entrepreneurial-revolution.

Iwerks, Leslie. "What Would Walt Do?" *The Imagineering Story.* Disney+, 2019.

James, Paul. "The Faces of svvr Conference and Expo 2014—New Speakers and Panellists Announced!" *Road to vr.* April 28, 2014. https:// www.roadtovr.com/faces-svvr-conference-expo-confirms-raft-new -speakers-panellists-exhibitors/.

Jameson, Fredric. *Postmodernism, or, The Cultural Logic of Late Capitalism.* Durham, NC: Duke University Press, 1991.

Jaschik, Scott. "What Larry Summers Said." *Inside Higher Ed.* February 17, 2005. https://www.insidehighered.com/news/2005/02/18/what-larry -summers-said.

Jenkins, Henry. *Convergence Culture: Where Old and New Media Collide.* New York: New York University Press, 2006.

Jobson, Ryan Cecil. "The Case for Letting Anthropology Burn: Sociocultural Anthropology in 2019." *American Anthropologist* 122, no. 2 (2020): 259–71.

Jones, Nick. *Spaces Mapped and Monstrous: Digital 3D Cinema and Visual Culture.* New York: Columbia University Press, 2020.

Kamau, W. Sebastian. "Rooms Full of Mirrors." *Real Life,* November 13, 2017. https://reallifemag.com/rooms-full-of-mirrors/.

Kantor, Jodi, and Megan Twohey. "Harvey Weinstein Paid Off Sexual Harassment Accusers for Decades." *New York Times,* October 5, 2017. https://www.nytimes.com/2017/10/05/us/harvey-weinstein -harassment-allegations.html.

Kantor, Jodi, and Megan Twohey. *She Said: Breaking the Sexual Harassment Story That Helped Ignite a Movement.* New York: Penguin Press, 2019.

Kenneally, Christopher. *Side by Side.* New York: Giant Pictures, 2012. https:// video.alexanderstreet.com/watch/side-by-side.

Kilston, Lyra. *Sun Seekers: The Cure of California.* Los Angeles: Atelier Éditions, 2019.

King, Homay. *Virtual Memory: Time-Based Art and the Dream of Digitality.* Durham, NC: Duke University Press, 2015.

Kirby, David A. *Lab Coats in Hollywood: Science, Scientists, and Cinema.* Cambridge, MA: MIT Press, 2011.

Klein, Norman M. *The History of Forgetting: Los Angeles and the Erasure of Memory.* New York: Verso, 1997.

Kleiner, Art. *The Age of Heretics: A History of the Radical Thinkers Who Reinvented Corporate Management.* San Francisco: John Wiley and Sons, 2008.

Kleinman, Arthur. "Caregiving: The Odyssey of Becoming More Human." *Lancet* 373, no. 9660 (2009): 292–93. Doi:10.1016/s0140–6736(09)60087–8.

Kofman, Ava. "Bruno Latour, the Post-Truth Philosopher, Mounts a Defense of Science." *New York Times Magazine*, October 25, 2018. https://www.nytimes.com/2018/10/25/magazine/bruno-latour-post-truth-philosopher-science.html.

Kokas, Aynne. *Hollywood Made in China*. Oakland: University of California Press, 2017.

Kraemer, Jordan. "Locating Emerging Media: Ethnographic Reflections on Culture, Selfhood, and Place." In *The Routledge Companion to Digital Ethnography*, edited by Larissa Hjorth, Heather Horst, Anne Galloway, and Genevieve Bell. New York: Routledge, 2017.

Krist, Gary. *The Mirage Factory: Illusion, Imagination, and the Invention of Los Angeles*. New York: Crown Publishers, 2018.

Kun, Josh, and Laura Pulido. "Introduction." In *Black and Brown in Los Angeles: Beyond Conflict and Coalition*, edited by Josh Kun and Laura Pulido. Berkeley: University of California Press, 2013.

Lakoff, Andrew. "The Generic Biothreat, or, How We Became Unprepared." *Cultural Anthropology* 23, no. 3 (2008): 399–428.

Lanier, Jaron. *Dawn of the New Everything: Encounters with Reality and Virtual Reality*. New York: Henry Holt and Company, 2017.

Lanzoni, Susan. *Empathy: A History*. New Haven, CT: Yale University Press, 2018.

Lasko-Harvill, Ann. "Identity and Mask in Virtual Reality." *Discourse: Journal for Theoretical Studies in Media and Culture* 14, no. 2 (1992): 222–34.

Latour, Bruno. *Down to Earth: Politics in the New Climatic Regime*. Translated by Catherine Porter. Cambridge, UK: Polity Press, 2018.

Latour, Bruno. *Science in Action: How to Follow Scientists and Engineers through Society*. Cambridge, MA: Harvard University Press, 1987.

Latour, Bruno. "Why Has Critique Run Out of Steam? From Matters of Fact to Matters of Concern." *Critical Inquiry* 30, no. 2 (2004.): 225–48. doi:10.1086/421123.

Layton, James, and David Pierce. *The Dawn of Technicolor, 1915–1935*. Edited by Paolo Cherchi Usai and Catherine A. Surowiec. Rochester, NY: George Eastman House, 2015.

Le Guin, Ursula K. "A Non-Euclidean View of California as a Cold Place to Be." *Yale Review* 72, no. 2 (1983): 161–80.

Lebkowsky, Jon, Paco Xander Nathan, and David C. MacKenzie. "Bait and Switch with Sandy Stone." *Mondo 2000*, 1993.

Lefebvre, Henri. *The Production of Space*. Translated by Donald Nicholson-Smith. Oxford: Blackwell Publishing, 1991.

Levy, Pierre. *Becoming Virtual: Reality in the Digital Age*. Translated by Robert Bononno. New York: Plenum Press, 1998.

Liboiron, Max. *Pollution Is Colonialism*. Durham, NC: Duke University Press, 2021.

Light, Jennifer S. *From Warfare to Welfare: Defense Intellectuals and Urban Problems in Cold War America*. Baltimore: John Hopkins University Press, 2005.

Light, Jennifer S. "When Computers Were Women." *Technology and Culture* 40, no. 3 (1999): 455–83.

Lithwick, Dahlia. "Stop Trying to Understand What Trump Says and Look at What His Followers Do." *Slate*, October 27, 2018. https://slate .com/news-and-politics/2018/10/squirrel-hill-shooting-trump-anti -semitism-america.html.

Loukissas, Yanni Alexander. *All Data Are Local: Thinking Critically in a Data-Driven Society*. Cambridge, MA: MIT Press, 2019.

Lui, Garding. *Inside Los Angeles Chinatown*. Los Angeles, 1948.

Madden Toby, Mekeisha. "'House of Lies' Producer Defends Shocking Death: Biggie and Tupac Murder Similarity Was Unintentional." *Wrap News Inc.*, March 26, 2014. https://www.thewrap.com/shocking-house -lies-death-unintentionally-similar-biggies-murder/.

Madianou, Mirca. "Nonhuman Humanitarianism: When 'AI for Good' Can Be Harmful." *Information, Communication and Society* 24, no. 6 (2021): 850–68.

Madianou, Mirca. "Technological Futures as Colonial Debris: 'Tech-for-Good' as Technocolonialism." In *The Future of Media*, edited by Joanna Zylinska. London: Goldsmiths Press, 2022.

Magalhães, João, and Nick Couldry. "Giving by Taking Away: Big Tech, Data Colonialism and the Reconfiguration of Social Good." *International Journal of Communication* 15 (2021): 343–62.

Manovich, Lev. *The Language of New Media*. Cambridge, MA: MIT Press, 2002.

Markley, Robert. "Boundaries: Mathematics, Alienation, and the Metaphysics of Cyberspace." In *Virtual Realities and Their Discontents*, edited by Robert Markley. Baltimore, MD: John Hopkins University Press, 1996.

Markley, Robert, ed. *Virtual Realities and Their Discontents*. Baltimore, MD: John Hopkins University Press, 1996.

Martin, Aryn, Natasha Myers, and Ana Viseu. "The Politics of Care in Technoscience." *Social Studies of Science* 45, no. 5 (2015): 625–41. doi:10.1177/0306312715602073.

Martin, Emily. "Meeting Polemics with Irenics in the Science Wars." *Social Text* 46/47 (1996): 43–60. doi:10.2307/466843.

Martin, Sylvia J. "Anthropology's Prophecy for #MeToo: From Hollywood to Hong Kong." *Visual Anthropology Review* 37, no. 1 (2021): 120–41.

Martin, Sylvia. *Haunted: An Ethnography of the Hollywood and Hong Kong Media Industries*. New York: Oxford University Press, 2017.

Marwick, Alice. "Silicon Valley and the Social Media Industry." In *The SAGE Handbook of Social Media*, edited by Jean Burgess, Alice Marwick, and Thomas Poell. London: SAGE Publications, 2018.

Marwick, Alice E. "None of This Is New (Media): Feminisms in the Social Media Age." In *The Routledge Handbook of Contemporary Feminism*, edited by Tasha Oren and Andrea L. Press. New York: Routledge, 2019.

Marx, Leo. "Does Improved Technology Mean Progress?" *Technology Review* 90, no. 1 (1987): 33–41.

Marx, Leo. "Technology: The Emergence of a Hazardous Concept." *Technology and Culture* 51, no. 3 (2010): 561–77.

Marzola, Luci. *Engineering Hollywood: Technology, Technicians, and the Science of Building the Studio System*. New York: Oxford University Press, 2021.

Massumi, Brian. *Parables for the Virtual: Movement, Affect, Sensation*. Durham, NC: Duke University Press, 2002.

Matney, Lucas. "Upload Exec Tasked with Turning Things around at the Troubled VR Startup Has Already Quit." *TechCrunch*, October 16, 2017. https://techcrunch.com/2017/10/16/upload-exec-tasked-with-turning -things-around-at-the-troubled-vr-startup-has-already-quit/.

Matney, Lucas. "VR Startup Upload Shuts Down Its Offices as Funding from Palmer Luckey Runs Out." *TechCrunch*, March 16, 2018. https:// techcrunch.com/2018/03/16/vr-startup-upload-shuts-down-its-offices -as-funding-from-oculus-founder-runs-out/.

Mattern, Shannon. "Maintenance and Care." *Places Journal*, November 2018. doi:10.22269/181120.

Mavhunga, Chakanetsa, ed. *What Do Science, Technology, and Innovation Mean from Africa?* Cambridge, MA: MIT Press, 2017.

McCray, W. Patrick. *Making Art Work: How Cold War Engineers and Artists Forged a New Creative Culture*. Cambridge, MA: MIT Press, 2020.

McDonald, Kevin, and Daniel Smith-Rowsey, eds. *The Netflix Effect: Technology and Entertainment in the 21st Century*. New York: Bloomsbury, 2016.

McDowell, Alex. "Storytelling Shapes the Future." *Journal of Futures Studies* 23, no. 3 (2019): 105–12. doi:10.6531/JFS.201903_23(3).0009.

McDowell, Alex, and Peter von Stackelberg. "What in the World? Story-worlds, Science Fiction, and Futures Studies." *Journal of Future Studies* 20, no. 2 (2015): 25–46. doi:10.6531/JFS.2015.20(2).A25.

McGowan, Todd. "Lost on Mulholland Drive: Navigating David Lynch's Panegyric to Hollywood." *Cinema Journal* 43, no. 2 (2004): 67–89.

McGowan, Todd. *The Real Gaze: Film Theory after Lacan*. Albany: SUNY Press, 2007.

McKittrick, Katherine. *Dear Science and Other Stories*. Durham, NC: Duke University Press, 2021.

McTighe, Laura, and Megan Raschig. "Introduction: An Otherwise Anthropology." *Society for Cultural Anthropology*, July 31, 2019. https://culanth .org/fieldsights/introduction-an-otherwise-anthropology.

McWilliams, Carey. *Southern California Country, an Island on the Land*. New York: Duell, Sloan and Pearce, 1946.

Meiri, Sandra, and Odeya Kohen-Raz. *Traversing the Fantasy: The Dialectic of Desire/Fantasy and the Ethics of Narrative Cinema.* New York: Bloomsbury, 2020.

Merrin, William. *Baudrillard and the Media: A Critical Introduction.* Cambridge, UK: Polity Press, 2005.

Messeri, Lisa. "The Man, the Myth, and the Metaverse." *Wired*, November 12, 2021. https://www.wired.com/story/the-man-the-myth-and-the-metaverse/.

Messeri, Lisa. *Placing Outer Space: An Earthly Ethnography of Other Worlds.* Durham, NC: Duke University Press, 2016.

Messeri, Lisa. "Realities of Illusion: Tracing an Anthropology of the Unreal from Torres Strait to Virtual Reality." *Journal of the Royal Anthropological Institute* 27, no. 2 (2021): 340–59. doi:10.1111/1467–9655.13495.

Metz, Christopher. *The Imaginary Signifier: Psychoanalysis and the Cinema.* Bloomington: Indiana University Press, 1982.

Milk, Chris. "How Virtual Reality Can Create the Ultimate Empathy Machine." Presented at TED2015, March 2015. https://www.ted.com/talks/chris_milk_how_virtual_reality_can_create_the_ultimate_empathy_machine/transcript.

Miller, Daniel, Elisabetta Costa, Nell Haynes, Tom McDonald, Razvan Nicolescu, Jolynna Sinanan, Juliano Spyer, Shriram Venkatraman, and Xinyuan Wang. *How the World Changed Social Media.* London: UCL Press, 2016.

Miller, Toby, Nitin Govil, John McMurria, Richard Maxwell, and Ting Wang. *Global Hollywood 2.* London: British Film Institute, 2005.

Minor, Jordan. "Virtual Reality Has a Bad Hair Problem." Geek.com. May 4, 2016. https://web.archive.org/web/20170424071636/https://www.geek.com/tech/vr-with-the-good-hair-1653973/.

Misa, Thomas J., ed. *Gender Codes: Why Women Are Leaving Computing.* Hoboken: John Wiley and Sons, 2010.

Mohanty, Chandra Talpade. "Under Western Eyes: Feminist Scholarship and Colonial Discourses." *boundary 2* 12, no. 3 (1984): 333–58.

Mol, Annemarie. "Ontological Politics. A Word and Some Questions." *The Sociological Review* 47, 1_suppl (1999): 74–89. doi:10.1111/j.1467–954X.1999.tb03483.x.

Molotch, Harvey. "L.A. as Design Product: How Art Works in a Regional Economy." In *The City: Los Angeles and Urban Theory at the End of the Twentieth Century*, edited by Allen Scott and Edward Soja. Los Angeles: University of California Press, 1996.

Morie, Jacquelyn Ford. "Female Artists and the VR Crucible: Expanding the Aesthetic Vocabulary." In *The Engineering Reality of Virtual Reality 2012*, 8289:828908. Burlingame, CA: International Society for Optics and Photonics, 2012. doi:10.1117/12.910974.

Morie, Jacquelyn Ford. "Meaning and Emplacement in Expressive Immersive Virtual Environments." PhD diss., University of East London, 2007.

Morie, Jacquelyn Ford. "Why Yes, Virginia, There Have Always Been Women in VR." VRScout. July 24, 2015. https://vrscout.com/news/why-yes-virginia-there-have-always-been-women-in-vr/.

Morie, Jacquelyn Ford, Brenda Laurel, and Margaret Dolinsky. "When VR Really Hits the Streets." In *The Engineering Reality of Virtual Reality 2014*, 9012:90120B. Burlingame, CA: International Society for Optics and Photonics, 2014.

Mullaney, Thomas, Benjamin Peters, Mar Hicks, and Kavita Philip. *Your Computer Is on Fire*. Cambridge, MA: MIT Press, 2020.

Murphy, Michelle. "Unsettling Care: Troubling Transnational Itineraries of Care in Feminist Health Practices." *Social Studies of Science* 45, no. 5 (2015): 717–37. doi:10.1177/0306312715589136.

Murray, Craig, and Judith Sixsmith. "The Corporeal Body in Virtual Reality." *Ethos* 27, no. 3 (1999): 315–43. doi:10.1525/eth.1999.27.3.315.

Murray, Janet H. *Hamlet on the Holodeck: The Future of Narrative in Cyberspace*. Cambridge, MA: MIT Press, 2017.

Murray, Janet H. "Virtual/Reality: How to Tell the Difference." *Journal of Visual Culture* 19, no. 1 (2020): 11–27. doi:10.1177/1470412920906253.

Murray, Susan. *Bright Signals: A History of Color Television*. Durham, NC: Duke University Press, 2018.

Nakamura, Lisa. *Cybertypes: Race, Ethnicity, and Identity on the Internet*. New York: Routledge, 2002.

Nakamura, Lisa. "Feeling Good about Feeling Bad: Virtuous Virtual Reality and the Automation of Racial Empathy." *Journal of Visual Culture* 19, no. 1 (2020): 47–64. doi:10.1177/1470412920906259.

Nakamura, Lisa. "Indigenous Circuits: Navajo Women and the Racialization of Early Electronic Manufacture." *American Quarterly* 66, no. 4 (2014): 919–41. doi:10.1353/aq.2014.0070.

Nakamura, Lisa. "'Where Do You Want to Go Today?' Cybernetic Tourism, the Internet, and Transnationality." In *Race in Cyberspace*, edited by Beth E. Kolko, Lisa Nakamura, and Gilbert B. Rodman. New York: Routledge, 2000.

Nardi, Bonnie. "Virtuality." *Annual Review of Anthropology* 44, no. 1 (2015): 15–31.

Nario-Redmond, Michelle R., Dobromir Gospodinov, and Angela Cobb. "Crip for a Day: The Unintended Negative Consequences of Disability Simulations." *Rehabilitation Psychology* 62, no. 3 (2017): 324–33. doi:10.1037/rep0000127.

Nash, Kate. "Virtual Reality Witness: Exploring the Ethics of Mediated Presence." *Studies in Documentary Film* 12, no. 2 (2018): 119–31. doi:10.1080/17503280.2017.1340796.

National Research Council. *Modeling and Simulation: Linking Entertainment and Defense*. Washington, DC: National Academies Press, 1997.

Nelson, Alondra. "Introduction: Future Texts." *Social Text* 20, no. 2 (2002): 1–15. doi:10.1215/01642472–20–2_71–1.

Noble, Safiya. *Algorithms of Oppression: How Search Engines Reinforce Racism.* New York: New York University Press, 2018.

Nusselder, André. *Interface Fantasy: A Lacanian Cyborg Ontology*. Cambridge, MA: MIT Press, 2009.

Obama, Barack. "Obama to Graduates: Cultivate Empathy." June 19, 2006. https://www.northwestern.edu/newscenter/stories/2006/06/barack .html.

Oreskes, Naomi, and Erik M. Conway. *Merchants of Doubt: How a Handful of Scientists Obscured the Truth on Issues from Tobacco Smoke to Global Warming*. New York: Bloomsbury, 2010.

Ortner, Sherry B. "Access: Reflections on Studying Up in Hollywood." *Ethnography* 11, no. 2 (2010): 211–33. doi:10.1177/1466138110362006.

Ortner, Sherry B. *Not Hollywood: Independent Film at the Twilight of the American Dream*. Durham, NC: Duke University Press, 2013.

Ortner, Sherry B. "Powdermaker's Anthropology." *Anthropology of This Century*, no. 15 (January 2016). http://aotcpress.com/articles /powdermaker/.

Oscars. "Alejandro González Iñárritu Accepts a Special Oscar for Carne Y Arena." YouTube. November 12, 2017. https://www.youtube.com/watch ?v=jGI-nCuQuFY.

Osworth, A. E. "I Thought I Understood My Trans Body—Then I Tried VR." *Quartz*, February 6, 2019, sec. Ideas. https://qz.com/1525158/i-thought -i-understood-my-trans-body-and-gender-then-i-tried-vr/.

Otsuki, Grant, "Human and Machine in Formation: An Ethnographic Study of Communication and Humanness in a Wearable Technology Laboratory in Japan." PhD diss., University of Toronto, 2015. https://tspace .library.utoronto.ca/handle/1807/71805.

Pacleb, Jocelyn A. "Hauntings of a Different Kind: Militarized Spaces and Memories of Containment." In *Anthropology of Los Angeles: Place and Agency in an Urban Setting*, edited by Jenny Banh and Melissa King. Lanham, MD: Lexington Books, 2019.

Pandian, Anand. *A Possible Anthropology: Methods for Uneasy Times*. Durham, NC: Duke University Press, 2019.

Pandian, Anand. *Reel World: An Anthropology of Creation*. Durham, NC: Duke University Press, 2015.

Parisi, Paula. "'Ready Player One' Juxtaposes Real, Virtual via VFX from Three Shops." *Variety*, February 21, 2019. https://variety.com/2019 /artisans/production/spielberg-ready-player-one-vfx-1203144265/.

Parvin, Nassim. "Doing Justice to Stories: On Ethics and Politics of Digital Storytelling." *Engaging Science, Technology, and Society* 4 (November 2018): 515–34. doi:10.17351/ests2018.248.

Paul, L. A. "The Paradox of Empathy." *Episteme*, 2021, 1–20. doi:10.1017/epi.2021.31.

Paxson, Heather. *The Life of Cheese: Crafting Food and Value in America*. Berkeley: University of California Press, 2013.

Pearlman, Karen, and Adelheid Heftberger. "Recognising Women's Work as Creative Work." *Apparatus. Film, Media and Digital Cultures of Central and Eastern Europe*, no. 6 (August 2018). doi:10.17892/app.2018.0006.124.

Peck, Tabitha C., Sofia Seinfeld, Salvatore M. Aglioti, and Mel Slater. "Putting Yourself in the Skin of a Black Avatar Reduces Implicit Racial Bias." *Consciousness and Cognition* 22, no. 3 (2013): 779–87. doi:10.1016/j.concog.2013.04.016.

Penny, Simon. "Virtual Bodybuilding." *Media Information Australia* 69, no. 1 (1993): 17–22. doi:10.1177/1329878X9306900105.

Pine, B. Joseph, II, and James H. Gilmore. "Welcome to the Experience Economy." *Harvard Business Review*, 1998. https://hbr.org/1998/07/welcome-to-the-experience-economy.

Pink, Sarah, Heather Horst, John Postill, Larissa Hjorth, Tania Lewis, and Jo Tacchi. *Digital Ethnography: Principles and Practice*. London: SAGE Publications, 2015.

Plagens, Peter. "Los Angeles: The Ecology of Evil." *Artforum*, 1972. https://www.artforum.com/print/197210/los-angeles-the-ecology-of-evil-36172.

Plant, Sadie. "On the Matrix: Cyberfeminist Simulations." In *Cultures of Internet: Virtual Spaces, Real Histories, Living Bodies*, edited by Rob Shields. London: SAGE Publications, 1996.

Pollock, Anne. *Synthesizing Hope: Matter, Knowledge, and Place in South African Drug Discovery*. Chicago: University of Chicago Press, 2019.

Pols, Jeannette. *Care at a Distance: On the Closeness of Technology*. Amsterdam: Amsterdam University Press, 2012.

Popper, Karl. *The Open Society and Its Enemies*. Princeton, NJ: Princeton University Press, 2020.

Povinelli, Elizabeth. *Geontologies: A Requiem to Late Liberalism*. Durham, NC: Duke University Press, 2016.

Povinelli, Elizabeth. "Routes/Worlds." *E-Flux Journal* 27 (2011): 1–12.

Powdermaker, Hortense. *Hollywood, the Dream Factory: An Anthropologist Looks at the Movie-Makers*. Boston: Little, Brown and Company, 1950.

Powdermaker, Hortense. *Stranger and Friend: The Way of an Anthropologist*. New York: W. W. Norton and Company, 1966.

Powers, Devon. *On Trend: The Business of Forecasting the Future*. Urbana: University of Illinois Press, 2019.

Pressberg, Matt. "How Joanna Popper Went from Investment Banking in Sao Paulo to Wearing Headsets in Silicon Valley." CSQ, October 28, 2020. https://csq.com/2020/10/how-joanna-popper-went-from -investment-banking-in-sao-paulo-to-wearing-headsets-in-silicon -valley/.

Prince, Stephen. *Digital Visual Effects in Cinema: The Seduction of Reality*. New Brunswick, NJ: Rutgers University Press, 2012.

Probst, Malia, Zeynep Abes, and Céline Tricart. "VRScout Creator Spotlight: Celine Tricart, Co-Director of Maria Bello's 'Sun Ladies.'" VRScout. 2018. https://directory.libsyn.com/episode/index/show/vrscout/id /6446597.

Puig de la Bellacasa, Maria. "Matters of Care in Technoscience: Assembling Neglected Things." *Social Studies of Science* 41, no. 1 (2011): 85–106. doi:10.1177/0306312710380301.

Puig de la Bellacasa, Maria. *Matters of Care: Speculative Ethics in More than Human Worlds*. Minneapolis: University of Minnesota Press, 2017.

Raab, Mark. "Political Ecology of Prehistoric Los Angeles." In *Land of Sunshine: An Environmental History of Metropolitan Los Angeles*, edited by William Deverell and Greg Hise. Pittsburgh: University of Pittsburgh Press, 2005.

Radin, Joanna. "Alternative Facts and States of Fear: Reality and STS in an Age of Climate Fictions." *Minerva* 57 (December 2019): 411–31. doi:doi .org/10.1007/s11024–019–09374–5.

Radin, Joanna. "The Speculative Present: How Michael Crichton Colonized the Future of Science and Technology." *Osiris* 34, no. 1 (2019): 297–315. doi:doi.org/10.1086/704047.

Rastegar, Roya. "A Cosmic Demonstration of Shari Frilot's Curatorial Practice." In *Sisters in the Life: A History of Out African American Lesbian Media-Making*, edited by Yvonne Welbon and Alexandra Juhasz. Durham, NC: Duke University Press, 2018.

Rastegar, Roya. "Curating 'Physical Cinema' at Sundance's New Frontier." Edited by Jonathan Beller. *S&F Online* 10, no. 3 (2012). https://sfonline .barnard.edu/feminist-media-theory/curating-physical-cinema-at -sundances-new-frontier/.

Raz, Guy. "Screen Time—Part I." TED *Radio Hour*. NPR, September 11, 2015.

Rees, Amanda, and Iwan Rhys Morus. "Presenting Futures Past: Science Fiction and the History of Science." *Osiris* 34, no. 1 (2019): 1–15. doi:doi .org/10.1086/704131.

Revkin, Andrew C. "Showing in Theaters: The Digital Revolution; Cinemas Test a Projector Prototype That Makes Spools of Film Obsolete." *New York Times*, July 3, 1999. https://www.nytimes.com/1999/07/03/nyregion /showing-theaters-digital-revolution-cinemas-test-projector -prototype-that-makes.html.

Rheingold, Howard. *Virtual Reality: The Revolutionary Technology of Computer-Generated Artificial Worlds—and How It Promises to Transform Society*. New York: Simon and Schuster, 1991.

Richardson, Ingrid, and Carly Harper. "Corporeal Virtuality: The Impossibility of a Fleshless Ontology." *Body, Space and Technology* 2, no. 2 (2002). doi:10.16995/bst.243.

Rider, Karina Alexis. "Volunteering the Valley: Designing Technology for the Common Good in the San Francisco Bay Area." PhD diss., Queen's University (Canada), 2021.

Robertson, Adi. "VR Was Sold as an 'Empathy Machine'—But Some Artists Are Getting Sick of It." *The Verge*, May 3, 2017. https://www.theverge.com/2017/5/3/15524404/tribeca-film-festival-2017-vr-empathy-machine-backlash.

Robertson, Jennifer. *Robo Sapiens Japanicus: Robots, Gender, Family, and the Japanese Nation*. Oakland: University of California Press, 2018.

Roettgers, Janko. "Van Jones Talks about His Lumiere Award-Winning, Winston Duke-Starring VR Experience 'The Messy Truth' (Exclusive)." *Variety*, January 31, 2019. https://variety.com/2019/digital/news/van-jones-talks-about-his-lumiere-award-winning-winston-duke-starring-vr-experience-the-messy-truth-exclusive-1203124713/.

Rogers, Ariel. "'Taking the Plunge': The New Immersive Screens." In *Screen Genealogies: From Optical Device to Environmental Medium*, edited by Craig Buckley, Rüdiger Campe, and Francesco Casetti. Amsterdam: Amsterdam University Press, 2019.

Roose, Kevin. "How the Biden Administration Can Help Solve Our Reality Crisis." *New York Times*, February 2, 2021, sec. Technology. https://www.nytimes.com/2021/02/02/technology/biden-reality-crisis-misinformation.html.

Roquet, Paul. "The Body Shop." *Logic(s) Magazine*, August 3, 2019. https://logicmag.io/bodies/the-body-shop/.

Roquet, Paul. "Empathy for the Game Master: How Virtual Reality Creates Empathy for Those Seen to Be Creating VR." *Journal of Visual Culture* 19, no. 1 (2020): 65–80. doi:10.1177/1470412920906260.

Roquet, Paul. *The Immersive Enclosure: Virtual Reality in Japan*. New York: Columbia University Press, 2022.

Rorty, James. "Dream Factory." *Forum and Century*, September 1935.

Rosane, Olivia. "Empathy Machines." *Real Life*, July 2, 2018. https://reallifemag.com/empathy-machines/.

Rose, Frank. *The Art of Immersion: How the Digital Generation Is Remaking Hollywood, Madison Avenue, and the Way We Tell Stories*. New York: W. W. Norton and Co., 2011.

Rossi, Michael. *The Republic of Color: Science, Perception, and the Making of Modern America*. Chicago: University of Chicago Press, 2019.

Rosten, Leo. *Hollywood: The Movie Colony, The Movie Makers.* New York: Harcourt, Brace and Company, 1941.

Salazar, Juan Francisco, Sarah Pink, Andrew Irving, and Johannes Sjöberg. *Anthropologies and Futures: Researching Emerging and Uncertain Worlds.* New York: Bloomsbury Publishing, 2017.

Saler, Michael. *As If: Modern Enchantment and the Literary Prehistory of Virtual Reality.* Oxford: Oxford University Press, 2012.

Salt, Barry. *Film Style and Technology: History and Analysis.* London: Starword, 1983.

Sanchez-Vives, Maria V., and Mel Slater. 2005. "From Presence to Consciousness through Virtual Reality." *Nature Reviews Neuroscience* 6 (2005): 332–39. doi:doi.org/10.1038/nrn1651.

Sandifer, Philip. "Out of the Screen and into the Theater: 3-D Film as Demo." *Cinema Journal* 50, no. 3 (2011): 62–78.

Schwartz, Raz, and Germaine R. Halegoua. "The Spatial Self: Location-Based Identity Performance on Social Media." *New Media and Society* 17, no. 10 (2015): 1643–60.

Scott, Allen. *On Hollywood: The Place, The Industry.* Princeton, NJ: Princeton University Press, 2005.

Scott, Allen. *Technopolis: High-Technology Industry and Regional Development in Southern California.* Berkeley: University of California Press, 1993.

Scott, Allen, and Edward W. Soja. *The City: Los Angeles and Urban Theory at the End of the Twentieth Century.* Berkeley: University of California Press, 1996.

Scott, Joan W. "Deconstructing Equality-versus-Difference: Or, the Uses of Poststructuralist Theory for Feminism." *Feminist Studies* 14, no. 1 (1988): 32–50. doi:10.2307/3177997.

Seaver, Nick. "Care and Scale: Decorrelative Ethics in Algorithmic Recommendation." *Cultural Anthropology* 36, no. 3 (2021): 509–37. doi:10.14506/ca36.3.11.

Serpell, Namwali. "The Banality of Empathy." *New York Review of Books,* March 2, 2019. https://www.nybooks.com/daily/2019/03/02/the-banality-of-empathy/.

Serpell, Namwali. "Race Off: The Fantasy of Race Transformation." *The Yale Review* 109, no. 3 (2021): 44–72.

Shields, Rob. *The Virtual.* New York: Routledge, 2003.

Sinclair, Kamal. "Making a New Reality: A Toolkit for Inclusive Media Futures." *Making a New Reality.* Accessed August 14, 2021. https://makinganewreality.org/.

Sinclair, Kamal. "Use the Amplification Strategy." Making a New Reality. February 1, 2018. https://makinganewreality.org/use-the-amplication-strategy-d1491158cd0d.

Sismondo, Sergio. "Post-Truth?" *Social Studies of Science* 47, no. 1 (2017): 3–6. doi:10.1177/0306312717692076.

Slate. "The Greatest Deliberative Body in the World." *Political Gab Fest*, podcast. Accessed September 2, 2021. https://slate.com/podcasts/political -gabfest/2021/01/senate-filibuster-obstruction-ahead.

Slater, Mel. "Place Illusion and Plausibility Can Lead to Realistic Behaviour in Immersive Virtual Environments." *Philosophical Transactions of the Royal Society of London. Series B, Biological Sciences* 364, no. 1535 (2009): 3549–57. doi:10.1098/rstb.2009.0138.

Slater, Mel, Daniel Pérez Marcos, Henrik Ehrsson, and Maria Sanchez-Vives. "Inducing Illusory Ownership of a Virtual Body." *Frontiers in Neuroscience* 3, no. 2 (2009): 214–20. doi:10.3389/neuro.01.029.2009.

Slater, Mel, Daniel Pérez-Marcos, Henrik Ehrsson, and Maria V. Sanchez-Vives. "Towards a Digital Body: The Virtual Arm Illusion." *Frontiers in Human Neuroscience* 2, no. 6 (2008). doi:10.3389/neuro.09.006.2008.

Slater, Mel, and Sylvia Wilbur. "A Framework for Immersive Virtual Environments (FIVE): Speculations on the Role of Presence in Virtual Environments." *Presence: Teleoperators and Virtual Environments* 6, no. 6 (1997): 603–16. doi:10.1162/pres.1997.6.6.603.

Smith-Doerr, Laurel, Sharla N. Alegria, and Timothy Sacco. "How Diversity Matters in the US Science and Engineering Workforce: A Critical Review Considering Integration in Teams, Fields, and Organizational Contexts." *Engaging Science, Technology, and Society* 3 (2017): 139–53. doi:10.17351/ests2017.142.

Sobchack, Vivian. "Science Fiction Film and the Technological Imagination." In *Technological Visions: The Hopes and Fears That Shape New Technologies*, edited by Marita Sturken, Douglas Thomas, and Sandra Ball-Rokeach. Philadelphia: Temple University Press, 2004.

Sobchack, Vivian. *Screening Space: The American Science Fiction Film*. New Brunswick, NJ: Rutgers University Press, 1997.

Soja, Edward W. *My Los Angeles: From Urban Restructuring to Regional Urbanization*. Berkeley: University of California Press, 2014.

Soja, Edward W. *Postmodern Geographies: The Reassertion of Space in Critical Social Theory*. London: Verso, 1989.

Soja, Edward W. *Thirdspace: Journeys to Los Angeles and Other Real-and-Imagined Places*. Oxford: Blackwell Publishers, 1996.

Solomon, Ben C., and Leslye Davis. "Finding Hope in the Vigils of Paris: A Virtual Reality Film." *New York Times*, November 20, 2015, sec. World. https://www.nytimes.com/2015/11/21/world/europe/finding-hope-in -the-vigils-of-paris.html.

Sontag, Susan. *Regarding the Pain of Others*. New York: Picador, 2003.

Sophia, Zoë. "Virtual Corporeality: A Feminist View." *Australian Feminist Studies* 7, no. 15 (1992): 11–24. doi:10.1080/08164649.1992.9994641.

Stanney, Kay, Cali Fidopiastis, and Linda Foster. "Virtual Reality Is Sexist: But It Does Not Have to Be." *Frontiers in Robotics and AI* 7, 2020. doi:10.3389/frobt.2020.00004.

Star, Susan Leigh, and James R. Griesemer. "Institutional Ecology, 'Translations' and Boundary Objects: Amateurs and Professionals in Berkeley's Museum of Vertebrate Zoology, 1907–39." *Social Studies of Science* 19, no. 3 (1989): 387–420. doi:10.1177/030631289019003001.

Starosielski, Nicole. *Media Hot and Cold*. Durham, NC: Duke University Press, 2021. doi:10.1215/9781478021841.

Staszak, Jean-François. "An Oriental Town Patterned upon Movies Concepts: China City, a Tourist Simulacrum in Los Angeles (1938–1948)." In *Tourism Fictions, Simulacra and Virtualities*, edited by Maria Gravari-Barbas, Nelson Graburn, and Jean-François Staszak. New York: Routledge, 2020.

Stone, Allucquére Rosanne. *The War of Desire and Technology at the Close of the Mechanical Age*. Cambridge, MA: MIT Press, 1996.

Stone, Allucquére Rosanne. "Will the Real Body Please Stand Up? Boundary Stories about Virtual Cultures." In *Cyberspace: First Steps*, edited by Michael Benedikt. Cambridge, MA: MIT Press, 1991.

Storper, Michael, and Susan Christopherson. "Flexible Specialization and Regional Industrial Agglomerations: The Case of the US Motion Picture Industry." *Annals of the Association of American Geographers* 77, no. 1 (1987): 104–17.

Street, Sarah. "'Colour Consciousness': Natalie Kalmus and Technicolor in Britain." *Screen* 50, no. 2 (2009): 191–215. doi:10.1093/screen/hjp010.

Streitfeld, David. "Lurid Lawsuit's Quiet End Leaves Silicon Valley Start-Up Barely Dented." *New York Times*, September 15, 2017. https://www.nytimes.com/2017/09/15/technology/lurid-lawsuits-quiet-end-leaves-silicon-valley-start-up-barely-dented.html.

Suchman, Lucy. "Configuring the Other: Sensing War through Immersive Simulation." *Catalyst: Feminism, Theory, Technoscience* 2, no. 1 (2016): 1–36.

Sutherland, Ivan E. "The Ultimate Display." In *Proceedings of the IFIP Congress*, 506–8, 1965.

Tal, Kali. "Life behind the Screen." *Wired*, October 1, 1996. https://www.wired.com/1996/10/screen/.

Telotte, J. P. *The Mouse Machine: Disney and Technology*. Urbana: University of Illinois Press, 2008.

Ticktin, Miriam. *Casualties of Care Immigration and the Politics of Humanitarianism in France*. Berkeley: University of California Press, 2011.

Todd, Zoe. "The Decolonial Turn 2.0: The Reckoning." *Anthro{dendum}*, June 15, 2018. https://anthrodendum.org/2018/06/15/the-decolonial-turn-2-0-the-reckoning/.

Trubek, Amy B. *The Taste of Place: A Cultural Journey into Terroir*. Berkeley: University of California Press, 2008.

Turkle, Sherry. *Alone Together: Why We Expect More from Technology and Less from Each Other*. New York: Basic Books, 2011.

Turkle, Sherry. "Empathy Machines: Forgetting the Body." In *A Psychoanalytic Exploration of the Body in Today's World: On the Body*, edited by Christine Anzieu-Premmereur and Vaia Tsolas. New York: Routledge, 2018.

Turner, Fred. "Burning Man at Google: A Cultural Infrastructure for New Media Production." *New Media and Society* 11, no. 1–2 (2009): 73–94. doi:10.1177/1461444808099575.

Turner, Fred. *From Counterculture to Cyberculture: Stewart Brand, the Whole Earth Network, and the Rise of Digital Utopianism*. Chicago: University of Chicago Press, 2006.

Turnock, Julie A. *Plastic Reality: Special Effects, Technology, and the Emergence of 1970s Blockbuster Aesthetics*. New York: Columbia University Press, 2015.

Underkoffler, John. "Pointing to the Future of UI." Presented at TED2010, February 2010. https://www.ted.com/talks/john_underkoffler _pointing_to_the_future_of_ui#t-511093.

Underman, Kelly. *Feeling Medicine: How the Pelvic Exam Shapes Medical Training*. New York: New York University Press, 2020.

Vaidhyanathan, Siva. *Antisocial Media: How Facebook Disconnects Us and Undermines Democracy*. Oxford: Oxford University Press, 2018.

Vaidhyanathan, Siva. "You Don't Change Your Name to 'Meta' If You Think Anyone Can Stop You." *Slate*, November 1, 2021. https://slate.com /technology/2021/11/meta-facebook-zuckerberg-metaverse-vision .html.

Valentine, David, and Amelia Hassoun. "Uncommon Futures." *Annual Review of Anthropology* 48 (2019): 243–60. doi:doi.org/10.1146/annurev -anthro-102218–011435.

"Van Jones, Lumiere Awards Winner, the Messy Truth VR Experience." 2019. https://www.youtube.com/watch?v=R8vhBoDneps&t=96s.

VandenBroek, Angela. "A Very Lengthy Swedish Introduction: Hype, Storytelling, and the Question of Entrepreneurial Allies." Platypus. August 3, 2021. https://blog.castac.org/2021/08/a-very-lengthy-swedish -introduction-hype-storytelling-and-the-question-of-entrepreneurial -allies/.

Volpe, J. "The Godmother of Virtual Reality: Nonny de La Peña." Engadget. January 24, 2015. https://www.engadget.com/2015-01-24-the -godmother-of-virtual-reality-nonny-de-la-pena.html.

Waldie, D. J. *Holy Land: A Suburban Memoir*. New York: W. W. Norton and Company, 2005.

Wanderer, Emily. *The Life of a Pest: An Ethnography of Biological Invasion in Mexico*. Oakland: University of California Press, 2020.

Ward, David, Jim Chabin, and Jonathan Miranda. "Jonathan Miranda @ XR Day on the Bay with Cisco and Disney." Presented at the XR on the Bay, June 2018. https://www.youtube.com/watch?v=CcckgVNkWAc.

Ward, Josi. "'Dreams of Oriental Romance': Reinventing Chinatown in 1930s Los Angeles." *Buildings and Landscapes: Journal of the Vernacular Architecture Forum* 20, no. 1 (2013): 19–42.

Ward, Priscilla. "Black Pain Isn't a Video Game: The Possibilities and Pitfalls of Virtual Reality in the Black Lives Matter Era." *Salon*, August 14, 2016. https://www.salon.com/2016/08/14/black-pain-isnt-a-video-game-the -possibilities-and-pitfalls-of-virtual-reality-in-the-black-lives-matter -era/.

Warzel, Charlie. "The Pro-Trump Movement Was Always Headed Here." *New York Times*, January 6, 2021, sec. Opinion. https://www.nytimes.com /2021/01/06/opinion/protests-trump-disinformation.html.

Whissel, Kristen. *Spectacular Digital Effects: CGI and Contemporary Cinema.* Durham, NC: Duke University Press, 2014.

Wiener, Anna. *Uncanny Valley: A Memoir.* New York: Farrar, Straus and Giroux, 2020.

Wilkie, Alex, Martin Savransky, and Marsha Rosengarten, eds. *Speculative Research: The Lure of Possible Futures.* New York: Routledge, 2017.

Winner, Langdon. "Do Artifacts Have Politics?" *Daedalus* 109, no. 1 (1980): 121–36.

Wolf, Mark J. P. *Building Imaginary Worlds: The Theory and History of Subcreation.* New York: Routledge, 2012.

Wolf-Meyer, Matthew J. *Theory for the World to Come: Speculative Fiction and Apocalyptic Anthropology.* Minneapolis: University of Minnesota Press, 2019.

Woolgar, Steve, and Javier Lezaun. "The Wrong Bin Bag: A Turn to Ontology in Science and Technology Studies?" *Social Studies of Science* 43, no. 3 (2013): 321–40. doi:10.1177/0306312713488820.

Wurgaft, Benjamin Aldes. "The Future of Futurism: A View from the Garden, Looking to the Stars." *Boom: A Journal of California* 3, no. 4 (2013): 35–45.

Wynter, Sylvia. "Towards the Sociogenic Principle: Fanon, Identity, the Puzzle of Conscious Experience, and What It Is Like to Be 'Black.'" In *National Identities and Sociopolitical Changes in Latin America*, by Antonio Gomez-Moriana and Mercedes Duran-Cogan, 30–66. New York: Routledge, 2001.

Wynter, Sylvia. "Unsettling the Coloniality of Being/Power/Truth/Freedom: Towards the Human, after Man, Its Overrepresentation—An Argument. *CR: The New Centennial Review*, 3, no. 3 (2003): 257–337.

Yang, Robert. "'If You Walk in Someone Else's Shoes, Then You've Taken Their Shoes': Empathy Machines as Appropriation Machines." Radiator. April 5, 2017. https://www.blog.radiator.debacle.us/2017/04/if-you -walk-in-someone-elses-shoes-then.html.

Yee, Nick, and Jeremy Bailenson. "The Proteus Effect: The Effect of Transformed Self-Representation on Behavior." *Human Communication Research* 33, no. 3 (2007): 271–90. doi:10.1111/j.1468–2958.2007.00299.x.

Yee, Nick, and Jeremy Bailenson. "Walk a Mile in Digital Shoes: The Impact
of Embodied Perspective-Taking on the Reduction of Negative Stereo-
typing in Immersive Virtual Environments." In *Proceedings of PRESENCE
2006: The 9th Annual International Workshop on Presence*, 2006.

Zeavin, Hannah. *The Distance Cure: A History of Teletherapy*. Cambridge, MA:
MIT Press, 2021.

Žižek, Slavoj. "Cyberspace, or, the Unbearable Closure of Being." In *The
Plague of Fantasies*, 127–70. New York: Verso, 1997.

Žižek, Slavoj. *Looking Awry: An Introduction to Jacques Lacan through Popular
Culture*. Cambridge, MA: MIT Press, 1991.

Zuckerberg, Mark. "Facebook Connect 2021." Facebook. October 28, 2021.
https://www.facebook.com/Meta/videos/577658430179350/.

Zuckerberg, Mark. "I Wanted to Share a Note." Facebook. October 5, 2021.
https://www.facebook.com/zuck/posts/10113961365418581/.

Zuckerman, Ethan. "Hey, Facebook, I Made a Metaverse 27 Years Ago."
Atlantic, October 29, 2021. https://www.theatlantic.com/technology
/archive/2021/10/facebook-metaverse-was-always-terrible/620546/.

INDEX

Beverly Hills, 41, 69, 71; Rodeo Drive, 55, 56, 57, 70, 219nn5–6

Biden, Joe, xvi, xviii, 241n30

Bigelow, Kathryn, 228n43

Big Tech, xviii, 9, 10, 92, 211n11, 245n3; technology otherwise and, 19, 203, 206–7. *See also* techlash

blockbusters, 46, 77–78, 90, 94, 227n36, 240n25

blockchain, 21, 84, 85, 225n25, 232n19, 245n42; "women in," 178, 179

Bloom, Paul, 234n51

body, 4–5, 103, 115, 119, 120, 148; Black, 126–29; mind and, 109–13, 175, 231n10, 231n18; ownership, 121, 126, 128, 234n44. *See also* avatars; embodied experiences

Boellstorff, Tom, 22, 116, 214n47, 230n5

Bolas, Mark, 116, 118, 232n30, 233n33

Bollmer, Grant, 124

Bonaventure Hotel, 61, 62, 63, 220n16

Brooks, Fred, 217n29

Brown, John, 128

Brown Derby, 54

Buch, Elana D., 241n35

Buchele, Fox, 204–6

Burke, Tarana, 212n18

Bye, Kent, 121, 122, 204–6, 234n46

Caldwell, John Thornton, 86, 224n14, 227n35, 228n42

Cameron, James, 89–91, 227n37, 227n39, 228n40, 240n25; cofounder of Digital Domain, 94, 96; *Strange Days* (1995), 228n43

care, concept of, 136–38, 152–54, 238nn4–5, 241n35

caregivers, 192, 239n15, 241n35; empathy and, 140, 152–54; medical training, 241n32; VR experiences for, 25, 102, 133–36, 147–49, 237n1

Carne y Arena (2017), 1–5, 12, 49, 113, 115, 210n7, 233n36

Castile, Philando, 127

Century City Mall, 73, 74, 109

Chin, Elizabeth, 235n55, 236n67

China City, 58–59, 219n12, 220n14. *See also* New Chinatown

Chinatown (1974), 220n14

Chun, Wendy Hui-Kyong, 231n10, 236n68

cinematic technology, 80, 86, 142, 158; analog-digital transition, 87–92, 227n37, 228n41; Caldwell on, 224n14, 227n35, 228n42; emerging technology and, 24, 78–79, 82, 84–86, 92, 96–97, 98–99, 183, 229n51

Cixous, Hélène, 172

class boundaries, 198

Cline, Ernest, 93–94

Cohan, Steven, 212n24

Cold War, 42, 216n18

Collbohm, Frank, 39

colonialism, 57, 131, 197; anthropology and, 17, 213n29

commercial VR market, 45, 112, 120, 186, 201

common reality, 7, 13, 33, 103, 152, 230n4. *See also* singular reality

composite shot, 146, 148, 240n26

computer-generated imagery (CGI), 82, 94, 142, 145–46, 220n20, 240n22; Cameron's films and, 89; first CG characters, 87

computers/computing, 161–62, 185, 195, 246n4, 247n14

Conn, Coco, 171, 243n12

Connor, J. D., 219n4, 228n41

content development, 21, 98, 160, 183, 187; in Hollywood, 95–96, 229n50

Coppola, Francis Ford, 226n30

COVID-19 pandemic, xvi, 12, 154, 205, 239n15

Craig, David, 229n51

Culver City, 79

Cunningham, Stuart, 229n51

cyberfeminism, 107, 162, 173–75, 237n80, 244nn28–29

cyberpunk, 110, 113; *Snow Crash* (Stephenson), 202, 232n19; *The Souls of Cyberfolk* (Foster), 131, 237n80

entertainment industries, 155–56, 221n34, 242n1; diversity and, 192, 247n16; hierarchies, 187, 188; military collaboration, 24, 28, 38–40, 43–45, 49, 218n32; technology relationship, 76–78, 82, 94, 169, 194, 196, 222nn1–2, 229n51

EPCOT, 40, 47, 217n29

Errand Boy, The (1961), 15–16, 66, 212n24

escapism, xiii, 37, 53, 80, 175, 202; desire for, 6, 65

Escobar, Arturo, 206

ethics, 85, 132, 137

façades, 70–72, 176, 199; empathy machine as, 102, 107, 108, 123, 125, 130, 132; high-tech, 239n19; LA's architectural, 24, 53, 54, 54–59, 61, 76, 219n7; Las Vegas and, 220n15; Skywalker Ranch and, 219n4; studio backlots as, 14–15, 15, 55; of the VR industry, 160, 205

Facebook, xiii, 9, 32, 155, 209n9; acquisition of Oculus, xviii, 52, 93, 119; Cambridge Analytica scandal, xv–xvi, 12, 130. *See also* Meta; Women in VR Facebook group; Zuckerberg, Mark

fake news, 64, 85

fantasy: of being someone else, 101–3, 106, 120, 122, 126, 131–32, 147; of a better world, 28, 45–46, 48, 125, 158; of care, 137; colonial and racial, 35, 37–38; color and, 226n29; Disney and, 40, 61; façade and, 54–55, 70, 176, 199; of a fantasy, 200; of a freed mind, 109–11, 115, 175, 231n17; of "good" VR technology, xvi, 11, 19, 25, 26, 45, 48–49, 178, 196; Hollywood and, 14–16; of knowing, 130; overview of types, 10–11, 24–26, 154, 183, 211n13; of place, 28, 52–53, 68, 74, 97, 101, 154, 211n15; reality of, 60, 157, 220n20; of representation, 154, 156–58, 161, 162, 176, 177, 178, 180; of tech otherwise, 185. *See also* utopian ideations

feminine approach, 172–73; feminist vs., 162, 173, 175, 177. *See also* cyberfeminism

film sets, 133, 144–45, 224n10; China City, 58–59, 219n12; LA cityscapes, 58, 70, 107, 219n6; for military purposes, 39, 39–40; Paramount studio backlots, 14–15, 15; women working on, 181–82

Fisher, Scott, 23, 45, 116, 232n30; NASA VR system, 43, 44, 109

Fogelson, Robert, 14

Ford, Christine Blasey, 12, 178

Foster, Thomas, 131, 237n80

Foucault, Michel, 63

fractured realities, 6–7, 8, 17, 26, 50, 103, 156, 206. *See also* unreal, the

Frilot, Shari, 118–20, 121, 128, 188, 189, 233n34

Furness, Tom, 43, 217n27, 233n33

future(s), 33, 78, 99, 158; Big Tech and, 202, 204, 206; blockchain, 84, 85, 225n25; building a better, 46–48, 50, 152; different or alternative, 19, 26, 34, 197, 205, 218n41; feminist, 175, 176; inclusive, 157; of LA, 38, 42, 45; rethinking the, 17, 207; of VR, 26, 92, 181, 204–7

futurists, 31–33, 40, 42, 69, 172, 217n18

Gabler, Neal, 216n2

Gaines, Alisha, 129, 236n78

game engines. *See* Unity

Gates, Bill, 230n3

Gellhorn, Martha, 114

gender: androgyny, 191; biology differences and, 190, 246n12; equality or parity, 161, 168, 172, 177, 247n15; essentialism, 162, 173, 177, 178, 190; experiencing sex and, 244n39; focus in VR, 200; hierarchies, 169, 175, 187, 188; innovators and fundraising and, 113, 119, 154, 161, 191, 232n22; labor tasks and, 185, 192, 246n5, 246n10; research and technology development and, 161–62, 242n1; storytelling and, 194

Ghamari-Tabrizi, Sharon, 40

Gibson, William, 110, 111, 174, 231n6

Iñárritu, Alejandro González, 7, 25, 128, 210n2; *Carne y Arena* (2017), 1–5, 12, 49, 113, 115, 210n7, 233n36; Oscar speech, 2, 10

Ince, Thomas, 58

independent film, 88–89, 224n8

Industrial Light and Magic (ILM), 94, 96, 98, 226n31

Infinity Film Festival, 69, 71

internet, 110–11, 174–75, 230n5

intersectionality, 107, 118, 130, 176–177

invisible witnessing, VR and, 2–4, 115, 119, 233n36

Irani, Lilly, 138, 148, 195, 215n4, 234n51

Iraq War, 13

Isaacs, Bruce, 240n25

Jameson, Fredric, 61–63, 220n16

Japan, 214n1, 222n45

Jastrow, Marcie, 84, 97–98, 99, 141, 188, 229n54; postproduction career, 87–88, 186; at TEC, 79, 80, 81–82, 86, 91–92, 149, 189; work with Cameron, 90–91, 227n37

Jemisin, N. K., 218n35

Jews, 216n2, 223n6; Pittsburgh synagogue attack, 193, 209n4

Jobson, Ryan, 17

Jones, Van, 127

journalism, 122, 129, 149; immersive, 25, 105, 114, 116, 118, 119, 186

JWT Intelligence, 64–65

Kahn, Herman, 40–42, 48, 217n18

Kalmus, Natalie, 86–87, 226n29

Kamau, W. Sebastian, 235n57

Kantor, Jodi, 168, 242n7

Kavanaugh, Brett, 12, 178

Kelley, H. Roy, 39

Kilston, Lyra, 216n6

King, Homay, 22

Kirby, David A., 222n2

Klein, Norman, 45, 49

Kleinman, Arthur, 152–53

Krist, Gary, 216n2

Kroeber, Alfred, 35

Kun, Josh, 37

labor, 78, 96, 246n11; analog-digital transition and, 89, 227n35; assistants, 88, 189, 225n22, 246n10; gendered, 185, 192, 246n5, 246n10; human vs. robotic, 137–38; tech workers, 157, 180, 181–86, 190, 194–95, 199, 211n11. *See also* caregivers

Lanier, Jaron, 43, 170–71, 243n13

LA School of Urbanism, 61, 216n16

Lasko-Harvill, Ann, 243n13

Latour, Bruno, 18, 136–37

Laurel, Brenda, 243n18

Lawnmower Man (1992), 92, 93, 196, 218n37, 237n81

Leahy, Tom, 139, 141–42, 143, 146, 147, 240n22

Lee's Hoagie House, 87–88

Lefebvre, Henri, 59, 63

Le Guin, Ursula, 35, 37, 38, 49–50

Lestz, Pat and Earl, 87

Lévi-Strauss, Claude, 49, 218n44

Light, Jennifer, 41

location-based entertainment (LBES), 52, 73, 84, 98, 160, 186

Los Angeles: architectural façades, 24, 53, 54, 54–59, 61, 76, 107, 219n7; conflict with Silicon Valley, 79, 95–97; entertainment and technology overlap, 38–41, 43–45; fantasy of place and, 28, 34, 52–53, 74, 97, 101, 154; fragment of, 14, 16, 53, 101, 198; hyperreality and unreality of, 12–16, 24, 59–61; neighborhoods and segregation, 41–42; phoniness of, 55; storytelling and, 194, 195; tech scene, 19, 20, 21–22, 184, 194, 245n3; Upload office, 167–68, 169; utopian and racial narratives, 34–35, 36, 37–38; VR community, 8, 11, 28, 45–46, 51–52, 156–57, 167–69, 198–200

Los Angeles County Museum of Art (LACMA), 1–2, 53

Los Angeles Times, 88, 221n36

Loukissas, Yanni, 29

Olvera Street, 58, 59

Once Upon a Time in Hollywood (2019), 91

Ortner, Sherry, 224n8, 224n10, 225n17

Pace, Vince, 90

Pacleb, Jocelyn, 45

Pandian, Anand, 17, 226n29

Paramount Pictures, 58, 69, 87, 88; back-lots, 14–15, *15*

Paul, L. A., 234n51

Pausch, Randy, 217n29

Paxson, Heather, 29, 215n9

Peña, Nonny de la. *See* de la Peña, Nonny

Penny, Simon, 111

perspective taking, 25, 121, 132, 169, 235n57, 238n3

physical cinema, 118, 119, 121, 128

physical disabilities, 237n1

"pink" companies, 191–92

Pixar Animation Studios, 2, 43, 226n31

place, fantasy of, 133, 157, 211n15, 216n6; LA's, 10, 28, 34, 52–53, 74, 97, 101, 154; overview of, 10, 27–30

Plagens, Peter, 55

Plant, Sadie, 175

pluriverse, 206, 207

Polar Express (2004), 84

politics: feminist, 177; identity, 103; of knowledge, 107, 136; liberal, 106; noir, 53; of place, 33; post-truth, 13, 18, 213n37; right and left, 103, 169, 206; of tech companies, 32; unreal and hyperreal, xvii, 12–13, 34, 63–64; of VR industry, 49, 54, 204–5; worldbuilding, 218n41. *See also* Trumpism

Popper, Joanna, 186–88, 191–93, 246n8

Popper, Karl, 205, 248n3

popular feminism, 176

postmodernity, 12, 59, 63, 216n16

postproduction, 79, 82, 87–91, 146, 185–86, 227n37

Powdermaker, Hortense, 222n5, 226n27, 242n9; *Hollywood, the Dream Factory*, 77, 86, 223n6

Powers, Devon, 64, 67

presence, duality of, 115–16, 120, 122

privilege, 38, 106, 131, 133, 137, 203

Puig de la Bellacasa, Maria, 136–37, 152, 153, 241n35

Pulido, Laura, 37

race: Blackness, 235n60; cyberfeminism and, 244n28; discrimination and inequality, 37, 41, 42, 106, 129, 231n10; embodied experiences and, 126–27, 129, 211n8; empathy critique and, 123–25, 127–29; leadership positions and, 176–77; science and, 197; utopian narratives of, 37–38. *See also* intersectionality

Radin, Joanna, 228n43

Rankin, John, 127–29

Ready Player One (2018), 92–96, *93*, 112, 130, 202, 228n47

real-and-imagined, the, 53, 59, 61, 63–64, 67; blending of, 69–70, 74, 85

reality. *See* alternative realities; common reality; deconstructing/reconstructing reality; fractured realities; hyperreality; multiple realities; singular reality; unreal, the

reality craft, 32, 48, 78

reality crisis, 6, 64, 102, 103, 156, 201, 204, 206; role of technology in, xviii, 8, 78

reality repair, 28, 49, 53, 101, 156–57, 185, 206; empathy machine and, 102; futurist debate on, 31–33, 50; history of LA and, 34, 37–38; worldbuilding projects and, 47–48

Reeves, Keanu, 89

refugees, xvi, 106, 148, 209n4; Syrian, xiii, 193

representation, fantasy of, 161, 162, 176, 178, 180; gender equality and, 177; overview of, 11, 25, 154, 156–58

Rheingold, Howard, 113, 114, 116, 119

Riveter, 159, 161, 163, 169, 178

robotics, 137–38, 222n45. *See also* animatronics

Printed and bound by CPI Group (UK) Ltd, Croydon, CR0 4YY

09/06/2025

14685751-0001